COLLECTED EDITION OF THE WORKS OF

JOSEPH CONRAD

ROMANCE

ROMANCE

by

JOSEPH CONRAD

in collaboration with

FORD MADOX HUEFFER

=LONDON=
J. M. DENT AND SONS LTD

J. M. Dent & Sons Ltd.
Aldine House · Bedford Street · London

Made in Great Britain
at
The Temple Press · Letchworth · Herts

First published 1903
Uniform Edition 1923
Present Collected Edition 1949

A chronological list of Conrad's books,
with brief biographical details and a
list of selected writings about him,
will be found at the end of this volume.

CONTENTS

PART FIRST

THE QUARRY AND THE BEACH

*

ROMANCE

CHAPTER ONE

To YESTERDAY and to to-day I say my polite
"vaya usted con Dios." What are these days to
me? But that far-off day of my romance, when
from between the blue and white bales in Don
Ramon's darkened storeroom, at Kingston, I saw the
door open before the figure of an old man with the tired,
long, white face, that day I am not likely to forget. I
remember the chilly smell of the typical West Indian
store, the indescribable smell of damp gloom, of locos,
of pimento, of olive oil, of new sugar, of new rum; the
glassy double sheen of Ramon's great spectacles, the
piercing eyes in the mahogany face, while the tap, tap,
tap of a cane on the flags went on behind the inner
door; the click of the latch; the stream of light. The
door, petulantly thrust inwards, struck against some
barrels. I remember the rattling of the bolts on that
door, and the tall figure that appeared there, snuffbox in
hand. In that land of white clothes, that precise, ancient, Castilian in black was something to remember.
The black cane that had made the tap, tap, tap dangled
by a silken cord from the hand whose delicate blue-
veined, wrinkled wrist ran back into a foam of lawn
ruffles. The other hand paused in the act of conveying
a pinch of snuff to the nostrils of the hooked nose that
had, on the skin stretched tight over the bridge, the
polish of old ivory; the elbow pressing the black

3

cocked hat against the side; the legs, one bent, the other bowing a little back—this was the attitude of Seraphina's father.

Having imperiously thrust the door of the inner room open, he remained immovable, with no intention of entering, and called in a harsh, aged voice: "Señor Ramon! Señor Ramon!" and then twice: "Seraphina—Seraphina!" turning his head back.

Then for the first time I saw Seraphina, looking over her father's shoulder. I remember her face of that day; her eyes were gray—the gray of black, not of blue. For a moment they looked me straight in the face, reflectively, unconcerned, and then travelled to the spectacles of old Ramon.

This glance—remember I was young on that day— had been enough to set me wondering what they were thinking of me; what they could have seen of me.

"But there he is—your Señor Ramon," she said to her father, as if she were chiding him for a petulance in calling; "your sight is not very good, my poor little father—there he is, your Ramon."

The warm reflection of the light behind her, gilding the curve of her face from ear to chin, lost itself in the shadows of black lace falling from dark hair that was not quite black. She spoke as if the words clung to her lips; as if she had to put them forth delicately for fear of damaging the frail things. She raised her long hand to a white flower that clung above her ear like the pen of a clerk, and disappeared. Ramon hurried with a stiffness of immense respect towards the ancient grandee. The door swung to.

I remained alone. The blue bales and the white, and the great red oil jars loomed in the dim light filtering through the jalousies out of the blinding sunlight of Jamaica. A moment after, the door opened once more and a young man came out to me; tall, slim, with very bright, very large black eyes aglow in an absolute pallor of face. That was Carlos Riego.

Well, that is my yesterday of romance, for the many things that have passed between those times and now have become dim or have gone out of my mind. And my day before yesterday was the day on which I, at twenty-two, stood looking at myself in the tall glass, the day on which I left my home in Kent and went, as chance willed it, out to sea with Carlos Riego.

That day my cousin Rooksby had become engaged to my sister Veronica, and I had a fit of jealous misery. I was rawboned, with fair hair, I had a good skin, tanned by the weather, good teeth, and brown eyes. I had not had a very happy life, and I had lived shut in on myself, thinking of the wide world beyond my reach, that seemed to hold out infinite possibilities of romance, of adventure, of love, perhaps, and stores of gold. In the family my mother counted; my father did not. She was the daughter of a Scottish earl who had ruined himself again and again. He had been an inventor, a projector, and my mother had been a poor beauty, brought up on the farm we still lived on—the last rag of land that had remained to her father. Then she had married a good man in his way; a good enough catch; moderately well off, very amiable, easily influenced, a dilettante, and a bit of a dreamer, too. He had taken her into the swim of the Regency, and his purse had not held out. So my mother, asserting herself, had insisted upon a return to our farm, which had been her dowry. The alternative would have been a shabby, ignominious life at Calais, in the shadow of Brummel and such.

My father used to sit all day by the fire, inscribing

"ideas" every now and then in a pocket-book. I think he was writing an epic poem, and I think he was happy in an ineffectual way. He had thin red hair, untidy for want of a valet, a shining, delicate, hooked nose, narrow-lidded blue eyes, and a face with the colour and texture of a white-heart cherry. He used to spend his days in a hooded chair. My mother managed everything, leading an out-of-door life which gave her face the colour of a wrinkled pippin. It was the face of a Roman mother, tight-lipped, brown-eyed, and fierce. You may understand the kind of woman she was from the hands she employed on the farm. They were smugglers and night-malefactors to a man—and she liked that. The decent, slow-witted, gently devious type of rustic could not live under her. The neighbours round declared that the Lady Mary Kemp's farm was a hotbed of disorder. I expect it was, too; three of our men were hung up at Canterbury on one day—for horse-stealing and arson. . . . Anyhow, that was my mother. As for me, I was under her, and, since I had my aspirations, I had a rather bitter childhood. And I had others to contrast myself with. First there was Rooksby: a pleasant, well-spoken, amiable young squire of the immediate neighbourhood; young Sir Ralph, a man popular with all sorts, and in love with my sister Veronica from early days. Veronica was very beautiful, and very gentle, and very kind; tall, slim, with sloping white shoulders and long white arms, hair the colour of amber, and startled blue eyes— a good mate for Rooksby. Rooksby had foreign relations, too. The uncle from whom he inherited the Priory had married a Riego, a Castilian, during the Peninsular war. He had been a prisoner at the time— he had died in Spain, I think. When Ralph made the grand tour, he had made the acquaintance of his

Spanish relations; he used to talk about them, the Riegos, and Veronica used to talk of what he said of them until they came to stand for Romance, the romance of the outer world, to me. One day, a little before Ralph and Veronica became engaged, these Spaniards descended out of the blue. It was Romance suddenly dangled right before my eyes. It was Romance; you have no idea what it meant to me to talk to Carlos Riego.

Rooksby was kind enough. He had me over to the Priory, where I made the acquaintance of the two maiden ladies, his second cousins, who kept house for him. Yes, Ralph was kind; but I rather hated him for it, and was a little glad when he, too, had to suffer some of the pangs of jealousy—jealousy of Carlos Riego.

Carlos was dark, and of a grace to set Ralph as much in the shade as Ralph himself set me; and Carlos had seen a deal more of the world than Ralph. He had a foreign sense of humour that made him forever ready to sacrifice his personal dignity. It made Veronica laugh, and even drew a grim smile from my mother; but it gave Ralph bad moments. How he came into these parts was a little of a mystery. When Ralph was displeased with this Spanish connection he used to swear that Carlos had cut a throat or taken a purse. At other times he used to say that it was a political matter. In fine, Carlos had the hospitality of the Priory, and the title of Count when he chose to use it. He brought with him a short, pursy, bearded companion, half friend, half servant, who said he had served in Napoleon's Spanish contingent, and had a way of striking his breast with a wooden hand (his arm had suffered in a cavalry charge), and exclaiming, "I, Tomas Castro! . . ." He was an Andalusian.

For myself, the first shock of his strangeness overcome, I adored Carlos, and Veronica liked him, and laughed at him, till one day he said good-by and rode off along the London road, followed by his Tomas Castro. I had an intense longing to go with him out into the great world that brooded all round our foot-hills.

You are to remember that I knew nothing whatever of that great world. I had never been further away from our farm than just to Canterbury school, to Hythe market, to Romney market. Our farm nestled down under the steep, brown downs, just beside the Roman road to Canterbury; Stone Street—the Street—we called it. Ralph's land was just on the other side of the Street, and the shepherds on the downs used to see of nights a dead-and-gone Rooksby, Sir Peter that was, ride upon it past the quarry with his head under his arm. I don't think I believed in him, but I believed in the smugglers who shared the highway with that horrible ghost. It is impossible for any one nowadays to conceive the effect these smugglers had upon life thereabouts and then. They were the power to which everything else deferred. They used to overrun the country in great bands, and brooked no interference with their business. Not long before they had defeated regular troops in a pitched battle on the Marsh, and on the very day I went away I remember we couldn't do our carting because the smugglers had given us notice they would need our horses in the evening. They were a power in the land where there was violence enough without them, God knows! Our position on that Street put us in the midst of it all. At dusk we shut our doors, pulled down our blinds, sat round the fire, and knew pretty well what was going on outside. There would be long whistles in the dark, and when we found men lurking in our barns we feigned not to see them—

it was safer so. The smugglers—the Free Traders, they called themselves—were as well organized for helping malefactors out of the country as for running goods in; so it came about that we used to have coiners and forgers, murderers and French spies—all sorts of malefactors—hiding in our straw throughout the day, wait-for the whistle to blow from the Street at dusk. I, born with my century, was familiar with these things; but my mother forbade my meddling with them. I expect she knew enough herself—all the resident gentry did. But Ralph—though he was to some extent of the new school, and used to boast that, if applied to, he would grant a warrant against any Free Trader—never did, as a matter of fact, or not for many years.

Carlos, then, Rooksby's Spanish kinsman, had come and gone, and I envied him his going, with his air of mystery, to some far-off lawless adventures—perhaps over there in Spain, where there were war and rebellion. Shortly afterwards Rooksby proposed for the hand of Veronica and was accepted—by my mother. Veronica went about looking happy. That upset me, too. It seemed unjust that she should go out into the great world—to Bath, to Brighton, should see the Prince Regent and the great fights on Hounslow Heath —whilst I was to remain forever a farmer's boy. That afternoon I was upstairs, looking at the reflection of myself in the tall glass, wondering miserably why I seemed to be such an oaf.

The voice of Rooksby hailed me suddenly from downstairs. "Hey, John—John Kemp; come down, I say!"

I started away from the glass as if I had been taken in an act of folly. Rooksby was flicking his leg with his switch in the doorway, at the bottom of the narrow flight of stairs.

He wanted to talk to me, he said, and I followed him

out through the yard on to the soft road that climbs the hill to westward. The evening was falling slowly and mournfully; it was dark already in the folds of the sombre downs.

We passed the corner of the orchard.

"I know what you've got to tell me," I said. "You're going to marry Veronica. Well, you've no need of my blessing. Some people have all the luck. Here am I . . . look at me!"

Ralph walked with his head bent down.

"Confound it," I said, "I shall run away to sea! I tell you, I'm rotting, rotting! There! I say, Ralph, give me Carlos' direction. . . ." I caught hold of his arm. "I'll go after him. He'd show me a little life. He said he would."

Ralph remained lost in a kind of gloomy abstraction, while I went on worrying him for Carlos' address.

"Carlos is the only soul I know outside five miles from here. Besides, he's friends in the Indies. That's where I want to go, and he could give me a cast. You remember what Tomas Castro said. . . ."

Rooksby came to a sudden halt, and began furiously to switch his corded legs.

"Curse Carlos, and his Castro, too. They'll have me in jail betwixt them. They're both in my red barn, if you want their direction. . . ."

He hurried on suddenly up the hill, leaving me gazing upwards at him. When I caught him up he was swearing—as one did in those days—and stamping his foot in the middle of the road.

"I tell you," he said violently, "it's the most accursed business! That Castro, with his Cuba, is nothing but a blasted buccaneer . . . and Carlos is no better. They go to Liverpool for a passage to Jamaica, and see what comes of it!"

It seems that on Liverpool docks, in the owl-light, they fell in with an elderly hunks just returned from West Indies, who asks the time at the door of a shipping agent. Castro pulls out a watch, and the old fellow jumps on it, vows it's his own, taken from him years before by some picaroons on his outward voyage. Out from the agent's comes another, and swears that Castro is one of the self-same crew. He himself purported to be the master of the very ship. Afterwards—in the solitary dusk among the ropes and bales—there had evidently been some play with knives, and it ended with a flight to London, and then down to Rooksby's red barn, with the runners in full cry after them.

"Think of it," Rooksby said, "and me a justice, and . . . oh, it drives me wild, this hole-and-corner work! There's a filthy muddle with the Free Traders—a whistle to blow after dark at the quarry. To-night of all nights, and me a justice . . . and as good as a married man!"

I looked at him wonderingly in the dusk; his high coat collar almost hid his face, and his hat was pressed down over his eyes. The thing seemed incredible to me. Here was an adventure, and I was shocked to see that Rooksby was in a pitiable state about it.

"But, Ralph," I said, "I would help Carlos."

"Oh, you," he said fretfully. "You want to run your head into a noose; that's what it comes to. Why, I may have to flee the country. There's the red-breasts poking their noses into every cottage on the Ashford road." He strode on again. A wisp of mist came stealing down the hill. "I can't give my cousin up. He could be smuggled out, right enough. But then I should have to get across salt water, too, for at least a year. Why——"

He seemed ready to tear his hair, and then I put in

my say.   He needed a little persuasion, though, in spite of Veronica.

I should have to meet Carlos Riego and Castro in a little fir-wood above the quarry, in half an hour's time. All I had to do was to whistle three bars of "Lillibulero," as a signal.   A connection had been already arranged with the Free Traders on the road beside the quarry, and they were coming down that night, as we knew well enough, both of us.   They were coming in force from Canterbury way down to the Marsh.   It had cost Ralph a pretty penny; but, once in the hands of the smugglers, his cousin and Castro would be safe enough from the runners; it would have needed a troop of horse to take them.   The difficulty was that of late the smugglers themselves had become demoralized.   There were ugly rumours of it; and there was a danger that Castro and Carlos, if not looked after, might end their days in some marsh-dyke.   It was desirable that someone well known in our parts should see them to the seashore.   A boat, there, was to take them out into the bay, where an outward-bound West Indiaman would pick them up. But for Ralph's fear for his neck, which had increased in value since its devotion to Veronica, he would have squired his cousin.   As it was, he fluttered round the idea of letting me take his place.   Finally he settled it; and I embarked on a long adventure.

CHAPTER TWO

Between moonrise and sunset I was stumbling
through the bracken of the little copse that was like
a tuft of hair on the brow of the great white
quarry. It was quite dark, in among the trees. I
made the circuit of the copse, whistling softly my three
bars of "Lillibulero." Then I plunged into it. The
bracken underfoot rustled and rustled. I came to a
halt. A little bar of light lay on the horizon in front
of me, almost colourless. It was crossed again and again
by the small fir-trunks that were little more than wands.
A woodpigeon rose with a sudden crash of sound, flapping away against the branches. My pulse was dancing with delight—my heart, too. It was like a game of
hide-and-seek, and yet it was life at last. Everything
grew silent again and I began to think I had missed
my time. Down below in the plain, a great way off,
a dog was barking continuously. I moved forward
a few paces and whistled. The glow of adventure began
to die away. There was nothing at all—a little mystery
of light on the tree-trunks.

I moved forward again, getting back towards the
road. Against the glimmer of dead light I thought I
caught the outlines of a man's hat down among the
tossing lines of the bracken. I whispered loudly:

"Carlos! Carlos!"

There was a moment of hoarse whispering; a sudden
gruff sound. A shaft of blazing yellow light darted
from the level of the ground into my dazed eyes. A
man sprang at me and thrust something cold and

knobby into my neckcloth. The light continued to blaze into my eyes; it moved upwards and shone on a red waistcoat dashed with gilt buttons. I was being arrested. . . . "In the King's name. . . ." It was a most sudden catastrophe. A hand was clutching my windpipe.

"Don't you so much as squeak, Mr. Castro," a voice whispered in my ear.

The lanthorn light suddenly died out, and I heard whispers.

"Get him out on to the road. . . . I'll tackle the other . . . Darbies. . . . Mind his knife."

I was like a confounded rabbit in their hands. One of them had his fist on my collar and jerked me out upon the hard road. We rolled down the embankment, but he was on the top. It seemed an abominable episode, a piece of bad faith on the part of fate. I ought to have been exempt from these sordid haps, but the man's hot leathery hand on my throat was like a foretaste of the other collar. And I was horribly afraid—horribly—of the sort of mysterious potency of the laws that these men represented, and I could think of nothing to do.

We stood in a little slanting cutting in the shadow. A watery light before the moon's rising slanted downwards from the hilltop along the opposite bank. We stood in utter silence.

"If you stir a hair," my captor said coolly, "I'll squeeze the blood out of your throat, like a rotten orange."

He had the calmness of one dealing with an everyday incident; yet the incident was—it should have been—tremendous. We stood waiting silently for an eternity, as one waits for a hare to break covert before the beaters. From down the long hill came a small sound of horses' hoofs—a sound like the beating of the heart, intermittent—a muffled thud on turf, and a faint clink of iron. It seemed to die away unheard by the runner beside me. Presently there was a crackling of the short pine branches, a rustle, and a hoarse whisper said from above:

"Other's cleared, Thoms. Got that one safe?"

"All serene."

The man from above dropped down into the road, a clumsy, cloaked figure. He turned his lanthorn upon me, in a painful yellow glare.

"What! 'Tis the young 'un," he grunted, after a moment. "Read the warrant, Thoms."

My captor began to fumble in his pocket, pulled out a paper, and bent down into the light. Suddenly he paused and looked up at me.

"This ain't—— Mr. Lillywhite, I don't believe this ain't a Jack Spaniard."

The clinks of bits and stirrup-irons came down in a waft again.

"That be hanged for a tale, Thoms," the man with the lanthorn said sharply. "If this here ain't Riego— or the other—I'll . . ."

I began to come out of my stupor.

"My name's John Kemp," I said.

The other grunted. "Hurry up, Thoms."

"But, Mr. Lillywhite," Thoms reasoned, "he don't speak like a Dago. Split me if he do! And we ain't in a friendly country either, you know that. We can't afford to rile the gentry!"

I plucked up courage.

"You'll get your heads broke," I said, "if you wait much longer. Hark to that!"

The approaching horses had turned off the turf on to the hard road; the steps of first one and then another

sounded out down the silent hill. I knew it was the
Free Traders from that; for except between banks they
kept to the soft roadsides as if it were an article of faith.
The noise of hoofs became that of an army.

The runners began to consult. The shadow called
Thoms was for bolting across country; but Lillywhite
was not built for speed. Besides he did not know the
lie of the land, and believed the Free Traders were mere
bogeys.

"They'll never touch us," Lillywhite grumbled.
"We've a warrant . . . King's name. . . ."
He was flashing his lanthorn aimlessly up the hill.

"Besides," he began again, "we've got this gallus
bird. If he's not a Spaniard, he knows all about them.
I heard him. Kemp he may be, but he spoke Spanish
up there . . . and we've got something for our
trouble. He'll swing, I'll lay you a——"

From far above us came a shout, then a confused
noise of voices. The moon began to get up; above the
cutting the clouds had a fringe of sudden silver. A
horseman, cloaked and muffled to the ears, trotted
warily towards us.

"What's up?" he hailed from a matter of ten yards.
"What are you showing that glim for? Anything
wrong below?"

The runners kept silence; we heard the click of a
pistol lock.

"In the King's name," Lillywhite shouted, "get off
that nag and lend a hand! We've a prisoner."

The horseman gave an incredulous whistle, and then
began to shout, his voice winding mournfully uphill,
"Hallo! Hallo—o—o." An echo stole back, "Hallo!
Hallo—o—o"; then a number of voices. The horse
stood, drooping its head, and the man turned in his
saddle. "Runners," he shouted, "Bow Street runners!

Come along, come along, boys! We'll roast 'em. . . . Runners! Runners!"

The sound of heavy horses at a jolting trot came to our ears.

"We're in for it," Lillywhite grunted. "D——n this county of Kent."

Thoms never loosed his hold of my collar. At the steep of the hill the men and horses came into sight against the white sky, a confused crowd of ominous things.

"Turn that lanthorn off'n me," the horseman said. "Don't you see you frighten my horse? Now, boys, get round them. . . ."

The great horses formed an irregular half-circle round us; men descended clumsily, like sacks of corn. The lanthorn was seized and flashed upon us; there was a confused hubbub. I caught my own name.

"Yes, I'm Kemp . . . John Kemp," I called. "I'm true blue."

"Blue be hanged!" a voice shouted back. "What be you a-doing with runners?"

The riot went on—forty or fifty voices. The runners were seized; several hands caught at me. It was impossible to make myself heard; a fist struck me on the cheek.

"Gibbet 'em," somebody shrieked; "they hung my nephew! Gibbet 'em all the three. Young Kemp's mother's a bad 'un. An informer he is. Up with 'em!"

I was pulled down on my knees, then thrust forward, and then left to myself while they rushed to bonnet Lillywhite. I stumbled against a great, quiet farm horse.

A continuous scuffling went on; an imperious voice cried: "Hold your tongues, you fools! Hold your

tongues! . . ." Someone else called: "Hear to
Jack Rangsley. Hear to him!"

There was a silence. I saw a hand light a torch at
the lanthorn, and the crowd of faces, the muddle of
limbs, the horses' heads, and the quiet trees above,
flickered into sight.

"Don't let them hang me, Jack Rangsley," I sobbed.
"You know I'm no spy. Don't let 'em hang me,
Jack."

He rode his horse up to me, and caught me by the
collar.

"Hold your tongue," he said roughly. He began to
make a set speech, anathematizing runners. He moved
to tie our feet, and hang us by our finger-nails over the
quarry edge.

A hubbub of assent and dissent went up; then the
crowd became unanimous. Rangsley slipped from his
horse.

"Blindfold 'em, lads," he cried, and turned me
sharply round.

"Don't struggle," he whispered in my ear; his silk
handkerchief came cool across my eyelids. I felt
hands fumbling with a knot at the back of my head.
"You're all right," he said again. The hubbub of
voices ceased suddenly. "Now, lads, bring 'em along."

A voice I knew said their watchword, "Snuff and
enough," loudly, and then, "What's agate?"

Someone else answered, "It's Rooksby, it's Sir
Ralph."

The voice interrupted sharply, "No names, now. I
don't want hanging." The hand left my arm; there
was a pause in the motion of the procession. I caught
a moment's sound of whispering. Then a new voice
cried, "Strip the runners to the shirt. Strip 'em.
That's it." I heard some groans and a cry, "You won't

murder us." Then a nasal drawl, "We will sure—*ly*."
Someone else, Rangsley, I think, called, "Bring 'em
along—this way now."

After a period of turmoil we seemed to come out of
the crowd upon a very rough, descending path; Rangsley had called out, "Now, then, the rest of you be off;
we've got enough here"; and the hoofs of heavy horses
sounded again. Then we came to a halt, and Rangsley
called sharply from close to me:

"Now, you runners—and you, John Kemp—here you
be on the brink of eternity, above the old quarry.
There's a sheer drop of a hundred feet. We'll tie your
legs and hang you by your fingers. If you hang long
enough, you'll have time to say your prayers. Look
alive, lads!"

The voice of one of the runners began to shout,
"You'll swing for this—you——"

As for me I was in a dream. "Jack," I said, "Jack,
you won't——"

"Oh, that's all right," the voice said in a whisper.
"Mum, now! It's all *right*."

It withdrew itself a little from my ear and called,
"Now then, ready with them. When I say three. . . ."

I heard groans and curses, and began to shout for
help. My voice came back in an echo, despairingly.
Suddenly I was dragged backward, and the bandage
pulled from my eyes.

"Come along," Rangsley said, leading me gently
enough to the road, which was five steps behind. "It's
all a joke," he snarled. "A pretty bad one for those
catchpolls. Hear 'em groan. The drop's not two
feet."

We made a few paces down the road; the pitiful voices
of the runners crying for help came plainly to my ears.

"You—they—aren't murdering them?" I asked.

"No, no," he answered. "Can't afford to. Wish we could; but they'd make it too hot for us."

We began to descend the hill. From the quarry a voice shrieked:

"Help—help—for the love of God—I can't. . . ."

There was a grunt and the sound of a fall; then a precisely similar sequence of sounds.

"That'll teach 'em," Rangsley said ferociously. "Come along—they've only rolled down a bank. They weren't over the quarry. It's all right, I swear it is."

And, as a matter of fact, that was the smugglers' ferocious idea of humour. They would hang any undesirable man, like these runners, whom it would make too great a stir to murder outright, over the edge of a low bank, and swear to him that he was clawing the brink of Shakespeare's Cliff or any other hundred-foot drop. The wretched creatures suffered all the tortures of death before they let go, and, as a rule, they never returned to our parts.

CHAPTER THREE

THE spirit of the age has changed; everything has changed so utterly that one can hardly believe in the existence of one's earlier self. But I can still remember how, at that moment, I made the acquaintance of my heart—a thing that bounded and leapt within my chest, a little sickeningly. The other details I forget.

Jack Rangsley was a tall, big-boned, thin man, with something sinister in the lines of his horseman's cloak, and something reckless in the way he set his spurred heel on the ground. He was the son of an old Marsh squire. Old Rangsley had been head of the last of the Owlers—the aristocracy of export smugglers—and Jack had sunk a little in becoming the head of the Old Bourne Tap importers. But he was hard enough, tyrannical enough, and had nerve enough to keep Free-trading alive in our parts until long after it had become an anachronism. He ended his days on the gallows, of course, but that was long afterwards.

"I'd give a dollar to know what's going on in those runners' heads," Rangsley said, pointing back with his crop. He laughed gayly. The great white face of the quarry rose up pale in the moonlight; the dusky red fires of the limekilns glowed at the base, sending up a blood-red dust of sullen smoke. "I'll swear they think they've dropped straight into hell.

"You'll have to cut the country, John," he added suddenly, "they'll have got your name uncommon pat. I did my best for you." He had had me tied up like that before the runners' eyes in order to take their suspicions off me. He had made a pretence to murder me with the same idea. But he didn't believe they were taken in. "There'll be warrants out before morning, if they ain't too shaken. But what were you doing in the business? The two Spaniards were lying in the fern looking on when you come blundering your clumsy nose in. If it hadn't been for Rooksby you might have—— Hullo, there!" he broke off.

An answer came from the black shadow of a clump of roadside elms. I made out the forms of three or four horses standing with their heads together.

"Come along," Rangsley said; "up with you. We'll talk as we go."

Someone helped me into a saddle; my legs trembled in the stirrups as if I had ridden a thousand miles on end already. I imagine I must have fallen into a stupor; for I have only a vague impression of somebody's exculpating himself to me. As a matter of fact, Ralph, after having egged me on, in the intention of staying at home, had had qualms of conscience, and had come to the quarry. It was he who had cried the watchword, "Snuff and enough," and who had held the whispered consultation. Carlos and Castro had waited in their hiding-place, having been spectators of the arrival of the runners and of my capture. I gathered this long afterwards. At that moment I was conscious only of the motion of the horse beneath me, of intense weariness, and of the voice of Ralph, who was lamenting his own cowardice.

"If it had come at any other time!" he kept on repeating. "But now, with Veronica to think of!—— You take me, Johnny, don't you?"

My companions rode silently. After we had passed the houses of a little village a heavy mist fell upon us, white, damp, and clogging. Ralph reined his horse beside mine.

"I'm sorry," he began again, "I'm miserably sorry I got you into this scrape. I swear I wouldn't have had it happen, not for a thousand pounds—not for ten."

"It doesn't matter," I said cheerfully.

"Ah, but," Rooksby said, "you'll have to leave the country for a time. Until I can arrange. I will. You can trust me."

"Oh, he'll have to leave the country, for sure," Rangsley said jovially, "if he wants to live it down. There's five-and-forty warrants out against me—but they dursent serve 'em. But he's not me."

"It's a miserable business," Ralph said. He had an air of the profoundest dejection. In the misty light he looked like a man mortally wounded, riding from a battle-field.

"Let him come with us," the musical voice of Carlos came through the mist in front of us. "He shall see the world a little."

"For God's sake hold your tongue!" Ralph answered him. "There's mischief enough. He shall go to France."

"Oh, let the young blade rip about the world for a year or two, squire," Rangsley's voice said from behind us.

In the end Ralph let me go with Carlos—actually across the sea, and to the West Indies. I begged and implored him; it seemed that now there was a chance for me to find my world of romance. And Ralph, who, though one of the most law-respecting of men, was not for the moment one of the most valorous, was wild to wash his hands of the whole business. He did his best for me; he borrowed a goodly number of guineas from Rangsley, who travelled with a bag of them at his saddle-bow, ready to pay his men their seven shillings a head for the run.

Ralph remembered, too—or I remembered for him— that he had estates and an agent in Jamaica, and he turned into the big inn at the junction of the London road to write a letter to his agent bidding him house me and employ me as an improver. For fear of compromising him we waited in the shadow of trees a furlong or two down the road. He came at a trot, gave me the letter, drew me aside, and began upbraiding himself again. The others rode onwards.

"Oh, it's all right," I said. "It's fine—it's fine. I'd have given fifty guineas for this chance this morning —and, Ralph, I say, you may tell Veronica why I'm going, but keep a shut mouth to my mother. Let her think I've run away—eh? Don't spoil your chance."

He was in such a state of repentance and flutter that he could not let me take a decent farewell. The sound of the others' horses had long died away down the hill when he began to tell me what he ought to have done.

"I knew it at once after I'd let you go. I ought to have kept you out of it. You came near being murdered. And to think of it—you, her brother—to be——"

"Oh, it's all right," I said gayly, "it's all right. You've to stand by Veronica. I've no one to my back. Good-night, good-by."

I pulled my horse's head round and galloped down the hill. The main body had halted before setting out over the shingle to the shore. Rangsley was waiting to conduct us into the town, where we should find a man to take us three fugitives out to the expected ship. We rode clattering aggressively through the silence of the long, narrow main street. Every now and then Carlos Riego coughed lamentably, but Tomas Castro rode in gloomy silence. There was a light here and there in a window, but not a soul stirring abroad. On the blind of an inn the shadow of a bearded man held the shadow of a rummer to its mouth.

"That'll be my uncle," Rangsley said. "He'll be the man to do your errand." He called to one of the men behind. "Here, Joe Pilcher, do you go into the White Hart and drag my Uncle Tom out. Bring 'un up to me—to the nest."

Three doors further on we came to a halt, and got down from our horses.

Rangsley knocked on a shutter-panel, two hard knocks with the crop and three with the naked fist. Then a lock clicked, heavy bars rumbled, and a chain rattled. Rangsley pushed me through the doorway. A side door opened, and I saw into a lighted room filled with wreaths of smoke. A paunchy man in a bob wig, with a blue coat and Windsor buttons, holding a church-warden pipe in his right hand and a pewter quart in his left, came towards us.

"Hullo, captain," he said, "you'll be too late with the lights, won't you?" He had a deprecatory air.

"Your watch is fast, Mr. Mayor," Rangsley answered surlily; "the tide won't serve for half an hour yet."

"Cht, cht," the other wheezed. "No offence. We respect you. But still, when one has a stake, one likes to know."

"My stake's all I have, and my neck," Rangsley said impatiently; "what's yours? A matter of fifty pun ten? . . . Why don't you make them bring they lanthorns?"

A couple of dark lanthorns were passed to Rangsley, who half-uncovered one, and lit the way up steep wooden stairs. We climbed up to a tiny cock-loft, of which the side towards the sea was all glazed.

"Now you sit there, on the floor," Rangsley com-

B

manded; "can't leave you below; the runners will be coming to the mayor for new warrants to-morrow, and he'd not like to have spent the night in your company."

He threw a casement open. The moon was hidden from us by clouds, but, a long way off, over the distant sea, there was an irregular patch of silver light, against which the chimneys of the opposite houses were silhouetted. The church clock began muffledly to chime the quarters behind us; then the hour struck— ten strokes.

Rangsley set one of his lanthorns on the window and twisted the top. He sent beams of yellow light shooting out to seawards. His hands quivered, and he was mumbling to himself under the influence of ungovernable excitement. His stakes were very large, and all depended on the flicker of those lanthorns out towards the men on the luggers that were hidden in the black expanse of the sea. Then he waited, and against the light of the window I could see him mopping his forehead with the sleeve of his coat; my heart began to beat softly and insistently—out of sympathy.

Suddenly, from the deep shadow of the cloud above the sea, a yellow light flashed silently out—very small, very distant, very short-lived. Rangsley heaved a deep sigh and slapped me heavily on the shoulder.

"All serene, my buck," he said; "now let's see after you. I've half an hour. What's the ship?"

I was at a loss, but Carlos said out of the darkness, "The ship the *Thames*. My friend Señor Ortiz, of the Minories, said you would know."

"Oh, I know, I know," Rangsley said softly; and, indeed, he did know all that was to be known about smuggling out of the southern counties of people who could no longer inhabit them. The trade was a survival of the days of Jacobite plots. "And it's a hanging job,

too? But it's no affair of mine." He stopped and
reflected for an instant.

I could feel Carlos' eyes upon us, looking out of the
thick darkness. A slight rustling came from the
corner that hid Castro.

"She passes down channel to-night, then?" Rangsley
said. "With this wind you'll want to be well out in the
Bay at a quarter after eleven."

An abnormal scuffling, intermingled with snatches of
jovial remonstrance, made itself heard from the bottom
of the ladder. A voice called up through the hatch,
"Here's your uncle, Squahre Jack," and a husky murmur corroborated.

"Be you drunk again, you old sinner?" Rangsley
asked. "Listen to me. . . . Here's three men to
be set aboard the *Thames* at a quarter after eleven."

A grunt came in reply.

Rangsley repeated slowly.

The grunt answered again.

"Here's three men to be set aboard the *Thames* at a
quarter after eleven. . . ." Rangsley said again.

"Here's . . . a-cop . . . three men to be
set aboard *Thames* at quarter after eleven," a voice
hiccoughed back to us.

"Well, see you do it," Rangsley said. "He's as
drunk as a king," he commented to us; "but when
you've said a thing three times, he remembers—hark to
him."

The drunken voice from below kept up a constant
babble of, "Three men to be set aboard *Thames* . . .
three men to be set . . ."

"He'll not stop saying that till he has you safe
aboard," Rangsley said. He showed a glimmer of
light down the ladder—Carlos and Castro descended.
I caught sight below me of the silver head and the deep

red ears of the drunken uncle of Rangsley. He had been one of the most redoubtable of the family, a man of immense strength and cunning, but a confirmed habit of consuming a pint and a half of gin a night had made him disinclined for the more arduous tasks of the trade. He limited his energies to working the underground passage, to the success of which his fox-like cunning, and intimate knowledge of the passing shipping, were indispensable. I was preparing to follow the others down the ladder when Rangsley touched my arm.

"I don't like your company," he said close behind my ear. "I know who they are. There were bills out for them this morning. I'd blow them, and take the reward, but for you and Squahre Rooksby. They're handy with their knives, too, I fancy. You mind me, and look to yourself with them. There's something unnatural."

His words had a certain effect upon me, and his manner perhaps more. A thing that was "unnatural" to Jack Rangsley—the man of darkness, who lived forever as if in the shadow of the gallows—was a thing to be avoided. He was for me nearly as romantic a figure as Carlos himself, but for his forbidding darkness, and he was a person of immense power. The silent flittings of lights that I had just seen, the answering signals from the luggers far out to sea, the enforced sleep of the towns and countryside whilst his plans were working out at night, had impressed me with a sense of awe. And his words sank into my spirit, and made me afraid for my future.

We followed the others downwards into a ground-floor room that was fitted up as a barber's shop. A rushlight was burning on a table. Rangsley took hold of a piece of wainscotting, part of the frame of a panel; he pulled it towards him, and, at the same moment, a glazed show-

case full of razors and brushes swung noiselessly forward
with an effect of the supernatural. A small opening,
just big enough to take a man's body, revealed itself.
We passed through it and up a sort of tunnel. The
door at the other end, which was formed of panels, had a
manger and straw crib attached to it on the outside, and
let us into a horse's stall. We found ourselves in the
stable of the inn.

"We don't use this passage for ourselves," Rangsley said. "Only the most looked up to need to—the
justices and such like. But gallus birds like you and
your company, it's best for us not to be seen in company
with. Follow my uncle now. Good-night."

We went into the yard, under the pillars of the town
hall, across the silent street, through a narrow passage,
and down to the sea. Old Rangsley reeled ahead of us
swiftly, muttering, "Three men to be set aboard of the
Thames . . . quarter past eleven. Three men to
be set aboard . . ." and in a few minutes we stood
upon the shingle beside the idle sea, that was nearly at
the full.

CHAPTER FOUR

It was, I suppose, what I demanded of Fate—to be gently wafted into the position of a hero of romance, without rough hands at my throat. It is what we all ask, I suppose; and we get it sometimes in ten-minute snatches. I didn't know where I was going. It was enough for me to sail in and out of the patches of shadow that fell from the moon right above our heads.

We embarked, and, as we drew further out, the land turned to a shadow, spotted here and there with little lights. Behind us a cock crowed. The shingle crashed, at intervals beneath the feet of a large body of men. I remembered the smugglers; but it was as if I had remembered them only to forget them forever. Old Rangsley, who steered with the sheet in his hand, kept up an unintelligible babble. Carlos and Castro talked under their breaths. Along the gunwale there was a constant ripple and gurgle. Suddenly old Rangsley began to sing; his voice was hoarse and drunken.

> "When Harol' war inva—a—ded,
> An' fallin', lost his crownd,
> An' Normun Willium wa—a—ded."

The water murmured without a pause, as if it had a million tiny facts to communicate in very little time. And then old Rangsley hove to, to wait for the ship, and sat half asleep, lurching over the tiller. He was a very unreliable scoundrel. The boat leaked like a sieve. The wind freshened, and we three began to ask ourselves how it was going to end. There were no lights upon the sea.

At last, well out, a blue gleam caught our eyes; but by this time old Rangsley was helpless, and it fell to me to manage the boat. Carlos was of no use—he knew it, and, without saying a word, busied himself in bailing the water out. But Castro, I was surprised to notice, knew more than I did about a boat, and, maimed as he was, made himself useful.

"To me it looks as if we should drown," Carlos said at one point, very quietly. "I am sorry for you, Juan."

"And for yourself, too," I answered, feeling very hopeless, and with a dogged grimness.

"Just now, my young cousin, I feel as if I should not mind dying under the water," he remarked with a sigh, but without ceasing to bail for a moment.

"Ah, you are sorry to be leaving home, and your friends, and Spain, and your fine adventures," I answered.

The blue flare showed a very little nearer. There was nothing to be done but talk and wait.

"No; England," he answered in a tone full of meaning —"things in England—people there. One person at least."

To me his words and his smile seemed to imply a bitter irony; but they were said very earnestly.

Castro had hauled the helpless form of old Rangsley forward. I caught him muttering savagely:

"I could kill that old man!"

He did not want to be drowned; neither assuredly did I. But it was not fear so much as a feeling of dreariness and disappointment that had come over me, the sudden feeling that I was going not to adventure, but to death; that here was not romance, but an end—a disenchanted surprise that it should soon be all over.

We kept a grim silence. Further out in the bay, we were caught in a heavy squall. Sitting by the tiller, I got as much out of her as I knew how. We would go as far as we could before the run was over. Carlos bailed unceasingly, and without a word of complaint, sticking to his self-appointed task as if in very truth he were careless of life. A feeling came over me that this, indeed, was the elevated and the romantic. Perhaps he was tired of his life; perhaps he really regretted what he left behind him in England, or somewhere else—some association, some woman. But he, at least, if we went down together, would go gallantly, and without complaint, at the end of a life with associations, movements, having lived and regretted. I should disappear ingloriously on the very threshold.

Castro, standing up unsteadily, growled, "We may do it yet! See, señor!"

The blue gleam was much larger—it flared smokily up towards the sky. I made out ghastly parallelograms of a ship's sails high above us, and at last many faces peering unseeingly over the rail in our direction. We all shouted together.

I may say that it was thanks to me that we reached the ship. Our boat went down under us whilst I was tying a rope under Carlos' arms. He was standing up with the baler still in his hand. On board, the women passengers were screaming, and as I clung desperately to the rope that was thrown me, it struck me oddly that I had never before heard so many women's voices at the same time. Afterwards, when I stood on the deck, they began laughing at old Rangsley, who held forth in a thunderous voice, punctuated by hiccoughs:

"They carried I aboard—a cop—theer lugger and sinks I in the cold, co—old sea."

It mortified me excessively that I should be tacked to

his tail and exhibited to a number of people, and I had a sudden conviction of my small importance. I had expected something altogether different—an audience sympathetically interested in my desire for a passage to the West Indies; instead of which people laughed while I spoke in panting jerks, and the water dripped out of my clothes. After I had made it clear that I wanted to go with Carlos, and could pay for my passage, I was handed down into the steerage, where a tallow candle burnt in a thick, blue atmosphere. I was stripped and filled with some fiery liquid, and fell asleep. Old Rangsley was sent ashore with the pilot.

It was a new and strange life to me, opening there suddenly enough. The *Thames* was one of the usual West Indiamen; but to me even the very ropes and spars, the sea, and the unbroken dome of the sky, had a rich strangeness. Time passed lazily and gliding. I made more fully the acquaintance of my companions, but seemed to know them no better. I lived with Carlos in the cabin—Castro in the half-deck; but we were all three pretty constantly together, and they being the only Spaniards on board, we were more or less isolated from the other passengers.

Looking at my companions at times, I had vague misgivings. It was as if these two had fascinated me to the verge of some danger. Sometimes Castro, looking up, uttered vague ejaculations. Carlos pushed his hat back and sighed. They had preoccupations, cares, interests in which they let me have no part.

Castro struck me as absolutely ruffianly. His head was knotted in a red, white-spotted handkerchief; his grizzled beard was tangled; he wore a black and rusty cloak, ragged at the edges, and his feet were often bare; at his side would lie his wooden right hand. As a rule,

*B

the place of his forearm was taken by a long, thin, steel blade, that he was forever sharpening.

Carlos talked with me, telling me about his former life and his adventures. The other passengers he discountenanced by a certain coldness of manner that made me ashamed of talking to them. I respected him so; he was so wonderful to me then. Castro I detested; but I accepted their relationship without in the least understanding how Carlos, with his fine grain, his high soul—I gave him credit for a high soul—could put up with the squalid ferocity with which I credited Castro. It seemed to hang in the air round the grotesque raggedness of the saturnine brown man.

Carlos had made Spain too hot to hold him in those tortuous intrigues of the Army of the Faith and Bourbon troops and Italian legions. From what I could understand, he must have played fast and loose in an insolent manner. And there was some woman offended. There was a gayness and gallantry in that part of it. He had known the very spirit of romance, and now he was sailing gallantly out to take up his inheritance from an uncle who was a great noble, owning the greater part of one of the Intendencias of Cuba.

"He is a very old man, I hear," Carlos said—"a little doting, and having need of me."

There were all the elements of romance about Carlos' story—except the actual discomforts of the ship in which we were sailing. He himself had never been in Cuba or seen his uncle; but he had, as I have indicated, ruined himself in one way or another in Spain, and it had come as a God-send to him when his uncle had sent Tomas Castro to bring him to Cuba, to the town of Rio Medio.

"The town belongs to my uncle. He is very rich; a Grand d'Espagne . . . everything; but he is now very old, and has left Havana to die in his palace in his own town. He has an only daughter, a Doña Seraphina, and I suppose that if I find favour in his eyes I shall marry her, and inherit my uncle's great riches; I am the only one that is left of the family to inherit." He waved his hand and smiled a little. "*Vaya;* a little of that great wealth would be welcome. If I had had a few pence more there would have been none of this worry, and I should not have been on this dirty ship in these rags." He looked down good-humouredly at his clothes.

"But," I said, "how do you come to be in a scrape at all?"

He laughed a little proudly.

"In a scrape?" he said. "I . . . I am in none. It is Tomas Castro there." He laughed affectionately. "He is as faithful as he is ugly," he said; "but I fear he has been a villain, too. . . . What do I know? Over there in my uncle's town, there are some villains— you know what I mean, one must not speak too loudly on this ship. There is a man called O'Brien, who mismanages my uncle's affairs. What do I know? The good Tomas has been in some villainy that is no affair of mine. He is a good friend and a faithful dependent of my family's. He certainly had that man's watch—the man we met by evil chance at Liverpool, a man who came from Jamaica. He had bought it—of a bad man, perhaps, I do not ask. It was Castro your police wished to take. But I, *bon Dieu,* do you think I would take watches?"

I certainly did not think he had taken a watch; but I did not relinquish the idea that he, in a glamorous, romantic way, had been a pirate. Rooksby had certainly hinted as much in his irritation.

He lost none of his romantic charm in my eyes. The

fact that he was sailing in uncomfortable circumstances detracted little; nor did his clothes, which, at the worst, were better than any I had ever had. And he wore them with an air and a grace. He had probably been in worse circumstances when campaigning with the Army of the Faith in Spain. And there was certainly the uncle with the romantic title and the great inheritance, and the cousin—the Miss Seraphina, whom he would probably marry. I imagined him an aristocratic scapegrace, a corsair—it was the Byronic period then— sailing out to marry a sort of shimmering princess with hair like Veronica's, bright golden, and a face like that of a certain keeper's daughter. Carlos, however, knew nothing about his cousin; he cared little more, as far as I could tell. "What can she be to me since I have seen your . . . ?" he said once, and then stopped, looking at me with a certain tender irony. He insisted, though, that his aged uncle was in need of him. As for Castro—he and his rags came out of a life of sturt and strife, and I hoped he might die by treachery. He had undoubtedly been sent by the uncle across the seas to find Carlos and bring him out of Europe; there was something romantic in that mission. He was now a dependent of the Riego family, but there were unfathomable depths in that tubby little man's past. That he had gone to Russia at the tail of the Grande Armée, one could not help believing. He had been most likely in the grand army of sutlers and camp-followers. He could talk convincingly of the cold, and of the snows and his escape. And from his allusions one could get glimpses of what he had been before and afterwards— apparently everything that was questionable in a secularly disturbed Europe; no doubt somewhat of a bandit; a guerrilero in the sixes and sevens; with the Army of the Faith near the French border, later on

There had been room and to spare for that sort of pike, in the muddy waters, during the first years of the century. But the waters were clearing, and now the good Castro had been dodging the gallows in the Antilles or in Mexico. In his heroic moods he would swear that his arm had been cut off at Somo Sierra; swear it with a great deal of asseveration, making one see the Polish lancers charging the gunners, being cut down, and his own sword arm falling suddenly.

Carlos, however, used to declare with affectionate cynicism that the arm had been broken by the cudgel of a Polish peasant while Castro was trying to filch a pig from a stable. . . . "I cut his throat out, though," Castro would grumble darkly; "so, like that, and it matters very little—it is even an improvement. See, I put on my blade. See, I transfix you that fly there. . . . See how astonished he was. He did never expect that." He had actually impaled a crawling cockroach. He spent his days cooking extraordinary messes, crouching for hours over a little charcoal brazier that he lit surreptitiously in the back of his bunk, making substitutes for eternal *gaspachos*.

All these things, if they deepened the romance of Carlos' career, enhanced, also, the mystery. I asked him one day, "But why do you go to Jamaica at all if you are bound for Cuba?"

He looked at me, smiling a little mournfully.

"Ah, Juan mio," he said, "Spain is not like your England, unchanging and stable. The party who reign to-day do not love me, and they are masters in Cuba as in Spain. But in his province my uncle rules alone. There I shall be safe." He was condescending to roll some cigarettes for Tomas, whose wooden hand incommoded him, and he tossed a fragment of tobacco to the wind with a laugh. "In Jamaica there is a merchant,

a Señor Ramon; I have letters to him, and he shall find
me a conveyance to Rio Medio, my uncle's town. He
is an *afiliado*."

He laughed again. "It is not easy to enter that
place, Juanino."

There was certainly some mystery about that town
of his uncle's. One night I overheard him say to
Castro:

"Tell me, O my Tomas, would it be safe to take this
caballero, my cousin, to Rio Medio?"

Castro paused, and then murmured gruffly:

"Señor, unless that Irishman is consulted beforehand,
or the English lord would undertake to join with the
picaroons, it is very assuredly not safe."

Carlos made a little exclamation of mild astonishment.

"*Pero?* Is it so bad as that in my uncle's own
town?"

Tomas muttered something that I did not catch, and
then:

"If the English *caballero* committed indiscretions, or
quarrelled—and all these people quarrel, why, God
knows—that Irish devil could hang many persons, even
myself, or take vengeance on your worship."

Carlos was silent as if in a reverie. At last he said:

"But if affairs are like this, it would be well to have
one more with us. The *caballero*, my cousin, is very
strong and of great courage."

Castro grunted, "Oh, of a courage! But as the
proverb says, 'If you set an Englishman by a hornets'
nest they shall not remain long within.'"

After that I avoided any allusion to Cuba, because
the thing, think as I would about it, would not grow
clear. It was plain that something illegal was going on
there, or how could "that Irish devil," whoever he was,

have power to hang Tomas and be revenged on Carlos? It did not affect my love for Carlos, though, in the weariness of this mystery, the passage seemed to drag a little. And it was obvious enough that Carlos was unwilling or unable to tell anything about what preoccupied him.

I had noticed an intimacy spring up between the ship's second mate and Tomas, who was, it seemed to me, forever engaged in long confabulations in the man's cabin, and, as much to make talk as for any other reason, I asked Carlos if he had noticed his dependent's familiarity. It was noticeable because Castro held aloof from every other soul on board. Carlos answered me with one of his nervous and angry smiles.

"Ah, Juan mine, do not ask too many questions! I wish you could come with me all the way, but I cannot tell you all I know. I do not even myself know all. It seems that the man is going to leave the ship in Jamaica, and has letters for that Señor Ramon, the merchant, even as I have. *Vaya;* more I cannot tell you."

This struck me as curious, and a little of the whole mystery seemed from that time to attach to the second mate, who before had been no more to me than a long, sallow Nova Scotian, with a disagreeable intonation and rather offensive manners. I began to watch him, desultorily, and was rather startled by something more than a suspicion that he himself was watching me. On one occasion in particular I seemed to observe this. The second mate was lankily stalking the deck, his hands in his pockets. As he paused in his walk to spit into the sea beside me, Carlos said:

"And you, my Juan, what will you do in this Jamaica?"

The sense that we were approaching land was already all over the ship. The second mate leered at me

enigmatically, and moved slowly away. I said that I
was going to the Horton Estates, Rooksby's, to learn
planting under a Mr. Macdonald, the agent. Carlos
shrugged his shoulders. I suppose I had spoken with
some animation.

"Ah," he said, with his air of great wisdom and varied
experience, of disillusionment, "it will be much the
same as it has been at your home—after the first days.
Hard work and a great sameness." He began to cough
violently.

I said bitterly enough, "Yes. It will be always the
same with me. I shall never see life. You've seen all
that there is to see, so I suppose you do not mind settling
down with an old uncle in a palace."

He answered suddenly, with a certain darkness of
manner, "That is as God wills. Who knows? Perhaps
life, even in my uncle's palace, will not be so safe."

The second mate was bearing down on us again.

I said jocularly, "Why, when I get very tired of life
at Horton Pen, I shall come to see you in your uncle's
town."

Carlos had another of his fits of coughing.

"After all, we are kinsmen. I dare say you would
give me a bed," I went on.

The second mate was quite close to us then.

Carlos looked at me with an expression of affection
that a little shamed my lightness of tone:

"I love you much more than a kinsman, Juan," he
said. "I wish you could come with me. I try to
arrange it. Later, perhaps, I may be dead. I am very
ill."

He was undoubtedly ill. Campaigning in Spain, exposure in England in a rainy time, and then the ducking
when we came on board, had done him no good. He
looked moodily at the sea.

"I wish you could come. I will try——"

The mate had paused, and was listening quite unaffectedly, behind Carlos' back.

A moment after Carlos half turned and regarded him with a haughty stare.

He whistled and walked away.

Carlos muttered something that I did not catch about "spies of that pestilent Irishman." Then:

"I will not selfishly take you into any more dangers," he said. "But life on a sugar plantation is not fit for you."

I felt glad and flattered that a personage so romantic should deem me a fit companion for himself. He went forward as if with some purpose.

Some days afterwards the second mate sent for me to his cabin. He had been on the sick list, and he was lying in his bunk, stripped to the waist, one arm and one leg touching the floor. He raised himself slowly when I came in, and spat. He had in a pronounced degree the Nova Scotian peculiarities and accent, and after he had shaved, his face shone like polished leather.

"Hallo!" he said. "See heeyur, young Kemp, does your neck just *itch* to be stretched?"

I looked at him with mouth and eyes agape.

He spat again, and waved a claw towards the forward bulkhead.

"They'll do it for yeh," he said. "You're such a green goose, it makes me sick a bit. You hevn't reckoned out the chances, not quite. It's a kind of dead reckoning yeh hevn't had call to make. Eh?"

"What do you mean?" I asked, bewildered.

He looked at me, grinning, half naked, with amused contempt, for quite a long time, and at last offered sardonically to open my eyes for me.

I said nothing.

"Do you know what will happen to you," he asked, "ef yeh don't get quit of that Carlos of yours?"

I was surprised into muttering that I didn't know.

"I can tell yeh," he continued. "Yeh will get hanged."

By that time I was too amazed to get angry. I simply suspected the Blue Nose of being drunk. But he glared at me so soberly that next moment I felt frightened.

"Hanged by the neck," he repeated; and then added, "Young fellow, you scoot. Take a fool's advice, and *scoot*. That Castro is a blame fool, anyhow. Yeh want men for that job. Men, I tell you." He slapped his bony breast.

I had no idea that he could look so ferocious. His eyes fascinated me, and he opened his cavernous mouth as if to swallow me. His lantern jaws snapped without a sound. He seemed to change his mind.

"I am done with yeh," he said, with a sort of sinister restraint. He rose to his feet, and, turning his back to me, began to shave, squinting into a broken looking-glass.

I had not the slightest inkling of his meaning. I only knew that going out of his berth was like escaping from the dark lair of a beast into a sunlit world. There is no denying that his words, and still more his manner, had awakened in me a sense of insecurity that had no precise object, for it was manifestly absurd and impossible to suspect my friend Carlos. Moreover, hanging was a danger so recondite, and an eventuality so extravagant, as to make the whole thing ridiculous. And yet I remembered how unhappy I felt, how inexplicably unhappy. Presently the reason was made clear. I was homesick. I gave no further thought to the second mate. I looked at the harbour we were entering, and thought of the home I had left so eagerly. After all, I was no more than a boy, and even younger in mind than in body.

Queer-looking boats crawled between the shores like tiny water beetles. One headed out towards us, then another. I did not want them to reach us. It was as if I did not wish my solitude to be disturbed, and I was not pleased with the idea of going ashore. A great ship, floating high on the water, black and girt with the two broad yellow streaks of her double tier of guns, glided out slowly from beyond a cluster of shipping in the bay. She passed without a hail, going out under her topsails with a flag at the fore. Her lofty spars overtopped our masts immensely, and I saw the men in her rigging looking down on our decks. The only sounds that came out of her were the piping of boatswain's calls and the tramping of feet. Imagining her to be going home, I felt a great desire to be on board. Ultimately, as it turned out, I went home in that very ship, but then it was too late. I was another man by that time, with much queer knowledge and other desires. Whilst I was looking and longing I heard Carlos' voice behind me asking one of our sailors what ship it was.

"Don't you know a flagship when you see it?" a voice grumbled surlily. "Admiral Rowley's," it continued. Then it rumbled out some remarks about "pirates, vermin, coast of Cuba."

Carlos came to the side, and looked after the man-of-war in the distance.

"*You* could help us," I heard him mutter.

CHAPTER FIVE

THERE was a lad called Barnes, a steerage passenger of about my own age, a raw, red-headed Northumbrian yokel, going out as a recruit to one of the West Indian regiments. He was a serious, strenuous youth, and I had talked a little with him at odd moments. In my great loneliness I went to say good-by to him after I had definitely parted with Carlos.

I had been in our cabin. A great bustle of shore-going, of leave-taking had sprung up all over the ship. Carlos and Castro had entered with a tall, immobile, gold-spectacled Spaniard, dressed all in white, and with a certain air of noticing and attentive deference, bowing a little as he entered the cabin in earnest conference with Tomas Castro. Carlos had preceded them with a certain nonchalance, and the Spaniard—it was the Señor Ramon, the merchant I had heard of—regarded him as if with interested curiosity. With Tomas he seemed already familiar. He stood in the doorway, against the strong light, bowing a little.

With a certain courtesy, touched with indifference, Carlos made him acquainted with me. Ramon turned his searching, quietly analytic gaze upon me.

"But is the *caballero* going over, too?" he asked.

Carlos said, "No. I think not, now."

And at that moment the second mate, shouldering his way through a white-clothed crowd of shore people, made up behind Señor Ramon. He held a letter in his hand.

"*I* am going over," he said, in his high nasal voice, and with a certain ferocity.

44

Ramon looked round apprehensively.

Carlos said, "The señor, my cousin, wishes for a Mr. Macdonald. You know him, señor?"

Ramon made a dry gesture of perfect acquaintance. "I think I have seen him just now," he said. "I will make inquiries."

All three of them had followed him, and became lost in the crowd. It was then, not knowing whether I should ever see Carlos again, and with a desperate, unhappy feeling of loneliness, that I had sought out Barnes in the dim immensity of the steerage.

In the square of wan light that came down the scuttle he was cording his hair-trunk—unemotional and very matter-of-fact. He began to talk in an everyday voice about his plans. An uncle was going to meet him, and to house him for a day or two before he went to the barracks.

"Mebbe we'll meet again," he said. "I'll be here many years, I think."

He shouldered his trunk and climbed unromantically up the ladder. He said he would look for Macdonald for me.

It was absurd to suppose that the strange ravings of the second mate had had an effect on me. "Hanged! Pirates!" Was Carlos really a pirate, or Castro, his humble friend? It was vile of me to suspect Carlos. A couple of men, meeting by the scuttle, began to talk loudly, every word coming plainly to my ears in the stillness of my misery, and the large deserted steerage. One of them, new from home, was asking questions. Another answered:

"Oh, I lost half a seroon the last voyage—the old thing."

"Haven't they routed out the scoundrels yet?" the other asked.

The first man lowered his voice. I caught only that "the admiral was an old fool—no good for this job. He's found out the name of the place the pirates come from—Rio Medio. That's the place, only he can't get in at it with his three-deckers. You saw his flagship?"

Rio Medio was the name of the town to which Carlos was going—which his uncle owned. They moved away from above.

What was I to believe? What could this mean? But the second mate's, "Scoot, young man," seemed to come to my ears like the blast of a trumpet. I became suddenly intensely anxious to find Macdonald— to see no more of Carlos.

From above came suddenly a gruff voice in Spanish. "Señor, it would be a great folly."

Tomas Castro was descending the ladder gingerly. He was coming to fetch his bundle. I went hastily into the distance of the vast, dim cavern of spare room that served for the steerage.

"I want him very much," Carlos said. "I like him. He would be of help to us."

"It's as your worship wills," Castro said gruffly. They were both at the bottom of the ladder. "But an Englishman there would work great mischief. And this youth——"

"I will take him, Tomas," Carlos said, laying a hand on his arm.

"Those others will think he is a spy. I know them," Castro muttered. "They will hang him, or work some devil's mischief. You do not know that Irish judge— the *canaille*, the friend of priests."

"He is very brave. He will not fear," Carlos said.

I came suddenly forward. "I will not go with you," I said, before I had reached them even.

Castro started back as if he had been stung, and

caught at the wooden hand that sheathed his steel blade.

"Ah, it is you, Señor," he said, with an air of relief and dislike. Carlos, softly and very affectionately, began inviting me to go to his uncle's town. His uncle, he was sure, would welcome me. Jamaica and a planter's life were not fit for me.

I had not then spoken very loudly, or had not made my meaning very clear. I felt a great desire to find Macdonald, and a simple life that I could understand.

"I am not going with you," I said, very loudly this time.

He stopped at once. Through the scuttle of the half-deck we heard a hubbub of voices, of people exchanging greetings, of Christian names called out joyously. A tumultuous shuffling of feet went on continuously over our heads. The ship was crowded with people from the shore. Perhaps Macdonald was amongst them, even looking for me.

"Ah, *amigo mio*, but you *must* now," said Carlos gently—"you must——" And, looking me straight in the face with a still, penetrating glance of his big, romantic eyes, "It is a good life," he whispered seductively, "and I like you, John Kemp. You are young— very young yet. But I love you very much for your own sake, and for the sake of one I shall never see again."

He fascinated me. He was all eyes in the dusk, standing in a languid pose just clear of the shaft of light that fell through the scuttle in a square patch.

I lowered my voice, too. "What life?" I asked.

"Life in my uncle's palace," he said, so sweetly and persuasively that the suggestiveness of it caused a thrill in me.

His uncle could nominate me to posts of honour fit for a *caballero*.

I seemed to wake up. "Your uncle the pirate!" I cried, and was amazed at my own words.

Tomas Castro sprang up, and placed his rough, hot hand over my lips.

"Be quiet, John Kemp, you fool!" he hissed with sudden energy.

He had spruced himself, but I seemed to see the rags still flutter about him. He had combed out his beard, but I could not forget the knots that had been in it.

"I told your worship how foolish and wrong-headed these English are," he said sardonically to Carlos. And then to me, "If the señor speaks loudly again, I shall kill him."

He was evidently very frightened of something.

Carlos, silent as an apparition at the foot of the ladder, put a finger to his lips and glanced upwards.

Castro writhed his whole body, and I stepped backwards. "I know what Rio Medio is," I said, not very loudly. "It is a nest of pirates."

Castro crept towards me again on the points of his toes. "Señor Don Juan Kemp, child of the devil," he hissed, looking very much frightened, "you must die!"

I smiled. He was trembling all over. I could hear the talking and laughing that went on under the break of the poop. Two women were kissing, with little cries, near the hatchway. I could hear them distinctly.

Tomas Castro dropped his ragged cloak with a grandiose gesture.

"By my hand!" he added with difficulty.

He was really very much alarmed. Carlos was gazing up the hatch. I was ready to laugh at the idea of dying by Tomas Castro's hand while, within five feet of me, people were laughing and kissing. I should have laughed had I not suddenly felt his hand on my throat. I kicked his shins hard, and fell backwards

over a chest. He went back a step or two, flourished
his arm, beat his chest, and turned furiously upon
Carlos.

"He will get us murdered," he said.   "Do you think
we are safe here? If these people here heard that name
they wouldn't wait to ask who your worship is. They
would tear us to pieces in an instant. I tell you—*moi*,
Tomas Castro—he will ruin us, this white fool——"

Carlos began to cough, shaken speechless as if by an
invisible devil. Castro's eyes ran furtively all round
him, then he looked at me. He made an extraordinary
swift motion with his right hand, and I saw that he was
facing me with a long steel blade displayed. Carlos
continued to cough. The thing seemed odd, laughable
still. Castro began to parade round me: it was as if
he were a cock performing its saltatory rites before
attacking. There was the same tenseness of muscle.
He stepped with extraordinary care on the points of
his toes, and came to a stop about four feet from me.
I began to wonder what Rooksby would have thought
of this sort of thing, to wonder why Castro himself
found it necessary to crouch for such a long time. Up
above, the hum of many people, still laughing, still
talking, faded a little out of mind. I understood,
horribly, how possible it would be to die within those
few feet of them. Castro's eyes were dusky yellow, the
pupils a great deal inflated, the lines of his mouth very
hard and drawn immensely tight. It seemed extraordinary that he should put so much emotion into such
a very easy killing. I had my back against the bulkhead, it felt very hard against my shoulder-blades. I
had no dread, only a sort of shrinking from the actual
contact of the point, as one shrinks from being tickled.
I opened my mouth. I was going to shriek a last, despairing call, to the light and laughter of meetings above,

when Carlos, still shaken, with one white hand pressed
very hard upon his chest, started forward and gripped
his hand round Castro's steel. He began to whisper
in the other's hairy ear. I caught:

"You are a fool. He will not make us to be molested,
he is my kinsman."

Castro made a reluctant gesture towards Barnes'
chest that lay between us.

"We could cram him into that," he said.

"Oh, bloodthirsty fool," Carlos answered, recovering
his breath; "is it always necessary to wash your hands in
blood? Are we not in enough danger? Up—up! Go
see if the boat is yet there. We must go quickly; up—
up——" He waved his hand towards the scuttle.

"But still," Castro said. He was reluctantly fitting
his wooden hand upon the blue steel. He sent a baleful
yellow glare into my eyes, and stooped to pick up his
ragged cloak.

"Up—mount!" Carlos commanded.

Castro muttered, "*Vamos*," and began clumsily to
climb the ladder, like a bale of rags being hauled from
above. Carlos placed his foot on the steps, preparing
to follow him. He turned his head round towards me,
his hand extended, a smile upon his lips.

"Juan," he said, "let us not quarrel. You are very
young; you cannot understand these things; you cannot
weigh them; you have a foolish idea in your head. I
wished you to come with us because I love you, Juan.
Do you think I wish you evil? You are true and brave,
and our families are united." He sighed suddenly.

"I do not want to quarrel!" I said. "I don't."

I did not want to quarrel; I wanted more to cry. I
was very lonely, and he was going away. Romance
was going out of my life.

He added musically, "You even do not understand.

There is someone else who speaks for you to me, always
—someone else. But one day you will. I shall come
back for you—one day." He looked at me and smiled.
It stirred unknown depths of emotion in me. I would
have gone with him, then, had he asked me. "One
day," he repeated, with an extraordinary cadence of
tone.

His hand was grasping mine; it thrilled me like a
woman's; he stood shaking it very gently.

"One day," he said, "I shall repay what I owe you.
I wished you with me, because I go into some danger.
I wanted you. Good-by. *Hasta mas ver*."

He leaned over and kissed me lightly on the cheek,
then climbed away. I felt that the light of Romance
was going out of my life. As we reached the top of the
ladder, somebody began to call harshly, startlingly. I
heard my own name and the words, "mahn ye were
speerin' after."

The light was obscured, the voice began clamouring
insistently.

"John Kemp, Johnnie Kemp, noo. Here's the
mahn ye were speerin' after. Here's Macdonald."

It was the voice of Barnes, and the voice of the every
day. I discovered that I had been tremendously upset.
The pulses in my temples were throbbing, and I wanted
to shut my eyes—to sleep! I was tired; Romance had
departed. Barnes and the Macdonald he had found
for me represented all the laborious insects of the world;
all the ants who are forever hauling immensely heavy
and immensely unimportant burdens up weary hillocks,
down steep places, getting nowhere and doing nothing.

Nevertheless I hurried up, stumbling at the hatchway against a man who was looking down. He said
nothing at all, and I was dazed by the light. Barnes
remarked hurriedly, "This 'll be your Mr. Mac-

donald"; and, turning his back on me, forgot my existence. I felt more alone than ever. The man in front of me held his head low, as if he wished to butt me.

I began breathlessly to tell him I had a letter from "my—my—Rooksby—brother-in-law—Ralph Rooksby"—I was panting as if I had run a long way. He said nothing at all. I fumbled for the letter in an inner pocket of my waistcoat, and felt very shy. Macdonald maintained a portentous silence; his enormous body was enveloped rather than clothed in a great volume of ill-fitting white stuff; he held in his hand a great umbrella with a vivid green lining. His face was very pale, and had the leaden transparency of a boiled artichoke; it was fringed by a red beard streaked with gray, as brown flood-water is with foam. I noticed at last that the reason for his presenting his forehead to me was an incredible squint—a squint that gave the idea that he was performing some tortuous and defiant feat with the muscles of his neck.

He maintained an air of distrustful inscrutability. The hand which took my letter was very large, very white, and looked as if it would feel horribly flabby. With the other he put on his nose a pair of enormous mother-of-pearl-framed spectacles—things exactly like those of a cobra's—and began to read. He had said precisely nothing at all. It was for him and what he represented that I had thrown over Carlos and what *he* represented. I felt that I deserved to be received with acclamation. I was not. He read the letter very deliberately, swaying, umbrella and all, with the slow movement of a dozing elephant. Once he crossed his eyes at me, meditatively, above the mother-of-pearl rims. He was so slow, so deliberate, that I own I began to wonder whether Carlos and Castro were still on board. It seemed to be at least half an hour before

Macdonald cleared his throat, with a sound resembling the coughing of a defective pump, and a mere trickle of a voice asked:

"Hwhat evidence have ye of identitee?"

I hadn't any at all, and began to finger my buttonholes as shamefaced as a pauper before a Board. The certitude dawned upon me suddenly that Carlos, even if he would consent to swear to me, would prejudice my chances.

I cannot help thinking that I came very near to being cast adrift upon the streets of Kingston. To my asseverations Macdonald returned nothing but a series of minute "humphs." I don't know what overcame his scruples; he had shown no signs of yielding, but suddenly turning on his heel made a motion with one of his flabby white hands. I understood it to mean that I was to follow him aft.

The decks were covered with a jabbering turmoil of negroes with muscular arms and brawny shoulders. All their shining black faces seemed to be momentarily gashed open to show rows of white, and were spotted with inlaid eyeballs. The sounds coming from them were a bewildering noise. They were hauling baggage about aimlessly. A large soft bundle of bedding nearly took me off my legs. There wasn't room for emotion. Macdonald laid about him with the handle of the umbrella a few inches from the deck; but the passage that he made for himself closed behind him.

Suddenly, in the pushing and hurrying, I came upon a little clear space beside a pile of boxes. Stooping over them was the angular figure of Nichols, the second mate. He looked up at me, screwing his yellow eyes together.

"Going ashore," he asked, "'long of that Puffing Billy?"

"What business is it of yours?" I mumbled sulkily.

Sudden and intense threatening came into his yellow eyes:

"Don't you ever come to you know where," he said; "I don't want no spies on what I do. There's a man there'll crack your little backbone if he catches you. Don't yeh come now. Never."

PART SECOND

THE GIRL WITH THE LIZARD

CHAPTER ONE

Rio Medio?" Señor Ramon said to me nearly two years afterwards. "The *caballero* is pleased to give me credit for a very great knowledge. What should I know of that town? There are doubtless good men there and very wicked, as in other towns. Who knows? Your worship must ask the boats' crews that the admiral has sent to burn the town. They will be back very soon now."

He looked at me, inscrutably and attentively, through his gold spectacles.

It was on the arcade before his store in Spanish Town. Long sunblinds flapped slightly. Before the next door a large sign proclaimed "Office of the *Buckatoro Journal.*" It was, as I have said, after two years—years which, as Carlos had predicted, I had found to be of hard work, and long, hot sameness. I had come down from Horton Pen to Spanish Town, expecting a letter from Veronica, and, the stage not being in, had dropped in to chat with Ramon over a consignment of Yankee notions, which he was prepared to sell at an extravagantly cheap price. It was just at the time when Admiral Rowley was understood to be going to make an energetic attempt upon the pirates who still infested the Gulf of Mexico and nearly ruined the Jamaica trade of those days. Naturally enough, we had talked of the mysterious town in which the pirates were supposed to have their headquarters.

"I know no more than others," Ramon said, "save, señor, that I lose much more because my dealings are much greater. But I do not even know whether those who take my goods are pirates, as you English say, or Mexican privateers, as the Havana authorities say. I do not very much care. *Basta*, what I know is that every week some ship with a letter of marque steals one of my consignments, and I lose many hundreds of dollars."

Ramon was, indeed, one of the most frequented merchants in Jamaica; he had stores in both Kingston and Spanish Town; his cargoes came from all the seas. All the planters and all the official class in the island had dealings with him.

"It was most natural that the hidalgo, your respected cousin, should consult me if he wished to go to any town in Cuba. Whom else should he go to? You yourself, señor, or the excellent Mr. Topnambo, if you desired to know what ships in a month's time are likely to be sailing for Havana, for New Orleans, or any Gulf port, you would ask me. What more natural? It is my business, my trade, to know these things. In that way I make my bread. But as for Rio· Medio, I do not know the place." He had a touch of irony in his composed voice. "But it is very certain," he went on, "that if your Government had not recognized the belligerent rights of the rebellious colony of Mexico, there would be now no letters of marque, no accursed Mexican privateers, and I and everyone else in the island should not now be losing thousands of dollars every year."

That was the eternal grievance of every Spaniard in the island—and of not a few of the English and Scotch planters. Spain was still in the throes of losing the Mexican colonies when Great Britain had acknowledged the existence of a state of war and a Mexican Government. Mexican letters of marque had immediately filled the Gulf. No kind of shipping was safe from them, and Spain was quite honestly powerless to prevent their swarming on the coast of Cuba—the Ever Faithful Island, itself.

"What can Spain do," said Ramon bitterly, "when even your Admiral Rowley, with his great ships, cannot rid the sea of them?" He lowered his voice. "I tell you, young señor, that England will lose this Island of Jamaica over this business. You yourself are a Separationist, are you not? . . . No? You live with Separationists. How could I tell? Many people say you are."

His words gave me a distinctly disagreeable sensation. I hadn't any idea of being a Separationist; I was loyal enough. But I understood suddenly, and for the first time, how very much like one I might look.

"I myself am nothing," Ramon went on impassively; "I am content that the island should remain English. It will never again be Spanish, nor do I wish that it should. But our little, waspish friend there"—he lifted one thin, brown hand to the sign of the *Buckatoro Journal*—"his paper is doing much mischief. I think the admiral or the governor will commit him to jail. He is going to run away and take his paper to Kingston; I myself have bought his office furniture."

I looked at him and wondered, for all his impassivity, what he knew—what, in the depths of his inscrutable Spanish brain, his dark eyes concealed.

He bowed to me a little. "There will come a very great trouble," he said.

Jamaica was in those days—and remained for many years after—in the throes of a question. The question was, of course, that of the abolition of slavery. The planters as a rule were immensely rich and overbearing. They said, "If the Home Government tries to abolish our slavery system, we will abolish the Home Govern-

ment, and go to the United States for protection." That
was treason, of course; but there was so much of it that
the governor, the Duke of Manchester, had to close his
ears and pretend not to hear. The planters had another grievance—the pirates in the Gulf of Mexico.
There was one in particular, a certain El Demonio or
Diableto, who practically sealed the Florida passage;
it was hardly possible to get a cargo underwritten, and
the planters' pockets felt it a good deal. Practically,
El Demonio had, during the last two years, gutted a
ship once a week, as if he wanted to help the Kingston
Separationist papers. The planters said, "If the Home
Government wishes to meddle with our internal affairs,
our slaves, let it first clear our seas. . . . Let it hang El
Demonio. . . ."

The Government had sent out one of Nelson's old
captains, Admiral Rowley, a good fighting man; but
when it came to clearing the Gulf of Mexico, he was
about as useless as a prize-fighter trying to clear a stable
of rats. I don't suppose El Demonio really did more
than a tithe of the mischief attributed to him, but in
the peculiar circumstances he found himself elevated
to the rank of an important factor in colonial politics.
The Ministerialist papers used to kill him once a
month; the Separationists made him capture one of
old Rowley's sloops five times a year. They both lied,
of course. But obviously Rowley and his frigates
weren't much use against a pirate whom they could not
catch at sea, and who lived at the bottom of a bottle-
necked creek with tooth rocks all over the entrance—
that was the sort of place Rio Medio was reported to
be. . . .

I didn't much care about either party—I was looking out for romance—but I inclined a little to the
Separationists, because Macdonald, with whom I lived

for two years at Horton Pen, was himself a Separationist, in a cool Scotch sort of way. He was an Argyleshire man, who had come out to the island as a lad in 1786, and had worked his way up to the position of agent to the Rooksby estate at Horton Pen. He had a little estate of his own, too, at the mouth of the River Minho, where he grew rice very profitably. He had been the first man to plant it on the island.

Horton Pen nestled down at the foot of the tall white scars that end the Vale of St. Thomas and are not much unlike Dover Cliffs, hanging over a sea of squares of the green cane, alternating with masses of pimento foliage. Macdonald's wife was an immensely stout, raven-haired, sloe-eyed, talkative body, the most motherly woman I have ever known—I suppose because she was childless.

What was anomalous in my position had passed away with the next outward mail. Veronica wrote to me; Ralph to his attorney and the Macdonalds. But by that time Mrs. Mac. had darned my socks ten times.

The surrounding gentry, the large resident land-owners, of whom there remained a sprinkling in the Vale, were at first inclined to make much of me. There was Mrs. Topnambo, a withered, very dried-up personage, who affected pink trimmings; she gave the *ton* to the countryside as far as *ton* could be given to a society that rioted with hospitality. She made efforts to draw me out of the Macdonald environment, to make me differentiate myself, because I was the grandson of an earl. But the Topnambos were the great Loyalists of the place, and the Macdonalds the principal Separationists, and I stuck to the Macdonalds. I was searching for romance, you see, and could find none in Mrs. Topnambo's white figure, with its dryish, gray skin, and pink patches round the neck, that lay forever in dark or darkened rooms, and talked querulously of "Your uncle, the earl," whom I had never seen. I didn't get on with the men any better. They were either very dried up and querulous, too, or else very liquorish or boisterous in an incomprehensible way. Their evenings seemed to be a constant succession of shouts of laughter, merging into undignified staggers of white trousers through blue nights—round the corners of ragged huts. I never understood the hidden sources of their humour, and I had not money enough to mix well with their lavishness. I was too proud to be indebted to them, too. They didn't even acknowledge me on the road at last; they called me poor-spirited, a thin-blooded nobleman's cub—a Separationist traitor—and left me to superintend niggers and save money. Mrs. Mac., good Separationist though she was, as became the wife of her husband, had the word "home" forever on her lips. She had once visited the Rooksbys at Horton; she had treasured up a host of tiny things, parts of my forgotten boyhood, and she talked of them and talked of them until that past seemed a wholly desirable time, and the present a dull thing.

Journeying in search of romance—and that, after all, is our business in this world—is much like trying to catch the horizon. It lies a little distance before us, and a little distance behind—about as far as the eye can carry. One discovers that one has passed through it just as one passed what is to-day our horizon. One looks back and says, "Why, there it is." One looks forward and says the same. It lies either in the old days when we used to, or in the new days when we shall. I look back upon those days of mine, and little things remain, come back to me, assume an atmosphere, take significance, go to the making of a *temps jadis*. Probably, when I look back upon what is the dull, arid waste of to-day, it will be much the same.

I could almost wish to take again one of the long, uninteresting night rides from the Vale to Spanish Town, or to listen once more to one of old Macdonald's interminable harangues on the folly of Mr. Canning's policy, or the virtues of Scotch thrift. "Jack, lad," he used to bellow in his curious squeak of a voice, "a gentleman you may be of guid Scots blood. But ye're a puir body's son for a' that." He was set on my making money and turning honest pennies. I think he really liked me.

It was with that idea that he introduced me to Ramon, "an esteemed Spanish merchant of Kingston and Spanish Town." Ramon had seemed mysterious when I had seen him in company with Carlos and Castro but re-introduced in the homely atmosphere of the Macdonalds, he had become merely a saturnine, tall, dusky-featured, gold-spectacled Spaniard, and very good company. I learnt nearly all my Spanish from him. The only mystery about him was the extravagantly cheap rate at which he sold his things under the flagstaff in front of Admiral Rowley's house, the King's House, as it was called. The admiral himself was said to have extensive dealings with Ramon; he had at least the reputation of desiring to turn an honest penny, like myself. At any rate, everyone, from the proudest planters to the editor of the *Buckatoro Journal* next door, was glad of a chat with Ramon, whose knowledge of an immense variety of things was as deep as a draw-well—and as placid.

I used to buy island produce through him, ship it to New Orleans, have it sold, and re-import parcels of "notions," making a double profit. He was always ready to help me, and as ready to talk, saying that he had an immense respect for my relations, the Riegos.

That was how, at the end of my second year in the island, I had come to talking to him. The stage should have brought a letter from Veronica, who was to have presented Rooksby with a son and heir, but it was unaccountably late. I had been twice to the coach office, and was making my way desultorily back to Ramon's. He was talking to the editor of the *Buckatoro Journal*— the man from next door—and to another who had, whilst I walked lazily across the blazing square, ridden furiously up to the steps of the arcade. The rider was talking to both of them with exaggerated gestures of his arms. He had ridden off, spurring, and the editor, a little, gleaming-eyed hunchback, had remained in the sunshine, talking excitedly to Ramon.

I knew him well, an amusing, queer, warped, Satanic member of society, who was a sort of nephew to the Macdonalds, and hand in glove with all the Scotch Separationists of the island. He had started an extraordinary, scandalous paper that, to avoid sequestration, changed its name and offices every few issues, and was said by Loyalists, like the Topnambos, to have an extremely bad influence.

He subsisted a good deal on the charity of people like the Macdonalds, and I used sometimes to catch sight of him at evenfall listening to Mrs. Macdonald; he would be sitting beside her hammock on the veranda, his head very much down on his breast, very much on one side, and his great hump portending over his little white face, and ruffling up his ragged black hair. Mrs. Macdonald clacked all the scandal of the Vale, and the *Buckatoro Journal* got the benefit of it all, with adornments.

For the last month or so the *Journal* had been more

than usually effective, and it was only because Rowley
was preparing to confound his traducers by the boat
attack on Rio Medio, that a warrant had not come
against David. When I saw him talking to Ramon, I
imagined that the rider must have brought news of a
warrant, and that David was preparing for flight. He
hopped nimbly from Ramon's steps into the obscurity
of his own door. Ramon turned his spectacles softly
upon me.

"There you have it," he said. "The folly; the folly!
To send only little boats to attack such a nest of villains.
It is inconceivable."

The horseman had brought news that the boats of
Rowley's squadron had been beaten off with great loss,
in their attack on Rio Medio.

Ramon went on with an air of immense superiority,
"And all the while we merchants are losing thousands."

His dark eyes searched my face, and it came dis-
agreeably into my head that he was playing some part;
that his talk was delusive, his anger feigned; that,
perhaps, he still suspected me of being a Separationist.
He went on talking about the failure of the boat attack.
All Jamaica had been talking of it, speculating about it,
congratulating itself on it. British valour was going to
tell; four boats' crews would do the trick. And now the
boats had been beaten off, the crews captured, half the
men killed! Already there was panic on the island. I
could see men coming together in little knots, talking
eagerly. I didn't like to listen to Ramon, to a Spaniard
talking in that way about the defeat of my countrymen
by his. I walked across the King's Square, and the
stage driving up just then, I went to the office, and got
my correspondence.

Veronica's letter came like a faint echo, like the
sound of very distant surf, heard at night; it seemed

*c

impossible that any one could be as interested as she in the things that were happening over there. She had had a son; one of Ralph's aunts was its godmother. She and Ralph had been to Bath last spring; the country wanted water very badly. Ralph had used his influence, had explained matters to a very great personage, had spent a little money on the injured runners. In the meanwhile I had nearly forgotten the whole matter; it seemed to be extraordinary that they should still be interested in it.

I was to come back; as soon as it was safe I was to come back; that was the main tenor of the letter.

I read it in a little house of call, in a whitewashed room that contained a cardboard cat labelled "The Best," for sole ornament. Four swarthy fellows, Mexican patriots, were talking noisily about their War of Independence, and the exploits of a General Trapelascis, who had been defeating the Spanish troops over there. It was almost impossible to connect them with a world that included Veronica's delicate handwriting with the pencil lines erased at the base of each line of ink. They seemed to be infinitely more real. Even Veronica's interest in me seemed a little strange; her desire for my return irritated me. It was as if she had asked me to return to a state of bondage, after having found myself. Thinking of it made me suddenly aware that I had become a man, with a man's aims, and a disillusionized view of life. It suddenly appeared very wonderful that I could sit calmly there, surveying, for instance, those four sinister fellows with daggers, as if they were nothing at all. When I had been at home the matter would have caused me extraordinary emotions, as many as if I had seen an elephant in a travelling show. As for going back to my old life, it didn't seem to be possible.

CHAPTER TWO

ONE night I was riding alone towards Horton Pen. A large moon hung itself up above me like an enormous white plate. Finally the sloping roof of the Ferry Inn, with one dishevelled palm tree drooping over it, rose into the disk. The window lights were reflected like shaken torches in the river. A mass of objects, picked out with white globes, loomed in the high shadow of the inn, standing motionless. They resolved themselves into a barouche, with four horses steaming a great deal, and an army of negresses with bandboxes on their heads. A great lady was on the road; her querulous voice was calling to someone within the open door that let down a soft yellow light from the top of the precipitous steps. A nondescript object, with apparently two horns and a wheel, rested inert at the foot of the sign-post; two negroes were wiping their foreheads beside it. That resolved itself into a man slumbering in a wheelbarrow, his white face turned up to the moon. A sort of buzz of voices came from above; then a man in European clothes was silhouetted against the light in the doorway. He held a full glass very carefully and started to descend. Suddenly he stopped emotionally. Then he turned half-right and called back, "Sir Charles! Sir Charles! Here's the very man! I protest, the very man!" There was an interrogative roar from within. It was like being outside a lion's cage.

People appeared and disappeared in front of the lighted door; windows stood open, with heads craning out all along the inn face. I was hurrying off the back of my horse when the admiral came out on to the steps. Someone lit a torch, and the admiral became a dark, solid figure, with the flash of the gold lace on his coat. He stood very high in the leg; had small white whiskers, and a large nose that threw a vast shadow on to his forehead in the upward light; his high collar was open, and a mass of white appeared under his chin; his head was uncovered. A third male face, very white, bobbed up and down beside his shining left shoulder. He kept on saying:

"What? what? what? Hey, what? . . . That man?" He appeared to be halfway between supreme content and violent anger. At last he delivered himself. "Let's duck him . . . hey? . . . Let's duck him!" He spoke with a sort of benevolent chuckle, then raised his voice and called, "Tinsley! Tinsley! Where the deuce is Tinsley?"

A high nasal sound came from the carriage window. "Sir Charles! Sir Charles! Let there be no scene in my presence, I beg."

I suddenly saw, halfway up, laboriously ascending the steps, a black figure, indistinguishable at first on account of deformities. It was David Macdonald. Since his last, really terrible comments on the failure of the boat-attack, he had been lying hidden somewhere. It came upon me in a flash that he was making his way from one hiding place to another. In making his escape from Spanish Town, either to Kingston or the Vale, he had run against the admiral and his party returning from the Topnambos' ball. It was hardly a coincidence: everyone on the road met at the Ferry Inn. But that hardly made the thing more pleasant.

Sir Charles continued to clamour for Tinsley, his flag lieutenant, who, as a matter of fact, was the man drunk in the wheelbarrow. When this was explained by the

shouts of the negroes, he grunted, "Umph!" turned
on the man at his side, and said, "Here, Oldham; you
lend a hand to duck the little toad." It was the sort
of thing that the thirsty climate of Jamaica rendered
frequent enough. Oldham dropped his glass and
protested. Macdonald continued silently and enigmatically to climb the steps; now he was in for it he
showed plenty of pluck. No doubt he recognized that,
if the admiral made a fool of himself, he would be
afraid to issue warrants in soberness. I could not
stand by and see them bully the wretched little creature.
At the same time I didn't, most decidedly, want to
identify myself with him.

I called out impulsively, "Sir Charles, surely you
would not use violence to a cripple."

Then, very suddenly, they all got to action, David
Macdonald reaching the top of the steps. Shrieks
came from the interior of the carriage, and from the
waiting negresses. I saw three men were falling upon
a little thing like a damaged cat. I couldn't stand
that, come what might of it.

I ran hastily up the steps, hoping to be able to make
them recover their senses, a force of purely conventional emotion impelling me. It was no business of
mine; I didn't want to interfere, and I felt like a man
hastening to separate half a dozen fighting dogs too
large to be pleasant.

When I reached the top, there was a sort of undignified scuffle, and in the end I found myself standing
above a ghastly white gentleman who, from a sitting
posture, was gasping out, "I'll commit you! . . . .
I swear I'll commit you! . . . ." I helped him
to his feet rather apologetically, while the admiral
behind me was asking insistently who the deuce I was.
The man I had picked up retreated a little, and then

turned back to look at me. The light was shining on my face, and he began to call out, "I know him. I know him perfectly well. He's John Kemp. I'll commit him at once. The papers are in the barouche." After that he seemed to take it into his head that I was going to assault him again. He bolted out of sight, and I was left facing the admiral. He stared at me contemptuously. I was streaming with perspiration and upbraiding him for assaulting a cripple.

The admiral said, "Oh, that's what you think? I will settle with you presently. This is rank mutiny."

I looked at Oldham, who was the admiral's secretary. He was extremely dishevelled about his neck, much as if a monkey had been clawing him thereabouts. Half of his roll collar flapped on his heaving chest; his stock hung down behind like a cue. I had seen him kneeling on the ground with his head pinned down by the hunchback. I said loftily:

"What did you set him on a little beggar like that for? You were three to one. What did you expect?"

The admiral swore. Oldham began to mop with a lace handkerchief at a damaged upper lip from which a stream of blood was running; he even seemed to be weeping a little. Finally, he vanished in at the door, very much bent together. The undaunted David hopped in after him coolly.

The admiral said, "I know your kind. You're a treasonous dog, sir. This is mutiny. You shall be made an example of."

All the same he must have been ashamed of himself, for presently he and the two others went down the steps without even looking at me, and their carriage rolled away.

Inside the inn I found a couple of merchant captains, one asleep with his head on the table and little rings shining in his great red ears; the other very spick and span—of what they called the new school then. His name was Williams—Captain Williams of the *Lion*, which he part owned; a man of some note for the dinners he gave on board his ship. His eyes sparkled blue and very round in a round rosy face, and he clawed effusively at my arm.

"Well done!" he bubbled over. "You gave it them; strike me, you did! It did me good to see and hear. I wasn't going to poke my nose in, not I. But I admire you, my boy."

He was a quite guileless man with a strong dislike for the admiral's blundering—a dislike that all the seamen shared—and for people of the Topnambo kidney who affected to be above his dinners. He assured me that I had burst upon those gentry roaring. . . "like the Bull of Bashan. You should have seen!" and he drank my health in a glass of punch.

David Macdonald joined us, looming through wreaths of tobacco smoke. He was always very nice in his dress, and had washed himself into a state of enviable coolness.

"They won't touch me now," he said. "I wanted that assault and battery. . . ." He suddenly turned vivid, sarcastic black eyes upon me. "But you," he said—"my dear Kemp! You're in a devil of a scrape! They'll have a warrant out against you under the Black Act. I know the gentry."

"Oh, he won't mind," Williams struck in, "I know him; he's a trump. Afraid of nothing."

David Macdonald made a movement of his head that did duty for an ominous shake:

"It's a devil of a mess," he said. "But I'll touch them up. Why did you hit Topnambo? He's the spitefullest beast in the island. They'll make it out

high treason. They are capable of sending you home
on this charge."

"Oh, never say die." Williams turned to me, "Come
and dine with me on board at Kingston to-morrow
night. If there's any fuss I'll see what I can do. Or
you can take a trip with me to Havana till it blows over.
My old woman's on board." His face fell. "But
there, you'll get round her. I'll see you through."

They drank some sangaree and became noisy. I
wasn't very happy; there was much truth in what
David Macdonald had said. Topnambo would certainly do his best to have me in jail—to make an
example of me as a Separationist to please the admiral
and the Duke of Manchester. Under the spell of his
liquor Williams became more and more pressing with
his offers of help.

"It's the devil that my missus should be on board,
just this trip. But hang it! come and dine with me.
I'll get some of the Kingston men—the regular hot
men—to stand up for you. They will when they hear
the tale."

There was a certain amount of sense in what he said.
If warrants were out against me, he or some of the
Kingston merchants whom he knew, and who had no
cause to love the admiral, might help me a good deal.

Accordingly, I did go down to Kingston. It happened to be the day when the seven pirates were hanged
at Port Royal Point. I had never seen a hanging, and
a man who hadn't was rare in those days. I wanted
to keep out of the way, but it was impossible to get a
boatman to row me off to the *Lion*. They were all
dying to see the show, and, half curious, half reluctant,
I let myself drift with the crowd.

.The gallows themselves stood high enough to be
seen—a long very stout beam supported by posts at

each end. There was a blazing sun, and the crowd pushed and shouted and craned its thousands of heads every time one heard the cry of "Here they come," for an hour or so. There was a very limpid sky, a very limpid sea, a scattering of shipping gliding up and down, and the very silent hills a long way away. There was a large flavour of Spaniards among the crowd. I got into the middle of a knot of them, jammed against the wheels of one of the carriages, standing, hands down, on tiptoe, staring at the long scaffold. There were a great many false alarms, sudden outcries, hushing again rather slowly. In between I could hear someone behind me talk Spanish to the occupants of the carriage. I thought the voice was Ramon's, but I could not turn, and the people in the carriage answered in French, I thought. A man was shouting "Cool Drinks" on the other side of them.

Finally, there was a roar, an irresistible swaying, a rattle of musket ramrods, a rhythm of marching feet, and the grating of heavy iron-bound wheels. Seven men appeared in sight above the heads, clinging to each other for support, and being drawn slowly along. The little worsted balls on the infantry shakos bobbed all round their feet. They were a sorry-looking group, those pirates; very wild-eyed, very ragged, dust-stained, weather-beaten, begrimed till they had the colour of unpolished mahogany. Clinging still to each other as they stood beneath the dangling ropes of the long beam, they had the appearance of a group of statuary to forlorn misery. Festoons of chains completed the "composition."

One was a very old man with long yellow-white hair, one a negro whose skin had no lustre at all. The rest were very dark-skinned, peak-bearded, and had long hair falling round their necks. A soldier with a ham-

mer and a small anvil climbed into the cart, and bent
down out of sight. There was a ring of iron on iron,
and the man next the very old man raised his arms and
began to speak very slowly, very distinctly, and very
mournfully. It was quite easy to understand him; he
declared his perfect innocence. No one listened to him;
his name was Pedro Nones. He ceased speaking, and
someone on a horse, the High Sheriff, I think, galloped
impatiently past the cart and shouted. Two men got
into the cart, one pulled the rope, the other caught the
pirate by the elbows. He jerked himself loose, and
began to cry out; he seemed to be lost in amazement,
and shrieked:

"*Adonde está el padre? . . . Adonde está el padre?*"

No one answered; there wasn't a priest of any de-
nomination; I don't know whether the omission was
purposed. The man's face grew convulsed with agony,
his eyeballs stared out very white and vivid, as he
struggled with the two men. He began to curse us
epileptically for compassing his damnation. A hoarse
patter of Spanish imprecations came from the crowd
immediately round me. The man with the voice like
Ramon's groaned in a lamentable way; someone else
said, "What infamy . . . what infamy!"

An aged voice said tremulously in the carriage, "This
shall be a matter of official remonstrance." Another
said, "Ah, these English heretics!"

There was a forward rush of the crowd, which carried
me away. Someone in front began to shout orders, and
the crowd swayed back again. The infantry muskets
rattled. The commotion lasted some time. When it
ceased, I saw that the man about to die had been kissing
the very old man; tears were streaming down the gray,
parchment-coloured cheeks. Pedro Nones had the rope
round his neck; it curved upwards loosely towards the

beam, growing taut as the cart jolted away. He shouted:

"*Adiós, viejo, para siempre adi*——"

My whole body seemed to go dead all over. I happened to look downwards at my hands; they were extraordinarily white, with the veins standing out all over them. They felt as if they had been sodden in water, and it was quite a long time before they recovered their natural colour. The rest of the men were hung after that, the cart jolting a little way backwards and forwards and growing less crowded after every journey. One man, who was very large framed and stout, had to go through it twice because the rope broke. He made a good deal of fuss. My head ached, and after the involuntary straining and craning to miss no details was over, I felt sick and dazed. The people talked a great deal as they streamed back, loosening over the broader stretch of pebbles; they seemed to wish to remind each other of details. I have an idea that one or two, in the sheer largeness of heart that seizes one after occasions of popular emotions, asked me in exulting voices if I had seen the nigger's tongue sticking out.

Others thought that there wasn't very much to be exultant over. We had not really captured the pirates; they had been handed over to the admiral by the Havana authorities—as an international courtesy I suppose, or else because they were pirates of no account and short in funds, or because the admiral had been making a fuss in front of the Morro. It was even asserted by the anti-admiral faction that the seven weren't pirates at all, but merely Cuban *mauvais sujets*, hawkers of derogatory *coplas*, and known freethinkers.

In any case, excited people cheered the High Sheriff

and the returning infantry, because it was pleasant to
hang any kind of Spaniard. I got nearly knocked down
by the kettle-drummers, who came through the scattering crowd at a swinging quick-step. As I cannoned off
the drums, a hand caught at my arm, and someone
else began to speak to me. It was old Ramon, who was
telling me that he had a special kind of Manchester
goods at his store. He explained that they had arrived
very lately, and that he had come from Spanish Town
solely on their account. One made the eighth of a
penny a yard more on them than on any other kind.
If I would deign to have some of it offered to my inspection, he had his little curricle just off the road.
He was drawing me gently towards it all the time, and
I had not any idea of resisting. He had been behind
in the crowd, he said, beside the carriage of the commissioner and the judge of the Marine Court sent by
the Havana authorities to deliver the pirates.

It was after that, that in Ramon's dusky store, I had
my first sight of Seraphina and of her father, and then
came my meeting with Carlos. I could hardly believe
my eyes when I saw him come out with extended hand.
It was an extraordinary sensation, that of talking to
Carlos again. He seemed to have worn badly. His
face had lost its moist bloom, its hardly distinguishable
subcutaneous flush. It had grown very, very pale.
Dark blue circles took away from the blackness and
sparkle of his eyes. And he coughed, and coughed.

He put his arm affectionately round my shoulders and
said, "How splendid to see you again, my Juan." His
eyes had affection in them, there was no doubt about
that, but I felt vaguely suspicious of him. I remembered how we had parted on board the *Thames*. "We
can talk here," he added; "it is very pleasant. You
shall see my uncle, that great man, the star of Cuban

law, and my cousin Seraphina, your kinsfolk. They love you; I have spoken well of you." He smiled gayly, and went on, "This is not a place befitting his greatness, nor my cousin's, nor, indeed, my own." He smiled again. "But I shall be very soon dead, and to me it matters little." He frowned a little, and then laughed. "But you should have seen the faces of your officers when my uncle refused to go to their governor's palace; there was to have been a *fiesta*, a 'reception'; is it not the word? It will cause a great scandal."

He smiled with a good deal of fine malice, and looked as if he expected me to be pleased. I said that I did not quite understand what had offended his uncle.

"Oh, it was because there was no priest," Carlos answered, "when those poor devils were hung. They were *canaille*. Yes; but one gives that much even to such. And my uncle was there in his official capacity as a—a plenipotentiary. He was very much distressed: we were all. You heard, my uncle himself had advised their being surrendered to your English. And when there was no priest he repented very bitterly. Why, after all, it was an infamy."

He paused again, and leant back against the counter. When his eyes were upon the ground and his face not animated by talking, there became lamentably insistent his pallor, the deep shadows under his eyes, and infinite sadness in the droop of his features, as if he were preoccupied by an all-pervading and hopeless grief. When he looked at me, he smiled, however.

"Well, at worst it is over, and my uncle is here in this dirty place instead of at your palace. We sail back to Cuba this very evening." He looked round him at Ramon's calicos and sugar tubs in the dim light, as if he accepted almost incredulously the fact that they could be in such a place, and the manner of his voice indicated that he thought our governor's palace would have been hardly less barbarous. "But I am sorry," he said suddenly, "because I wanted you—you and all your countrymen—to make a good impression on him. You must do it yourself alone. And you will. You are not like these others. You are our kinsman, and I have praised you very much. You saved my life."

I began to say that I had done nothing at all, but he waved his hand with a little smile.

"You are very brave," he said, as if to silence me. "I am not ungrateful."

He began again to ask for news from home—from my home. · I told him that Veronica had a baby, and he sighed.

"She married the excellent Rooksby?" he asked. "Ah, what a waste." He relapsed into silence again. "There was no woman in your land like her. She might have—— And to marry that—that excellent personage, my good cousin. It is a tragedy."

"It was a very good match," I answered.

He sighed again. "My uncle is asleep in there, now," he said, after a pause, pointing at the inner door. "We must not wake him; he is a very old man. You do not mind talking to me? You will wait to see them? Doña Seraphina is here, too."

"You have not married your cousin?" I asked.

I wanted very much to see the young girl who had looked at me for a moment, and I certainly should have been distressed if Carlos had said she was married.

He answered, "What would you have?" and shrugged his shoulders gently. A smile came into his face. "She is very willful. I did not please her, I do not know why. Perhaps she has seen too many men like me."

He told me that, when he reached Cuba, after parting with me on the *Thames*, his uncle, "in spite of certain influences," had received him quite naturally as his heir, and the future head of the family. But Seraphina, whom by the laws of convenience he ought to have married, had quite calmly refused him.

"I did not impress her; she is romantic. She wanted a very bold man, a Cid, something that it is not easy to have."

He paused again, and looked at me with some sort of challenge in his eyes.

"She could have met no one better than you," I said.

He waved his hand a little. "Oh, for that——" he said deprecatingly. "Besides, I am dying. I have never been well since I went into your cold sea, over there, after we left your sister. You remember how I coughed on board that miserable ship."

I did remember it very well.

He went to the inner door, looked in, and then came back to me.

"Seraphina needs a guide—a controller—someone very strong and gentle, and kind and brave. My uncle will never ask her to marry against her wish; he is too old and has too little will. And for any man who would marry her—except one—there would be great dangers, for her and for him. It would need a cool man, and a brave man, and a good one, too, to hazard, perhaps even life, for her sake. She will be very rich. All our lands, all our towns, all our gold." There was a suggestion of fabulousness in his dreamy voice. "They shall never be mine," he added. "*Vaya.*"

He looked at me with his piercing eyes set to an expression that might have been gentle mockery. At any rate, it also contained intense scrutiny, and, perhaps, a little of appeal. I sighed myself.

"There is a man called O'Brien in there," he said. "He does us the honour to pretend to my cousin's hand."

I felt singularly angry. "Well, he's not a Spaniard," I said.

Carlos answered mockingly, "Oh, for Spaniard, no. He is a descendant of the Irish kings."

"He's an adventurer," I said. "You ought to be on your guard. You don't know these bog-trotting fortune-hunters. They're the laughter of Europe, kings and all."

Carlos smiled again. "He's a very dangerous man for all that," he said. "I should not advise any one to come to Rio Medio, my uncle's town, without making a friend of the Señor O'Brien."

He went once more to the inner door, and, after a moment's whispering with someone within, returned to me.

"My uncle still sleeps," he said. "I must keep you a little longer. Ah, yes, the Señor O'Brien. He shall marry my cousin, I think, when I am dead."

"You don't know these fellows," I said.

"Oh, I know them very well," Carlos smiled, "there are many of them at Havana. They came there after what they call the '98, when there was great rebellion in Ireland, and many good Catholics were killed and ruined."

"Then he's a rebel, and ought to be hung," I said.

Carlos laughed as of old. "It may be, but, my good Juan, we Christians do not see eye to eye with you. This man rebelled against your government, but, also, he suffered for the true faith. He is a good Catholic; he has suffered for it; and in the Ever Faithful Island, that is a passport. He has climbed very high; he is a judge of the Marine Court at Havana. That is why he is here to-day, attending my uncle in this affair of delivering up the pirates. My uncle loves him very much. O'Brien was at first my uncle's clerk, and my uncle made him a *juez*, and he is also the intendant of my uncle's estates, and he has a great influence in my uncle's town of Rio Medio. I tell you, if you come to visit us, it will be as well to be on good terms with the Señor Juez O'Brien. My uncle is a very old man, and if I die before him, this O'Brien, I think, will end by marrying my cousin, because my poor uncle is very much in his hands. There are other pretenders, but they have little chance, because it is so very dangerous to come to my uncle's town of Rio Medio, on account of this man's intrigues and of his power with the populace."

I looked at Carlos intently. The name of the town had seemed to be familiar to me. Now I suddenly remembered that it was where Nicolas el Demonio, the pirate who was so famous as to be almost mythical, had beaten off Admiral Rowley's boats.

"Come, you had better see this Irish hidalgo who wants to do us so much honour,"—he gave an inscrutable glance at me,—"but do not talk loudly till my uncle wakes."

He threw the door open. I followed him into the room, where the vision of the ancient Don and the charming apparition of the young girl had retreated only a few moments before.

CHAPTER THREE

THE room was very lofty and coldly dim; there were great bars in front of the begrimed windows. It was very bare, containing only a long black table, some packing cases, and half a dozen rocking chairs. Of these, five were very new and one very old, black and heavy, with a green leather seat and a coat of arms worked on its back cushions. There were little heaps of mahogany sawdust here and there on the dirty tiled floor, and a pile of sacking in one corner. Beneath a window the flap of an open trap-door half hid a large green damp-stain; a deep recess in the wall yawned like a cavern, and had two or three tubs in the right corner; a man with a blond head, slightly bald as if he had been tonsured, was rocking gently in one of the new chairs.

Opposite him, with his aged face towards us, sat the old Don asleep in the high chair. His delicate white hands lay along the arms, one of them holding a gold vinaigrette; his black, silver-headed cane was between his silk-stockinged legs. The diamond buckles of his shoes shot out little vivid rays, even in that gloomy place. The young girl was sitting with her hands to her temples and her elbows on the long table, minutely examining the motionlessness of a baby lizard, a tiny thing with golden eyes, whom fear seemed to have turned into stone.

We entered quietly, and after a moment she looked up candidly into my eyes, and placed her finger on her lips, motioning her head towards her father. She placed her hand in mine, and whispered very clearly:

"Be welcome, my English cousin," and then dropped her eyes again to the lizard.

She knew all about me from Carlos. The man of whom I had seen only the top of his head, turned his chair suddenly and glinted at me with little blue eyes. He was rather small and round, with very firm flesh, and very white, plump hands. He was dressed in the black clothes of a Spanish judge. On his round face there was always a smile like that which hangs around the jaws of a pike—only more humorous. He bowed a little exaggeratedly to me and said:

"Ah, ye are that famous Mr. Kemp."

I said that I imagined him the more famous Señor Juez O'Brien.

"It's little use saying ye arren't famous," he said. His voice had the faint, infinitely sweet twang of certain Irishry; a thing as delicate and intangible as the scent of lime flowers. "Our noble friend"—he indicated Carlos with a little flutter of one white hand—"has told me what make of a dare-devil gallant ye are; breaking the skulls of half the Bow Street runners for the sake of a friend in distress. Well, I honour ye for it; I've done as much myself." He added, "In the old days," and sighed.

"You mean in the '98," I said, a little insolently.

O'Brien's eyes twinkled. He had, as a matter of fact, nearly lost his neck in the Irish fiasco, either in Clonmel or Sligo, bolting violently from the English dragoons, in the mist, to a French man-of-war's boats in the bay. To him, even though he was now a judge in Cuba, it was an episode of heroism of youth—of romance, in fact. So that, probably, he did not resent my mention of it. I certainly wanted to resent something that was slighting in his voice, and patronizing in his manner.

The old Don slumbered placidly, his face turned up to the distant begrimed ceiling.

"Now, I'll make you a fair offer," O'Brien said suddenly, after an intent study of the insolent glance that I gave him. I disliked him because I knew nothing about the sort of man he was. He was, as a matter of fact, more alien to me than Carlos. And he gave me the impression that, if perhaps he were not absolutely the better man, he could still make a fool of me, or at least make me look like a fool.

"I'm told you are a Separationist," he said. "Well, it's like me. I am an Irishman; there has been a price on my head in another island. And there are warrants out against you here for assaulting the admiral. We can work together, and there's nothing low in what I have in mind for you."

He had heard frequently from Carlos that I was a desperate and aristocratically lawless young man, who had lived in a district entirely given up to desperate and murderous smugglers. But this was the first I had heard definitely of warrants against me in Jamaica. That, no doubt, he had heard from Ramon, who knew everything. In all this little sardonic Irishman said to me, it seemed the only thing worth attention. It stuck in my mind while, in persuasive tones, and with airy fluency, he discoursed of the profits that could be made, nowadays, in arming privateers under the Mexican flag. He told me I needn't be surprised at their being fitted out in a Spanish colony. "There's more than one aspect to disloyalty like this," said he dispassionately, but with a quick wink contrasting with his tone.

Spain resented our recognition of their rebellious colonies. And with the same cool persuasiveness, relieved by humorous smiles, he explained that the loyal Spaniards of the Ever Faithful Island thought there was no sin in doing harm to the English, even under the Mexican flag, whose legal existence they did not recognize.

"Mind ye, it's an organized thing, I have something to say in it. It hurts Mr. Canning's Government at home, the curse of Cromwell on him and them. They will be dropping some of their own colonies directly. And as you are a Separationist, small blame to you, and I am an Irishman, we shan't cry our eyes out over it. Come, Mr. Kemp, 'tis all for the good of the Cause. . . . And there's nothing *low*. You are a gentleman, and I wouldn't propose anything that was. The very best people in Havana are interested in the matter. Our schooners lie in Rio Medio, but I can't be there all the time myself."

Surprise deprived me of speech. I glanced at Carlos. He was watching us inscrutably. The young girl touched the lizard gently, but it was too frightened to move. O'Brien, with shrewd glances, rocked his chair. . . . What did I want? he inquired. To see life? What he proposed was the life for a fine young fellow like me. Moreover, I was half Scotch. Had I forgotten the wrongs of my own country? Had I forgotten the '45?

"You'll have heard tell of a Scotch Chief Justice whose son spent in Amsterdam the money his father earned on the justice seat in Edinb'ro'—money paid for rum and run silks . . ."

Of course I had heard of it; everybody had; but it had been some years before.

"We're backwards hereabouts," O'Brien jeered. "But over there they winked and chuckled at the judge, and they do the same in Havana at us."

Suddenly from behind us the voice of the young girl said, "Of what do you discourse, my English cousin?"

O'Brien interposed deferentially. "Señorita, I ask him to come to Rio," he said.

She turned her large dark eyes scrutinizingly upon me, then dropped them again. She was arranging some melon seeds in a rayed circle round the lizard that looked motionlessly at her.

"Do not speak very loudly, lest you awaken my father," she warned us.

The old Don's face was still turned to the ceiling. Carlos, standing behind his chair, opened his mouth a little in a half smile. I was really angry with O'Brien by that time, with his air of omniscience, superiority, and self-content, as if he were talking to a child or someone very credulous and weak-minded.

"What right have you to speak for me, Señor Juez?" I said in the best Spanish I could.

The young girl looked at me once more, and then again looked down.

"Oh, I can speak for you," he answered in English, "because I know. Your position's this." He sat down in his rocking chair, crossed his legs, and looked at me as if he expected me to show signs of astonishment at his knowing so much. "You're in a hole. You must leave this island of Jamaica—surely it's as distressful as my own dear land—and you can't go home, because the runners would be after you. You're 'wanted' here as well as there, and you've nowhere to go."

I looked at him, quite startled by this view of my case. He extended one plump hand towards me, and still further lowered his voice.

"Now, I offer you a good berth, a snug berth. And 'tis a pretty spot." He got a sort of languorous honey into his voice, and drawled out, "The—the Señorita's." He took an air of businesslike candour. "You can help

us, and we you; we could do without you better than
you without us. Our undertaking—there's big names
in it, just as in the Free Trading you know so well, don't
be saying you don't—is worked from Havana. What
we need is a man we can trust. We had one—Nichols.
You remember the mate of the ship you came over in.
He was Nicola el Demonio; he won't be any longer—I
can't tell you why, it's too long a story."

I did remember very vividly that cadaverous Nova
Scotian mate of the *Thames*, who had warned me with
truculent menaces against showing my face in Rio
Medio. I remembered his sallow, shiny cheeks, and the
exaggerated gestures of his claw-like hands.

O'Brien smiled. "Nichols is alive right enough, but
no more good than if he were dead. And that's the
truth. He pretends his nerve's gone; he was a devil
among tailors for a time, but he's taken to crying now.
It was when your blundering old admiral's boats had
to be beaten off that his zeal cooled. He thinks the
British Government will rise in its strength." There
was a bitter contempt in his voice, but he regained his
calm business tone. "It will do nothing of the sort.
I've given them those seven poor devils that had to die
to-day without absolution. So Nichols is done for, as
far as we are concerned. I've got him put away to keep
him from blabbing. You can have his place—and
better than his place. He was only a sailor, which you
are not. However, you know enough of ships, and
what we want is a man with courage, of course, but
also a man we can trust. Any of the Creoles would
bolt into the bush the moment they'd five dollars
in hand. We'll pay you well; a large share of all you
take."

I laughed outright. "You're quite mistaken in your
man," I said. "You are, really."

He shook his head gently, and brushed an invisible speck from his plump black knees.

"You *must* go somewhere," he said. "Why not go with us?"

I looked at him, puzzled by his tenacity and assurance.

"Ramon here has told us you battered the admiral last night; and there's a warrant out already against you for attempted murder. You're hand and glove with the best of the Separationists in this island, I know, but they won't save you from being committed —for rebellion, perhaps. You know it as well as I do. You were down here to take a passage to-day, weren't you, now?"

I remembered that the Island Loyalists said that the pirates and Separationists worked together to bother the admiral and raise discontent. Living in the centre of Separationist discontent with the Macdonalds, I knew it was not true. But nothing was too bad to say against the planters who clamoured for union with the United States.

O'Brien leaned forward. His voice had a note of disdain, and then took one of deeper earnestness; it sank into his chest. He extended his hand; his eyebrows twitched. He looked—he was—a conspirator.

"I tell you I do it for the sake of Ireland," he said passionately. "Every ship we take, every clamour they raise here, is a stroke and is disgrace for them over there that have murdered us and ruined my own dear land." His face worked convulsively; I was in the presence of one of the primeval passions. But he grew calm immediately after. "*You* want Separation for reasons of your own. I don't ask what they are. No doubt you and your crony Macdonald and the rest of them will feather your own nests; I don't ask. But help me

to be a thorn in their sides—just a little—just a little
longer. What do I put in your way? Just what you
want. Have your Jamaica joined to the United States.
You'll be able to come back with your pockets full, and
I'll be joyful—for the sake of my own dear land."

I said suddenly and recklessly—if I had to face one
race-passion, he had to look at another; we were cat and
dog—Celt and Saxon, as it was in the beginning:

"I am not a traitor to my country."

Then I realized with sudden concern that I had
probably awakened the old Don. He stirred uneasily
in his chair, and lifted one hand.

"The moment I go out from here I'll denounce you,"
I said very low; "I swear I will. You're here; you
can't get away; you'll swing."

O'Brien started. His eyes blazed at me. Then he
frowned. "I've been misled," he muttered, with a
dark glance at Carlos. And recovering his jocular
serenity, "Ye mean it?" he asked; "it's not British
heroics?"

The old Don stirred again and sighed.

The young girl glided swiftly to his side. "Señor
O'Brien," she said, "you have so irritated my English
cousin that he has awakened my father."

O'Brien grinned gently. "'Tis ever the way," he
said sardonically. "The English fools do the harm and
the Irish fool gets the kicking." He rose to his feet,
quite collected, a spick-and-span little man. "I suppose I've said too much. Well, well! You are going to
denounce the senior judge of the Marine Court of
Havana as a pirate. I wonder who will believe you!"
He went behind the old Don's chair with the gliding
motion of a Spanish lawyer, and slipped down the open
trap-hatch near the window.

It was the disappearance of a shadow. I heard some

D

guttural mutterings come up through the hatch, a rustling, then silence. If he was afraid of me at all he
carried it off very well. I apologized to the young girl
for having awakened her father. Her colour was very
high, and her eyes sparkled. If she had not been so
very beautiful I should have gone away at once. She
said angrily:

"He is odious to me, the Señor Juez. Too long my
father has suffered his insolence." She was very small,
but she had an extraordinary dignity of command. "I
could see, Señor, that he was annoying you. Why
should you consider such a creature?" Her head
drooped. "But my father is very old."

I turned upon Carlos, who stood all black in the light
of the window.

"Why did you make me meet him? He may be a
judge of your Marine Court, but he's nothing but a
scoundrelly bog-trotter."

Carlos said a little haughtily, "You must not denounce him. You should not leave this place if I
feared you would try thus to bring dishonour on this
gray head, and involve this young girl in a public
scandal." His manner became soft. "For the honour
of the house you shall say nothing. And you shall
come with us. I need you."

I was full of mistrust now. If he did countenance
this unlawful enterprise, whose headquarters were in
Rio Medio, he was not the man for me. Though it was
big enough to be made, by the papers at home, of
political importance, it was, after all, neither more nor
less than piracy. The idea of my turning a sort of
Irish traitor was so extravagantly outrageous that now
I could smile at the imbecility of that fellow O'Brien.
As to turning into a sea-thief for lucre—my blood
boiled.

No. There was something else there. Something
deep; something dangerous; some intrigue, that I could
not conceive even the first notion of. But that Carlos
wanted anxiously to make use of me for some purpose
was clear. I was mystified to the point of forgetting
how heavily I was compromised even in Jamaica,
though it was worth remembering, because at that time
an indictment for rebellion—under the Black Act—was
no joking matter. I might be sent home under arrest;
and even then, there was my affair with the runners.

"It is coming to pay a visit," he was saying
persuasively, "while your affair here blows over, my
Juan—and—and—making my last hours easy, perhaps."

I looked at him; he was worn to a shadow—a shadow
with dark wistful eyes. "I don't understand you," I
faltered.

The old man stirred, opened his lids, and put a gold
vinaigrette to his nostrils.

"Of course I shall not denounce O'Brien," I said.
"I, too, respect the honour of your house."

"You are even better than I thought you. And if I
entreat you, for the love of your mother—of your
sister? Juan, it is not for myself, it is——"

The young girl was pouring some drops from a green
phial into a silver goblet; she passed close to us, and
handed it to her father, who had leant a little forward in
his chair. Every movement of hers affected me with an
intimate joy; it was as if I had been waiting to see just
that carriage of the neck, just that proud glance from
the eyes, just that droop of eyelashes upon the cheeks,
for years and years.

"No, I shall hold my tongue, and that's enough," I
said.

At that moment the old Don sat up and cleared his

throat. Carlos sprang towards him with an infinite
grace of tender obsequiousness. He mentioned my
name and the relationship, then rehearsed the innumerable titles of his uncle, ending "and patron of the
Bishopric of Pinar del Rio."

I stood stiffly in front of the old man. He bowed his
head at intervals, holding the silver cup carefully whilst
his chair rocked a little. When Carlos' mellow voice
had finished the rehearsing of the sonorous styles, I
mumbled something about "transcendent honour."

He stopped me with a little, deferentially peremptory
gesture of one hand, and began to speak, smiling with a
contraction of the lips and a trembling of the head.
His voice was very low, and quavered slightly, but
every syllable was enunciated with the same beauty of
clearness that there was in his features, in his hands, in
his ancient gestures.

"The honour is to me," he said, "and the pleasure. I
behold my kinsman, who, with great heroism, I am told,
rescued my dearly loved nephew from great dangers; it
is an honour to me to be able to give him thanks. My
beloved and lamented sister contracted a union with an
English hidalgo, through whose house your own very
honourable family is allied to my own; it is a pleasure to
me to meet after many years with one who has seen the
places where her later life was passed."

He paused, and breathed with some difficulty, as if
the speech had exhausted him. Afterwards he began
to ask me questions about Rooksby's aunt—the
lamented sister of his speech. He had loved her
greatly, he said. I knew next to nothing about her,
and his fine smile and courtly, aged, deferential manners
made me very nervous. I felt as if I had been taken to
pay a ceremonial visit to a supreme pontiff in his dotage.
He spoke about Horton Priory with some animation for

a little while, and then faltered, and forgot what he was speaking of. Suddenly he said:

"But where is O'Brien? Did he write to the Governor here? I should like you to know the Señor O'Brien. He is a spiritual man."

I forbore to say that I had already seen O'Brien, and the old man sank into complete silence. It was beginning to grow dark, and the noise of suppressed voices came from the open trap-door. Nobody said anything.

I felt a sort of uneasiness; I could by no means understand the connection between the old Don and what had gone before, and I did not, in a purely conventional sense, know how long I ought to stop. The sky through the barred windows had grown pallid.

The old Don said suddenly, "You must visit my poor town of Rio Medio," but he gave no specific invitation and said nothing more.

Afterwards he asked, rather querulously, "But where is O'Brien? He must write those letters for me."

The young girl said, "He has preceded us to the ship; he will write there."

She had gone back to her seat. Don Balthasar shrugged his shoulders to his ears, and moved his hands from his knees.

"Without doubt, he knows best," he said, "but he should ask me."

It grew darker still; the old Don seemed to have fallen asleep again. Save for the gleam of the silver buckle of his hat, he had disappeared into the gloom of the place. I remembered my engagement to dine with Williams on board the *Lion*, and I rose to my feet. There did not seem to be any chance of my talking to the young girl. She was once more leaning nonchalantly over the lizard, and her hair drooped right across her face like clusters of grapes. There was a gleam on a little piece of white

forehead, and all around and about her there were
shadows deepening. Carlos came concernedly towards
me as I looked at the door.

"But you must not go yet," he said a little suavely;
"I have many things to say. Tell me——"

His manner heightened my uneasiness to a fear. The
expression of his eyes changed, and they became fixed
over my shoulder, while on his lips the words "You
must come, you must come," trembled, hardly audible.
I could only shake my head. At once he stepped back
as if resigning. He was giving me up—and it occurred
to me that if the danger of his seduction was over, there
remained the danger of arrest just outside the door.

Someone behind me said peremptorily, "It is time,"
and there was a flickering diminution of the light. I
had a faint instantaneous view of the old Don dozing,
with his head back—of the tall windows, cut up into
squares by the black bars. Something hairily coarse
ran harshly down my face; I grew blind; my mouth, my
eyes, my nostrils were filled with dust; my breath shut
in upon me became a flood of warm air. I had no time
to resist. I kicked my legs convulsively; my elbows
were drawn tight against my sides. Someone grunted
under my weight; then I was carried—down, along, up,
down again; my feet were knocking along a wall, and
the top of my head rubbed occasionally against what
must have been the roof of a low stone passage, issuing
from under the back room of Ramon's store. Finally,
I was dropped upon something that felt like a heap of
wood-shavings. My surprise, rage, and horror had
been so great that, after the first stifled cry, I had made
no sound. I heard the footsteps of several men going
away.

CHAPTER FOUR

I REMAINED lying there, bound hand and foot, for a long time; for quite long enough to allow me to collect my senses and see that I had been a fool to threaten O'Brien. I had been nobly indignant, and behold! I had a sack thrown over my head for my pains, and was put away safely somewhere or other. It seemed to be a cellar.

I was in search of romance, and here were all the elements; Spaniards, a conspirator, and a kidnapping; but I couldn't feel a fool and romantic as well. True romance, I suppose, needs a whirl of emotions to extinguish all the senses except that of sight, which it dims. Except for sight, which I hadn't at all, I had the use of them all, and all reported unpleasant things.

I ached and smarted with my head in a sack, with my mouth full of flour that had gone mouldy and offended my nostrils; I had a sense of ignominy, and I was extremely angry; I could see that the old Don was in his dotage—but Carlos I was bitter against.

I was not really afraid; I could not suppose that the Riegos would allow me to be murdered or seriously maltreated. But I was incensed against Fate or Chance or whatever it is—on account of the ignominious details, the coarse sack, the mouldy flour, the stones of the tunnel that had barked my shins, the tightness of the ropes that bound my ankles together, and seemed to cut into my wrists behind my back.

I waited, and my fury grew in a dead silence. How would it end—with what outrage? I would show my contempt and preserve my dignity by submitting without a struggle—I despised this odious plot. At last there were voices, footsteps; I found it very hard to carry out my resolution and refrain from stifled cries and kicks. I was lifted up and carried, like a corpse, with many stumbles, by men who sometimes growled as they hastened along. From time to time somebody murmured "Take care." Then I was deposited into a boat. The world seemed to be swaying, splashing, jarring— and it became obvious to me that I was being taken to some ship. The Spanish ship, of course. Suddenly I broke into cold perspiration at the thought that, after all, their purpose might be to drop me quickly overboard. "Carlos!" I cried. I felt the point of a knife on my breast. "Silence, Señor!" said a gruff voice.

This fear vanished when we came alongside a ship evidently already under way; but I was handled so roughly and clumsily that I was thoroughly exhausted and out of breath, by the time I was got on board. All was still around me; I was left alone on a settee in the main cabin, as I imagined. For a long time I made no movement; then a door opened and shut. There was a murmured conversation between two voices. This went on in animated whispers for a time. At last I felt as if someone were trying, rather ineffectually, to remove the sack itself. Finally, that actually did rub its way over my head, and something soft and silken began to wipe my eyes with a surprising care, and even tenderness. "This was stupidly done," came a discontented remark; "you do not handle a *caballero* like this."

"And how else was it to be done, to that kind of *caballero*?" was the curt retort.

By that time I had blinked my eyes into a condition for remaining open for minute stretches. Two men were bending over me—Carlos and O'Brien himself. The latter said:

"Believe me, your mistake made this necessary. This young gentleman was about to become singularly inconvenient, and he is in no way harmed."

He spoke in a velvety voice, and walked away gently through the darkness. Carlos followed with the lanthorn dangling at arm's length; strangely enough he had not even looked at me. I suppose he was ashamed, and I was too proud to speak to him, with my hands and feet tied fast. The door closed, and I remained sitting in the darkness. Long small windows grew into light at one end of the place, curved into an outline that suggested a deep recess. The figure of a crowned woman, that moved rigidly up and down, was silhouetted over my body. Groaning creaks of wood and the faint swish of water made themselves heard continuously.

I turned my head to a click, I saw a door open a little way, and the small blue flame of a taper floated into the room. Then the door closed with a definite sound of shutting in. The light shone redly through protecting fingers, and upwards on to a small face. It came to a halt, and I made out the figure of a girl leaning across a table and looking upwards. There was a click of glass, and then a great blaze of light created a host of shining things; a glitter of gilded carvings, red velvet couches, a shining table, a low ceiling, painted white, on carved rafters. A large silver lamp she had lighted kept on swinging to the gentle motion of the ship.

She stood just in front of me; the girl that I had seen through the door; the girl I had seen play with the melon seeds. She was breathing fast—it agitated me to be alone with her—and she had a little shining dagger in her hand.

*D

She cut the rope round my ankles, and motioned me imperiously to turn round.

"Your hands—your hands!"

I turned my back awkwardly to her, and felt the grip of small, cool, very firm fingers upon my wrists. My arms fell apart, numb and perfectly useless; I was half aware of pain in them, but it passed unnoticed among a cloud of other emotions. I didn't feel my finger-tips because I had the agitation, the flutter, the tantalization of looking at her.

I was all the while conscious of the—say, the irregularity of my position, but I felt very little fear. There were the old Don, an ineffectual, silver-haired old gentleman, who obviously was not a pirate; the sleek O'Brien, and Carlos, who seemed to cough on the edge of a grave—and this young girl. There was not any future that I could conceive, and the past seemed to be cut off from me by a narrow, very dark tunnel through which I could see nothing at all.

The young girl was, for the moment, what counted most on the whole, the only thing the eye could rest on. She affected me as an apparition familiar, yet absolutely new in her charm. I had seen her gray eyes; I had seen her red lips; her dark hair, her lithe gestures; the carriage of her head; her throat, her hands. I knew her; I seemed to have known her for years. A rush of strange, sweet feeling made me dumb. She was looking at me, her lips set, her eyes wide and still; and suddenly she said:

"Ask nothing. The land is not far yet. You can escape, Carlos thought. . . . But no! You would only perish for nothing. Go with God." She pointed imperiously towards the square stern-ports of the cabin.

Following the direction of her hand, my eyes fell upon the image of a Madonna; rather large—perhaps a third life-size; with a gilt crown, a pink serious face bent a little forward over a pink naked child that perched on her lift arm and raised one hand. It stood on a bracket, against the rudder casing, with fat cherubs' heads carved on the supports. The young girl crossed herself with a swift motion of the hand. The stern-ports, glazed in small panes, were black, and gleaming in a white frame-work.

"Go—go—go with God," the girl whispered urgently. "There is a boat——"

I made a motion to rise; I wanted to go. The idea of having my liberty, of its being again a possibility, made her seem of less importance; other things began to have their share. But I could not stand, though the blood was returning, warm and tingling, in my legs and hands. She looked at me with a sharp frown puckering her brows a little; beat a hasty tattoo with one of her feet, and cast a startled glance towards the forward door that led on deck. Then she walked to the other side of the table, and sat looking at me in the glow of the lamp.

"Your life hangs on a thread," she murmured.

I answered, "You have given it to me. Shall I never repay?" I was acutely conscious of the imperfection of my language.

She looked at me sharply; then lowered her lids. Afterwards she raised them again. "Think of yourself. Every moment is important."

"I will be as quick as I can," I said.

I was chafing my ankles and looking up at her. I wanted, very badly, to thank her for taking an interest in me, only I found it very difficult to speak to her. Suddenly she sprang to her feet:

"That man thinks he can destroy you. I hate him—I detest him! You have seen how he treats my father."

It struck me, like a blow, that she was merely aveng-
ing O'Brien's insolence to her father. I had been kidnapped against Don Balthasar Riego's will. It gave
me very well the measure of the old man's powerlessness
in face of his intendant—who was obviously confident
of afterwards soothing the resentment.

I was glad I had not thanked her for taking an interest in me. I was distressed, too, because once more I
had missed Romance by an inch.

Someone kicked at the locked door. A voice cried—
I could not help thinking—warningly, "Seraphina,
Seraphina," and another voice said with excessive soft-
ness, "*Señorita! Voynos! quelle folie.*"

She sprang at me. Her hand hurt my wrist as she
dragged me aft. I scrambled clumsily into the recess
of the counter, and put my head out. The night air
was very chilly and full of brine; a little boat towing by a
long painter was sheering about in the phosphorescent
wake of the ship. The sea itself was pallid in the light
of the moon, invisible to me. A little astern of us, on
our port quarter, a vessel under a press of canvas seemed
to stand still; looming up like an immense pale ghost.
She might have been coming up with us, or else we had
just passed her—I couldn't tell. I had no time to find
out, and I didn't care. The great thing was to get hold
of the painter. The whispers of the girl urged me, but
the thing was not easy; the rope, fastened higher up,
streamed away out of reach of my hand. At last, by
watching the moment when it slacked, and throwing
myself half out of the stern window, I managed to hook
it with my finger-tips. Next moment it was nearly
jerked away from me, but I didn't lose it, and the boat
taking a run just then under the counter, I got a good
hold. The sound of another kick at the door made me
swing myself out, head first, without reflection. I got

soused to the waist before I had reached the bows of
the boat. With a frantic effort I clambered up and
rolled in. When I got on my legs, the jerky motion of
tossing had ceased, the boat was floating still, and the
light of the stern windows was far away already. The
girl had managed to cut the painter.

The other vessel was heading straight for me, rather
high on the water, broad-beamed, squat, and making
her way quietly, like a shadow. The land might have
been four or five miles away—I had no means of knowing exactly. It looked like a high black cloud, and
purple-gray mists here and there among the peaks hung
like scarves.

I got an oar over the stern to scull, but I was not fit
for much exertion. I stared at the ship I had left.
Her stern windows glimmered with a slight up-and-
down motion; her sails seemed to fall into black confusion against the blaze of the moon; faint cries came to
me out of her, and by the alteration of her shape I
understood that she was being brought to, preparatory
to lowering a boat. She might have been half a mile
distant when the gleam of her stern windows swung
slowly round and went out. I had no mind to be re-
captured, and began to scull frantically towards the
other vessel. By that time she was quite near—near
enough for me to hear the lazy sound of the water at her
bows, and the occasional flutter of a sail. The land
breeze was dying away, and in the wake of the moon
I perceived the boat of my pursuers coming over, black
and distinct; but the other vessel was nearly upon me.
I sheered under her starboard bow and yelled, "Ship
ahoy! Ship ahoy!"

There was a lot of noise on board, and no one seemed
to hear my shouts. Several voices yelled. "That
cursed Spanish ship ahead is heaving-to athwart our

hawse." The crew and the officers seemed all to be forward shouting abuse at the "lubberly Dago," and it looked as though I were abandoned to my fate. The ship forged ahead in the light air; I failed in my grab at her fore chains, and my boat slipped astern, bumping against the side. I missed the main chain, too, and yelled all the time with desperation, "For God's sake! Ship ahoy! For God's sake throw me a rope, somebody, before it's too late!"

I was giving up all hope when a heavy coil—of a brace, I suppose—fell upon my head, nearly knocking me over. Half stunned as I was, desperation lent me strength to scramble up her side hand over hand, while the boat floated away from under my feet. I was done up when I got on the poop. A yell came from forward, "Hard aport." Then the same voice addressed itself to abusing the Spanish ship very close to us now. "What do you mean by coming-to right across my bows like this?" it yelled in a fury.

I stood still in the shadows on the poop. We were drawing slowly past the stern of the Spaniard, and O'Brien's voice answered in English:

"We are picking up a boat of ours that's gone adrift with a man. Have you seen anything of her?"

"No—confound you and your boat."

Of course those forward knew nothing of my being on board. The man who had thrown me the rope—a passenger, a certain Major Cowper, going home with his wife and child—had walked away proudly, without deigning as much as to look at me twice, as if to see a man clamber on board a ship ten miles from the land was the most usual occurrence. He was, I found afterwards, an absurd, pompous person, as stiff as a ramrod, and so full of his own importance that he imagined he had almost demeaned himself by his condescension in throwing down the rope in answer to my despairing cries. On the other hand, the helmsman, the only other person aft, was so astounded as to become quite speechless. I could see, in the light of the binnacle thrown upon his face, his staring eyes and his open mouth.

The voice forward had subsided by then, and as the stern of the Spanish ship came abreast of the poop, I stepped out of the shadow of the sails, and going close to the rail I said, not very loud—there was no need to shout—but very distinctly:

"I am out of your clutches, Mr. O'Brien, after all. I promise you that you shall hear of me yet."

Meanwhile, another man had come up from forward on the poop, growling like a bear, a short, rotund little man, the captain of the ship. The Spanish vessel was dropping astern, silent, with her sails all black, hiding the low moon. Suddenly a hurried hail came out of her.

"What ship is this?"

"What's that to you, blank your eyes? The *Breeze*, if you want to know. What are you going to do about it?" the little skipper shouted fiercely. In the light wind the ships were separating slowly.

"Where are you bound to?" hailed O'Brien's voice again.

The little skipper laughed with exasperation. "Dash your blanked impudence. To Havana, and be hanged to you. Anything more you want to know? And my name's Lumsden, and I am sixty years old, and if I had you here, I would put a head on you for getting in my way, you——"

He stopped, out of breath. Then, addressing himself to his passenger:

"That's the Spanish chartered ship that brought these sanguinary pirates that were hanged this morning,

major. She's taking the Spanish commissioner back.
I suppose they had no man-of-war handy for the service
in Cuba. Did you ever——"

He had caught sight of me for the first time, and
positively jumped a foot high with astonishment.

"Who on earth's that there?"

His astonishment was comprehensible. The major,
without deigning to enlighten him, walked proudly
away. He was too dignified a person to explain.

It was left to me. Frequenting, as I had been doing,
Ramon's store, which was a great gossiping centre of
the maritime world in Kingston, I knew the faces and
the names of most of the merchant captains who used
to gather there to drink and swap yarns. I was not
myself quite unknown to little Lumsden. I told him
all my story, and all the time he kept on scratching his
bald head, full of incredulous perplexity. Old Señor
Ramon! Such a respectable man. And I had been
kidnapped? From his store!

"If I didn't see you here in my cuddy before my eyes,
I wouldn't believe a word you say," he declared absurdly.

But he was ready enough to take me to Havana.
However, he insisted upon calling down his mate, a
gingery fellow, short, too, but wizened, and as stupid
as himself.

"Here's that Kemp, you know. The young fellow
that Macdonald of the Horton Pen picked up somewhere two years ago. The Spaniards in that ship kidnapped him—so he says. He says they are pirates. But
that's a government chartered ship, and all the pirates
that have ever been in her were hanged this morning in
Kingston. But here he is, anyhow. And he says that
at home he had throttled a Bow Street runner before
he went off with the smugglers. Did you ever hear the

likes of it, Mercer? I shouldn't think he was telling us a parcel of lies; hey, Mercer?"

And the two grotesque little chaps stood nodding their heads at me sagaciously.

"He's a desperate character, then," said Mercer at last, cautiously. "This morning, the very last thing I heard ashore, as I went to fetch the fresh beef off, is that he had been assaulting a justice of the peace on the highroad, and had been trying to knock down the admiral, who was coming down to town in a chaise with Mr. Topnambo. There's a warrant out against him under the Black Act, sir."

Then he brightened up considerably. "So he must have been kidnapped or something after all, sir, or he would be in chokey now."

It was true, after all. Romance reserved me for another fate, for another sort of captivity, for more than one sort. And my imagination had been captured, enslaved already by the image of that young girl who had called me her English cousin, the girl with the lizard, the girl with the dagger! And with every word she uttered romance itself, if I had only known it, the romance of persecuted lovers, spoke to me through her lips.

That night the Spanish ship had the advantage of us in a freshening wind, and overtook the *Breeze*. Before morning dawned she passed us, and before the close of the next day she was gone out of sight ahead, steering, apparently, the same course with ourselves.

Her superior sailing had an enormous influence upon my fortunes; and I was more adrift in the world than ever before, more in the dark as to what awaited me than when I was lugged along with my head in a sack. I gave her but little thought. A sort of numbness had come over me. I could think of the girl who had cut me free, and for all my resentment at the indignity of my treatment, I had hardly a thought to spare for the man who had me bound. I was pleased to remember that she hated him; that she had said so herself. For the rest, I had a vague notion of going to the English Consul in Havana. After all, I was not a complete nobody. I was John Kemp, a gentleman, well connected; I could prove it. The Bow Street runner had not been dead as I had thought. The last letter from Veronica informed me that the man had given up thief-catching, and was keeping, now, a little inn in the neighbourhood. Ralph, my brother-in-law, had helped him to it, no doubt. I could come home safely now.

And I had discovered I was no longer anxious to return home.

CHAPTER FIVE

THERE wasn't any weirdness about the ship when I woke in the sunlight. She was old and slow and rather small. She carried Lumsden (master), Mercer (mate), a crew that seemed no better and no worse than any other crew, and the old gentleman who had thrown me the rope the night before, and who seemed to think that he had derogated from his dignity in doing it. He was a Major Cowper, retiring from a West Indian regiment, and had with him his wife and a disagreeable little girl, with a yellow pigtail and a bony little chest and arms.

On the whole, they weren't the sort of people that one would have chosen for companions on a pleasure-trip. Major Cowper's wife lay all day in a deck chair, alternately drawing to her and repulsing the whining little girl. The major talked to me about the scandals with which the world was filled, and kept a suspicious eye upon his wife. He spent the morning in shaving what part of his face his white whiskers did not cover, the afternoon in enumerating to me the subjects on which he intended to write to the Horse Guards. He had grown entirely amiable, perhaps for the reason that his wife ignored my existence.

Meantime I let the days slip by idly, only wondering how I could manage to remain in Havana and breathe the air of the same island with the girl who had delivered me. Perhaps some day we might meet—who knows? I was not afraid of that Irishman.

It never occurred to me to bother about the course

we were taking, till one day we sighted the Cuban coast, and I heard Lumsden and Mercer pronounce the name of Rio Medio. The two ridiculous old chaps talked of Mexican privateers, which seemed to rendezvous off that place. They pointed out to me the headland near the bay. There was no sign of privateer or pirate, as far as the eye could reach. In the course of beating up to windward we closed in with the coast, and then the wind fell.

I remained motionless against the rail for half the night, looking at the land. Not a single light was visible. A wistful and dreamy longing pervaded me, as though I had been drugged. I dreamed, as young men dream, of a girl's face. She was sleeping there within this dim vision of land. Perhaps this was as near as I should ever be able to approach her. I felt a sorrow without much suffering. A great stillness reigned around the ship, over the whole earth. At last I went below and fell asleep.

I was awakened by the idea that I had heard an extraordinary row—shouting and stamping. But there was a dead silence, to which I was listening with all my ears. Suddenly there was a little pop, as if someone had spat rather vigorously; then a succession of shouts, then another little pop, and more shouts, and the stamping overhead. A woman began to shriek on the other side of the bulkhead, then another woman somewhere else, then the little girl. I hurried on deck, but it was some minutes before I could make things fit together. I saw Major Cowper on the poop; he was brandishing a little pistol and apostrophizing Lumsden, who was waving ineffectual arms towards the sky; and there was a great deal of shouting, forward and overhead. Cowper rushed at me, and explained that something was an abominable scandal, and that there were women on board. He waved his pistol towards the side; I noticed that the butt was inlaid with mother-of-pearl. Lumsden rushed at him and clawed at his clothes, imploring him not to be rash.

We were so close in with the coast that the surf along the shore gleamed and sparkled in full view.

Someone shouted aloft, "Look out! They are firing again."

Then only I noticed, a quarter of a mile astern and between the land and us, a little schooner, rather low in the water, curtseying under a cloud of white canvas —a wonderful thing to look at. It was as if I had never seen anything so instinct with life and the joy of it. A snowy streak spattered away from her bows at each plunge. She came at a great speed, and a row of faces looking our way became plain, like a beady decoration above her bulwarks. She swerved a little out of her course, and a sort of mushroom of smoke grew out of her side; there was a little gleam of smouldering light hidden in its heart. The spitting bang followed again, and something skipped along the wave-tops beside us, raising little pillars of spray that drifted away on the wind. The schooner came back on her course, heading straight for us; a shout like groaned applause went up from on board us. Lumsden hid his face in his hands.

I could hear little Mercer shrieking out orders forwards. We were shortening sail. The schooner, luffing a little, ranged abreast. A hail like a metal blare came out of her.

"If you donn'd heef-to we seenk you! We seenk you! By God!"

Major Cowper was using abominable language beside me. Suddenly he began to call out to someone:

"Go down . . . go down, I say."

A woman's face disappeared into the hood of the

companion like a rabbit's tail into its burrow. There was
a great volley of cracks from the loose sails, and the ship
came to. At the same time the schooner, now on our
beam and stripped of her light kites, put in stays and
remained on the other tack, with her foresheet to windward.

Major Cowper said it was a scandal. The country
was going to the dogs because merchantmen were not
compelled by law to carry guns. He spluttered into
my ears that there wasn't so much as a twopenny signal
mortar on board, and no more powder than enough to
load one of his duelling pistols. He was going to write
to the Horse Guards.

A blue-and-white ensign fluttered up to the main gaff
of the schooner; a boat dropped into the water. It all
went breathlessly—I hadn't time to think. I saw
old Cowper run to the side and aim his pistol overboard; there was an ineffectual click; he made a gesture
of disgust, and tossed it on deck. His head hung dejectedly down upon his chest.

Lumsden said, "Thank God, oh, thank God!" and
the old man turned on him like a snarling dog.

"You infernal coward," he said. "Haven't you got
a spark of courage?"

A moment after, our decks were invaded by men,
brown and ragged, leaping down from the bulwarks
one after the other.

They had come out at break of day (we must have
been observed the evening before), a big schooner—full
of as ill-favoured, ragged rascals as the most vivid imagination could conceive. Of course, there had been no
resistance on our part. We were outsailed, and at the
first ferocious hail the halyards had been let go by the
run, and all our crew had bolted aloft. A few bronzed
bandits posted abreast of each mast kept them there

by the menace of bell-mouthed blunderbusses pointed upwards. Lumsden and Mercer had been each tied flat down to a spare spar. They presented an appearance too ridiculous to awaken genuine compassion. Major Cowper was made to sit on a hen-coop, and a bearded pirate, with a red handkerchief tied round his head and a cutlass in his hand, stood guard over him. The major looked angry and crestfallen. The rest of that infamous crew, without losing a moment, rushed into the cuddy to loot the cabins for wearing apparel, jewellery, and money. They squabbled amongst themselves, throwing the things on deck into a great heap of booty.

The schooner flying the Mexican flag remained hove to abeam. But in the man in command of the boarding party I recognized Tomas Castro!

He *was* a pirate. My surmises were correct. He looked the part to the life, in a plumed hat, cloaked to the chin, and standing apart in a saturnine dignity.

"Are you going to have us all murdered, Castro?" I asked, with indignation. To my surprise he did not seem to recognize me; indeed, he pretended not to see me at all. I might have been thin air for any sign he gave of being aware of my presence; but, turning his back on me, he addressed himself to the ignobly captive Lumsden, telling him that he, Castro, was the commander of that Mexican schooner, and menacing him with dreadful threats of vengeance for what he called the resistance we had offered to a privateer of the Republic. I suppose he was pleased to qualify with the name of armed resistance the miserable little pop of the major's pocket pistol. To punish that audacity he announced that no private property would be respected.

"You shall have to give up all the money on board,"

he yelled at the wretched man lying there like a sheep
ready for slaughter. The other could only gasp and
blink. Castro's ferocity was so remarkable that for
a moment it struck me as put on. There was no necessity for it. We were meek and silent enough, only
poor Major Cowper muttered:

"My wife and child. . . ."

The ragged brown men were pouring on deck from
below; their arms full of bundles. Half a dozen of
them started to pull off the main hatch tarpaulin. Up
aloft the crew looked down with scared eyes. I began
to say excitedly, in my indignation, almost into his very
ear:

"I know you, Tomas Castro—I know you—Tomas
Castro."

Even then he seemed not to hear; but at last he looked
into my face balefully, as if he wished to convey the
plague to me.

"Hold your tongue," he said very quickly in Spanish.
"This is folly!" His little hawk's beak of a nose nestled
in his moustache. He waved his arm and declared
forcibly, "I don't know you. I am Nicola el Demonio,
the Mexican."

Poor old Cowper groaned. The reputation of Nicola
el Demonio, if rumours were to be trusted, was a horrible
thing for a man with women depending on him.

Five or six of these bandits were standing about
Lumsden, the major, and myself, fingering the locks of
their guns. Poor old Cowper, breaking away from his
guard, was raging up and down the poop; and the big
pirate kept him off the companion truculently. The
major wanted to get below; the little girl was screaming
in the cuddy, and we could hear her very plainly. It
was rather horrible. Castro had gone forward into the
crowd of scoundrels round the hatchway. It was only

then that I realized that Major Cowper was in a state of delirious apprehension and fury; I seemed to remember at last that for a long time he had been groaning somewhere near me. He kept on saying:

"Oh, for God's sake—for God's sake—my poor wife."

I understood that he must have been asking me to do something.

It came as a shock to me. I had a vague sensation of his fears. Up till then I hadn't realized that any one could be much interested in Mrs. Cowper.

He caught hold of my arm, as if he wanted support, and stuttered:

"Couldn't you—couldn't you speak to——" He nodded in the direction of Tomas Castro, who was bent and shouting down the hatch. "Try to——" the old man gasped. "Didn't you hear the child scream?" His face was pallid and wrinkled, like a piece of crumpled paper; his mouth was drawn on one side, and his lips quivered one against the other.

I went to Castro and caught him by the arm. He spun round and smiled discreetly.

"We shall be using force upon you directly. Pray resist, Señor; but not too much. What? His wife? Teli that stupid Inglez with whispers that she is safe." He whispered with an air of profound intelligence, "We shall be ready to go as soon as these foul swine have finished their stealing. I cannot stop them," he added.

I could not pause to think what he might mean. The child's shrieks resounding louder and louder, I ran below. There were a couple of men in the cabin with the women. Mrs. Cowper was lying back upon a sofa, her face very white and drawn, her eyes wide open. Her useless hands twitched at her dress; otherwise she was absolutely motionless, like a frozen woman. The black nurse was panting convulsively in a corner—a palpitating bundle of orange and purple and white clothes. The child was rushing round and round, shrieking. The two men did nothing at all. One of them kept saying in Spanish:

"But—we only want your rings. But—we only want your rings."

The other made feeble efforts to catch the child as it rushed past him. He wanted its earrings—they were contraband of war, I suppose.

Mrs. Cowper was petrified with terror. Explaining the desires of the two men was like shouting things into the ear of a very deaf woman. She kept on saying:

"Will they go away then? Will they go away then?" All the while she was drawing the rings off her thin fingers, and handing them to me. I gave them to the ruffians whose presence seemed to terrify her out of her senses. I had no option. I could do nothing else. Then I asked her whether she wished me to remain with her and the child. She said:

"Yes. No. Go away. Yes. No—let me think."

Finally it came into my head that in the captain's cabin she would be able to talk to her husband through the deck ventilator, and, after a time, the idea filtered through to her brain. She could hardly walk at all. The child and the nurse ran in front of us, and, practically, I carried her there in my arms. Once in the stateroom she struggled loose from me, and, rushing in, slammed the door violently in my face. She seemed to hate me.

CHAPTER SIX

I WENT on deck again. On the poop about twenty men had surrounded Major Cowper; his white head was being jerked backwards and forwards above their bending backs; they had got his old uniform coat off, and were fighting for the buttons. I had just time to shout to him, "Your wife's down there, she's all right!" when very suddenly I became aware that Tomas Castro was swearing horribly at these thieves. He drove them away, and we were left quite alone on the poop, I holding the major's coat over my arm. Major Cowper stooped down to call through the skylight. I could hear faint answers coming up to him.

Meantime, some of the rascals left on board the schooner had filled on her in a light wind, and, sailing round our stern, had brought their vessel alongside. Ropes were thrown on board and we lay close together, but the schooner with her dirty decks looked to me, now, very sinister and very sordid.

Then I remembered Castro's extraordinary words; they suggested infinite possibilities of a disastrous nature, I could not tell just what. The explanation seemed to be struggling to bring itself to light, like a name that one has had for hours on the tip of a tongue without being able to formulate it. Major Cowper rose stiffly, and limped to my side. He looked at me askance, then shifted his eyes away. Afterwards, he took his coat from my arm. I tried to help him, but he refused my aid, and jerked himself painfully into it. It was too tight for him. Suddenly, he said:

115

"You seem to be deuced intimate with that man—deuced intimate."

His tone caused me more misgiving than I should have thought possible. He took a turn on the deserted deck; went to the skylight; called down, "All well, still?" waited, listening with his head on one side, and then came back to me.

"You drop into the ship," he said, "out of the clouds. Out of the clouds, I say. You tell us some sort of cock-and-bull story. I say it looks deuced suspicious." He took another turn and came back. "My wife says that you took her rings and—and—gave them to——" He had an ashamed air. It came into my head that that hateful woman had been egging him on to this through the skylight, instead of saying her prayers.

"Your wife!" I said. "Why, she might have been murdered—if I hadn't made her give them up. I believe I saved her life."

He said suddenly, "Tut, tut!" and shrugged his shoulders. He hung his head for a minute, then he added, "Mind, I don't say—I don't say that it mayn't be as you say. You're a very nice young fellow. . . . But what I say is—I am a public man—you ought to clear yourself." He was beginning to recover his military bearing.

"Oh! don't be absurd," I said.

One of the Spaniards came up to me and whispered, "You must come now. We are going to cast off." At the same time Tomas Castro prowled to the other side of the ship, within five yards of us. I called out, "Tomas Castro! Tomas Castro! I will not go with you." The man beside me said, "Come Señor! *Vamos!*"

Suddenly Castro, stretching his arm out at me, cried, "Come, *hombres*. This is the *caballero;* seize

him." And to me in his broken English he shouted,
"You may resist, if you like."

This was what I meant to do with all my might. The
ragged crowd surrounded me; they chattered like
monkeys. One man irritated me beyond conception.
He looked like an inn-keeper in knee-breeches, had a
broken nose that pointed to the left, and a double chin.
More of them came running up every minute. I made
a sort of blind rush at the fellow with the broken nose;
my elbow caught him on the soft folds of flesh and he
skipped backwards; the rest scattered in all directions,
and then stood at a distance, chattering and waving
their hands. And beyond them I saw old Cowper
gesticulating approval. The man with the double
chin drew a knife from his sleeve, crouched instantly,
and sprang at me. I hadn't fought anybody since I
had been at school; raising my fists was like trying a
dubious experiment in an emergency. I caught him
rather hard on the end of his broken nose; I felt the
contact on my right, and a small pain in my left hand.
His arms went up to the sky; his face, too. But I had
started forward to meet him, and half a dozen of them
flung their arms round me from behind.

I seemed to have an exaggerated clearness of vision;
I saw each brown dirty paw reach out to clutch some
part of me. I was not angry any more; it wasn't any
good being angry, but I made a fight for it. There
were dozens of them; they clutched my wrists, my
elbows, and in between my wrists and my elbows, and
my shoulders. One pair of arms was round my neck,
another round my waist, and they kept on trying to
catch my legs with ropes. We seemed to stagger all
over the deck; I expect they got in each other's way;
they would have made a better job of it if they hadn't
been such a multitude. I must then have got a crack

on the head, for everything grew dark; the night seemed to fall on us, as we fought.

Afterwards I found myself lying gasping on my back on the deck of the schooner; four or five men were holding me down. Castro was putting a pistol into his belt. He stamped his foot violently, and then went and shouted in Spanish:

"Come you all on board. You have done mischief enough, fools of *Lugareños*. Now we go."

I saw, as in a dream of stress and violence, some men making ready to cast off the schooner, and then, in a supreme effort, an effort of lusty youth and strength, which I remember to this day, I scattered men like chaff, and stood free.

For the fraction of a second I stood, ready to fall myself, and looking at prostrate men. It was a flash of vision, and then I made a bolt for the rail. I clambered furiously; I saw the deck of the old barque; I had just one exulting sight of it, and then Major Cowper uprose before my eyes and knocked me back on board the schooner, tumbling after me himself.

Twenty men flung themselves upon my body. I made no movement. The end had come. I hadn't the strength to shake off a fly, my heart was bursting my ribs. I lay on my back and managed to say, "Give me air." I thought I should die.

Castro, draped in his cloak, stood over me, but Major Cowper fell on his knees near my head, almost sobbing:

"My papers! My papers! I tell you I shall starve. Make them give me back my papers. They ain't any use to them—my pension—mortgages—not worth a penny piece to you."

He crouched over my face, and the Spaniards stood around, wondering. He begged me to intercede, to save him those papers of the greatest importance.

Castro preserved his attitude of a conspirator. I was touched by the major's distress, and at last I condescended to address Castro on his behalf, though it cost me an effort, for I was angry, indignant, and humiliated.

"Whart—whart? What do I know of his papers? Let him find them." He waved his hand loftily.

The deck was hillocked with heaps of clothing, of bedding, casks of rum, old hats, and tarpaulins. Cowper ran in and out among the plunder, like a pointer in a turnip field. He was groaning.

Beside one of the pumps was a small pile of shiny cases; ship's instruments, a chronometer in its case, a medicine chest.

Cowper tottered at a black dispatch-box. "There, there!" he said; "I tell you I shall starve if I don't have it. Ask him—ask him——" He was clutching me like a drowning man.

Castro raised the inevitable arm towards heaven, letting his round black cloak fall into folds like those of an umbrella. Cowper gathered that he might take his japanned dispatch-box; he seized the brass handles and rushed towards the side, but at the last moment he had the good impulse to return to me, holding out his hand, and spluttering distractedly, "God bless you, God bless you." After a time he remembered that I had rescued his wife and child, and he asked God to bless me for that too. "If it is ever necessary," he said, "on my honour, if you escape, I will come a thousand miles to testify. On my honour—remember." He said he was going to live in Clapham. That is as much as I remember. I was held pinned down to the deck, and he disappeared from my sight. Before the ships had separated, I was carried below in the cabin of the schooner.

They left me alone there, and I sat with my head on

my arms for a long time. I did not think of anything at all; I was too utterly done up with my struggles, and there was nothing to be thought about. I had grown to accept the meanness of things as if I had aged a great deal. I had seen men scratch each other's faces over coat buttons, old shoes—over Mercer's trousers. My own future did not interest me at this stage. I sat up and looked round me.

I was in a small, bare cabin, roughly wainscotted and exceedingly filthy. There were the grease-marks from the backs of heads all along a bulkhead above a wooden bench; the rough table, on which my arms rested, was covered with layers of tallow spots. Bright light shone through a porthole. Two or three ill-assorted muskets slanted about round the foot of the mast—a long old piece, of the time of Pizarro, all red velvet and silver chasing, on a swivelled stand, three English fowling-pieces, and a coachman's blunderbuss. A man was rising from a mattress stretched on the floor; he placed a mandolin, decorated with red favours, on the greasy table. He was shockingly thin, and so tall that his head disturbed the candle-soot on the ceiling. He said: "Ah, I was waiting for the cavalier to awake."

He stalked round the end of the table, slid between it and the side, and grasped my arm with wrapt earnestness as he settled himself slowly beside me. He wore a red shirt that had become rather black where his long brown ringlets fell on his shoulders; it had tarnished gilt buttons ciphered "G. R.," stolen, I suppose, from some English ship.

"I beg the Señor Caballero to listen to what I have to record," he said, with intense gravity. "I cannot bear this much longer—no, I cannot bear my sufferings much longer."

His face was of a large, classical type; a close-featured,

rather long face, with an immense nose that from the front resembled the section of a bell; eyebrows like horseshoes, and very large-pupilled eyes that had the purplish-brown lustre of a horse's. His air was mournful in the extreme, and he began to speak resonantly as if his chest were a sounding-board. He used immensely long sentences, of which I only understood one-half.

"What, then, is the difference between me, Manuel-del-Popolo Isturiz, and this Tomas Castro? The Señor Caballero can tell at once. Look at me. I am the finer man. I would have you ask the ladies of Rio Medio, and leave the verdict to them. This Castro is an Andalou—a foreigner. And we, the braves of Rio Medio, will suffer no foreigner to make headway with our ladies. Yet this Andalusian is preferred because he is a humble friend of the great Don, and because he is for a few days given the command. I ask you, Señor, what is the radical difference between me, the sailing captain of this vessel, and him, the fighting captain for a few days. Is it not I that am, as it were, the brains of it, and he only its knife? I ask the Señor Caballero."

I didn't in the least know what to answer. His great eyes wistfully explored my face. I expect I looked bewildered.

"I lay my case at your feet," he continued. "You are to be our chief leader, and, on account of your illustrious birth and renowned intelligence, will occupy a superior position in the council of the notables. Is it not so? Has not the Señor Juez O'Brien so ordained? You will give ear to me, you will alleviate my indignant sufferings?" He implored me with his eyes for a long time.

Manuel-del-Popolo, as he called himself, pushed the hair back from his forehead. I had noticed that the

E

love-locks were plaited with black braid, and that he wore large dirty silk ruffles.

"The *caballero*," he continued, marking his words with a long, white finger a-tap on the table, "will represent my views to the notables. My position at present, as I have had the honour to observe, is become unbearable. Consider, too, how your worship and I would work together. What lightness for you and me. You will find this Castro unbearably gross. But I—I assure you I am a man of taste—an *improvisador*—an artist. My songs are celebrated. And yet! . . ."

He folded his arms again, and waited; then he said, employing his most impressive voice:

"I have influence with the men of Rio. I could raise a riot. We Cubans are a jealous people; we do not love that foreigners should take our best from us. We do not love it; we will not suffer it. Let this Castro bethink himself and go in peace, leaving us our ladies. As the proverb says, 'It is well to build a bridge for a departing enemy.'"

He began to peer at me more wistfully, and his eyes grew more luminous than ever. This man, in spite of his grotesqueness, was quite in earnest, there was no doubting that.

"I have a gentle spirit," he began again, "a gentle spirit. I am submissive to the legitimate authorities. What the Señor Juez O'Brien asks me to do, I do. I would put a knife into any one who inconvenienced the Señor Juez O'Brien, who is a good Catholic; we would all do that, as is right and fitting. But this Castro—this Andalou, who is nearly as bad as a heretic! When my day comes, I will have his arms flayed and the soles of his feet, and I will rub red pepper into them; and all the men of Rio who do not love foreigners will applaud. And I will stick little thorns under his tongue, and I will cut off his eyelids with little scissors, and set him facing the sun. *Caballero*, you would love me; I have a gentle spirit. I am a pleasant companion." He rose and squeezed round the table. "Listen"—his eyes lit up with rapture—"you shall hear me. It is divine—ah, it is very pleasant, you will say."

He seized his mandolin, slung it round his neck, and leant against the bulkhead. The bright light from the port-hole gilded the outlines of his body, as he swayed about and moved his long fingers across the strings; they tinkled metallically. He sang in a nasal voice:

"'Listen!' the young girls say as they hasten to the barred window.
  'Listen! Ah, surely that is the guitar of
  Man—u—el—del-Popolo,
  As he glides along the wall in the twilight.'"

It was a very long song. He gesticulated freely with his hand in between the scratching of the strings, which seemed to be a matter of luck. His eyes gazed distantly at the wall above my head. The performance bewildered and impressed me; I wondered if this was what they had carried me off for. It was like being mad. He made a decrescendo tinkling, and his lofty features lapsed into their normal mournfulness.

At that moment Castro put his face round the door, then entered altogether. He sighed in a satisfied manner, and had an air of having finished a laborious undertaking.

"We have arranged the confusion up above," he said to Manuel-del-Popolo; "you may go and see to the sailing. . . . Hurry; it is growing late."

Manuel blazed silently, and stalked out of the door as if he had an electric cloud round his head. Tomas Castro turned towards me.

"You are better?" he asked benevolently. "You

exerted yourself too much. . . . But still, if you liked——" He picked up the mandolin, and began negligently scratching the strings. I noticed an alteration in him; he had grown softer in the flesh in the past years; there were little threads of gray in the knotted curls of his beard. It was as if he had lived well, on the whole. He bent his head over the strings, plucked one, tightened a peg, plucked it again, then set the instrument on the table, and dropped on to the mattress. "Will you have some rum?" he said. "You have grown broad and strong, like a bull. . . . You made those men fly, *sacré nom d'une pipe*. . . . One would have thought you were in earnest. . . . Ah, well!" He stretched himself at length on the mattress, and closed his eyes.

I looked at him to discover traces of irony. There weren't any. He was talking quietly; he even reproved me for having carried the pretence of resistance beyond a joke.

"You fought too much; you struck many men—and hard. You will have made enemies. The *picaros* of this dirty little town are as conceited as pigs. You must take care, or you will have a knife in your back."

He lay with his hands crossed on his stomach, which was round like a pudding. After a time he opened his eyes, and looked at the dancing white reflection of the water on the grimy ceiling.

"To think of seeing you again, after all these years," he said. "I did not believe my ears when Don Carlos asked me to fetch you like this. Who would have believed it? But, as they say," he added philosophically, "'The water flows to the sea, and the little stones find their places.'" He paused to listen to the sounds that came from above. "That Manuel is a fool," he said without rancour; "he is mad with jealousy because for this day I have command here. But, all the same, they are dangerous pigs, these slaves of the Señor O'Brien. I wish the town were rid of them. One day there will be a riot—a function—with their jealousies and madness."

I sat and said nothing, and things fitted themselves together, little patches of information going in here and there like the pieces of a puzzle map. O'Brien had gone on to Havana in the ship from which I had escaped, to render an account of the pirates that had been hung at Kingston; the Riegos had been landed in boats at Rio Medio, of course.

"That poor Don Carlos!" Castro moaned lamentably. "They had the barbarity to take him out in the night, in that raw fog. He coughed and coughed; it made me faint to hear him. He could not even speak to me—his Tomas; it was pitiful. He could not speak when we got to the Casa."

I could not really understand why I had been a second time kidnapped. Castro said that O'Brien had not been unwilling that I should reach Havana. It was Carlos that had ordered Tomas to take me out of the *Breeze*. He had come down in the raw morning, before the schooner had put out from behind the point, to impress very elaborate directions upon Tomas Castro; indeed, it was whilst talking to Tomas that he had burst a blood-vessel.

"He said to me: 'Have a care now. Listen. He is my dear friend, that Señor Juan. I love him as if he were my only brother. Be very careful, Tomas Castro. Make it appear that he comes to us much against his will. Let him be dragged on board by many men. You are to understand, Tomas, that he is a youth of noble family, and that you are to be as careful of compromising him as you are of the honour of Our Lady.'"

Tomas Castro looked across at me. "You will be able to report well of me," he said; "I did my best. If you are compromised, it was you who did it by talking to me as if you knew me."

I remembered, then, that Tomas certainly had resented my seeming to recognize him before Cowper and Lumsden. He closed his eyes again. After a time he added:

"*Vaya!* After all, it is foolishness to fear being compromised. You would never believe that his Excellency Don Balthasar had led a riotous life—to look at him with his silver head. It is said he had three friars killed once in Seville, a very, very long time ago. It was dangerous in those days to come against our Mother, the Church." He paused, and undid his shirt, laying bare an incredibly hairy chest; then slowly kicked off his shoes. "One stifles here," he said. "Ah! in the old days——"

Suddenly he turned to me and said, with an air of indescribable interest, as if he were gloating over an obscene idea:

"So they would hang a gentleman like you, if they caught you? What savages you English people are!— what savages! Like cannibals! You did well to make that comedy of resisting. *Quel pays!* . . . What a people . . . I dream of them still. . . . The eyes; the teeth! Ah, well! in an hour we shall be in Rio. I must sleep. . . ."

CHAPTER SEVEN

BY TWO of the afternoon we were running into the inlet of Rio Medio. I had come on deck when Tomas Castro had started out of his doze. I wanted to see. We went round violently as I emerged, and, clinging to the side, I saw, in a whirl, tall, baked, brown hills dropping sheer down to a strip of flat land and a belt of dark-green scrub at the water's edge; little pink squares of house-walls dropped here and there, mounting the hillside among palms, like men standing in tall grass, running back, hiding in a steep valley; silver-gray huts with ragged dun roofs, like dishevelled shocks of hair; a great pink church-face, very tall and narrow, pyramidal towards the top, and pierced for seven bells, but having only three. It looked as if it had been hidden for centuries in the folds of an ancient land, as it lay there asleep in the blighting sunlight.

When we anchored, Tomas, beside me in saturnine silence, grunted and spat into the water.

"Look here," I said. "What is the meaning of it all? What is it? What is at the bottom?"

He shrugged his shoulders gloomily. "If your worship does not know, who should?" he said. "It is not for me to say why people should wish to come here."

"Then take me to Carlos," I said. "I must get this settled."

Castro looked at me suspiciously. "You will not excite him?" he said. "I have known people die right out when they were like that."

"Oh, I won't excite him," I said.

As we were rowed ashore, he began to point out the houses of the notables. Rio Medio had been one of the principal ports of the Antilles in the seventeenth century, but it had failed before the rivalry of Havana because its harbour would not take the large vessels of modern draft. Now it had no trade, no life, no anything except a bishop and a great monastery, a few retired officials from Havana. A large settlement of ragged thatched huts and clay hovels lay to the west of the cathedral. The Casa Riego was an enormous palace, with windows like loopholes, facing the shore. Don Balthasar practically owned the whole town and all the surrounding country, and, except for his age and feebleness, might have been an absolute monarch.

He had lived in Havana with great splendour, but now, in his failing years, had retired to his palace, from which he had since only twice set foot. This had only been when official ceremonies of extreme importance, such as the international execution of pirates that I had witnessed, demanded the presence of someone of his eminence and lustre. Otherwise he had lived shut up in his palace. There was nowhere in Rio Medio for him to go to.

He was said to regard his intendente O'Brien as the apple of his eye, and had used his influence to get him made one of the judges of the Marine Court. The old Don himself probably knew nothing about the pirates. The inlet had been used by buccaneers ever since the days of Columbus; but they were below his serious consideration, even if he had ever seen them, which Tomas Castro doubted.

There was no doubting the sincerity of his tone.

"Oh, you thought *I* was a pirate!" he muttered. "For a day—yes—to oblige a Riego, my friend—yes! Moreover, I hate that familiar of the priests, that soft-

spoken Juez, intendente, intriguer—that O'Brien. A
sufferer for the faith! *Que picardía!* Have I, too, not
suffered for the faith? I am the trusted humble friend
of the Riegos. But, perhaps, you think Don Balthasar
is himself a pirate! He who has in his veins the blood
of the Cid Campeador; whose ancestors have owned
half this island since the days of Christopher himself. . . ."

"Has he nothing whatever to do with it?" I asked.
"After all, it goes on in his own town."

"Oh, you English," he muttered; "you are all mad!
Would one of your great nobles be a pirate? Perhaps
they would—God knows. Alas, alas!" he suddenly
broke off, "when I think that my Carlos shall leave his
bones in this ungodly place. . . ."

I gave up questioning Tomas Castro; he was too
much for me.

We entered the grim palace by the shore through an
imposing archway, and mounted a broad staircase. In
a lofty room, giving off the upper gallery round the
central court of the Casa Riego, Carlos lay in a great
bed. I stood before him, having pushed aside Tomas
Castro, who had been cautiously scratching the great
brilliant mahogany panels with a dirty finger-nail.

"Damnation, Carlos!" I said. "This is the third
of your treacheries. What do you want with me?"

You might well have imagined he was a descendant
of the Cid Campeador, only to look at him lying there
without a quiver of a feature, his face stainlessly white,
a little bluish in extreme lack of blood, with all the
nobility of death upon it, like an alabaster effigy of an
old knight in a cathedral. On the red-velvet hangings
of the bed was an immense coat-of-arms, worked in silk
and surrounded by a collar, with the golden sheep
hanging from the ring. The shield was patched in

*E

with an immense number of quarterings—lions rampant, leopards courant, fleurs de lis, castles, eagles, hands, and arms. His eyes opened slowly, and his face assumed an easy, languorous smile of immense pleasure.

"Ah, Juan," he said, "*sé bienvienido*, be welcome, be welcome."

Castro caught me roughly by the shoulder, and gazed at me with blazing, yellow eyes.

"You should not speak roughly to him," he said. "English beast! He is dying."

"No, I won't speak roughly to him," I answered. "I see."

I did see. At first I had been suspicious; it might have been put on to mollify me. But one could not put on that blueness of tinge, that extra—nearly final— touch of the chisel to the lines round the nose, that air of restfulness that nothing any more could very much disturb. There was no doubt that Carlos was dying.

"Treacheries—no. You had to come," he said suddenly. "I need you. I am glad, dear Juan." He waved a thin long hand a little towards mine. "You shall not long be angry. It had to be done—you must forgive the means."

His air was so gay, so uncomplaining, that it was hard to believe it came from him.

"You could not have acted worse if you had owed me a grudge, Carlos," I said. "I want an explanation. But I don't want to kill you. . . ."

"Oh, no, oh, no," he said; "in a minute I will tell."

He dropped a gold ball into a silver basin that was by the bedside, and it sounded like a great bell. A nun in a sort of coif that took the lines of a buffalo's horns glided to him with a gold cup, from which he drank, raising himself a little. Then the religious went out with

Tomas Castro, who gave me a last ferocious glower from his yellow eyes. Carlos smiled.

"They try to make my going easy," he said. "*Vamos!* The pillow is smooth for him who is well loved." He shut his eyes. Suddenly he said, "Why do you, alone, hate me, John Kemp? What have I done?"

"God knows I don't hate you, Carlos," I answered.

"You have always mistrusted me," he said. "And yet I am, perhaps, nearer to you than many of your countrymen, and I have always wished you well, and you have always hated and mistrusted me. From the very first you mistrusted me. Why?"

It was useless denying it; he had the extraordinary incredulity of his kind. I remembered how I had idolized him as a boy at home.

"Your brother-in-law, my cousin Rooksby, was the very first to believe that I was a pirate. I, a vulgar pirate! I, Carlos Riego! Did he not believe it—and you?" He glanced a little ironically, and lifted a thin white finger towards the great coat-of-arms. "That sort of thing," he said, "*amigo mio*, does not allow one to pick pockets." He suddenly turned a little to one side, and fixed me with his clear eyes. "My friend," he said, "if I told you that Rooksby and your greatest Kent earls carried smugglers' tubs, you would say I was an ignorant fool. Yet they, too, are magistrates. The only use I have ever made of these ruffians was to-day, to bring you here. It was a necessity. That O'Brien had gone on to take you when you arrived. You would never have come alive out of Havana. I was saving your life. Once there, you could never have escaped from that man."

I saw suddenly that this might be the truth. There had been something friendly in Tomas Castro's desire not to compromise me before the people on board the ship. Obviously he had been acting a part, with a visible contempt for the pilfering that he could not prevent. He *had* been sent merely to bring me to Rio Medio.

"I never disliked you," I protested. "I do not understand what you mean. All I know is, that you have used me ill—outrageously ill. You have saved my life now, you say. That may be true; but why did you ever make me meet with that man O'Brien?"

"And even for that you should not hate me," he said, shaking his head on the silk pillows. "I never wished you anything but well, Juan, because you were honest and young, of noble blood, good to look upon; you had done me and my friend good service, to your own peril, when my own cousin had deserted me. And I loved you for the sake of another. I loved your sister. We have a proverb: 'A man is always good to the eyes in which the sister hath found favour.'"

I looked at him in amazement. "You loved Veronica!" I said. "But Veronica is nothing at all. There was the Señorita."

He smiled wearily. "Ah, the Señorita; she is very well; a man could love her, too. But we do not command love, my friend."

I interrupted him. "I want to know why you brought me here. Why did you ask me to come here when we were on board the *Thames?*"

He answered sadly, "Ah, then! · Because I loved your sister, and you reminded me always of her. But that is all over now—done with for good. . . . I have to address myself to dying as it becomes one of my race to die." He smiled at me. "One must die in peace to die like a Christian. Life has treated me rather scurvily, only the gentleman must not repine like a poor man of low birth. I would like to do a good turn to the friend who is the brother of his sister, to the girl-cousin whom I do not love with love, but whom I understand with affection—to the great inheritance that is not for my wasted hands."

I looked out of the open door of the room. There was the absolutely quiet inner court of the palace, a colonnade of tall square pillars, in the centre the little thread of a fountain. Round the fountain were tangled bushes of flowers—enormous geraniums, enormous hollyhocks, a riot of orange marigolds.

"How like our flowers at home!" I said mechanically.

"I brought the seeds from there—from your sister's garden," he said.

I felt horribly hipped. "But all these things tell me nothing," I said, with an attempt towards briskness.

"I have to husband my voice." He closed his eyes.

There is no saying that I did not believe him; I did, every word. I had simply been influenced by Rooksby's suspicions. I had made an ass of myself over that business on board the *Thames*. The passage of Carlos and his faithful Tomas had been arranged for by some agent of O'Brien in London, who was in communication with Ramon and Rio Medio. The same man had engaged Nichols, that Nova Scotian mate, an unscrupulous sailor, for O'Brien's service. He was to leave the ship in Kingston, and report himself to Ramon, who furnished him with the means to go to Cuba. That man, seeing me intimate with two persons going to Rio Medio, had got it into his head that I was going there, too. And, very naturally, he did not want an Englishman for a witness of his doings.

But Rooksby's behaviour, his veiled accusations, his innuendoes against Carlos, had influenced me more than anything else. I remembered a hundred little things now that I knew that Carlos loved Veronica. I understood Rooksby's jealous impatience, Veronica's friendly glances at Carlos, the fact that Rooksby had proposed to Veronica on the very day that Carlos had come again into the neighbourhood with the runners after him. I saw very well that there was no more connection between the Casa Riego and the rascality of Rio Medio than there was between Ralph himself and old drunken Rangsley on Hythe beach. There was less, perhaps.

"Ah, you have had a sad life, my Carlos," I said, after a long time.

He opened his eyes, and smiled his brave smile. "Ah, as to that," he said, "one kept on. One has to husband one's voice, though, and not waste it over lamentations. I have to tell you—ah, yes. . . ." He paused and fixed his eyes upon me. "Figure to yourself that this house, this town, an immense part of this island, much even yet in Castile itself, much gold, many slaves, a great name—a very great name—are what I shall leave behind me. Now think that there is a very noble old man, one who has been very great in the world, who shall die very soon; then all these things shall go to a young girl. That old man is very old, is a little foolish with age; that young girl knows very little of the world, and is very passionate, very proud, very helpless.

"Add, now, to that a great menace—a very dangerous, crafty, subtle personage, who has the ear of that old man; whose aim it is to become the possessor of that young girl and of that vast wealth. The old man is much subject to the other. Old men are like that, especially the very great. They have many things to think of; it is necessary that they rely on somebody. I am, in fact, speaking of my uncle and the man called O'Brien. You have seen him." Carlos spoke in a

voice hardly above a whisper, but he stuck to his task
with indomitable courage. "If I die and leave him
here, he will have my uncle to himself. He is a terrible
man. Where would all that great fortune go? For the
re-establishing of the true faith in Ireland? *Quien sabe?*
Into the hands of O'Brien, at any rate. And the daughter, too—a young girl—she would be in the hands of
O'Brien, too. If I could expect to live, it might be
different. That is the greatest distress of all." He
swallowed painfully, and put his frail hand on to the
white ruffle at his neck. "I was in great trouble to find
how to thwart this O'Brien. My uncle went to Kingston because he was persuaded it was his place to see that
the execution of those unhappy men was conducted with
due humanity. O'Brien came with us as his secretary.
I was in the greatest horror of mind. I prayed for
guidance. Then my eyes fell upon you, who were
pressed against our very carriage wheels. It was like
an answer to my prayers." Carlos suddenly reached
out and caught my hand.

I thought he was wandering, and I was immensely
sorry for him. He looked at me so wistfully with his
immense eyes. He continued to press my hand.

"But when I saw you," he went on, after a time, "it
had come into my head, 'That is the man who is sent in
answer to my prayers.' I knew it, I say. If you could
have my cousin and my lands, I thought, it would be
like my having your sister—not quite, but good enough
for a man who is to die in a short while, and leave no
trace but a marble tomb. Ah, one desires very much to
leave a mark under God's blessed sun, and to be able to
know a little how things will go after one is dead. . . .
I arranged the matter very quickly in my mind. There
was the difficulty of O'Brien. If I had said, 'Here is
the man who is to marry my cousin,' he would have had

you or me murdered; he would stop at nothing. So I said to him very quietly, 'Look here, Señor Secretary, that is the man you have need of to replace your Nichols—a devil to fight; but I think he will not consent without a little persuasion. Decoy him, then, to Ramon's, and do your persuading.' O'Brien was very glad, because he thought that at last I was coming to take an interest in his schemes, and because it was bringing humiliation to an Englishman. And Seraphina was glad, because I had often spoken of you with enthusiasm, as very fearless and very honourable. Then I made that man Ramon decoy you, thinking that the matter would be left to me."

That was what Carlos had expected. But O'Brien, talking with Ramon, had heard me described as an extreme Separationist so positively that he had thought it safe to open himself fully. He must have counted, also, on my youth, my stupidity, or my want of principle. Finding out his mistake, he very soon made up his mind how to act; and Carlos, fearing that worse might befall me, had let him.

But when the young girl had helped me to escape, Carlos, who understood fully the very great risks I ran in going to Havana in the ship that picked me up, had made use of O'Brien's own picaroons to save me from him. That was the story.

Towards the end his breath came fast and short; there was a flush on his face; his eyes gazed imploringly at me.

"You will stay here, now, till I die, and then—I want you to protect——" He fell back on the pillows.

PART THIRD
CASA RIEGO

CHAPTER ONE

ALL this is in my mind now, softened by distance, by the tenderness of things remembered—the wonderful dawn of life, with all the mystery and promise of the young day breaking amongst heavy thunder-clouds. At the time I was overwhelmed—I can't express it otherwise. I felt like a man thrown out to sink or swim, trying to keep his head above water. Of course, I did not suspect Carlos now; I was ashamed of ever having done so. I had long ago forgiven him his methods. "In a great need, you must," he had said, looking at me anxiously, "recur to desperate remedies." And he was going to die. I had made no answer, and only hung my head—not in resentment, but in doubt of my strength to bear the burden of the great trust that this man whom I loved for his gayety, his recklessness and romance, was going to leave in my inexperienced hands.

He had talked till, at last exhausted, he sank back gently on the pillows of the enormous bed emblazoned like a monument. I went out, following a gray-headed negro, and the nun glided in, and stood at the foot with her white hands folded patiently.

"Señor!" I heard her mutter reproachfully to the invalid.

"Do not scold a poor sinner, Doña Maria," he addressed her feebly, with valiant jocularity. "The days are not many now."

The strangeness and tremendousness of what was happening came over me very strongly whilst, in a large chamber with barred loopholes, I was throwing off the rags in which I had entered this house. The night had come already, and I was putting on some of Carlos' clothes by the many flames of candles burning in a tall bronze candelabrum, whose three legs figured the paws of a lion. And never, since I had gone on the road to wait for the smugglers, and be choked by the Bow Street runners, had I remembered so well the house in which I was born. It was as if, till then, I had never felt the need to look back. But now, like something romantic and glamorous, there came before me Veronica's sweet, dim face, my mother's severe and resolute countenance. I had need of all her resoluteness now. And I remembered the figure of my father in the big chair by the ingle, powerless and lost in his search for rhymes. He might have understood the romance of my situation.

It grew upon me as I thought. Don Balthasar, I understood, was apprised of my arrival. As in a dream, I followed the old negro, who had returned to the door of my room. It grew upon me in the silence of this colonnaded court. We walked along the upper gallery; his cane tapped before me on the tessellated pavement; below, the water splashed in the marble basins; glass lanthorns hung glimmering between the pillars and, in wrought silver frames, lighted the broad white staircase. Under the inner curve of the vaulted gateway a black-faced man on guard, with a bell-mouthed gun, rose from a stool at our passing. I thought I saw Castro's peaked hat and large cloak flit in the gloom into which fell the light from the small doorway of a sort of guardroom near the closed gate. We continued along the arcaded walk; a double curtain was drawn to right and left before me, while my guide stepped aside.

In a vast white apartment three black figures stood about a central glitter of crystal and silver. At once the aged, slightly mechanical voice of Don Balthasar rose thinly, putting himself and his house at my disposition.

The formality of movement, of voices, governed and checked the unbounded emotions of my wonder. The two ladies sank, with a rustle of starch and stiff silks, in answer to my profound bow. I had just enough control over myself to accomplish that, but mentally I was out of breath; and when I felt the slight, trembling touch of Don Balthasar's hand resting on my inclined head, it was as if I had suddenly become aware for a moment of the earth's motion. The hand was gone; his face was averted, and a corpulent priest, all straight and black below his rosy round face, had stepped forward to say a Latin grace in solemn tones that wheezed a little. As soon as he had done he withdrew with a circular bow to the ladies, to Don Balthasar, who inclined his silvery head. His lifeless voice pronounced:

"Our excellent Father Antonio, in his devotion, dines by the bedside of our beloved Carlos." He sighed. The heavy carvings of his chair rose upright at his back; he sat with his head leaning forward over his silver plate. A heavy silence fell. Death hovered over that table—and also, as if the breath of past ages. The multitude of lights, the polished floor of costly wood, the bare whiteness of walls wainscotted with marble, the vastness of the room, the imposing forms of furniture, carved heavily in ebony, impressed me with a sense of secular and austere magnificence. For centuries there had always been a Riego living in this fortress-like palace, ruling this portion of the New World with the whole majesty of his race. And I

thought of the long, loop-holed, buttressed walls that
this abode of noble adventurers presented foursquare to
the night outside, standing there by the seashore like a
tomb of warlike glories. They built their houses thus,
centuries ago, when the bands of buccaneers, indomitable and atrocious, had haunted their conquest with a
reminder of mortality and weakness.

It was a tremendous thing for me, this dinner. The
portly duenna on my left had a round eye and an
irritated, parrot-like profile, crowned by a high comb,
a head shaded by black lace. I dared hardly lift my
eyes to the dark and radiant presence facing me across
a table furniture that was like a display of treasure.

But I did look. She was the girl of the lizard, the
girl of the dagger, and, in the solemnity of the silence,
she was like a fabulous apparition from a half-forgotten
tale. I watched covertly the youthful grace of her
features. The curve of her cheek filled me with delight.
From time to time she shook the heavy clusters of her
curls, and I was amazed, as though I had never before
seen a woman's hair. Each parting of her lips was a
distinct anticipation of a great felicity; when she said a
few words to me, I felt an inward trembling. They
were indifferent words.

Had she forgotten she was the girl with the dagger?
And the old Don? What did that old man know?
What did he think? What did he mean by that touch
of a blessing on my head? Did *he* know how I had come
to his house? But every turn of her head troubled my
thoughts. The movements of her hands made me
forget myself. The gravity of her eyes above the smile
of her lips suggested ideas of adoration.

We were served noiselessly. A battalion of young
lusty negroes, in blue jackets laced with silver, walked
about barefooted under the command of the old major-

domo. He, alone, had white silk stockings, and shoes
with silver buckles; his wide-skirted maroon velvet
coat, with gold on the collar and cuffs, hung low about
his thin shanks; and, with a long ebony staff in his hand,
he directed the service from behind Don Balthasar's
chair. At times he bent towards his master's ear.
Don Balthasar answered with a murmur: and those two
faces brought close together, one like a noble ivory
carving, the other black with the mute pathos of the
African faces, seemed to commune in a fellowship of age,
of things far off, remembered, lived through together.
There was something mysterious and touching in this
violent contrast, toned down by the near approach to
the tomb—the brotherhood of master and slave.

At a given moment an enormous iron key was brought
in on a silver salver, and, bending over the chair, the
gray-headed negro laid it by Don Balthasar's plate.

"Don Carlos' orders," he muttered.

The old Don seemed to wake up; a little colour
mounted to his cheeks.

"There was a time, young *caballero*, when the gates of
Casa Riego stood open night and day to the griefs and
poverty of the people, like the doors of a church—and as
respected. But now it seems . . ."

He mumbled a little peevishly, but seemed to recollect himself. "The safety of his guest is like the
breath of life to a Castilian," he ended, with a benignant
but attentive look at me.

He rose, and we passed out through the double lines
of the servants ranged from table to door. By the
splash of the fountain, on a little round table between
two chairs, stood a many-branched candlestick. The
duenna sat down opposite Don Balthasar. A multitude
of stars was suspended over the breathless peace of the
court.

"Señorita," I began, mustering all my courage, and all my Spanish, "I do not know——"

She was walking by my side with upright carriage and a nonchalant step, and shut her fan smartly.

"Don Carlos himself had given me the dagger," she said rapidly.

The fan flew open; a touch of the wind fanning her person came faintly upon my cheek with a suggestion of delicate perfume.

She noticed my confusion, and said, "Let us walk to the end, Señor."

The old man and the duenna had cards in their hands now. The intimate tone of her words ravished me into the seventh heaven.

"Ah," she said, when we were out of ear-shot, "I have the spirit of my house; but I am only a weak girl. We have taken this resolution because of your *hidalguidad*, because you are our kinsman, because you are English. *Ay de mi!* Would I had been a man. My father needs a son in his great, great age. Poor father! Poor Don Carlos!"

There was the catch of a sob in the shadow of the end gallery. We turned back, and the undulation of her walk seemed to throw me into a state of exaltation.

"On the word of an Englishman——" I began.

The fan touched my arm. The eyes of the duenna glittered over the cards.

"This woman belongs to that man, too," muttered Seraphina. "And yet she used to be faithful—almost a mother. *Misericordia!* Señor, there is no one in this unhappy place that he has not bought, corrupted, frightened, or bent to his will—to his madness of hate against England. Of our poor he has made a rabble. The bishop himself is afraid."

Such was the beginning of our first conversation in

this court suggesting the cloistered peace of a convent. We strolled to and fro; she dropped her eyelids, and the agitation of her mind, pictured in the almost fierce swiftness of her utterance, made a wonderful contrast to the leisurely rhythm of her movements, marked by the slow beating of the fan. The retirement of her father from the world after her mother's death had made a great solitude round his declining years. Yes, that sorrow, and the base intrigues of that man—a fugitive, a hanger-on of her mother's family—recommended to Don Balthasar's grace by her mother's favour. Yes! He had, before she died, thrown his baneful influence even upon that saintly spirit, by the piety of his practices and these sufferings for his faith he always paraded. His faith! Oh, hypocrite, hypocrite, hypocrite! His only faith was hate—the hate of England. He would sacrifice everything to it. He would despoil and ruin his greatest benefactors, this fatal man!

"Señor, my cousin," she said picturesquely, "he would, if he could, drop poison into every spring of clear water in your country. . . . Smile, Don Juan."

Her repressed vehemence had held me spellbound, and the silvery little burst of laughter ending her fierce tirade had the bewildering effect of a crash on my mind. The other two looked up from their cards.

"I pretend to laugh to deceive that woman," she explained quickly. "I used to love her."

She had no one now about her she could trust or love. It was as if the whole world were blind to the nefarious nature of that man. He had possessed himself of her little father's mind. I glanced towards the old Don, who at that moment was brokenly taking a pinch of snuff out of a gold snuff-box, while the duenna, very sallow and upright, waited, frowning loftily at her cards.

"It seemed as if nothing could restrain that man," Seraphina's voice went on by my side, "neither fear nor gratitude." He seemed to cast a spell upon people. He was the plenipotentiary of a powerful religious order—no matter. Don Carlos knew these things better than she did. He had the ear of the Captain-General through that. "Sh! But the intrigues, the intrigues!" I saw her little hand clenched on the closed fan. There were no bounds to his audacity. He wasted their wealth. "The audacity!" He had overawed her father's mind; he claimed descent from his Irish kings, he who—— "Señor, my English cousin, he even dares aspire to my person."

The game of cards was over.

"Death rather," she let fall in a whisper of calm resolution.

She dropped me a deep curtsey. Servants were ranging themselves in a row, holding upright before their black faces wax lights in tall silver candlesticks inherited from the second Viceroy of Mexico. I bowed profoundly, with indignation on her behalf and horror in my breast; and, turning away from me, she sank low, bending her head to receive her father's blessing. The major-domo preceded the *cortège*. The two women moved away with an ample rustling of silk, and with lights carried on each side of their black, stiff figures. Before they had disappeared up the wide staircase, Don Balthasar, who had stood perfectly motionless with his old face over his snuff-box, seemed to wake up, and made in the air a hasty sign of the cross after his daughter.

They appeared again in the upper gallery between the columns. I saw her head, draped in lace, carried proudly, with the white flower in her hair. I raised my eyes. All my being seemed to strive upwards in that glance. Had she turned her face my way just a little? Illusion! And the double door above closed with an echoing sound along the empty galleries. She had disappeared.

Don Balthasar took three turns in the courtyard, no more. It was evidently a daily custom. When he withdrew his hand from my arm to tap his snuff-box, we stood still till he was ready to slip it in again. This was the strangest part of it, the most touching, the most startling—that he should lean like this on me, as if he had done it for years. Before me there must have been somebody else. Carlos? Carlos, no doubt. And in this placing me in that position there was apparent the work of death, the work of life, of time, the pathetic realization of an inevitable destiny. He talked a little disjointedly, with the uncertain swaying of a shadow on his thoughts, as if the light of his mind had flickered like an expiring lamp. I remember that once he asked me, in a sort of senile worry, whether I had ever heard of an Irish king called Brian Boru; but he did not seem to attach any importance to my reply, and spoke no more till he said good-night at the door of my chamber.

He went on to his apartment, surrounded by lights and preceded by his major-domo, who walked as bowed with age as himself; but the African had a firmer step.

I watched him go; there was about his progress in state something ghostlike and royal, an old-time, decayed majesty. It was as if he had arisen before me after a hundred years' sleep in his retreat—that man who, in his wild and passionate youth, had endangered the wealth of the Riegos, had been the idol of the Madrid populace, and a source of dismay to his family. He had carried away, *vi et armis*, a nun from a convent, incurring the enmity of the Church and the displeasure of his sovereign. He had sacrificed all his fortune in

Europe to the service of his king, had fought against the French, had a price put upon his head by a special proclamation. He had known passion, power, war, exile, and love. He had been thanked by his returned king, honoured for his wisdom, and crushed with sorrow by the death of his young wife—Seraphina's mother.

What a life! And what was my arm—my arm on which he had leaned in his decay? I looked at it with a sort of surprise, dubiously. What was expected of it? I asked myself. Would it have the strength? Ah, let *her* only lean on it!

It seemed to me that I would have the power to shake down heavy pillars of stone, like Samson, in her service; to reach up and take the stars, one by one, to lay at her feet. I heard a sigh. A shadow appeared in the gallery.

The door of my room was open. Leaning my back against the balustrade, I saw the black figure of the Father Antonio, muttering over his breviary, enter the space of the light.

He crossed himself, and stopped with a friendly, "You are taking the air, my son. The night is warm." He was rubicund, and his little eyes looked me over with priestly mansuetude.

I said it was warm indeed. I liked him instinctively.

He lifted his eyes to the starry sky. "The orbs are shining excessively," he said; then added, "To the greater glory of God. One is never tired of contemplating this sublime spectacle."

"How is Don Carlos, your reverence?" I asked.

"My beloved penitent sleeps," he answered, peering at me benevolently; "he reposes. Do you know, young *caballero*, that I have been a prisoner of war in your country, and am acquainted with Londres? I was chaplain of the ship *San José* at the battle of Trafalgar.

On my soul, it is, indeed, a blessed, fertile country, full of beauty and of well-disposed hearts. I have never failed since to say every day an especial prayer for its return to our holy mother, the Church. Because I love it."

I said nothing to this, only bowing; and he laid a short, thick hand on my shoulder.

"May your coming amongst us, my son, bring calmness to a Christian soul too much troubled with the affairs of this world." He sighed, nodded to me with a friendly, sad smile, and began to mutter his prayers as he went.

CHAPTER TWO

DON BALTHASAR accepted my presence without a question. Perhaps he fancied he had invited me; of my manner of coming he was ignorant, of course. O'Brien, who had gone on to Havana in the ship which had landed the Riegos in Rio Medio, gave no sign of life. And yet, on the arrival of the *Breeze*, he must have found out I was no longer on board. I forgot the danger suspended over my head. For a fortnight I lived as if in a dream.

"What is the action you want me to take, Carlos?" I asked one day.

Propped up with pillows, he looked at me with the big eyes of his emaciation.

"I would like best to see you marry my cousin. Once before a woman of our race had married an Englishman. She had been happy. English things last forever— English peace, English power, English fidelity. It is a country of much serenity, of order, of stable affection. . . ."

His voice was very weak and full of faith. I remained silent, overwhelmed at this secret of my innermost heart, voiced by his bloodless lips—as if a dream had come to pass, as if a miracle had taken place. He added, with an indefinable smile of an almost unearthly wistfulness:

"I would have married your sister, my Juan."

He had on him the glamour of things English—of English power emerging from the dust of wars and revolution; of England stable and undismayed, like a strong

man who had kept his feet in the tottering of secular
edifices shaken to their foundations by an earthquake.
It was as if for him that were something fine, something
romantic, just as for me romance had always seemed
to be embodied in his features, in his glance, and to live
in the air he breathed. On the other side of the bed
the old Don, lost in a high-backed armchair, remained
plunged in that meditation of the old which resembles
sleep, as sleep resembles death. The priest, lighted up
by the narrow, bright streak of the window, was reading his breviary through a pair of enormous spectacles.
The white coif of the nun hovered in distant corners of
the room.

We were constantly talking of O'Brien. He was the
only subject of all our conversations; and when Carlos
inveighed against the Intendente, the old Don nodded
sadly in his chair. He was dishonouring the name of the
Riegos, Carlos would exclaim feebly, turning his head
towards his uncle. His uncle's own province, the
name of his own town, stood for a refuge of the scum of
the Antilles. It was a shameful sanctuary. Every
ruffian, rascal, murderer, and thief of the West Indies
had come to think of this ancient and honourable town
as a safe haven.

I myself could very well remember the Jamaica
household expression, "The Rio Medio piracies," and
all these paragraphs in the home papers that reached us
a month old headed, "The Activity of the So-called
Mexican Privateers," and urging upon our Government the necessity of energetic remonstrances in Madrid. "The fact, incredible as it may appear," said the
writers, "seeming to be that the nest of these Picaroons
is actually within the loyal dominions of the Spanish
Crown." If Spain, our press said, resented our recognition of South American independence, let it do so

openly, not by countenancing criminals. It was unworthy of a great nation. "Our West Indian trade is being stabbed in the back," declaimed the *Bristol Mirror*. "Where is our fleet?" it asked. "If the Cuban authorities are unable or unwilling, let us take the matter in our own hands."

There was a great deal of mystery about this peculiar outbreak of lawlessness that seemed to be directed so pointedly against the British trade. The town of Rio Medio was alluded to as one of the unapproachable towns of the earth—closed, like the capital of Prester John to the travellers, or Mecca to the infidels. Nobody I ever met in Jamaica had set eyes on the place. The impression prevailed that no stranger could come out of it alive. Incredible stories were told of it in the island, and indignation at its existence grew at home and in the colonies.

Admiral Rowley, an old fighter, grown a bit lazy, no diplomatist (the stories of his being venial, I take it, were simply abominable calumnies), unable to get anything out of the Cuban authorities but promises and lofty protestations, had made up his mind, under direct pressure from home, to take matters into his own hands. His boat attack had been a half-and-half affair, for all that. He intended, he had said, to go to the bottom of the thing, and find out what there was in the place; but he could not believe that anybody would dare offer resistance to the boats of an English squadron. They were sent in as if for an exploration rather than for an armed landing.

It ended in a disaster, and a sense of wonder had been added to the mystery of the fabulous Rio Medio organization. The Cuban authorities protested against the warlike operations attempted in a friendly country; at the same time, they had delivered the seven pirates—

the men whom I saw hanged in Kingston. And Rowley was recalled home in disgrace.

It was my extraordinary fate to penetrate into this holy city of the last organized piracy the world would ever know. I beheld it with my eyes; I had stood on the point behind the very battery of guns which had swept Rowley's boats out of existence.

The narrow entrance faced, across the water, the great portal of the cathedral. Rio Medio had been a place of some splendour in its time. The ruinous heavy buildings clung to the hillsides, and my eyes plunged into a broad vista of an empty and magnificent street. Behind many of the imposing and escutcheoned frontages there was nothing but heaps of rubble; the footsteps of rare passers-by woke lonely echoes, and strips of grass outlined in parallelograms the flagstones of the roadway. The Casa Riego raised its buttressed and loop-holed bulk near the shore, resembling a defensive outwork; on my other hand the shallow bay, vast, placid, and shining, extended itself behind the strip of coast like an enormous lagoon. The fronds of palm-clusters dotted the beach over the glassy shimmer of the far distance. The dark and wooded slopes of the hills closed the view inland on every side.

Under the palms the green masses of vegetation concealed the hovels of the rabble. There were three so-called villages at the bottom of the bay; and that good Catholic and terrible man, Señor Juez O'Brien, could with a simple nod send every man in them to the gallows.

The respectable population of Rio Medio, leading a cloistered existence in the ruins of old splendour, used to call that thievish rabble *Lugareños*—villagers. They were sea-thieves, but they were dangerous.

At night, from these clusters of hovels surrounded by

F

the banana plantations, there issued a villainous noise, the humming of hived scoundrels. Lights twinkled. One could hear the thin twanging of guitars, uproarious songs, all the sounds of their drinking, singing, gambling, quarrelling, love-making, squalor. Sometimes the long shriek of a woman rent the air, or shouting tumults rose and subsided; while, on the other side of the cathedral, the houses of the past, the houses without life, showed no light and made no sound.

There would be no strollers on the beach in the daytime; the masts of the two schooners (bought in the United States by O'Brien to make war with on the British Empire) appeared like slender sticks far away up the empty stretch of water; and that gathering of ruffians, thieves, murderers, and runaway slaves slept in their noisome dens. Their habits were obscene and nocturnal. Cruel without hardihood, and greedy without courage, they were no skull-and-crossbones pirates of the old kind, that, under the black flag, neither gave nor expected quarter. Their usual practice was to hang in rowboats round some unfortunate ship becalmed in sight of their coast, like a troop of vultures hopping about the carcass of a dead buffalo on a plain. When they judged the thing was fairly safe, they would attack with a great noise and show of ferocity; do some hasty looting amongst the cargo; break into the cabins for watches, wearing apparel, and so on; perpetrate at times some atrocity, such as singeing the soles of some poor devil of a ship-master, when they had positive information (from such affiliated helpers as Ramon, the storekeeper in Jamaica) that there was coined money concealed on board; and take themselves off to their sordid revels on shore, and to hold auctions of looted property on the beach. These were attended by people from the interior of the province, and now and then even the Havana dealers would come on the quiet to secure a few pieces of silk or a cask or two of French wine. Tomas Castro could not mention them without spitting in sign of contempt. And it was with that base crew that O'Brien imagined himself to be making war on the British Empire!

In the time of Nichols it did look as if they were really becoming enterprising. They had actually chased and boarded ships sixty miles out at sea. It seems he had inspired them with audacity by means of kicks, blows, and threats of instant death, after the manner of Bluenose sailors. His long limbs, the cadaverous and menacing aspect, the strange nasal ferocity of tone, something mocking and desperate in his aspect, had persuaded them that this unique sort of heretic was literally in league with the devil. He had been the most efficient of the successive leaders O'Brien had imported to give some sort of effect to his warlike operations. I laugh and wonder as I write these words; but the man did look upon it as a war and nothing else. What he had had the audacity to propose to me had been treason, not thieving. It had a glamour for him which, he supposed, a Separationist (as I had the reputation of being) could not fail to see. He was thinking of enlarging his activity, of getting really in touch with the Mexican Junta of rebels. As he had said, he needed a gentleman now. These were Carlos' surmises.

Before Nichols there had been a rather bloodthirsty Frenchman, but he got himself stabbed in an *aguardiente* shop for blaspheming the Virgin. Nichols, as far as I could understand, had really grown scared at O'Brien's success in repulsing Rowley's boats; he had mysteriously disappeared, and neither of the two schooners had been out till the day of my kidnapping, when Castro, by order of Carlos, had taken the command. The freebooters of Rio Medio had returned to their cautious and petty pilfering in boats, from such unlucky ships as the chance of the weather had delivered into their hands. I heard, also, during my walks with Castro (he attended me wrapped in his cloak, and with two pistols in his belt), that there were great jealousies and bickerings amongst that base populace. They were divided into two parties. For instance, the rascals living in the easternmost village accepted tacitly the leadership of a certain Domingo, a mulatto, keeper of a vile grogshop, who was skilled in the art of throwing a knife to a great distance. Manuel-del-Popolo, the extraordinary *improvisador* with the guitar, was an aspirant for power with a certain following of his own. Words could not express Castro's scorn for these fellows. *Ladrones!* vermin of the earth, scum of the sea, he called them.

His position, of course, was exceptional. A dependent of the Riegos, a familiar of the Casa, he was infinitely removed from a Domingo or a Manuel. He lived soberly, like a Spaniard, in some hut in the nearest of the villages, with an old woman who swept the earth floor and cooked his food at an outside fire—his *puchero* and *tortillas*—and rolled for him his provision of cigarettes for the day. Every morning he marched up to the Casa, like a courtier, to attend on his king. I never saw him eat or drink anything there. He leaned a shoulder against the wall, or sat on the floor of the gallery with his short legs stretched out near the big mahogany door of Carlos' room, with many cigarettes stuck behind his ears and in the band of his hat. When these were gone he grubbed for more in the depths of his clothing, somewhere near his skin. Puffs of smoke issued from his pursed lips; and the desolation of his pose, the sorrow of his round, wrinkled face, was so great that it seemed were he to cease smoking, he would die of grief.

The general effect of the place was of vitality exhausted, of a body calcined, of romance turned into stone. The still air, the hot sunshine, the white beach curving around the deserted sheet of water, the sombre green of the hills, had the motionlessness of things petrified, the vividness of things painted, the sadness of things abandoned, desecrated. And, as if alone intrusted with the guardianship of life's sacred fire, I was moving amongst them, nursing my love for Seraphina. The words of Carlos were like oil upon a flame; it enveloped me from head to foot with a leap. I had the physical sensation of breathing it, of seeing it, of being at the same time driven on and restrained. One moment I strode blindly over the sand, the next I stood still; and Castro, coming up panting, would remark from behind that, on such a hot day as this, it was a shame to disturb even a dog sleeping in the shade. I had the feeling of absolute absorption into one idea. I was ravaged by a thought. It was as if I had never before imagined, heard spoken of, or seen a woman.

It was true. She was a revelation to my eye and my ear, as much as to my heart and mind. Indeed, I seemed never before to have seen a woman. Whom had I seen? Veronica? We had been too poor, and my mother too proud, to keep up a social intercourse with our neighbours; the village girls had been devoid of even the most rustic kind of charm; the people were too poor to be handsome. I had never been tempted to look at a woman's face; and the manner of my going from home is known. In Jamaica, sharing with an exaggerated loyalty the unpopularity of the Macdonalds, I had led a lonely life; for I had no taste for their friends' society, and the others, after a time, would have nothing to do with me. I had made a sort of hermitage for myself out of a house in a distant plantation, and sometimes I would see no white face for whole weeks together. She was the first woman to me—a strange new being, a marvel as great as Eve herself to Adam's wondering awakening.

It may be that a close intimacy stands in the way of love springing up between two young people, but in our case it was different. My passion seemed to spring from our understanding, because the understanding was in the face of danger. We were like two people in a slowly sinking ship; the feeling of the abyss under our feet was our bond, not the real comprehension of each other. Apart from that, she remained to me always unattainable and romantic—unique, with all the unexpressed promises of love such as no world had ever known. And naturally, because for me, hitherto, the world had held no woman. She was an apparition of dreams—the girl with the lizard, the girl with the dagger, a wonder to stretch out my hands to from afar; and yet I was permitted to whisper intimately to this my dream, to this vision. We had to put our heads close together, talking of the enemy and of the shadow over the house; while under our eyes Carlos waited for death, made cruel by his anxieties, and the old Don walked in the darkness of his accumulated years.

As to me, what was I to her?

Carlos, in a weak voice, and holding her hand with a feeble and tenacious grasp, had told her repeatedly that the English cousin was ready to offer up his life to her happiness in this world. Many a time she would turn her glance upon me—not a grateful glance, but, as it were, searching and pensive—a glance of penetrating candour, a young girl's glance, that, by its very trustfulness, seems to look one through and through. And then the sense of my unworthiness made me long for her love as a sinner, in his weakness, longs for the saving grace.

"Our English cousin is worthy of his great nation. He is very brave, and very chivalrous to a poor girl," she would say softly.

One day, I remember, going out of Carlos' room, she had just paused on the threshold for an almost imperceptible moment, the time to murmur, with feeling, "May Heaven reward you, Don Juan." This sound, faint and enchanting, like a breath of sweet wind, staggered me. Castro, sitting outside as usual, had scrambled to his feet and stood by, hat in hand, his head bent slightly with saturnine deference. She smiled at him. I think she felt kindly towards the tubby little bandit of a fellow. After all, there was something touching and pathetic in his mournful vigil at the door of our radiant Carlos. I could have embraced that figure of grotesque and truculent devotion. Had she not smiled upon him?

The rest of that memorable day I spent in a state of delightful distraction, as if I had been ravished into the seventh heaven, and feared to be cast out again presently, as my unworthiness deserved. What if it were possible, after all?—this, what Carlos wished, what he had said. The heavens shook; the constellations above the court of Casa Riego trembled at the thought.

Carlos fought valiantly. There were days when his courage seemed to drive the grim presence out of the chamber, where Father Antonio with his breviary, and the white coif of the nun, seemed the only reminders of illness and mortality. Sometimes his voice was very strong, and a sort of hopefulness lighted his wasted features. Don Balthasar paid many visits to his nephew in the course of each day. He sat apparently attentive, and nodding at the name of O'Brien. Then Carlos would talk against O'Brien from amongst his pillows as if inspired, till the old man, striking the floor with his gold-headed cane, would exclaim, in a quavering voice, that he, alone, had made him, had raised him up from the dust, and could abase him to the dust again. He would instantly go to Havana; orders would be given to Cesar for the journey this very moment. He would then take a pinch of snuff with shaky energy, and lean back in the armchair. Carlos would whisper to me, "He will never leave the Casa again," and an air of solemn, brooding helplessness would fall upon the funereal magnificence of the room. Presently we would hear the old Don muttering dotingly to himself the name of Seraphina's mother, the young wife of his old days, so saintly, and snatched away from him in punishment of his early sinfulness. It was impossible that she should have been deceived in Don Patricio (O'Brien's Christian name was Patrick). The intendente was a man of great intelligence, and full of reverence for her memory. Don Balthasar admitted that he himself was growing old; and, besides, there was that sorrow of his life. . . . He had been fortunate in his affliction to have a man of his worth by his side. There might have been slight irregularities, faults of youth (O'Brien was five-and-forty if a day). The archbishop himself was edified by the life of the upright judge—all Havana, all the island. The intendente's great zeal for the House might have led him into an indiscretion or two. So many years now, so many years. A noble himself. Had we heard of an Irish king? A king . . . king . . . he could not recall the name at present. It might be well to hear what a man of such abilities had to say for himself.

Carlos and I looked at each other silently.

"And his life hangs on a thread," whispered the dying man with something like despair.

The crisis of all these years of plotting would come the moment the old Don closed his eyes. Meantime, why was it that O'Brien did not show himself in Rio Medio? What was it that kept him in Havana?

"Already I do not count, my Juan," Carlos would say. "And he prepares all things for the day of my uncle's death."

The dark ways of that man were inscrutable. He must have known, of course, that I was in Rio Medio. His presence was to be feared, and his absence itself was growing formidable.

"But what do you think he will do? How do you think he will act?" I would ask, a little bewildered by my responsibility.

Carlos could not tell precisely. It was not till some time after his arrival from Europe that he became clearly aware of all the extent of that man's ambition. At the same time, he had realized all his power. That man aimed at nothing less than the whole Riego fortune, and, of course, through Seraphina. I would feel a rage at this—a sort of rage that made my head spin as if the ground had reeled. "He would have found means of getting rid of me if he had not seen I was not long for this world," Carlos would say. He had gained an un-limited ascendency over his uncle's mind; he had made a solitude round this solemn dotage in which ended so much power, a great reputation, a stormy life of romance and passion—so picturesque and excessive even in his old man's love, whose after-effect, as though the work of a Nemesis resenting so much brilliance, was casting a shadow upon the fate of his daughter.

Small, fair, plump, concealing his Irish vivacity of
*F

intelligence under the taciturn gravity of a Spanish lawyer, and backed by the influence of two noble houses, O'Brien had attained to a remarkable reputation of sagacity and unstained honesty. Hand in glove with the clergy, one of the judges of the Marine Court, procurator to the cathedral chapter, he had known how to make himself so necessary to the highest in the land that everybody but the very highest looked upon him with fear. His occult influence was altogether out of proportion to his official position. His plans were carried out with an unswerving tenacity of purpose. Carlos believed him capable of anything but a vulgar peculation. He had been reduced to observe his action quietly, hampered by the weakness of ill-health. As an instance of O'Brien's methods, he related to me the manner in which, faithful to his purpose of making a solitude about the Riegos, he had contrived to prevent overtures for an alliance from the Salazar family. The young man Don Vincente himself was impossible, an evil liver, Carlos said, of dissolute habits. Still, to have even that shadow of a rival out of the way, O'Brien took advantage of a sanguinary affray between that man and one of his boon companions about some famous guitar-player girl. The encounter having taken place under the wall of a convent, O'Brien had contrived to keep Don Vincente in prison ever since—not on a charge of murder (which for a young man of that quality would have been a comparatively venial offence), but of sacrilege. The Salazars were a powerful family, but he was strong enough to risk their enmity. "Imagine that, Juan!" Carlos would exclaim, closing his eyes. What had caused him the greatest uneasiness was the knowledge that Don Balthasar had been induced lately to write some letter to the archbishop in Havana. Carlos was afraid it was simply an expression of affection and unbounded trust in his intendente, practically dictated to the old man by O'Brien. "Do you not see, Juan, how such a letter would strengthen his case, should he ask the guardians for Seraphina's hand?" And perhaps he was appointed one of the guardians himself. It was impossible to know what were the testamentary dispositions; Father Antonio, who had learned many things in the confessional, could tell us nothing, but, when the matter was mentioned, only rolled his eyes up to heaven in an alarming manner. It was startling to think of all the unholy forces awakened by the temptation of Seraphina's helplessness and her immense fortune. Incorruptible himself, that man knew how to corrupt others. There might have been combined in one dark intrigue the covetousness of religious orders, the avarice of high officials—God knows what conspiracy—to help O'Brien's ambition, his passions. He could make himself necessary; he could bribe; he could frighten; he was able to make use of the highest in the land and of the lowest, from the present Captain-General to the *Lugareños*. In Havana he had for him the reigning powers; in Rio Medio the lowest outcasts of the island.

This last was the most dangerous aspect of his power for us, and also his weakest point. This was the touch of something fanciful and imaginative; a certain grim childishness in the idea of making war on the British Empire; a certain disregard of risk; a bizarre illusion of his hate for the abhorred Saxon. That he risked his position by his connection with such a nest of scoundrels, there could be no doubt. It was he who had given them such organization as they had, and he stood between them and the law. But whatever might have been suspected of him, he was cautious

enough not to go too far. He never appeared personally; his agents directed the action—men who came
from Havana rather mysteriously. They were of all
sorts; some of them were friars. But the rabble, who
knew him really only as the intendente of the great
man, stood in the greatest dread of him. Who was it
procured the release of some of them who had got into
trouble in Havana? The intendente. Who was it
who caused six of their comrades, who had been taken
up on a matter of street-brawling in the capital, to be
delivered to the English as pirates? Again, the intendente, the terrible man, the Juez, who apparently had
the power to pardon and condemn.

In this way he was most dangerous to us in Rio
Medio. He had that rabble at his beck and call. He
could produce a rising of cut-throats by lifting his little
finger. He was not very likely to do that, however.
He was intriguing in Havana—but how could we unmask him there? "He has cut us off from the world,"
Carlos would say. "It is so, my Juan, that, if I tried
to write, no letter of mine would reach its destination;
it would fall into his hands. And if I did manage to
make my voice heard, he would appeal to my uncle
himself in his defence."

Besides, to whom could he write?—who would believe
him? O'Brien would deny everything, and go on his
way. He had been accepted too long, had served too
many people and known so many secrets. It was
terrible. And if I went myself to Havana, no one
would believe me. But I should disappear; they would
never see me again. It was impossible to unmask that
man unless by a long and careful action. And for this
he—Carlos—had no time; and I—I had no standing,
no relations, no skill even. . . .

"But what is my line of conduct, Carlos?" I insisted; while Father Antonio, from whom Carlos had, of course, no secrets, stood by the bed, his round, jolly face almost comical in its expression of compassionate concern.

Carlos passed his thin, wasted hand over a white brow pearled with the sweat of real anguish.

Carlos thought that while Don Balthasar lived, O'Brien would do nothing to compromise his influence over him. Neither could I take any action; I must wait and watch. O'Brien would, no doubt, try to remove me; but as long as I kept within the Casa, he thought I should be safe. He recommended me to try to please his cousin, and even found strength to smile at my transports. Don Balthasar liked me for the sake of his sister, who had been so happy in England. I was his kinsman and his guest. From first to last, England, the idea of my country, of my home, played a great part in my life then; it seemed to rest upon all our thoughts. To me it was but my boyhood, the farm at the foot of the downs—Rooksby's Manor—all within a small nook between the quarry by the side of the Canterbury road and the shingle beach, whose regular crashing under the feet of a smuggling band was the last sound of my country I had heard. For Carlos it was the concrete image of stability, with the romantic feeling of its peace and of Veronica's beauty; the unchangeable land where he had loved. To O'Brien's hate it loomed up immense and odious, like the form of a colossal enemy. Father Antonio, in the naïve benevolence of his heart, prayed each night for its conversion, as if it were a loved sinner. He believed this event to be not very far off accomplishment, and told me once, with an amazing simplicity of certitude, that "there will be a great joy amongst the host of heaven on that day." It is marvellous how that distant land, from which I had escaped as if from a prison to go in search of romance, appeared romantic and perfect in these days—all things to all men! With Seraphina I talked of it and its denizens as of a fabulous country. I wonder what idea she had formed of my father, of my mother, my sister—"Señora Doña Veronica Rooksby," she called her—of the landscape, of the life, of the sky. Her eyes turned to me seriously. Once, stooping, she plucked an orange marigold for her hair; and at last we came to talk of our farm as of the only perfect refuge for her.

CHAPTER THREE

ONE evening Carlos, after a silence of distress, had said, "There's nothing else for it. When the crisis comes, you must carry her off from this unhappiness and misery that hangs over her head. You must take her out of Cuba; there is no safety for her here."

This took my breath away. "But where are we to go, Carlos?" I asked, bending over him.

"To—to England," he whispered.

He was utterly worn out that evening by all the perplexities of his death-bed. He made a great effort and murmured a few words more—about the Spanish ambassador in London being a near relation of the Riegos; then he gave it up and lay still under my amazed eyes. The nun was approaching, alarmed, from the shadows. Father Antonio, gazing sadly upon his beloved penitent, signed me to withdraw.

Castro had not gone away yet; he greeted me in low tones outside the big door.

"Señor," he went on, "I make my report usually to his Señoria Don Carlos; only I have not been admitted to-day into his rooms at all. But what I have to say is for your ear, also. There has arrived a friar from Havana convent amongst the *Lugareños* of the bay. I have known him come like this before."

I remembered that in the morning, while dressing, I had glanced out of the narrow outside window of my room, and had seen a brown, mounted figure passing on the sands. Its sandalled feet dangled against the flanks of a powerful mule.

Castro shook his head. "Malediction on his green eyes! He baptizes the offspring of this vermin some-times, and sits for hours in the shade before the door of Domingo's posada telling his beads as piously as a devil that had turned monk for the greater undoing of us Christians. These women crowd there to kiss his oily paw. What else they—— *Basta!* Only I wanted to tell you, Señor, that this evening (I just come from taking a pasear that way) there is much talk in the villages of an evil-intentioned heretic that has intro-duced himself into this our town; of an *Inglez* hungry for men to hang—of you, in short."

The moon, far advanced in its first quarter, threw an ashen, bluish light upon one-half of the courtyard; and the straight shadow upon the other seemed to lie at the foot of the columns, black as a broad stroke of Indian ink.

"And what do you think of it, Castro?" I asked.

"I think that Domingo has his orders. Manuel has made a song already. And do you know its burden, Señor? Killing is its burden. I would the devil had all these *Improvisadores*. They gape round him while he twangs and screeches, the wind-bag! And he knows what words to sing to them, too. He has talent. *Maladetta!*"

"Well, and what do you advise?"

"I advise the señor to keep, now, within the Casa. No songs can give that vermin the audacity to seek the señor here. The gate remains barred; the firearms are always loaded; and Cesar is a sagacious African. But methinks this moon would fall out of the heaven first before they would dare. . . . Keep to the Casa, I say—I, Tomas Castro."

He flung the corner of his cloak over his left shoulder, and preceded me to the door of my room; then, after a

"God guard you, Señor," continued along the colonnade. Before I had shut my door it occurred to me that he was going on towards the part of the gallery on which Seraphina's apartments opened. Why? What could he want there?

I am not so much ashamed of my sudden suspicion of him—one did not know whom to trust—but I am a little ashamed to confess that, kicking off my shoes, I crept out instantly to spy upon him.

This part of the house was dark in the inky flood of shadow; and before I had come to a recess in the wall, I heard the discreet scratching of a finger-nail on a door. A streak of light darted and disappeared, like a signal for the murmurs of two voices.

I recognized the woman's at once. It belonged to one of Seraphina's maids, a pretty little quadroon—a favourite of hers—called La Chica. She had slipped out, and her twitter-like whispering reached me in the still solemnity of the quadrangle. She addressed Castro as "His Worship" at every second word, for the saturnine little man, in his unbrushed cloak and battered hat, was immensely respected by the household. Had he not been sent to Europe to fetch Don Carlos? He was in the confidence of the masters—their humble friend. The little tire-woman twittered of her mistress. The señorita had been most anxious all day—ever since she had heard the friar had come. Castro muttered:

"Tell the Excellency that her orders have been obeyed. The English *caballero* has been warned. I have been sleepless in my watchfulness over the guest of the house, as the señorita has desired—for the honour of the Riegos. Let her set her mind at ease."

The girl then whispered to him with great animation. Did not his worship think that it was the señorita's heart which was not at ease?

Then the quadrangle became dumb in its immobility, half sheen, half night, with its arcades, the soothing plash of water, with its expiring lights, in a suggestion of Castilian severity, enveloped by the exotic softness of the air.

"What folly!" uttered Castro's sombre voice. "You women do not mind how many corpses come into your imaginings of love. The mere whisper of such a thing——"

She murmured swiftly. He interrupted her.

"Thine eyes, La Chica—thine eyes see only the silliness of thine own heart. Think of thine own lovers, _niña_. _Por Dios!_—he changed to a tone of severe appreciation—"thy foolish face looks well by moonlight."

I believe he was chucking her gravely under the chin. I heard her soft, gratified cooing in answer to the compliment; the streak of light flashed on the polished shaft of a pillar; and Castro went on, going round to the staircase, evidently so as not to pass again before my open door.

I forgot to shut it. I did not stop until I was in the middle of my room; and then I stood still for a long time in a self-forgetful ecstasy, while the many wax candles of the high candelabrum burned without a flicker in a rich cluster of flames, as if lighted to throw the splendour of a celebration upon the pageant of my thoughts.

For the honour of the Riegos!

I came to myself. Well, it was sweet to be the object of her anxiety and care, even on these terms—on any terms. And I felt a sort of profound, inexpressible, grateful emotion, as though no one, never, on no day, on no occasion, had taken thought of me before.

I should not be able to sleep. I went to the window, and leaned my forehead on the iron bar. There was no glass; the heavy shutter was thrown open; and, under the faint crescent of the moon I saw a small part of the beach, very white, the long streak of light lying mistily on the bay, and two black shapes, cloaked, moving and stopping all of a piece like pillars, their immensely long shadows running away from their feet, with the points of the hats touching the wall of the Casa Riego. Another, a shorter, thicker shape, appeared, walking with dignity. It was Castro. The other two had a movement of recoil, then took off their hats.

"*Buenas noches, caballeros*," his voice said, with grim politeness. "You are out late."

"So is your worship. *Vaya, Señor, con Dios*. We are taking the air."

They walked away, while Castro remained looking after them. But I, from my elevation, noticed that they had suddenly crouched behind some scrubby bushes growing on the edge of the sand. Then Castro, too, passed out of my sight in the opposite direction, muttering angrily.

I forgot them all. Everything on earth was still, and I seemed to be looking through a casement out of an enchanted castle standing in the dreamland of romance. I breathed out the name of Seraphina into the moonlight in an increasing transport.

"Seraphina! Seraphina! Seraphina!"

The repeated beauty of the sound intoxicated me.

"Seraphina!" I cried aloud, and stopped, astounded at myself. And the moonlight of romance seemed to whisper spitefully from below:

"Death to the traitor! Vengeance for our brothers dead on the English gallows!"

"Come away, Manuel."

"No. I am an artist. It is necessary for my soul."

"Be quiet!"

Their hissing ascended along the wall from under the window. The two *Lugareños* had stolen in unnoticed by me. There was a stifled metallic ringing, as of a guitar carried under a cloak.

"Vengeance on the heretic *Inglez!*

"Come away! They may suddenly open the gate and fall upon us with sticks."

"My gentle spirit is roused to the accomplishment of great things. I feel in me a valiance, an inspiration. I am no vulgar seller of *aguardiente*, like Domingo. I was born to be the *capataz* of the *Lugareños.*"

"We shall be set upon and beaten, oh, thou Manuel. Come away!"

There were no footsteps, only a noiseless flitting of two shadows, and a distant voice crying:

"Woe, woe, woe to the traitor!"

I had not needed Castro's warning to understand the meaning of this. O'Brien was setting his power to work, only this Manuel's restless vanity had taught me exactly how the thing was to be done. The friar had been exciting the minds of this rabble against me; awakening their suspicions, their hatred, their fears.

I remained at the casement, lost in rather sombre reflections. I was now a prisoner within the walls of the Casa. After all, it mattered little. I did not want to go away unless I could carry off Seraphina with me. What a dream! What an impossible dream! Alone, without friends, with no place to go to, without means of going; without, by Heaven, the right of even as much as speaking of it to her. Carlos—Carlos dreamed— a dream of his dying hours. England was so far, the enemy so near; and—Providence itself seemed to have forgotten me.

A sound of panting made me turn my head. Father Antonio was mopping his brow in the doorway. Though a heavy man, he was noiseless of foot. A wheezing would be heard along the dark galleries some time before his black bulk approached you with a gliding motion. He had the outward placidity of corpulent people, a natural artlessness of demeanour which was amusing and attractive, and there was something shrewd in his simplicity. Indeed, he must have displayed much tact and shrewdness to have defeated all O'Brien's efforts to oust him from his position of confessor to the household. What had helped him to hold his ground was that, as he said to me once, "I, too, my son, am a legacy of that truly pious and noble lady, the wife of Don Riego. I was made her spiritual director soon after her marriage, and I may say that she showed more discretion in the choice of her confessor than in that of her man of affairs. But what would you have? The best of us, except for Divine grace, is liable to err; and, poor woman, let us hope that, in her blessed state, she is spared the knowledge of the iniquities going on here below in the Casa."

He used to talk to me in that strain, coming in almost every evening on his way from the sick room. He, too, had his own perplexities, which made him wipe his forehead repeatedly; afterwards he used to spread his red bandanna handkerchief over his knees.

He sympathized with Carlos, his beloved penitent, with Seraphina, his dear daughter, whom he had baptized and instructed in the mysteries of "our holy religion," and he allowed himself often to drop the remark that his "illustrious spiritual son," Don Balthasar, after a stormy life of which men knew only too much, had attained to a state of truly childlike and God-fearing innocence—a sign, no doubt, of Heaven's forgiveness for those excesses. He ended, always, by sighing heartily, to sit with his gaze on the floor.

That night he came in silently, and after shutting the door with care, took his habitual seat, a broad wooden armchair.

"How did your reverence leave Don Carlos?" I asked.

"Very low," he said. "The disease is making terrible ravages, and my ministrations—— I ought to be used to the sight of human misery, but——" He raised his hands; a genuine emotion overpowered him; then, uncovering his face to stare at me, "He is lost, Don Juan," he exclaimed.

"Indeed, I fear we are about to lose him, your reverence," I said, surprised at this display. It seemed inconceivable that he should have been in doubt up to this very moment.

He rolled his eyes painfully. I was forgetting the infinite might of God. Still, nothing short of a miracle —— But what had we done to deserve miracles?

"Where is the ancient piety of our forefathers which made Spain so great?" he apostrophized the empty air, a little wildly, as if in distraction. "No, Don Juan; even I, a true servant of our faith, am conscious of not having had enough grace for my humble ministrations to poor sailors and soldiers—men naturally inclined to sin, but simple. And now—there are two great nobles, the fortune of a great house. . . ."

I looked at him and wondered, for he was, in a manner, wringing his hands, as if in immense distress.

"We are all thinking of that poor child—*mas que*, Don Juan, imagine all that wealth devoted to the iniquitous purposes of that man. Her happiness sacrificed."

"I cannot imagine this—I will not," I interrupted, so violently that he hushed me with both hands uplifted.

"To these wild enterprises against your own country," he went on vehemently, disregarding my exasperated and contemptuous laugh. "And she herself, the *niña*. I have baptized her; I have instructed her; and a more noble disposition, more naturally inclined to the virtues and proprieties of her sex—— But, Don Juan, she has pride, which doubtless is a gift of God, too, but it is made a snare of by Satan, the roaring lion, the thief of souls. And what if her feminine rashness—women are rash, my son," he interjected with unction—"and her pride were to lead her into—I am horrified at the thought—into an act of mortal sin for which there is no repentance?"

"Enough!" I shouted at him.

"No repentance," he repeated, rising to his feet excitedly, and I stood before him, my arms down my sides, with my fists clenched.

Why did the stupid priest come to talk like this to me, as if I had not enough of my own unbearable thoughts?

He sat down and began to flourish his handkerchief. There was depicted on his broad face—depicted simply and even touchingly—the inward conflict of his benevolence and of his doubts.

"I observe your emotion, my son," he said. I must have been as pale as death. And, after a pause, he meditated aloud, "And, after all, you English are a reverent nation. You, a scion of the nobility, have been brought up in deplorable rebellion against the authority of God on this earth; but you are not a scoffer—not a scoffer. I, a humble priest—— But, after all, the Holy Father himself, in his inspired wisdom—— I have prayed to be enlightened. . . ."

He spread the square of his damp handkerchief on his knees, and bowed his head. I had regained command over myself, but I did not understand in the least. I had passed from my exasperation into a careworn fatigue of mind that was like utter darkness.

"After all," he said, looking up naïvely, "the business of us priests is to save souls. It is a solemn time when death approaches. The affairs of this world should be cast aside. And yet God surely does not mean us to abandon the living to the mercy of the wicked."

A sadness came upon his face, his eyes; all the world seemed asleep. He made an effort. "My son," he said with decision, "I call you to follow me to the bedside of Don Carlos at this very hour of night. I, a humble priest, the unworthy instrument of God's grace, call upon you to bring him a peace which my ministrations cannot give. His time is near."

I rose up, startled by his solemnity, by the hint of hidden significance in these words.

"Is he dying now?" I cried.

"He ought to detach his thoughts from this earth; and if there is no other way——"

"What way? What am I expected to do?"

"My son, I had observed your emotion. We, the appointed confidants of men's frailties, are quick to discern the signs of their innermost feelings. Let me tell you that my cherished daughter in God, Señorita Doña Seraphina Riego, is with Don Carlos, the virtual head of the family, since his Excellency Don Balthasar is in a state of, I may say, infantile innocence."

"What do you mean, father?" I faltered.

"She is waiting for you with him," he pronounced, looking up. And as his solemnity seemed to have deprived me of my power to move, he added, with his ordinary simplicity, "Why, my son, she is, I may say, not wholly indifferent to your person."

I could not have dropped more suddenly into the chair had the good *padre* discharged a pistol into my

breast. He went away; and when I leapt up, I saw a
young man in black velvet and white ruffles staring at
me out of the large mirror set frameless into the wall,
like the apparition of a Spanish ghost with my own
English face.

When I ran out, the moon had sunk below the ridge
of the roof; the whole quadrangle of the Casa had turned
black under the stars, with only a yellow glimmer of
light falling into the well of the court from the lamp
under the vaulted gateway. The form of the priest
had gone out of sight, and a far-away knocking, mingling with my footfalls, seemed to be part of the tumult
within my heart. Below, a voice at the gate challenged,
"Who goes there?" I ran on. Two tiny flames burned
before Carlos' door at the end of the long vista, and
two of Seraphina's maids shrank away from the great
mahogany panels at my approach. The candlesticks
trembled askew in their hands; the wax guttered down,
and the taller of the two girls, with an uncovered long
neck, gazed at me out of big sleepy eyes in a sort of
dumb wonder. The teeth of the plump little one—La
Chica—rattled violently like castanets. She moved
aside with a hysterical little laugh, and glanced upwards
at me.

I stopped, as if I had intruded; of all the persons in
the sick-room, not one turned a head. The stillness of
the lights, of things, of the air, seemed to have passed
into Seraphina's face. She stood with a stiff carriage
under the heavy hangings of the bed, looking very
Spanish and romantic in her short black skirt, a black
lace shawl enveloping her head, her shoulders, her
arms, as low as the waist. Her bare feet, thrust into
high-heeled slippers, lent to her presence an air of flight,
as if she had run into that room in distress or fear.
Carlos, sitting up amongst the snowy pillows of eider-

down at his back, was not speaking to her. He had done; and the flush on his cheek, the eager lustre of his eyes, gave him an appearance of animation, almost of joy, a sort of consuming, flame-like brilliance. They were waiting for me. With all his eagerness and air of life, all he could do was to lift his white hand an inch or two off the silk coverlet that spread over his limbs smoothly, like a vast crimson pall. There was something joyous and cruel in the shimmer of this piece of colour, contrasted with the dead white of the linen, the duskiness of the wasted face, the dark head with no visible body, symbolically motionless. The confused shadows and the tarnished splendour of emblazoned draperies, looped up high under the ceiling, fell in heavy and unstirring folds right down to the polished floor, that reflected the lights like a sheet of water, or rather like ice.

I felt it slippery under my feet. I, alone, had to move, in this great chamber, with its festive patches of colour amongst the funereal shadows, with the expectant, still figures of priest and nun, servants of passionless eternity, as if immobilized and made mute by hostile wonder before the perishable triumph of life and love. And only the impatient tapping of the sick man's hand on the stiff silk of the coverlet was heard.

It called to me. Seraphina's unstirring head was lighted strongly by a two-branched sconce on the wall; and when I stood by her side, not even the shadow of the eyelashes on her cheek trembled. Carlos' lips moved; his voice was almost extinct; but for all his emaciation, the profundity of his eyes, the sunken cheeks, the hollow temples, he remained attractive, with the charm of his gallant and romantic temper worn away to an almost unearthly fineness.

He was going to have his desire because, on the threshold of his spiritual inheritance, he refused, or was unable, to turn his gaze away from this world. Father Antonio's business was to save this soul; and with a sort of simple and sacerdotal shrewdness, in which there was much love for his most noble penitent, he would try to appease its trouble by a romantic satisfaction. His voice, very grave and profound, addressed me:

"Approach, my son—nearer. We trust the natural feelings of pity which are implanted in every human breast, the nobility of your extraction, the honour of your *hidalguidad*, and that inextinguishable courage which, as by the unwearied mercy of God, distinguishes the sons of your fortunate and unhappy nation." His bass voice, deepened in solemn utterance, vibrated huskily. There was a rustic dignity in his uncouth form, in his broad face, in the gesture of the raised hand. "You shall promise to respect the dictates of our conscience, guided by the authority of our faith; to defer to our scruples, and to the procedure of our Church in matters which we believe touch the welfare of our souls. . . . You promise?"

He waited. Carlos' eyes burned darkly on my face. What were they asking of me? This was nothing. Of course I would respect her scruples—her scruples—if my heart should break. I felt her living intensely by my side; she could be brought no nearer to me by anything they could do, or I could promise. She had already all the devotion of my love and youth, the unreasoning and potent devotion, without a thought or hope of reward. I was almost ashamed to pronounce the two words they expected.

"I promise."

And suddenly the meaning pervading this scene, something that was in my mind already, and that I had hardly dared to look at till now, became clear to me in its awful futility against the dangers, in all its remote consequences. It was a betrothal. The priest—Carlos, too—must have known that it had no binding power. To Carlos it was symbolic of his wishes. Father Antonio was thinking of the papal dispensation. I was a heretic. What if it were refused? But what was that risk to me, who had never dared to hope? Moreover, they had brought her there, had persuaded her; she had been influenced by her fears, impressed by Carlos. What could she care for me? And I repeated:

"I promise. I promise, even at the cost of suffering and unhappiness, never to demand anything from her against her conscience."

Carlos' voice sounded weak. "I answer for him, good father." Then he seemed to wander in a whisper, which we two caught faintly, "He resembles his sister. O Divine——"

And on this ghostly sigh, on this breath, with the feeble click of beads in the nun's hands, a silence fell upon the room, vast as the stillness of a world of unknown faiths, loves, beliefs, of silent illusions, of unexpressed passions and secret motives that live in our unfathomable hearts.

Seraphina had given me a quick glance—the first glance—which I had rather felt than seen. Carlos made an effort, and, raising himself, put her hand in mine.

Father Antonio, trying to pronounce a short allocution, broke down, naïve in his emotion, as he had been in his dignity. I could at first catch only the words, "Beloved child—Holy Father—poor priest. . . ." He had taken this upon himself; and he would attest the purity of our intentions, the necessity of the case, the assent of the head of the family, my excellent dis-

position. All the Englishmen had excellent dispositions. He would, personally, go to the foot of the Holy
See—on his knees, if necessary. Meantime, a document—he should at once prepare a justificative document. The archbishop, it is true, did not like him on
account of the calumnies of that man O'Brien. But
there was, beyond the seas, the supreme authority of
the Church, unerring and inaccessible to calumnies.

All that time Seraphina's hand was lying passive
in my palm—warm, soft, living; all the life, all the
world, all the happiness, the only desire—and I dared
not close my grasp, afraid of the vanity of my hopes,
shrinking from the intense felicity in the audacious act.
Father Antonio—I must say the word—blubbered. He
was now only a tender-hearted, simple old man, nothing more.

"Before God now, Don Juan. . . . I am only
a poor priest, but invested with a sacred office, an
enormous power. Tremble, Señor, it is a young girl . . .
I have loved her like my own; for, indeed, I have in
baptism given her the spiritual life. You owe her
protection; it is for that, before God, Señor——"

It was as if Carlos had swooned; his eyes were closed,
his face like a carving. But gradually the suggestion
of a tender and ironic smile appeared on his lips. With
a slow effort he raised his arm and his eyelids, in an
appeal of all his weariness for my ear. I made a movement to stoop over him, and the floor, the great bed,
the whole room, seemed to heave and sway. I felt a
slight, a fleeting pressure of Seraphina's hand before it
slipped out of mine; I thought, in the beating rush of
blood to my temples, that I was going mad.

He had thrown his arm over my neck; there was the
calming austerity of death on his lips, that just touched
my ear and departed, together with the far-away sound

of the words, losing themselves in the remoteness of another world:

"Like an Englishman, Juan."

"On my honour, Carlos."

His arm, releasing my neck, fell stretched out on the coverlet. Father Antonio had mastered his emotion; with the trail of undried tears on his face, he had become a priest again, exalted above the reach of his earthly sorrow by the august concern of his sacerdoce.

"Don Carlos, my son, is your mind at ease, now?"

Carlos closed his eyes slowly.

"Then turn all your thoughts to heaven." Father Antonio's bass voice rose, aloud, with an extraordinary authority. "You have done with the earth."

The arm of the nun touched the cords of the curtains, and the massive folds shook and fell expanded, hiding from us the priest and the penitent.

CHAPTER FOUR

Seraphina and I moved towards the door sadly, as if
under the oppression of a memory, as people go back
from the side of a grave to the cares of life. No exultation possessed me. Nothing had happened. It had
been a sick man's whim.

"Señorita," I said low, with my hand on the wrought
bronze of the door-handle, "Don Carlos might have
died in full trust of my devotion to you—without this."

"I know it," she answered, hanging her head.

"It was his wish," I said. "And I deferred."

"It was his wish," she repeated.

"Remember he had asked you for no promise."

"Yes, it is you only he has asked. You have remembered it very well, Señor. And you—you ask for
nothing."

"No," I said; "neither from your heart nor from your
conscience—nor from your gratitude. Gratitude from
you! As if it were not I that owe you gratitude for having condescended to stand with your hand in mine—
if only for a moment—if only to bring peace to a dying
man; for giving me the felicity, the illusion of this wonderful instant, that, all my life, I shall remember as
those who are suddenly stricken blind remember the
great glory of the sun. I shall live with it, I shall
cherish it in my heart to my dying day; and I promise
never to mention it to you again."

Her lips were slightly parted, her eyes remained
downcast, her head drooped as if in extreme attention.

"I asked for no promise," she murmured coldly.

My heart was heavy. "Thank you for that proof of your confidence," I said. "I am yours without any promises. Wholly yours. But what can I offer? What help? What refuge? What protection? What can I do? I can only die for you. Ah, but this was cruel of Carlos, when he knew that I had nothing else but my poor life to give."

"I accept that," she said unexpectedly.

"Señorita, it is generous of you to accept so worthless a gift—a life I value not at all save for one unique memory which I owe to you."

I knew she was looking at me while I swung open the door with a low bow. I did not trust myself to look at her. An unreasonable disenchantment, like the awakening from a happy dream, oppressed me. I felt an almost angry desire to seize her in my arms—to go back to my dream. If I had looked at her then, I believed I could not have controlled myself.

She passed out; and when I looked up there was O'Brien booted and spurred, but otherwise in his lawyer's black, inclining his dapper figure profoundly before her in the dim gallery. She had stopped short. The two maids, huddled together behind her, stared with terrified eyes. The flames of their candles vacillated very much.

I closed the door quietly. Carlos was done with the earth. This had become my affair; and the necessity of coming to an immediate decision almost deprived me of my power of thinking. The necessity had arisen too swiftly; the arrival of that man acted like the sudden apparition of a phantom. It had been expected, however; only, from the moment we had turned away from Carlos' bedside, we had thought of nothing but ourselves; we had dwelt alone in our emotions, as if there had been no inhabitant of flesh and blood on the earth but we two. Our danger had been present, no doubt, in our minds, because we drew it in with every breath. It was the indispensable condition of our contact, of our words, of our thoughts; it was the atmosphere of our feelings; a something as all-pervading and impalpable as the air we drew into our lungs. And suddenly this danger, this breath of our life, had taken this material form. It was material and expected, and yet it had the effect of an evil spectre, inasmuch as one did not know where and how it was vulnerable, what precisely it would do, how one should defend one's self.

His bow was courtly; his gravity was all in his bearing, which was quiet and confident: the manner of a capable man, the sort of man the great of this earth find invaluable and are inclined to trust. His full-shaven face had a good-natured, almost a good-humored expression, which I have come to think must have depended on the cast of his features, on the setting of his eyes—on some peculiarity not under his control, or else he could not have preserved it so well. In certain occasions, as this one, for instance, it affected me as a refinement of cynicism; and, generally, it was startling, like the assumption of a mask inappropriate to the action and the speeches of the part.

He had journeyed in his customary manner overland from Havana, arriving unexpectedly at night, as he had often done before; only this time he had found the little door, cut out in one of the sides of the big gate, bolted fast. It was his knocking I had heard, as I hurried after the priest. The major-domo, who had been called up to let him in, told me afterwards that the señor intendente had put no question whatever to him as to this, and had gone on, as usual, towards his own room. Nobody knew what was going on in Carlos' chamber, but, of course, he came upon the two

G

girls at the door. He said nothing to them either, only just stopped there and waited, leaning with one elbow on the balustrade with his good-tempered, gray eyes fixed on the door. He had fully expected to see Seraphina come out presently, but I think he did not count on seeing me as well. When he straightened himself up after the bow, we two were standing side by side.

I had stepped quickly towards her, asking myself what he would do. He did not seem to be armed; neither had I any weapon about me. Would he fly at my throat? I was the bigger, and the younger man. I wished he would. But he found a way of making me feel all his other advantages. He did not recognize my existence. He appeared not to see me at all. He seemed not to be aware of Seraphina's startled immobility, of my firm attitude; but turning his good-humoured face towards the two girls, who appeared ready to sink through the floor before his gaze, he shook his fore-finger at them slightly.

This was all. He was not menacing; he was almost playful; and this gesture, marvellous in its economy of effort, disclosed all the might and insolence of his power. It had the unerring efficacy of an act of instinct. It was instinct. He could not know how he dismayed us by that shake of the finger. The tall girl dropped her candlestick with a clatter, and fled along the gallery like a shadow. La Chica cowered under the wall. The light of her candle just touched dimly the form of a negro boy, waiting passively in the background with O'Brien's saddle-bags over his shoulder.

"You see," said Seraphina to me, in a swift, desolate murmur. "They are all like this—all, all."

Without a change of countenance, without emphasis, he said to her in French:

"*Votre père dort sans doute, Señorita.*"

And she intrepidly replied, "You know very well, Señor Intendente, that nothing can make him open his eyes."

"So it seems," he muttered between his teeth, stooping to pick up the dropped candlestick. It was lying at my feet. I could have taken him at a disadvantage, then; I could have felled him with one blow, thrown myself upon his back. Thus may an athletic prisoner set upon a jailer coming into his cell, if there were not the prison, the locks, the bars, the heavy gates and the walls, all the apparatus of captivity, and the superior weight of the idea chaining down the will, if not the courage.

It might have been his knowledge of this, or his absolute disdain of me. The unconcerned manner in which he busied himself—his head within striking distance of my fist—in lighting the extinguished candle from the trembling Chica's humiliated me beyond expression. He had some difficulty with that, till he said to her just audibly, "Calm thyself, *niña*," and she became rigid in her appearance of excessive terror.

He turned then towards Seraphina, candlestick in hand, courteously saying in Spanish:

"May I be allowed to help light you to your door, since that silly Juanita—I think it was Juanita—has taken leave of her senses? She is not fit to remain in your service—any more than this one here."

With a gasp of desolation, La Chica began to sob limply against the wall. I made one step forward; and, holding the candle well up, as though for the purpose of examining my face carefully, he never looked my way, while he and Seraphina were exchanging a few phrases in French which I did not understand well enough to follow.

He was politely interrogatory, it seemed to me.   The natural, good-humoured expression never left his face, as though he had a fund of inexhaustible patience for dealing with the unaccountable trifles of a woman's conduct.   Seraphina's shawl had slipped off her head. The Chica sidled towards her, sobbing a deep sob now and then, without any sign of tears; and with their scattered hair, their bare arms, the disorder of their attire, they looked like two women discovered in a secret flight for life.   Only the mistress stood her ground firmly; her voice was decided; there was resolution in the way one little white hand clutched the black lace on her bosom.   Only once she seemed to hesitate in her replies.   Then, after a pause he gave her for reflection, he appeared to repeat his question.   She glanced at me apprehensively, as I thought, before she confirmed the previous answer by a slow inclination of her head.

Had he allowed himself to make a provoking movement, a dubious gesture of any sort, I would have flung myself upon him at once; but the nonchalant manner in which he looked away, while he extended to me his hand with the candlestick, amazed me.   I simply took it from him.   He stepped back, with a ceremonious bow for Seraphina.   La Chica ran up close to her elbow.   I heard her voice saying sadly, "You need fear nothing for yourself, child"; and they moved away slowly.   I remained facing O'Brien, with a vague notion of protecting their retreat.

This time it was I who was holding the light before his face.   It was calm and colourless; his eyes were fixed on the ground reflectively, with the appearance of profound and quiet absorption.   But suddenly I perceived the convulsive clutch of his hand on the skirt of his coat.   It was as if accidentally I had looked inside the man—

upon the strength of his illusions, on his desire, on his passion. Now he will fly at me, I thought, with a tremendously convincing certitude. Now—— All my muscles, stiffening, answered the appeal of that thought of battle.

He said, "Won't you give me that light?"

And I understood he demanded a surrender.

"I would see you die first where you stand," was my answer.

This object in my hand had become endowed with moral meaning—significant, like a symbol—only to be torn from me with my life.

He lifted his head; the light twinkled in his eyes. "Oh, *I* won't die," he said, with that bizarre suggestion of humour in his face, in his subdued voice. "But it is a small thing; and you are young; it may be yet worth your while to try and please me—this time."

Before I could answer, Seraphina, from some little distance, called out hurriedly:

"Don Juan, your arm."

Her voice, sounding a little unsteady, made me forget O'Brien, and, turning my back on him, I ran up to her. She needed my support; and before us La Chica tottered and stumbled along with the lights, moaning:

"*Madre de Dios!* What will become of us now! Oh, what will become of us now!"

"You know what he had asked me to let him do," Seraphina talked rapidly. "I made answer, 'No; give the light to my cousin.' Then he said, 'Do you really wish it, Señorita? I am the older friend.' I repeated, 'Give the light to my cousin, Señor.' He, then, cruelly, 'For the young man's own sake, reflect, Señorita.' And he waited before he asked me again, 'Shall I surrender it to him?' I felt death upon my heart, and all my fear for you—there." She touched her beautiful throat with a swift movement of a hand that disappeared at once under the lace. "And because I could not speak, I—— Don Juan, you have just offered me your life—I—— *Misericordia!* What else was possible? I made with my head the sign 'Yes.'"

In the stress, hurry, and rapture encompassing my immense gratitude, I pressed her hand to my side familiarly, as if we had been two lovers walking in a lane on a serene evening.

"If you had not made that sign, it would have been worse than death—in my heart," I said. "He had asked me, too, to renounce my trust, my light."

We walked on slowly, accompanied in our sudden silence by the plash of the fountain at the bottom of the great square of darkness on our left, and by the piteous moans of the Chica.

"That is what he meant," said the enchanting voice by my side. "And you refused. That is your valour."

"From no selfish motives," I said, troubled, as if all the great incertitude of my mind had been awakened by the sound that brought so much delight to my heart. "My valour is nothing."

"It has given me a new courage," she said.

"You did not want more," I said earnestly.

"Ah! I was very much alone. It is difficult to——" She hesitated.

"To live alone," I finished.

"More so to die," she whispered, with a new note of timidity. "It is frightful. Be cautious, Don Juan, for the love of God, because I could not——"

We stopped. La Chica, silent, as if exhausted, drooped lamentably, with her shoulder against the wall, by Seraphina's door; and the pure crystalline sound of the fountain below, enveloping the parting pause, seemed to wind its coldness round my heart.

"Poor Don Carlos!" she said. "I had a great affection for him. I was afraid they would want me to marry him. He loved your sister."

"He never told her," I murmured. "I wonder if she ever guessed."

"He was poor, homeless, ill already, in a foreign land."

"We all loved him at home," I said.

"He never asked her," she breathed out. "And, perhaps—but he never asked her."

"I have no more force," sighed La Chica, suddenly, and sank down at the foot of the wall, putting the candlesticks on the floor.

"You have been very good to him," I said; "only he need not have demanded this from you. Of course, I understood perfectly. . . . I hope you understand, too, that I——"

"Señor, my cousin," she flashed out suddenly, "do you think that I would have consented only from my affection for him?"

"Señorita," I cried, "I am poor, homeless, in a foreign land. How can I believe? How can I dare to dream?—unless your own voice——"

"Then you are permitted to ask. Ask, Don Juan."

I dropped on one knee, and, suddenly extending her arm, she pressed her hand to my lips. Lighted up from below, the picturesque aspect of her figure took on something of a transcendental grace; the unusual upward shadows invested her beauty with a new mystery of fascination. A minute passed. I could hear her rapid breathing above, and I stood up before her, holding both her hands.

"How very few days have we been together," she whispered. "Juan, I am ashamed."

"I did not count the days. I have known you always. I have dreamed of you since I can remember—for days, for months, a year, all my life."

The crash of a heavy door flung to, exploded, filling the galleries all round the *patio* with the sonorous reminder of our peril.

"Ah! We had forgotten."

I heard her voice, and felt her form in my arms. Her lips at my ear pronounced:

"Remember, Juan. Two lives, but one death only."

And she was gone so quickly that it was as though she had passed through the wocd of the massive panels.

The Chica crouched on her knees. The lights on the floor burned before her empty stare, and with her bare shoulders the tone of old ivory emerging from the white linen, with wisps of raven hair hanging down her cheeks, the abandonment of her whole person embodied every outward mark and line of desolation.

"What do you fear from him?" I asked.

She looked up; moved nearer to me on her knees. "I have a lover outside."

She seized her hair wildly, drew it across her face, tried to stuff handfuls of it into her mouth, as if to stop herself from shrieking.

"He shook his finger at me," she moaned.

Her terror, as incomprehensible as the emotion of an animal, was gaining upon me. I said sternly:

"What can he do, then?"

"I don't know."

She did not know. She was like me. She feared for her love. Like myself! Was there anything in the way of our undoing which it was not in his power to achieve?

"Try to be faithful to your mistress," I said, "and all may be well yet."

She made no answer, but staggered to her feet, and

went away blindly through the door, which opened just wide enough to let her through. There were clouds on the sky. The *patio*, in its blackness, was like the rectangular mouth of a bottomless pit. I picked up the candlesticks, and lighted myself to my room, walking upon air, upon tempestuous air, in a feeling of insecurity and exultation.

The lights of my candelabrum had gone out. I stood the two candlesticks on a table, and the shadows of the room, uplifted above the two flames as high as the ceiling, filled the corners heavily like gathered draperies, descended to the foot of the four walls in the shape of a military tent, in which warlike objects vaguely gleamed: a trophy of ancient arquebuses and conquering swords, arranged with bows, the spears, the stick and stone weapons of an extinct race, a war collar of shells or pebbles, a round wicker-work shield in a halo of arrows, with a matchlock piece on each side—of the sort that had to be served by two men.

I had left the door of my room open on purpose, so that he should know I was back there, and ready for him. I took down a long straight blade, like a rapier, with a basket hilt. It was a cumbrous weapon, and with a blunt edge; still, it had a point, and I was ready to thrust and parry against the world. I called upon my foes. No enemy appeared, and by the light of two candles, with a sword in my hand, I lost myself in the foreshadowings of the future.

It was positive and uncertain. I wandered in it like a soul outside the gates of paradise, with an anticipation of bliss, and the pain of my exclusion. There was only one man in the way. I was certain he had been watching us across the blackness of the *patio*. He must have seen the dimly-lit dumb show of our parting at Seraphina's door. I hoped he had understood, and that my

*G

shadow, bearing the two lights, had struck him as triumphant and undismayed, walking upon air. I strained my ears. I had heard. . . .

Somebody was coming towards me along the silent galleries. It was he; I knew it. He was coming nearer and nearer. In the profound, tomb-like stillness of the great house, I had heard the sound of his footsteps on the tessellated pavement from afar. Now he had turned the corner, and the calm, strolling pace of his approach was enough to strike awe into an adversary's heart. It never hesitated, not once; never hurried; never slowed till it stopped. He stood in the doorway.

I suppose, in that big room, by the light of two candles, I must have presented an impressive picture of a menacing youth all in black, with a tense face, and holding a naked, long rapier in his hand. At any rate, he stood still, eying me from the doorway, the picture of a dapper Spanish lawyer in a lofty frame; all in black, also, with a fair head and a well-turned leg advanced in a black silk stocking. He had taken off his riding boots. For the rest, I had never seen him dressed otherwise. There was no weapon in his hand, or at his side.

I lowered the point, and, seeing he remained on the doorstep, as if not willing to trust himself within, I said disdainfully:

"You don't suppose I would murder a defenceless man."

"Am I defenceless?" He had a slight lift of the eyebrows. "That is news, indeed. It is you who are supposing. I have been a very certain man for this many a year."

"How can you know how an English gentleman would feel and act? I am neither a murderer nor yet an intriguer."

He walked right in rapidly, and, getting round to the other side of the table, drew a small pistol out of his breeches pocket.

"You see—I am not trusting too much to your English generosity."

He laid the pistol negligently on the table. I had turned about on my heels. As we stood, by lunging between the two candlesticks, I should have been able to run him through the body before he could cry out.

I laid the sword on the table.

"Would you trust a damned Irish rebel?" he asked.

"You are wrong in your surmise. I would have nothing to do with a rebel, even in my thoughts and suppositions. I think that the Intendente of Don Balthasar Riego would look twice before murdering in a bedroom the guest of the house—a relation, a friend of the family."

"That's sensible," he said, with that unalterable air of good nature, which sometimes was like the most cruel mockery of humour. "And do you think that even a relation of the Riegos would escape the scaffold for killing Don Patricio O'Brien, one of the Royal Judges of the Marine Court, member of the Council, Procurator to the Chapter. . . ."

"Intendente of the Casa," I threw in.

"That's my gratitude," he said gravely. "So you see. . . ."

"Supreme chief of thieves and picaroons," I suggested again.

He answered this by a gesture of disdainful superiority.

"I wonder if you—if any of you English—would have the courage to risk your all—ambition, pride, position, wealth, peace of mind, your dearest hope, your self-respect—like this. For an idea."

His tone, that revealed something exalted and sad behind everything that was sordid and base in the acts of that man's villainous tools, struck me with astonishment. I beheld, as an inseparable whole, the contemptible result, the childishness of his imagination, the danger of his recklessness, and something like loftiness in his pitiful illusion.

"Nothing's too hot, too dirty, too heavy. Any way to get at you English; any means. To strike! That's the thing. I would die happy if I knew I had helped to detach from you one island—one little island of all the earth you have filched away, stolen, taken by force, got by lying. . . . Don't taunt me with your taunts of thieves. What weapons better worthy of you could I use? Oh, I am modest. I am modest. This is a little thing, this Jamaica. What do I care for the Separationist blatherskite more than for the loyal fools? You are all English to me. If I had my way, your Empire would die of pin-pricks all over its big, overgrown body. Let only one bit drop off. If robbing your ships may help it, then, as you see me standing here, I am ready to go myself in a leaky boat. I tell you Jamaica's gone. And that may be the beginning of the end."

He lifted his arm not at me, but at England, if I may judge from his burning stare. It was not to me he was speaking. There we were, Irish and English, face to face, as it had been ever since we had met in the narrow way of the world that had never been big enough for the tribes, the nations, the races of man.

"Now, Mr. O'Brien, I don't know what you may do to me, but I won't listen to any of this," I said, very red in the face.

"Who wants you to listen?" he muttered absently, and went away from the table to look out of the loophole, leaving me there with the sword and the pistol.

Whatever he might have said of the scaffold, this was very imprudent of him. It was characteristic of the man—of that impulsiveness which existed in him side by side with his sagacity, with his coolness in intrigue, with his unmerciful and revengeful temper. By my own feelings I understood what an imprudence it was. But he was turning his back on me, and how could I? . . . His imprudence was so complete that it made for security. He did not, I am sure, remember my existence. I would just as soon have jumped with a dagger upon a man in the dark.

He was really stirred to his depths—to the depths of his hate, and of his love—by seeing me, an insignificant youth (I was no more), surge up suddenly in his path. He turned where he stood at last, and contemplated me with a sort of thoughtful surprise, as though he had tried to account to himself for my existence.

"No," he said, to himself really, "I wonder when I look at you. How did you manage to get that pretty reputation over there? Ramon's a fool. He shall know it to his cost. But the craftiness of that Carlos! Or is it only my confounded willingness to believe?"

He was putting his finger nearly on the very spot. I said nothing.

"Why," he exclaimed, "when it's all boiled down, you are only an English beggar boy."

"I've come to a man's estate since we met last," I said meaningly.

He seemed to meditate over this. His face never changed, except, perhaps, to an even more amused benignity of expression.

"You have lived very fast by that account," he remarked artlessly. "Is it possible now? Well, life, as you know, can't last forever; and, indeed, taking a

better look at you in this poor light, you do seem to be
very near death."

I did not flinch; and, with a very dry mouth, I uttered
defiantly:

"Such talk means nothing."

"Bravely said. But this is not talk. You've gone
too fast. I am giving you a chance to turn back."

"Not an inch," I said fiercely. "Neither in thought,
in deed; not even in semblance."

He seemed as though he wanted to swallow a bone in
his throat.

"Believe me, there is more in life than you think.
There is at your age, more than . . ." he had a
strange contortion of the body, as though in a sudden
access of internal pain; that humorous smile, that
abode in the form of his lips, changed into a ghastly,
forced grin . . . "than one love in a life—more
than one woman."

I believe he tried to leer at me, because his voice was
absolutely dying in his throat. My indignation was
boundless. I cried out with the fire of deathless conviction:

"It is not true. You know it is not true."

He was speechless for a time; then, shaking and
stammering with that inward rage that seemed to heave
like molten lava in his breast, without ever coming to
the surface of his face:

"What! Is it I, then, who have to go back? For—
for you—a boy—come from devil knows where—an
English, beggarly. . . . For a girl's whim. . . .
I—a man."

He calmed down. "No; you are mad. You are
dreaming. You don't know. You can't—you! You
don't know what a man is; you with your calf-love a
day old. How dare you look at me who have breathed

for years in the very air? You fool—you little, wretched fool! For years sleeping, and waking, and working. . . ."

"And intriguing," I broke in, "and plotting, and deceiving—for years."

This calmed him altogether. "I am a man; you are but a boy; or else I would not have to tell you that your love"—he choked at the word—"is to mine like— like——"

His eyes fell on a cut-glass water-ewer, and, with a convulsive sweep of his arm, he sent it flying far away from the table. It fell heavily, shattering itself with the unringing thud of a piece of ice.

"Like this."

He remained for some time with his eyes fixed on the table, and when he looked up at me it was with a sort of amused incredulity. His tone was not resentful. He spoke in a business-like manner, a little contemptuously. I had only Don Carlos to thank for the position in which I found myself. What the "poor devil over there" expected from me, he, O'Brien, would not inquire. It was a ridiculous boy-and-girl affair. If those two—meaning Carlos and Seraphina—had not been so mighty clever, I should have been safe now in Jamaica jail, on a charge of treasonable practices. He seemed to find the idea funny. Well, anyhow, he had meant no worse by me than my own dear countrymen. When he, O'Brien, had found how absurdly he had been hoodwinked by Don Carlos—the poor devil—and misled by Ramon—he would make him smart for it, yet—all he had intended to do was to lodge me in Havana jail. On his word of honour. . . .

"Me in jail!" I cried angrily. "You—you would dare! On what charge? You could not. . . ."

"You don't know what Pat O'Brien can do in Cuba."

The little country solicitor came out in a flash from under the Spanish lawyer. Then he frowned slightly at me. "You being an Englishman, I would have had you taken up on a charge of stealing."

Blood rushed to my face. I lost control over myself. "Mr. O'Brien," I said, "I dare say you could have trumped up anything against me. You are a very great scoundrel."

"Why? Because I don't lie about my motives, as you all do? I would wish you to know that I would scorn to lie either to myself or to you."

I touched the haft of the sword on the table. It was lying with the point his way.

"I had been thinking," said I, in great heat, "to propose to you that we should fight it out between us two, man to man, rebel and traitor as you have been."

"The devil you have!" he muttered.

"But really you are too much of a Picaroon. I think the gallows should be your end."

I gave reins to my exasperation, because I felt myself hopelessly in his power. What he was driving at, I could not tell. I had an intolerable sense of being as much at his mercy as though I had been lying bound hand and foot on the floor. It gave me pleasure to tell him what I thought. And, perhaps, I was not quite candid, either. Suppose I provoked him enough to fire his pistol at me. He had been fingering the butt, absently, as we talked. He might have missed me, and then. . . . Or he might have shot me dead. But surely there was some justice in Cuba. It was clear enough that he did not wish to kill me himself. Well, this was a desperate strait; to force him to do something he did not wish to do, even at the cost of my own life, was the only step left open to me to thwart his purpose; the only thing I could do just then for the furtherance of my mission to save Seraphina from his intrigues. I was oppressed by the misery of it all. As to killing him as he stood—if I could do it by being very quick with the old rapier—my bringing up, my ideas, my very being, recoiled from it. I had never taken a life. I was very young. I was not used to scenes of violence; and to begin like this in cold blood! Not only my conscience, but my very courage faltered. Truth to tell, I was afraid; not for myself—I had the courage to die; but I was afraid of the act. It was the unknown for me—for my nerve—for my conscience. And then the Spanish gallows! That, too, revolted me. To kill him, and then kill myself. . . . No, I must live. "Two lives, one death," she had said. . . . For a second or two my brain reeled with horror; I was certainly losing my self-possession. His voice broke upon that nightmare.

"It may be your lot, yet," it said.

I burst into a nervous laugh. For a moment I could not stop myself.

"I won't murder you," I cried.

To this he said astonishingly, "Will you go to Mexico?"

It sounded like a joke. He was very serious. "I shall send one of the schooners there on a little affair of mine. I can make use of you. I give you this chance."

It was as though he had thrown a bucketful of water over me. I had an inward shiver, and became quite cool. It was his turn now to let himself go.

It was a matter of delivering certain papers to the Spanish Commandant in Timaulipas. There would be some employment found for me with the Royal troops. I was a relation of the Riegos. And there came upon his voice a strange ardour; a swiftness into his utterance. He walked away from the table; came back, and gazed into my face in a marked, expectant manner. He was not prompted by any love for me, he said, and had an uncertain laugh.

My wits had returned to me wholly; and as he repeated "No love for you—no love for you," I had the intuition that what influenced him was his love for Seraphina. I saw it. I read it in the workings of his face. His eyes retained his good-humoured twinkle. He did not attach any importance to a boy-and-girl affair; not at all—pah! The lady, naturally young, warm-hearted, full of kindness. I mustn't think. . . . Ha, ha! A man of his age, of course, understood. . . . No importance at all.

He walked away from the table trying to snap his fingers, and, suddenly, he reeled; he reeled, as though he had been overcome by the poison of his jealousy—as though a thought had stabbed him to the heart. There was an instant when the sight of that man moved me more than anything I had seen of passionate suffering before (and that was nothing), or since. He longed to kill me—I felt it in the very air of the room; and he loved her too much to dare. He laughed at me across the table. I had ridiculously misunderstood a very proper and natural kindness of a girl with not much worldly experience. He had known her from the earliest childhood.

"Take my word for it," he stammered.

It seemed to me that there were tears in his eyes. A stiff smile was parting his lips. He took up the pistol, and evidently not knowing anything about it, looked with an air of curiosity into the barrel.

It was time to think of making my career. That's what I ought to be thinking of at my age. "At your age—at your age," he repeated aimlessly. I was an Englishman. He hated me—and it was easy to believe this, though he neither glared nor grimaced. He smiled.

He smiled continuously and rather pitifully. But his devotion to a—a—person who. . . . His devotion was great enough to overcome even that, even that. Did I understand? I owed it to the lady's regard, which, for the rest, I had misunderstood—stupidly misunderstood.

"Well, at your age it's excusable!" he mumbled. "A career that . . ."

"I see," I said slowly. Young as I was, it was impossible to mistake his motives. Only a man of mature years, and really possessed by a great passion—by a passion that had grown slowly, till it was exactly as big as his soul—could have acted like this—with that profound simplicity, with such resignation, with such horrible moderation. But I wanted to find out more. "And when would you want me to go?" I asked, with a dissimulation of which I would not have suspected myself capable a moment before. I was maturing in the fire of love, of danger; in the lurid light of life piercing through my youthful innocence.

"Ah," he said, banging the pistol on to the table hurriedly. "At once. To-night. Now."

"Without seeing anybody?"

"Without seeing . . . Oh, of course. In your own interest."

He was very quiet now. "I thought you looked intelligent enough," he said, appearing suddenly very tired. "I am glad you see your position. You shall go far in the Royal service, on the faith of Pat O'Brien, English as you are. I will make it my own business for the sake of—the Riego family. There is only one little condition."

He pulled out of his pocket a piece of paper, a pen, a travelling inkstand. He looked the lawyer to the life; the Spanish family lawyer grafted on an Irish attorney.

"You can't see anybody. But you ought to write. Doña Seraphina naturally would be interested. A cousin and . . . I shall explain to Don Balthasar, of course. . . . I will dictate: 'Out of regard for your future, and the desire for active life, of your own will, you accept eagerly Señor O'Brien's proposition.' She'll understand."

"Oh, yes, she'll understand," I said.

"Yes. And that you will write of your safe arrival in Timaulipas. You must promise to write. Your word . . ."

"By heavens, Señor O'Brien!" I burst out with inexpressible scorn, "I thought you meant your villains to cut my throat on the passage. I should have deserved no better fate."

He started. I shook with rage. A change had come upon both of us as sudden as if we had been awakened by a violent noise. For a time we did not speak a word. One look at me was enough for him. He passed his hand over his forehead.

"What devil's in you, boy?" he said. "I seem to make nothing but mistakes."

He went to the loophole window, and, advancing his head, cried out:

"The schooner does not sail to-night."

He had some of his cut-throats posted under the window. I could not make out the reply he got; but after a while he said distinctly, so as to be heard below:

"I give up that spy to you." Then he came back, put the pistol in his pocket, and said to me, "Fool! I'll make you long for death yet."

"You've given yourself away pretty well," I said. "Some day I shall unmask you. It will be my revenge on you for daring to propose to me . . ."

"What?" he interrupted, over his shoulder. "You?

Not you—and I'll tell you why.   It's because dead men tell no tales."

He passed through the door—a back view of a dapper Spanish lawyer, all in black, in a lofty frame. The calm, strolling footsteps went away along the gallery. He turned the corner. The tapping of his heels echoed in the *patio*, into whose blackness filtered the first suggestion of the dawn.

CHAPTER FIVE

I REMEMBER walking about the room, and thinking to myself, "This is bad, this is very bad; what shall I do now?" A sort of mad meditation that in this meaningless way became so tense as positively to frighten me. Then it occurred to me that I could do nothing whatever at present, and I was soothed by this sense of powerlessness, which, one would think, ought to have driven me to distraction. I went to sleep ultimately, just as a man sentenced to death goes to sleep, lulled in a sort of ghastly way by the finality of his doom. Even when I awoke it kept me steady, in a way. I washed, dressed, walked, ate, said "Good-morning, Cesar," to the old major-domo I met in the gallery; exchanged grins with the negro boys under the gateway, and watched the mules being ridden out barebacked by other nearly naked negro boys into the sea, with great splashing of water and a noise of voices. A small knot of men, unmistakably *Lugareños*, stood on the beach, also, watching the mules, and exchanging loud jocular shouts with the blacks. Rio Medio, the dead, forsaken, and desecrated city, was lying, as bare as a skeleton, on the sands. They were yellow; the bay was very blue, the wooded hills very green.

After the mules had been ridden uproariously back to the stables, wet and capering, and shaking their long ears, all the life of the land seemed to take refuge in this vivid colouring. As I looked at it from the outer balcony above the great gate, the small group of *Lugareños* turned about to look at the Casa Riego.

They recognized me, no doubt, and one of them flourished, threateningly, an arm from under his cloak. I retreated indoors.

This was the only menacing sign, absolutely the only one sign that marked this day. It was a day of pause. Seraphina did not leave her apartments; Don Balthasar did not show himself; Father Antonio, hurrying towards the sick room, greeted me with only a wave of the hand. I was not admitted to see Carlos; the nun came to the door, shook her head at me, and closed it gently in my face. Castro, sitting on the floor not very far away, seemed unaware of me in so marked a manner that it inspired me with the idea of not taking the slightest notice of him. Now and then the figure of a maid in white linen and bright petticoat flitted in the upper gallery, and once I fancied I saw the black, rigid carriage of the duenna disappearing behind a pillar.

Señor O'Brien, old Cesar whispered, without looking at me, was extremely occupied in the *Cancilleria*. His midday meal was served him there. I had mine all alone, and then the sunny, heat-laden stillness of siesta-time fell upon the Castilian dignity of the house.

I sank into a kind of reposeful belief in the work of accident. Something would happen. I did not know how soon and how atrociously my belief was to be justified. I exercised my ingenuity in the most approved lover-fashion—in devising means how to get secret speech with Seraphina. The confounded silly maids fled from my most distant appearance, as though I had the pest. I was wondering whether I should not go simply and audaciously and knock at her door, when I fancied I heard a scratching at mine. It was a very stealthy sound, quite capable of awakening my dormant emotions.

I went to the door and listened. Then, opening it the

merest crack, I saw the inexplicable emptiness of the gallery. Castro, on his hands and knees, startled me by whispering at my feet:

"Stand aside, Señor."

He entered my room on all-fours, and waited till I got the door closed before he stood up.

"Even he may sleep sometimes," he said. "And the balustrade has hidden me."

To see this little saturnine bandit, who generally stalked about haughtily, as if the whole Casa belonged to him by right of fidelity, crawl into my room like this was inexpressibly startling. He shook the folds of his cloak, and dropped his hat on the floor.

"Still, it is better so. The very women of the house are not safe," he said. "Señor, I have no mind to be delivered to the English for hanging. But I have not been admitted to see Don Carlos, and, therefore, I must make my report to you. These are Don Carlos' orders. 'Serve him, Castro, when I am dead, as if my soul had passed into his body.'"

He nodded sadly. "*Si!* But Don Carlos is a friend to me and you—you." He shook his head, and drew me away from the door. "Two *Lugareños*," he said, "Manuel and another one, did go last night, as directed by the friar"—he supposed—"to meet the *Juez* in the bush outside Rio Medio."

I had guessed that much, and told him of Manuel's behaviour under my window. How did they know my chamber?

"Bad, bad," muttered Castro. "La Chica told her lover, no doubt." He hissed, and stamped his foot.

She was pretty, but flighty. The lover was a silly boy of decent, Christian parents, who was always hanging about in the low villages. No matter.

What he could not understand was why some boats

should have been held in readiness till nearly the morning to tow a schooner outside. Manuel came along at dawn, and dismissed the crews. They had separated, making a great noise on the beach, and yelling, "Death to the *Inglez!*"

I cleared up that point for him. He told me that O'Brien had the duenna called to his room that morning. Nothing had been heard outside, but the woman came out staggering, with her hand on the wall. He had terrified her. God knows what he had said to her. The widow—as Castro called her—had a son, an *escrivano* in one of the Courts of Justice. No doubt it was that.

"There it is, Señor," murmured Castro, scowling all round, as if every wall of the room was an enemy. "He holds all the people in his hand in some way. Even I must be cautious, though I am a humble, trusted friend of the Casa!"

"What harm could he do you?" I asked.

"He is civil to me. *Amigo Castro* here, and *Amigo Castro* there. Bah! The devil, alone, is his friend! He could deliver me to justice, and get my life sworn away. He could—— *Quien sabe?* What need he care what he does—a man that can get absolution from the archbishop himself if he likes."

He meditated. "No! there is only one remedy for him." He tiptoed to my ear. "The knife!"

He made a pass in the air with his blade, and I remembered vividly the cockroach he had impaled with such accuracy on board the *Thames*. His baneful glance reminded me of his murderous capering in the steerage, when he had thought that the only remedy for *me* was the knife.

He went to the loop-hole, and passed the steel thoughtfully on the stone edge. I had not moved.

"The knife; but what would you have? Before,

when I talked of this to Don Carlos, he only laughed at me. That was his way in matters of importance. Now they will not let me come in to him. He is too near God—and the señorita—why, she is too near the saints for all the great nobility of her spirit. But, *que diableria*, when I—in my devotion—opened my mouth to her I saw some of that spirit in her eyes. . . ."

There was a slight irony in his voice. "No! Me—Castro! to be told that an English señora would have dismissed me forever from her presence for such a hint. 'Your Excellency,' I said, 'deign, then, to find it good that I should avoid giving offence to that man. It is not my desire to run my neck into the iron collar.'"

He looked at me fixedly, as if expecting me to make a sign, then shrugged his shoulders.

"*Bueno.* You see this? Then look to it yourself, Señor. You are to me even as Don Carlos—all except for the love. No English body is big enough to receive his soul. No friend will be left that would risk his very honour of a noble for a man like Tomas Castro. Let me warn you not to leave the Casa, even if a shining angel stood outside the gate and called you by name. The gate is barred, now, night and day. I have dropped a hint to Cesar, and that old African knows more than the señor would suppose. I cannot tell how soon I may have the opportunity to talk to you again."

He peeped through the crack of the door, then slipped out, suddenly falling at once on his hands and knees, so as to be hidden by the stone balustrade from anybody in the *patio*. He, too, did not think himself safe.

Early in the evening I descended into the court, and Father Antonio, walking up and down the *patio* with his eyes on his breviary, muttered to me:

"Sit on this chair," and went on without stopping.

I took a chair near the marble rim of the basin with

its border of English flowers, its splashing thread of water. The goldfishes that had been lying motionless, with their heads pointing different ways, glided into a bunch to the fall of my shadow, waiting for crumbs of bread.

Father Antonio, his head down, and the open breviary under his nose, brushed my foot with the skirt of his cassock.

"Have you any plan?"

When he came back, walking very slowly, I said, "None."

At this next turn I pronounced rapidly, "I should like to see Carlos."

He frowned over the edge of the book.

I understood that he refused to let me in. And, after all, why should I disturb that dying man? The news about him was that he felt stronger that day. But he was preparing for eternity. Father Antonio's business was to save souls. I felt horribly crushed and alone. The priest asked, hardly moving his lips:

"What do you trust to?"

I had the time to meditate my reply. "Tell Carlos I think of escape by sea."

He made a little sign of assent, turned off towards the staircase, and went back to the sick room.

"The folly of it," I thought. How could I think of it? Escape where? I dared not even show myself outside the Casa. My safety within depended on old Cesar more than on anybody else. He had the key of the gate, and the gate was practically the only thing between me and a miserable death at the hands of the first ruffian I met outside. And with the thought I seemed to stifle in that *patio* open to the sky.

That gate seemed to cut off the breath of life from me. I was there, as if in a trap. Should I—I asked myself—

try to enlighten Don Balthasar? Why not? He would
understand me. I would tell him that in his own town,
as he always called Rio Medio, there lurked assassination for his guest. That would move him if anything
could.

He was then walking with O'Brien after dinner, as he
had walked with me on the day of my arrival. Only
Seraphina had not appeared, and we three men had sat
out the silent meal alone.

They stopped as I approached, and Don Balthasar
listened to me benignantly. "Ah, yes, yes! Times
have changed." But there was no reason for alarm.
There were some undesirable persons. Had they not
arrived lately? He turned to O'Brien, who stood by,
in readiness to resume the walk, and answered, "Yes,
quite lately. Very undesirable," in a matter-of-fact
tone. The excellent Don Patricio would take measures
to have them removed, the old man soothed me. But
it was not really dangerous for any one to go out. Again
he addressed O'Brien, who only smiled gently, as much
as to say, "What an absurdity!" I must not forget,
continued the old man, the veneration for the very
name of Riego that still, thank Heaven, survived in these
godless and revolutionary times in the Riegos' own town.

He straightened his back a little, looking at me with
dignity, and then glanced at the other, who inclined his
head affirmatively. The utter and complete hopelessness of the position appalled me for a moment. The
old man had not put foot outside his door for years, not
even to go to church. Father Antonio said Mass for
him every day in the little chapel next the dining room.
When O'Brien—for his own purposes, and the better to
conceal his own connection with the Rio Medio piracies
—had persuaded him to go to Jamaica officially, he had
been rowed in state to the ship waiting outside. For

many years now it had been impossible to enlighten him as to the true condition of affairs. He listened to people's talk as though it had been children's prattle. I have related how he received Carlos' denunciations. If one insisted, he would draw himself up in displeasure. But in his decay he had preserved a great dignity, a grave firmness that intimidated me a little.

I did not, of course, insist that evening, and, after giving me my dismissal in a gesture of blessing, he resumed his engrossing conversation with O'Brien. It related to the services commemorating his wife's death, those services that, once every twelve months, draped in black all the churches in Havana. A hundred masses, no less, had to be said that day; a distribution of alms had to be made. O'Brien was charged with all the arrangements, and I caught, as they crept past me up and down the *patio*, snatches of phrases relating to this mournful function, when all the capital was invited to pray for the soul of the illustrious lady. The priest of the church of San Antonio had said this and that; the grand vicar of the diocese had made difficulties about something; however, by the archbishop's special grace, no less than three altars would be draped in the cathedral.

I saw Don Balthasar smile with an ineffable satisfaction; he thanked O'Brien for his zeal, and seemed to lean more familiarly on his arm. His voice trembled with eagerness. "And now, my excellent Don Patricio, as to the number of candles. . . ."

I stood for a while as if rooted to the spot, overwhelmed by my insignificance. O'Brien never once looked my way. Then, hanging my head, I went slowly up the white staircase towards my room.

Cesar, going his rounds along the gallery, shuffled his silk-clad shanks smartly between two young negroes balancing lanthorns suspended on the shafts of their halberds. That little group had a mediæval and outlandish aspect. Cesar carried a bunch of keys in one hand, his staff of office in the other. He stood aside, in his maroon velvet and gold lace, holding the three-cornered hat under his arm, bowing his gray, woolly head—the most venerable and deferential of major-domos. His attendants, backing against the wall, grounded their halberds heavily at my approach.

He stepped out to intercept me, and, with great discretion, "Señor, a word," he said in his subdued voice. "A moment ago I have been called within the door of our señorita's apartments. She has given me this for your worship, together with many compliments. It is a seal. The señor will understand."

I took it; it was a tiny seal with her monogram on it. "Yes," I said.

"And Señorita Doña Seraphina has charged me to repeat"—he made a stealthy sign, as if to counteract an evil influence—"the words, 'Two lives—one death.' The señor will understand."

"Yes," I said, looking away with a pang at my heart.

He touched my elbow. "And to trust Cesar. Señor, I dandled her when she was quite little. Let me most earnestly urge upon your worship not to go near the windows, especially if there is light in your worship's room. Evil men are gazing upon the house, and I have seen myself the glint of a musket at the end of the street. The moon grows fast, too. The señorita begs you to trust Cesar."

"Are there many men?" I asked.

"Not many in sight; I have seen only one. But by signs, open to a man of my experience, I suspect many more to be about." Then, as I looked down on the ground, he added parenthetically, "They are poor shots, one and all, lacking the very firmness of manhood necessary to discharge a piece with a good aim. Still, Señor, I am ordered to entreat you to be cautious. Strange it is that to-night, from the great revelry at the Aldea Bajo, one might think they had just visited an English ship outside."

A ship! a ship! of any sort. But how to get out of the Casa? Murder forbade me even as much as to look out of the windows. Was there a ship outside? Cesar was positive there was not—not since I had arrived. Besides, the empty sea itself was unattainable, it seemed.

I pressed the seal to my lips. "Tell the señorita how I received her gift," I said; and the old negro inclined his head lower still. "Tell her that as the letters of her name are graved on this, so are all the words she has spoken graven on my heart."

They went away busily, the lanthorns swinging about the ax-heads of the halberds, Cesar's staff tapping the stones.

I shut my door, and buried my face in the pillows of the state bed. My mental anguish was excessive; action, alone, could relieve it. I had been battling with my thoughts like a man fighting with shadows. I could see no issue to such a struggle, and I prayed for something tangible to encounter—something that one could overcome or go under to. I must have fallen suddenly asleep, because there was a lion in front of me. It lashed its tail, and beyond the indistinct agitation of the brute I saw Seraphina. I tried to shout to her; no voice came out of my throat. And the lion produced a strange noise; he opened his jaws like a door. I sat up.

It was like a change of dream. A glare filled my eyes. In the wide doorway of my room, in a group of attendants, I saw a figure in a short black cloak standing, hat on head, and an arm outstretched. It was Don

Balthasar. He held himself more erect than I had ever seen him before. Stifled sounds of weeping, a vast, confused rumour of lamentations, running feet and slamming doors, came from behind him; his aged, dry voice, much firmer and very distinct, was speaking to me.

"You are summoned to attend the bedside of Don Carlos Riego at the hour of death, to help his soul struggling on the threshold of eternity, with your prayers—as a kinsman and a friend."

A great draught swayed the lights about that black and courtly figure. All the windows and doors of the palace had been flung open for the departure of the struggling soul. Don Balthasar turned; the group of attendants was gone in a moment, with a tramp of feet and jostling of lights in the long gallery.

I ran out after them. A wavering glare came from under the arch, and, through the open gate, I saw the bulky shape of the bishop's coach waiting outside in the moonlight. A strip of cloth fell from step to step down the middle of the broad white stairs. The staircase was brilliantly lighted, and quite empty. The household was crowding the upper galleries; the sobbing murmurs of their voices fell into the deserted *patio* The strip of crimson cloth laid for the bishop ran across it from the arch of the stairway to the entrance.

The door of Carlos' room stood wide open; I saw the many candles on a table covered with white linen, the side of the big bed, surpliced figures moving within the room. There was the ringing of small bells, and sighing groans from the kneeling forms in the gallery through which I was making my way slowly.

Castro appeared at my side suddenly. "Señor," he began, with saturnine stoicism, "he is dead. I have seen battlefields——" His voice broke.

I saw, through the large portal of the death-chamber, Don Balthasar and Seraphina standing at the foot of the bed; the bowed heads of two priests; the bishop, a tiny old man, in his vestments; and Father Antonio, burly and motionless, with his chin in his hand, as if left behind after leading that soul to the very gate of Eternity. All about me, women and men were crossing themselves; and Castro, who for a moment had covered his eyes with his hand, touched my elbow.

"And you live," he said, with sombre emphasis; then, warningly, "You are in great danger now."

I looked around, as if expecting to see an uplifted knife. I saw only a lot of people—household negroes and the women—rising from their knees. Below, the *patio* was empty.

"The house is defenceless," Castro continued.

We heard tumultuous voices under the gate.

O'Brien appeared in the doorway of Carlos' room with an attentive and dismayed expression on his face. I do not really think he had anything to do with what then took place. He meant to have me killed outside; but the rabble, excited by Manuel's inflammatory speeches, had that night started from the villages below with the intention of clamouring for my life. Many of their women were with them. Some of the *Lugareños* carried torches, others had pikes; most of them, how-ever, had nothing but their long knives. They came in a disorderly, shouting mob along the beach, intending this not for an attack, but as a simple demonstration.

The sight of the open gate struck them with wonder. The bishop's coach blocked the entrance, and for a time they hesitated, awed by the mystery of the house and by the rites going on in there. Then two or three bolder spirits stole closer. The bishop's people, of course, did not think of offering any resistance. The very de-

H

fencelessness of the house restrained the mob for a while. A few more men from outside ran in. Several women began to clamour scoldingly to them to bring the *Inglez* out. Then the men, encouraging each other in their audacity, advanced further under the arch.

A solitary black, the only guard left at the gate, shouted at them, "*Arria!* Go back." It had no effect. More of them crowded in, though, of course, the greater part of that mob remained outside. The black rolled big eyes. He could not stop them; he did not like to leave his post; he dared not fire. "Go back; go back," he repeated.

"Not without the *Inglez*," they answered.

The tumult we had heard arose when the *Lugareños* suddenly fell upon the sentry, and wrenched his musket from him.

This man, when disarmed, ran away. I saw him running across the *patio*, on the crimson pathway, to the foot of the staircase. His shouting, "The *Lugareños* have risen!" broke upon the hush of mourning. Father Antonio made a brusque movement, and Seraphina sent a startled glance in my direction.

The cloistered court, with its marble basin and a jet of water in the centre, remained empty for a moment after the negro had run across; a growing clamour penetrated into it. In the midst of it I heard O'Brien's voice saying. "Why don't they shut the gate?" Immediately afterwards a woman in the gallery cried out in surprise, and I saw the *Lugareños* pour into the *patio*.

For a time that motley group of bandits stood in the light, as if intimidated by the great dignity of the house, by the mysterious prestige of the Casa whose interior, probably, none of them had ever seen before. They gazed about silently, as if surprised to find themselves there.

It looked as if they would have retired if they had not caught sight of me. A murmur of "the *Inglez*" arose at once. By that time the household negroes had occupied the staircase with what weapons they could find upstairs.

Father Antonio pushed past O'Brien out of the room, and shook his arms over the balustrade.

"Impious men," he cried, "begone from this house of death." His eyes flashed at the ruffians, who stared stupidly from below.

"Give us the *Inglez*," they growled.

Seraphina, from within, cried, "Juan." I was then near the door, but not within the room.

"The *Inglez!* The heretic! The traitor!" came in sullen, subdued mutter. A hoarse, reckless voice shouted, "Give him to us, and we shall go!"

"You are putting in danger all the lives in this house!" O'Brien hissed at me. "Señorita, pray do not." He stood in the way of Seraphina, who wished to come out.

"It is you!" she cried. "It is you! It is your voice, it is your hand, it is your iniquity!"

He was confounded by her vehemence.

"Who brought him here?" he stammered. "Am I to find one of that accursed brood forever in my way? I take him to witness that for your sake——"

A formidable roar, "Throw us down the *Inglez!*" filled the *patio*. They were gaining assurance down there; and the ferocious clamouring of the mob outside came faintly upon our ears.

O'Brien barred the way. Don Balthasar leaned on his daughter's arm—she very straight, with tears still on her face and indignation in her eye, he bowed, and with his immovable fine features set in the calmness of age. Behind that group there were two priests, one with a scared, white face, another, black-browed, with an exalted and fanatical aspect. The light of the candles from the improvised altar fell on the bishop's small, bald head, emerging with a patient droop from the wide spread of his cope, as though he had been inclosed in a portable gold shrine. He was ready to go.

Don Balthasar, who seemed to have heard nothing, as if suddenly waking up to his duty, left his daughter, and muttering to O'Brien, "Let me precede the bishop," came out, bare-headed, into the gallery. Father Antonio had turned away, and his heavy hand fell on O'Brien's shoulder.

"Have you no heart, no reverence, no decency?" he said. "In the name of everything you respect, I call upon you to stop this sacrilegious outbreak."

O'Brien shook off the priestly hand, and fixed his eyes upon Seraphina. I happened to be looking at his face; he seemed to be ready to go out of his mind. His jealousy, the awful torment of soul and body, made him motionless and speechless.

Seeing Don Balthasar appear by the balustrade, the ruffians below had become silent for a while. His aged, mechanical voice was heard asking distinctly:

"What do these people want?"

Seraphina, from within the room, said aloud, "They are clamouring for the life of our guest." She looked at O'Brien contemptuously, "They are doing this to please you."

"Before God, I have nothing to do with this."

It was true enough, he had nothing to do with this outbreak; and I believe he would have interfered, but, in his dismay at having lost himself in the eyes of Seraphina, in his rage against myself, he did not know how to act. No doubt he had been deceiving himself as to his position with Seraphina. He was a man who lived on illusions, and was inclined to put implicit faith in his wishes. His desire of revenge on me, the downfall of his hopes (he could no longer deceive himself), a desperate striving of thought for their regaining, his impulse towards the impossible—all these emotions paralyzed his will.

Don Balthasar beckoned to me.

"Don't go near him," said O'Brien, in a thick, mumbling voice. "I shall—— I must——"

I put him aside. Don Balthasar took my arm. "Misguided populace," he whispered. "They have been a source of sorrow to me lately. But this wicked folly is incredible. I shall call upon them to come to their senses. My voice——"

The court below was strongly lighted, so that I saw the bearded, bronzed, wild faces of the *Lugareños* looking up. We, also, were strongly shown by the light of the doorway behind us, and by the torches burning in the gallery.

That morning, in my helplessness, I had come to put my trust in accident—in some accident—I hardly knew of what nature—my own death, perhaps—that would find a solution for my responsibilities, put an end to my tormenting thoughts. And now the accident came with a terrible swiftness, at which I shudder to this day.

We were looking down into the *patio*. Don Balthasar had just said, "You are nowhere as safe as by my side," when I noticed a *Lugareño* withdrawing himself from the throng about the basin. His face came to me familiarly. He was the pirate with the broken nose, who had had a taste of my fist. He had the sentry's musket on his shoulder, and was slinking away towards the gate.

Don Balthasar extended his hand over the balustrade, and there was a general movement of recoil below. I wondered why the slaves on the stairs did not charge and clear the *patio;* but I suppose with such a mob outside there was a natural hesitation in bringing the position to an issue. The *Lugareños* were muttering, "Look at the *Inglez!*" then cried out together, "Excellency, give up this *Inglez!*"

Don Balthasar seemed ten years younger suddenly. I had never seen him so imposingly erect.

"Insensate!" he began, without any anger.

"He is going to fire!" yelled Castro's voice somewhere in the gallery.

I saw a red dart in the shadow of the gate. The broken-nosed pirate had fired at me. The report, deadened in the vault, hardly reached my ears. Don Balthazar's arm seemed to swing me back. Then I felt him lean heavily on my shoulder. I did not know what had happened till I heard him say:

"Pray for me, gentlemen."

Father Antonio received him in his arms.

For a second after the shot, the most dead silence prevailed in the court. It was broken by an affrighted howl below: and Seraphina's voice cried piercingly:

"Father!"

The priest, dropping on one knee, sustained the silvery head, with its thin features already calm in death. Don Balthasar had saved my life; and his daughter flung herself upon the body. O'Brien pressed his hands to his temples, and remained motionless.

I saw the bishop, in his stiff cope, creep up to the group with the motion of a tortoise. And, for a moment, his quavering voice pronouncing the absolution was the only sound in the house.

Then a most fiendish noise broke out below. The negroes had charged, and the *Lugareños*, struck with terror at the unforeseen catastrophe, were rushing helter-skelter through the gate. The screaming of the maids was frightful. They ran up and down the galleries with their hair streaming. O'Brien passed me by swiftly, muttering like a madman.

I, also, got down into the courtyard in time to strike some heavy blows under the gateway;. but I don't know who it was that thrust into my hands the musket which I used as a club. The sudden burst of shrieks, the cries of terror under the vault of the gate, yells of rage and consternation, silenced the mob outside. The *Lugareños*, appalled at what had happened, shouted most pitifully. They squeaked like the vermin they were. I brought down the clubbed musket; two went down.. Of two I am sure. The rush of flying feet swept through between the walls, bearing me along. For a time a black stream of men eddied in the moonlight round the bishop's coach, like a torrent breaking round a boulder. The great heavy machine rocked, mules plunged, torches swayed.

The archway had been cleared. Outside, the slaves were forming in the open space before the Casa, while Cesar, with a few others, laboured to swing the heavy gates to. Hats, torn cloaks, knives strewed the flagstones, and the dim light of the lamps, fastened high up on the walls, fell on the faces of three men stretched out on their backs. Another, lying huddled up in a heap, got up suddenly and rushed out.

The thought of Seraphina clinging to the lifeless body of her father upstairs came to me; it came over me in horror, and I let the musket fall out of my hand. A silence like the silence of despair reigned in the house. She would hate me now. I felt as if I could walk out and give myself up, had it not been for the sight of O'Brien.

He was leaning his shoulders against the wall in the

posture of a man suddenly overcome by a deadly disease. No one was looking at us. It came to me that he could not have many illusions left to him now. He looked up wearily, saw me, and, waking up at once, thrust his hands into the pockets of his breeches. I thought of his pistol. No wild hope of love would prevent him, now, from killing me outright. The fatal shot that had put an end to Don Balthasar's life must have brought to him an awakening worse than death. I made one stride, caught him by both arms swiftly, and pinned him to the wall with all my strength. We struggled in silence.

I found him much more vigorous than I had expected; but, at the same time, I felt at once that I was more than a match for him. We did not say a word. We made no noise. But, in our struggle, we got away from the wall into the middle of the gateway I dared not let go of his arms to take him by the throat. He only tried to jerk and wrench himself away. Had he succeeded, it would have been death for me. We never moved our feet from the spot, fairly in the middle of the archway but nearer to the gate than to the *patio*. The slaves, formed outside, guarded the bishop's coach, and I do not know that there was anybody else actually with us under the vault of the entrance. We glared into each other's faces, and the world seemed very still around us. I felt in me a passion—not of hate, but of determination to be done with him; and from his face it was impossible to guess his suffering, his despair, or his rage.

In the midst of our straining I heard a sibilant sound. I detached my eyes from his; his struggles redoubled, and, behind him, stealing in towards us from the court, black on the strip of crimson cloth, I saw Tomas Castro. He flung his cloak back. The light of the lanthorn under the keystone of the arch glimmered feebly on the blade of his maimed arm. He made a discreet and bloodcurdling gesture to me with the other.

How could I hold a man so that he should be stabbed from behind in my arms? Castro was running up swiftly, his cloak opening like a pair of sable wings. Collecting all my strength, I forced O'Brien round, and we swung about in a flash. Now he had his back to the gate. My effort seemed to have uprooted him. I felt him give way all over.

As soon as our position had changed, Castro checked himself, and stepped aside into the shadow of the guardroom doorway. I don't think O'Brien had been aware of what had been going on. His strength was overborne by mine. I drove him backwards. His eyes blinked wildly. He bared his teeth. He resisted, as though I had been forcing him over the brink of perdition. His feet clung to the flagstones. I shook him till his head rolled.

"Viper brood!" he spluttered.

"Out you go!" I hissed.

I had found nothing heroic, nothing romantic to say —nothing that would express my desperate resolve to rid the world of his presence. All I could do was to fling him out. The Casa Riego was all my world—a world full of great pain, great mourning, and love. I saw him pitch headlong under the wheels of the bishop's enormous carriage. The black coachman who had sat aloft, unmoved through all the tumult, in his white stockings and three-cornered hat, glanced down from his high box. And the two parts of the gate came together with a clang of ironwork and a heavy crash that seemed as loud as thunder under that vault.

*H

CHAPTER SIX

Not even in memory am I willing to live over again those three days when Father Antonio, the old majordomo, and myself would meet each other in the galleries, in the *patio*, in the empty rooms, moving in the stillness of the house with heavy hearts and desolate eyes, which seemed to demand, "What is there to do?"

Of course, precautions were taken against the *Lugareños*. They were besieging the Casa from afar. They had established a sort of camp at the end of the street, and they prowled about amongst the old, barricaded houses in their pointed hats, in their rags and finery; women, with food, passed constantly between the villages and the panic-stricken town; there were groups on the beach; and one of the schooners had been towed down the bay, and was lying, now, moored stem and stern opposite the great gate. They did nothing whatever active against us. They lay around and watched, as if in pursuance of a plan traced by a superior authority. They were watching for me. But when, by some mischance, they burnt the roof off the outbuildings that were at some distance from the Casa, their chiefs sent up a deputation of three, with apologies. Those men came unarmed, and, as it were, under Castro's protection, and absolutely whimpered with regrets before Father Antonio. "Would his reverence kindly intercede with the most noble señorita? . . ."

"Silence! Dare not pronounce her name!" thundered the good priest, snatching away his hand, which they attempted to grab and kiss.

I, in the background, noted their black looks at me,
even as they cringed. The man who had fired the shot,
they said, had expired of his wounds after great torments. Their other dead had been thrust out of the
gate before. A long fellow, with slanting eyebrows
and a scar on his cheek, called El Rechado, tried to
inform Cesar, confidentially, that Manuel, his friend,
had been opposed to any encroachment of the Casa's
offices, only: "That Domingo——"

As soon as we discovered what was their object
(their apparent object, at any rate), they were pushed
out of the gate unceremoniously,—still protesting their
love and respect—by the Riego negroes. Castro
followed them out again, after exchanging a meaning
look with Father Antonio. To live in the two camps,
as it were, was a triumph of Castro's diplomacy, of
his saturnine mysteriousness. He kept us in touch
with the outer world, coming in under all sorts of
pretences, mostly with messages from the bishop, or
escorting the priests that came in relays to pray by
the bodies of the two last Riegos lying in state, side
by side, rigid in black velvet and white lace ruffles,
on the great bed dragged out into the middle of the
room.

Two enormous wax torches in iron stands flamed and
guttered at the door; a black cloth draped the emblazoned shields; and the wind from the sea, blowing
through the open casement, inclined all together the
flames of a hundred candles, pale in the sunlight, extremely ardent in the night. The murmur of prayers
for these souls went on incessantly; I have it in my
ears now. There would be always some figure of the
household kneeling in prayer at the door; or the old
major-domo would come in to stand at the foot, motionless for a time; or, through the open door, I would

see the cassock of Father Antonio, flung on his knees, with his forehead resting on the edge of the bed, his hands clasped above his tonsure.

Apart from what was necessary for defence, all the life of the house seemed stopped. Not a woman appeared; all the doors were closed; and the numbing desolation of a great bereavement was symbolized by Don Balthasar's chair in the *patio*, which had remained lying overturned in full view of every part of the house, till I could bear the sight no longer, and asked Cesar to have it put away. "*Si, Señor*," he said deferentially, and a few tears ran suddenly down his withered cheeks. The English flowers had been trampled down; an unclean hat floated on the basin, now here, now there, frightening the goldfish from one side to the other.

And Seraphina. It seems not fitting that I should write of her in these days. I hardly dared let my thoughts approach her, but I had to think of her all the time. Her sorrow was the very soul of the house.

Shortly after I had thrown O'Brien out the bishop had left, and then I learned from Father Antonio that Seraphina had been carried away to her own apartments in a fainting condition. The excellent man was almost incoherent with distress and trouble of mind, and walked up and down, his big head drooping on his capacious chest, the joints of his entwined fingers cracking. I had met him in the gallery, as I was making my way back to Carlos' room in anxiety and fear, and we had stepped aside into a large saloon, seldom used, above the gateway. I shall never forget the restless, swift pacing of that burly figure, while, feeling utterly crushed, now the excitement was over, I leaned against a console. Three long bands of moonlight fell, chilly bluish, into the vast room, with its French Empire furniture stiffly arranged about the white walls.

"And that man?" he asked me at last.

"I could have killed him with my own hands," I said. "I was the stronger. He had his pistols on him, I am certain, only I could not be a party to an assassination. . . ."

"Oh, my son, it would have been no sin to have exerted the strength which God had blessed you with," he interrupted. "We are allowed to kill venomous snakes, wild beasts; we are given our strength for that, our intelligence. . . ." And all the time he walked about, wringing his hands.

"Yes, your reverence," I said, feeling the most miserable and helpless of lovers on earth; "but there was no time. If I had not thrown him out, Castro would have stabbed him in the back in my very hands. And that would have been——" Words failed me.

I had been obliged not only to desist myself, but to save his life from Castro. I had been obliged! There had been no option. Murderous enemy as he was, it seemed to me I should never have slept a wink all the rest of my life.

"Yes, it is just, it is just. What else? Alas!" Father Antonio repeated disconnectedly. "Those feelings implanted in your breast—— I have served my king, as you know, in my sacred calling, but in the midst of war, which is the outcome of the wickedness natural to our fallen state. I understand; I understand. It may be that God, in his mercy, did not wish the death of that evil man—not yet, perhaps. Let us submit. He may repent." He snuffled aloud. "I think of that poor child," he said through his handkerchief. Then, pressing my arm with his vigorous fingers, he murmured, "I fear for her reason."

It may be imagined in what state I spent the rest of that sleepless night. At times, the thought that I was the cause of her bereavement nearly drove me mad.

And there was the danger, too.

But what else could I have done? My whole soul had recoiled from the horrible help Castro was bringing us at the point of his blade. No love could demand from me such a sacrifice.

Next day Father Antonio was calmer. To my trembling inquiries he said something consolatory as to the blessed relief of tears. When not praying fervently in the mortuary chamber, he could be seen pacing the gallery in a severe aloofness of meditation. In the evening he took me by the arm, and, without a word, led me up a narrow and winding staircase. He pushed a small door, and we stepped out on a flat part of the roof, flooded in moonlight.

The points of land dark with the shadows of trees and broken ground clasped the waters of the bay, with a body of shining white mists in the centre; and, beyond, the vast level of the open sea, touched with glitter, appeared infinitely sombre under the luminous sky.

We stood back from the parapet, and Father Antonio threw out a thick arm at the splendid trail of the moon upon the dark water.

"This is the only way," he said.

He had a warm heart under his black robe, a simple and courageous comprehension of life, this priest who was very much of a man; a certain grandeur of resolution when it was a matter of what he regarded as his principal office.

"This is the way," he repeated.

Never before had I been struck so much by the gloom, the vastness, the emptiness of the open sea, as on that moonlight night. And Father Antonio's deep voice went on:

"My son, since God has made use of the nobility of your heart to save that sinner from an unshriven death——"

He paused to mutter, "Inscrutable! inscrutable!" to himself, sighed, and then:

"Let us rejoice," he continued, with a completely unconcealed resignation, "that you have been the chosen instrument to afford him an opportunity to repent."

His tone changed suddenly.

"He will never repent," he said with great force. "He has sold his soul and body to the devil, like these magicians of old of whom we have records."

He clicked his tongue with compunction, and regretted his want of charity. It was proper for me, however, as a man having to deal with a world of wickedness and error, to act as though I did not believe in his repentance.

"The hardness of the human heart is incredible; I have seen the most appalling examples." And the priest meditated. "He is not a common criminal, however," he added profoundly.

It was true. He was a man of illusions, ministering to passions that uplifted him above the fear of consequences. Young as I was, I understood that, too. There was no safety for us in Cuba while he lived. Father Antonio nodded dismally.

"Where to go?" I asked. "Where to turn? Whom can we trust? In whom can we repose the slightest confidence? Where can we look for hope?"

Again the *padre* pointed to the sea. The hopeless aspect of its moonlit and darkling calm struck me so forcibly that I did not even ask how he proposed to get us out there. I only made a gesture of discouragement. Outside the Casa, my life was not worth ten

minutes' purchase. And how could I risk her there?
How could I propose to her to follow me to an almost
certain death? What could be the issue of such an
adventure? How could we hope to devise such secret
means of getting away as would prevent the *Lugareños*
pursuing us? I should perish, then, and she . . .

Father Antonio seemed to lose his self-control suddenly.

"Yes," he cried. "The sea is a perfidious element,
but what is it to the blind malevolence of men?" He
gripped my shoulder. "The risk to her life," he cried;
"the risk of drowning, of hunger, of thirst—that is all
the sea can do. I do not think of that. I love her too
much. She is my very own spiritual child; and I tell
you, Señor, that the unholy intrigue of that man endangers not her happiness, not her fortune alone—it
endangers her innocent soul itself."

A profound silence ensued. I remembered that his
business was to save souls. This old man loved that
young girl whom he had watched growing up, defenceless in her own home; he loved her with a great strength
of paternal instinct that no vow of celibacy can extinguish, and with a heroic sense of his priestly duty. And
I was not to say him nay. The sea—so be it. It was
easier to think of her dead than to think of her im-
mured; it was better that she should be the victim of
the sea than of evil men; that she should be lost with
me than to me.

Father Antonio, with that naïve sense of the poetry
of the sky he possessed, apostrophized the moon, the
"gentle orb," as he called it, which ought to be weary
of looking at the miseries of the earth. His immense
shadow on the leads seemed to fling two vast fists over
the parapet, as if to strike at the enemies below, and
without discussing any specific plan we descended. It

was understood that Seraphina and I should try to escape—I won't say by sea, but to the sea. At best, to ask the charitable help of some passing ship, at worst to go out of the world together.

I had her confidence. I will not tell of my interview with her; but I shall never forget my sensations of awe, as if entering a temple, the melancholy and soothing intimacy of our meeting, the dimly lit loftiness of the room, the vague form of La Chica in the background, and the frail, girlish figure in black with a very pale, delicate face. Father Antonio was the only other person present, and chided her for giving way to grief. "It is like rebellion—like rebellion," he denounced, turning away his head to wipe a tear hastily; and I wondered and thanked God that I should be a comfort to that tender young girl, whose lot on earth had been difficult, whose sorrow was great but could not overwhelm her indomitable spirit, which held a promise of sweetness and love.

Her courage was manifest to me in the gentle and sad tones of her voice. I made her sit in a vast armchair of tapestry, in which she looked lost like a little child, and I took a stool at her feet. This is an unforgettable hour in my life in which not a word of love was spoken, which is not to be written of. The burly shadow of the priest lay motionless from the window right across the room; the flickering flame of a silver lamp made an unsteady white circle of light on the lofty ceiling above her head. A clock was beating gravely somewhere in the distant gloom, like the unperturbed heart of that silence, in which our understanding of each other was growing, even into a strength fit to withstand every tempest.

"Escape by the sea," I said aloud. "It would be, at least, like two lovers leaping hand in hand off a high rock, and nothing else."

Father Antonio's bass voice spoke behind us.

"It is better to jeopardize the sinful body that returns to the dust of which it is made than the redeemed soul, whose awful lot is eternity. Reflect."

Seraphina hung her head, but her hand did not tremble in mine.

"My daughter," the old man continued, "you have to confide your fate to a noble youth of elevated sentiments, and of a truly chivalrous heart. . . ."

"I trust him," said Seraphina.

And, as I heard her say this, it seemed really to me as if, in very truth, my sentiments were noble and my heart chivalrous. Such is the power of a girl's voice. The door closed on us, and I felt very humble.

But in the gallery Father Antonio leaned heavily on my shoulder.

"I shall be a lonely old man," he whispered faintly. "After all these years! Two great nobles; the end of a great house—a child I had seen grow up. . . . But I am less afraid for her now."

I shall not relate all the plans we made and rejected. Everything seemed impossible. We knew from Castro that O'Brien had gone to Havana, either to take the news of Don Balthasar's death himself, or else to prevent the news spreading there too soon. Whatever his motive for leaving Rio Medio, he had left orders that the house should be respected under the most awful penalties, and that it should be watched so that no one left it. The Englishman was to be killed at sight. Not a hair on anybody else's head was to be touched.

To escape seemed impossible; then on the third day the thing came to pass. The way was found. Castro, who served me as if Carlos' soul had passed into my body, but looked at me with a saturnine disdain, had arranged it all with Father Antonio.

It was the day of the burial of Carlos and Don Balthasar. That same day Castro had heard that a ship had been seen becalmed a long way out to sea. It was a great opportunity; and the funeral procession would give the occasion for my escape. There was in Rio Medio, as in all Spanish towns amongst the respectable part of the population, a confraternity for burying the dead, "The Brothers of Pity," who, clothed in black robes and cowls, with only two holes for the eyes, carried the dead to their resting-place, unrecognizable and unrecognized in that pious work. A "Brother of Pity" dress would be brought for me into Father Antonio's room. Castro was confident as to his ability of getting a boat. It would be a very small and dangerous one, but what would I have, if I neither killed my enemy, nor let any one else kill him for me, he commented with sombre sarcasm.

A truce of God had been called, and the burial was to take place in the evening when the mortal remains of the last of the Riegos would be laid in the vault of the cathedral of what had been known as their own province, and had, in fact, been so for a time under a grant from Charles V.

Early in the day I had a short interview with Seraphina. She was resolute. Then, long before dark, I slipped into Father Antonio's room, where I was to stay until the moment to come out and mingle with the throng of other Brothers of Pity. Once with the bodies in the crypt of the cathedral, I was to await Seraphina there, and, together, we should slip through a side door on to the shore. Cesar, to throw any observer off the scent (three *Lugareños* were to be admitted to see the bodies put in their coffins), posted two of the Riego negroes with loaded muskets on guard before the door of my empty room, as if to protect me.

Then, just as dusk fell, Father Antonio, who had been praying silently in a corner, got up, blew his nose, sighed, and suddenly enfolded me in his powerful arms for an instant.

"I am an old man—a poor priest," he whispered jerkily into my ear, "and the sea is very perfidious. And yet it favours the sons of your nation. But, remember—the child has no one but you. Spare her."

He went off; stopped. "Inscrutable! inscrutable!" he murmured, lifting upwards his eyes. He raised his hand with a solemn slowness. "An old man's blessing can do no harm," he said humbly. I bowed my head. My heart was too full for speech, and the door closed. I never saw him again, except later on in his surplice for a moment at the gate, his great bass voice distinct in the chanting of the priests conducting the bodies.

The *Lugareños* would respect the truce arranged by the bishop.

No man of them but the three had entered the Casa. Already, early in the night, their black-haired women, with coarse faces and melancholy eyes, were kneeling in rows under the black *mantillas* on the stone floor of the cathedral, praying for the repose of the soul of Seraphina's father, of that old man who had lived among them, unapproachable, almost invisible, and as if infinitely removed. They had venerated him, and many of them had never set eyes on his person.

It strikes me, now, as strange and significant of a mysterious human need, the need to look upwards towards a superiority inexpressibly remote, the need of something to idealize in life. They had only that and, maybe, a sort of love as idealized and as personal for the mother of God, whom, also, they had never seen, to whom they trusted to save them from a devil as real. And they had, moreover, a fear even more real of O'Brien.

And, when one comes to think of it, in putting on the long spectacled robe of a Brother of Pity, in walking before the staggering bearers of the great coffin with a tall crucifix in my hand, in thus taking advantage of their truce of God, I was, also, taking advantage of what was undoubtedly their honour—a thing that handicapped them quite as much as had mine when I found myself unable to strike down O'Brien. At that time, I was a great deal too excited to consider this, however. I had many things to think of, and the immense necessity of keeping a cool head.

It was, after all, Tomas Castro to whom all the credit of the thing belonged. Just after it had fallen very dark, he brought me the black robes, a pair of heavy pistols to gird on under them, and the heavy staff topped by a crucifix. He had an air of sarcastic protest in the dim light of my room, and he explained with exaggeratedly plain words precisely what I was to do—which, as a matter of fact, was neither more nor less than merely following in his own footsteps.

"And, oh, Señor," he said sardonically, "if you desire again to pillow your head upon the breast of your mother; if you would again see your sister, who, alas! by bewitching my Carlos, is at the heart of all our troubles; if you desire again to see that dismal land of yours, which politeness forbids me to curse, I would beg of you not to let the mad fury of your nation break loose in the midst of these thieves and scoundrels."

He peered intently into the spectacled eyeholes of my cowl, and laid his hand on his sword-hilt. His small figure, tightly clothed in black velvet from chin to knee, swayed gently backwards and forwards in the light of the dim candle, and his grotesque shadow flitted over the ghostly walls of the great room. He stood gazing silently for a minute, then turned smartly on his heels, and, with a gesture of sardonic respect, threw open the door for me.

"Pray, Señor," he said, "that the moon may not rise too soon."

We went swiftly down the colonnades for the last time, in the pitch darkness and into the blackness of the vast archway. The clumping staff of my heavy crucifix drew hollow echoes from the flagstones. In the deep sort of cave behind us, lit by a dim lanthorn, the negroes waited to unbar the doors. Castro himself began to mutter over his beads. Suddenly he said:

"It is the last time I shall stand here. Now, there is not any more a place for me on the earth."

Great flashes of light began to make suddenly visible the tall pillars of the immense mournful place, and after a long time, absolutely without a sound, save the sputter of enormous torches, an incredibly ghostly body of figures, black-robed from head to foot, with large eyeholes peering fantastically, swayed into the great arch of the hall. Above them was the enormous black coffin. It was a sight so appalling and unexpected that I stood gazing at them without any power to move, until I remembered that I, too, was such a figure. And then, with an ejaculation of impatience, Tomas Castro caught at my hand, and whirled me round.

The great doors had swung noiselessly open, and the black night, bespangled with little flames, was framed in front of me. He suddenly unsheathed his portentous sword, and, hanging his great hat upon his maimed arm, stalked, a pathetic and sinister figure of grief, down the great steps. I followed him in the vivid and extraordinary compulsion of the sinister body that, like one fabulous and enormous monster, swayed impenetrably after me.

My heart beat till my head was in a tumultuous whirl, when thus, at last, I stepped out of that house— but I suppose my grim robes cloaked my emotions— though, seeing very clearly through the eyeholes, it was almost incredible to me that I was not myself seen. But these Brothers of Pity were a secret society, known to no man except their spiritual head, who chose them in turn, and not knowing even each other. Their good deeds of charity were, in that way, done by pure stealth. And it happened that their spiritual director was the Father Antonio himself. At that foot of the palace steps, drawn back out of our way, stood the great glass coach of state, containing, even then, the woman who was all the world to me, invisible to me, unattainable to me, not to be comforted by me, even as her great griefs were to me invisible and unassuageable. And there between us, in the great coffin, held on high by the grim, shadowy beings, was all that she loved, invisible, unattainable, too, and beyond all human comfort. Standing there, in the midst of the whispering, bare-headed, kneeling, and villainous crowd, I had a vivid vision of her pale, dim, pitiful face. Ah, poor thing! she was going away for good from all that state, from all that seclusion, from all that peace, mutely, and with a noble pride of quietness, into a world of dangers, with no head but mine to think for her, no arm but mine to ward off all the great terrors, the immense and dangerous weight of a new world.

In the twinkle of innumerable candles, the priceless harness of the white mules, waiting to draw the great coach after us, shone like streaks of ore in an infinitely rich silver mine. A double line of tapers kept the road to the cathedral, and a crowd of our negroes, the bell muzzles of their guns suggested in the twinkling light, massed themselves round the coach. Outside the lines were the crowd of rapscallions in red jackets, their women and children—all the population of the Aldea Bajo, groaning. The whole crowd got into motion round us, the white mules plunging frantically, the coach swaying. Ahead of me marched the sardonic, gallantly grotesque figure of true Tomas, his sword point up, his motions always jaunty. Ahead of him, again, were the white robes of many priests, a cluster of tall candles, a great jewelled cross, and a tall saint's figure swaying, more than shoulder high, and disappearing up above into the darkness. For me, under my cowl, it was suffocatingly hot; but I seemed to move forward, following, swept along without any volition of my own. It appeared an immensely long journey; and then, as we went at last up the cathedral steps, a voice cried harshly, "Death to the heretic!" My heart stood still. I clutched frantically at the handle of a pistol that I could not disengage from folds of black cloth. But, as a matter of fact, the cry was purely a general one; I was supposed to be shut up in the palace still.

The sudden glow, the hush, the warm breath of incense, and the blaze of light turned me suddenly faint; my ears buzzed, and I heard strange sounds.

The cathedral was a mass of heads. Everyone in Rio Medio was present, or came trooping in behind us. The better class was clustered near the blaze of gilding, mottled marble, wax flowers, and black and purple drapery that vaulted over the two black coffins in the choir. Down in the unlit body of the church the riff-raff of O'Brien kept the doors.

I followed the silent figure of Tomas Castro to the bishop's own stall, right up in the choir, and we became hidden from the rest by the forest of candles round the catafalque. Up the centre of the great church, and high over the heads of the kneeling people, came the great coffin, swaying, its bearers robbed of half their grimness by the blaze of lights. Tomas Castro suddenly caught at my sleeve whilst they were letting the coffin down on to the bier. He drew me unnoticed into the shadow behind the bishop's stall. In the swift transit, I had a momentary glance of a small, black figure, infinitely tiny in that quiet place, and infinitely solitary, veiled in black from head to foot, coming alone up the centre of the nave.

I stood hidden there beside the bishop's stall for a long time, and then suddenly I saw the black figure alone in the gallery, looking down upon me—from the *loggia* of the Riegos. I felt suddenly an immense calm; she was looking at me with unseeing eyes, but I knew and felt that she would follow me now to the end of the world. I had no more any doubts as to the issue of our enterprise; it was open to no unsuccess with a figure so steadfast engaged in it; it was impossible that blind fate should be insensible to her charm, impossible that any man could strike at or thwart her.

Monks began to sing; a great brass instrument grunted lamentably; in the body of the building there was silence. The bishop and his supporters moved about, as if aimlessly, in front of the altar; the chains of the gold censors clicked ceaselessly. Seraphina's head had sunk forward out of my sight. All the heads of the cathedral bowed down, and suddenly, from round the side of the stall, a hand touched mine, and a voice said, "It is time." Very softly, as if it were part of the rite, I was drawn round the stall through a door in the side of the screen. As we went out, in his turnings, the old bishop gave us the benediction. Then the door closed on the glory of his robes, and in a minute, in the

darkness we were rustling down a circular narrow staircase into the dimness of a crypt, lit by the little blue
flame of an oil lamp. From above came sounds like
thunder, immense, vibrating; we were immediately
under the choir. Through the cracks round a large
stone showed a parallelogram of light.

In the dimness I had a glimpse of the face of my con-
ductor—a thin, wonderfully hollow-cheeked lay brother.
He began, with great gentleness, to assist me out of
my black robes, and then he said:

"The señorita will be here very soon with the Señor
Tomas," and then added, with an infinitely sad and
tender, dim smile:

"Will not the Señor Caballero, if it is not repugnant,
say a prayer for the repose of . . ." He pointed
gently upwards to the great flagstone above which was
the coffin of Don Balthasar and Carlos. The priest
himself was one of those very holy, very touching—
perhaps, very stupid—men that one finds in such
places. With his dim, wistful face he is very present
in my memory. He added: "And that the good God
of us all may keep it in the Señor Caballero's heart to
care well for the soul of the dear señorita."

"I am a very old man," he whispered, after a pause.
He was indeed an old man, quite worn out, quite without hope on earth. "I have loved the señorita since
she was a child. The Señor Caballero takes her from
us. I would have him pray—to be made worthy."

Whilst I was doing it, the place began to be alive with
whispers of garments, of hushed footsteps, a small
exclamation in a gruff voice. Then the stone above
moved out of its place, and a blaze of light fell down
from the choir above.

I saw beside me Seraphina's face, brilliantly lit,
looking upwards. Tomas Castro said:

"Come quickly . . . come quickly . . . the prayers are ending; there will be people in the street." And from above an enormous voice intoned: "*Tu . . u . . ba mi . . i . . i . . irum . . .*" And the serpent groaned discordantly. The end of a great box covered with black velvet glided forward above our heads; ropes were fastened round it. The priest had opened a door in the shadowy distance, beside a white marble tablet in the thick walls. The coffin up above moved forward a little again; the ropes were readjusted with a rattling, wooden sound. A dry, formal voice intoned from above:

"*Erit . . justus . . Ab . . . auditione . . .*"

From the open door the priest rattled his keys, and said, "Come, come," impatiently.

I was horribly afraid that Seraphina would shriek or faint, or refuse to move. There was very little time. The pirates might stream out of the front of the cathedral as we came from the back; the bishop had promised to accentuate the length of the service. But Seraphina glided towards the open door; a breath of fresh air reached us. She looked back once. The coffin was swinging right over the hole, shutting out the light. Tomas Castro took her hand and said, "Come . . . come," with infinite tenderness.

He had been sobbing convulsedly. We went up some steps, and the door shut behind us with a sound like a sigh of relief.

We walked fast, in perfect blackness and solitude, on the deserted beach between the old town and the village. Every soul was near the cathedral. A boat lay half afloat. To the left in the distance the light of the schooner opposite the Casa Riego wavered on the still water.

Suddenly Tomas Castro said:

"The señorita never before set foot to the open ground."

At once I lifted her into the boat. "Shove off, Tomas," I said, with a beating heart.

PART FOURTH

BLADE AND GUITAR

CHAPTER ONE

THERE was a slight, almost imperceptible jar, a faint grating noise, a whispering sound of sand—and the boat, without a splash, floated.

The earth, slipping as it were away from under the keel, left us borne upon the waters of the bay, which were as still as the windless night itself. The pushing off of that boat was like a launching into space, as a bird opens its wings on the brow of a cliff, and remains poised in the air. A sense of freedom came to me, the unreasonable feeling of exultation—as if I had been really a bird essaying its flight for the first time. Everything, sudden and evil and most fortunate, had been arranged for me, as though I had been a lay figure on which Romance had been wreaking its bewildering unexpectedness; but with the floating clear of the boat, I felt somehow that this escape I had to manage myself.

It was dark. Dipping cautiously the blade of the oar, I gave another push against the shelving shore. Seraphina sat, cloaked and motionless, and Tomas Castro, in the bows, made no sound. I didn't even hear him breathe. Everything was left to me. The boat, impelled afresh, made a slight ripple, and my elation was replaced in a moment by all the torments of the most acute anxiety.

I gave another push, and then lost the bottom. Success depended upon my resource, readiness, and courage. And what was this success? Immediately, it meant getting out of the bay, and into the open sea in a twelve-foot dinghy looted from some ship years ago by the Rio Medio pirates, if that miserable population of sordid and ragged outcasts of the Antilles deserved such a romantic name. They were sea-thieves.

Already the wooded shoulder of a mountain was thrown out intensely black by the glow in the sky behind. The moon was about to rise. A great anguish took my heart as if in a vice. The stillness of the dark shore struck me as unnatural. I imagined the yell of the discovery breaking it, and the fancy caused me a greater emotion than the thing itself, I flatter myself, could possibly have done. The unusual silence in which, through the open portals, the altar of the cathedral alone blazed with many flames upon the bay, seemed to enter my very heart violently, like a sudden access of anguish. The two in the boat with me were silent, too. I could not bear it.

"Seraphina," I murmured, and heard a stifled sob.

"It is time to take the oars, Señor," whispered Castro suddenly, as though he had fallen asleep as soon as he had scrambled into the bows, and only had awaked that instant. "The mists in the middle of the bay will hide us when the moon rises."

It was time—if we were to escape. Escape where? Into the open sea? With that silent, sorrowing girl by my side! In this miserable cockleshell, and without any refuge open to us? It was not really a hesitation; she could not be left at the mercy of O'Brien. It was as though I had for the first time perceived how vast the world was; how dangerous; how unsafe. And there was no alternative. There could be no going back.

Perhaps, if I had known what was before us, my heart would have failed me utterly out of sheer pity. Suddenly my eyes caught sight of the moon making like the glow of a bush fire on the black slope of the mountain. In a moment it would flood the bay with light, and the schooner anchored off the beach before the Casa Riego was not eighty yards away. I dipped my oar without a splash. Castro pulled with his one hand.

The mists rising on the lowlands never filled the bay, and I could see them lying in moonlight across the outlet like a silvery white ghost of a wall. We penetrated it, and instantly became lost to view from the shore.

Castro, pulling quickly, turned his head, and grunted at a red blurr very low in the mist. A fire was burning on the low point of land where Nichols—the Nova Scotian—had planted the battery which had worked such havoc with Admiral Rowley's boats. It was a mere earthwork and some of the guns had been removed. The fire, however, warned us that there were some people on the point. We ceased rowing for a moment, and Castro explained to me that a fire was always lit when any of these thieves' boats were stirring. There would be three or four men to keep it up. On this very night Manuel-del-Popolo was outside with a good many rowboats, waiting on the *Indiaman*. The ship had been seen nearing the shore since noon. She was becalmed now. Perhaps they were looting her already.

This fact had so far favoured our escape. There had been no strollers on the beach that night. Since the investment of the Casa Riego, Castro had lived amongst the besiegers on his prestige of a superior person, of a *caballero* skilled in war and diplomacy. No one knew how much the tubby, saturnine little man was in the confidence of the Juez O'Brien; and there was no doubt that he was a good Catholic. He was a very grave, a very silent *caballero*. In reality his heart had been broken by the death of Carlos, and he did not care what happened to him. His action was actuated by his

I

scorn and hate of the Rio Medio population, rather than by any friendly feeling towards myself.

On that night Domingo's partisans were watching the Casa Riego, while Manuel (who was more of a seaman) had taken most of his personal friends, and all the larger boats that would float, to do a bit of "outside work," as they called it, upon the becalmed West Indiaman.

This had facilitated Castro's plan, and it also accounted for the smallness of the boat, which was the only one of the refuse lot left on the beach that did not gape at every seam. She was not tight by any means, though. I could hear the water washing above the bottom-boards, and I remember how concern about keeping Seraphina's feet dry mingled with the grave apprehensions of our enterprise.

We had been paddling an easy stroke. The red blurr of the fire on the point was growing larger, while the diminished blaze of lights on the high altar of the cathedral pierced the mist with an orange ray.

"The boat should be baled out," I remarked in a whisper.

Castro laid his oar in and made his way to the thwart. It shows how well we were prepared for our flight, that there was not even a half-cocoanut shell in the boat. A gallon earthenware jar, stoppered with a bunch of grass, contained all our provision of fresh water. Castro displaced it, and, bending low, tried to bale with his big, soft hat. I should imagine that he found it impracticable, because, suddenly, he tore off one of his square-toed shoes with a steel buckle. He used it as a scoop, blaspheming at the necessity, but in a very low mutter, out of respect for Seraphina.

Standing up in the stern-sheets by her side, I kept on sculling gently. Once before I had gone desperately to sea—escaping the gallows, perhaps—in a very small

boat, with the drunken song of Rangsley's uncle herald-
ing the fascination of the unknown to a very callow
youth. That night had been as dark, but the danger
had been less great. The boat, it is true, had actually
sunk under us, but then it was only the sea that might
have swallowed me who knew nothing of life, and was as
much a stranger to fate as the animals on our farm.
But now the world of men stood ready to devour us,
and the Gulf of Mexico was of no more account than
a puddle on a road infested by robbers. What were the
dangers of the sea to the passions amongst which I was
launched—with my high fortunes in my hand, and, like
all those who live and love, with a sword suspended
above my head?

The danger had been less great on that old night,
when I had heard behind me the soft crash of the
smugglers' feet on the shingle. It had been less great,
and, if it had had a touch of the sordid, it had led me
to this second and more desperate escape—in a cockle-
shell, carrying off a silent and cloaked figure, which
quickened my heart-beats at each look. I was carrying her off from the evil spells of the Casa Riego, as a
knight a princess from an enchanted castle. But she
was more to me than any princess to any knight.

There was never anything like that in the world.
Lovers might have gone, in their passion, to a certain
death; but never, it seemed to me, in the history of
youth, had they gone in such an atmosphere of cautious
stillness upon such a reckless adventure. Everything
depended upon slipping out through the gullet of the
bay without a sound. The men on the point had no
means of pursuit, but, if they heard or saw anything,
they could shout a warning to the boats outside. There
were the real dangers—my first concern.

Afterwards . . . I did not want to think of

afterwards. There were only the open sea and the perilous coast. Perhaps, if I thought of them, I should give up.

I thought only of gaining each successive moment and concentrated all my faculties into an effort of stealthiness. I handled the boat with a deliberation full of tense prudence, as if the oar had been a stalk of straw, as if the water of the bay had been the film of a glass bubble an unguarded movement could have shivered to atoms. I hardly breathed, for the feeling that a deeper breath would have blown away the mist that was our sole protection now.

It was not blown away. On the contrary, it clung closer to us, with the enveloping chill of a cloud wreathing a mountain crag. The vague shadows and dim outlines that had hung around us began, at last, to vanish utterly in an impenetrable and luminous whiteness. And through the jumble of my thoughts darted the sudden knowledge that there was a sea-fog outside —a thing quite different from the nightly mists of the bay. It was rolling into the passage inexplicably, for no stir of air reached us. It was possible to watch its endless drift by the glow of the fire on the point, now much nearer us. Its edges seemed to melt away in the flight of the water-dust. It was a sea-fog coming in. Was it disastrous to us, or favourable? It, at least, answered our immediate need for concealment, and this was enough for me, when all our future hung upon every passing minute.

The Rio picaroons, when engaged in thieving from some ship becalmed on the coast, began by towing one of their schooners as far as the entrance. They left her there as a rallying point for the boats, and to receive the booty.

One of these schooners, as I knew, was moored op-

posite the Casa Riego. The other might be lying at
anchor somewhere right in the fairway ahead, within a
few yards. I strained my ears for some revealing sound
from her, if she were there—a cough, a voice, the
creak of a block, or the fall of something on her deck.
Nothing came. I began to fear lest I should run stem
on into her side without a moment's warning. I could
see no further than the length of our twelve-foot boat.

To make certain of avoiding that danger, I decided
to shave close the spit of sand that tipped the narrow
strip of lowland to the south. I set my teeth, and
sheered in resolutely.

Castro remained on the after-thwart, with his elbows
on his knees. His head nearly touched my leg. I
could distinguish the woeful, bent back, the broken
swaying of the plume in his hat. Seraphina's perfect
immobility gave me the measure of her courage, and the
silence was so profoundly pellucid that the flutter of the
flames that we were nearing began to come loud out
of the blur of the glow. Then I heard the very crackling of the wood, like a fusillade from a great distance.
Even then Castro did not deign to turn his head.

Such as he was—a born vagabond, *contrabandista*,
spy in armed camps, sutler at the tail of the *Grande
Armée* (escaped, God only knows how, from the snows of
Russia), beggar, *guerillero*, bandit, sceptically murderous, draping his rags in saturnine dignity—he had
ended by becoming the sinister and grotesque squire of
our quixotic Carlos. There was something romantically
sombre in his devotion. He disdained to turn round
at the danger, because he had left his heart on the
coffin as a lesser affection would have laid a wreath.
I looked down at Seraphina. She too, had left a heart
in the vaults of the cathedral. The edge of the heavy
cloak drawn over her head concealed her face from me,

and, with her face, her ignorance, her great doubts, her great fears.

I heard, above the crackling of dry wood, a husky exclamation of surprise, and then a startled voice exclaiming:

"Look! *Santissima Madre!* What is this?"

Sheer instinct altered at once the motion of my hand so as to incline the bows of the dinghy away from the shore; but a sort of stupefying amazement seized upon my soul. We had been seen. It was all over. Was it possible? All over, already?

In my anxiety to keep clear of the schooner which, for all I know to this day, may not have been there at all, I had come too close to the sand, so close that I heard soft, rapid footfalls stop short in the fog. A voice seemed to be asking me in a whisper:

"Where, oh, where?"

Another cried out irresistibly, "I see it."

It was a subdued cry, as if hushed in sudden awe.

My arm swung to and fro; the turn of my wrist went on imparting the propelling motion of the oar. All the rest of my body was gripped helplessly in the dead expectation of the end, as if in the benumbing seconds of a fall from a towering height. And it was swift, too. I felt a draught at the back of my neck—a breath of wind. And instantly, as if a battering-ram had been let swing past me at many layers of stretched gauze, I beheld, through a tattered deep hole in the fog, a roaring vision of flames, borne down and springing up again; a dance of purple gleams on the strip of unveiled water, and three coal-black figures in the light.

One of them stood high on lank black legs, with long black arms thrown up stiffly above the black shape of a hat. The two others crouched low on the very edge of the water, peering as if from an ambush.

The clearness of this vision was contained by a thick and fiery atmosphere, into which a soft white rush and swirl of fog fell like a sudden whirl of snow. It closed down and overwhelmed at once the tall flutter of the flames, the black figures, the purple gleams playing round my oar. The hot glare had struck my eyeballs once, and had melted away again into the old, fiery stain on the mended fabric of the fog. But the attitudes of the crouching men left no room for doubt that we had been seen. I expected a sudden uplifting of voices on the shore, answered by cries from the sea, and I screamed excitedly at Castro to lay hold of his oar.

He did not stir, and after my shout, which must have fallen on the scared ears with a weird and unearthly note, a profound silence attended us—the silence of a superstitious fear. And, instead of howls, I heard, before the boat had travelled its own short length, a voice that seemed to be the voice of fear itself asking, "Did you hear that?" and a trembling mutter of an invocation to all the saints. Then a strangled throat trying to pronounce firmly, "The souls of the dead *Inglez*. Crying from pain."

Admiral Rowley's seamen, so miserably thrown away in the ill-conceived attack on the bay, were making a ghostly escort for our escape. Those dead boats'-crews were supposed to haunt the fatal spot, after the manner of spectres that linger in remorse, regret, or revenge, about the gates of departure. I had blundered; the fog, breaking apart, had betrayed us. But my obscure and vanquished countrymen held possession of the outlet by the memory of their courage. In this critical moment it was they, I may say, who stood by us.

We, on our part, must have been disclosed, dark, indistinct, utterly inexplicable; completely unexpected;

an apparition of stealthy shades. The painful voice in the fog said:

"Let them be. Answer not. They shall pass on, for none of them died on the shore—all in the water. Yes, all in the water."

I suppose the man was trying to reassure himself and his companions. His meaning, no doubt, was that, being on shore, they were safe from the ghosts of those *Inglez* who had never achieved a landing. From the enlarging and sudden deepening of the glow, I knew that they were throwing more brushwood on the fire.

I kept on sculling, and gradually the sharp fusillade of dry twigs grew more distant, more muffled in the fog. At last it ceased altogether. Then a weakness came over me, and, hauling my oar in, I sat down by Seraphina's side. I longed for the sound of her voice, for some tender word, for the caress of a murmur upon my perplexed soul. I was sure of her, as of a conquered and rare treasure, whose possession simplifies life into a sort of adoring guardianship—and I felt so much at her mercy that an overwhelming sense of guilt made me afraid to speak to her. The slight heave of the open sea swung the boat up and down.

Suddenly Castro let out a sort of lugubrious chuckle, and, in low tones, I began to upbraid him with his apathy. Even with his one arm he should have obeyed my call to the oar. It was incomprehensible to me that we had not been fired at. Castro enlightened me, in a few moody and scornful words. The Rio Medio people, he commented upon the incident, were fools, of bestial nature, afraid of they knew not what.

"Castro, the valour of these dead countrymen of mine was not wasted; they have stood by us like true friends," I whispered in the excitement of our escape.

"These insensate English," he grumbled. . . .

"A dead enemy would have served the turn better. If the *caballero* had none other than dead friends. . . ."

His harsh, bitter mumble stopped. Then Seraphina's voice said softly:

"It is you who are the friend, Tomas Castro. To you shall come a friend's reward."

"Alas, Señorita!" he sighed. "What remains for me in this world—for me who have given for two masses for the souls of that illustrious man, and of your cousin Don Carlos, my last piece of silver?"

"We shall make you very rich, Tomas Castro," she said with decision, as if there had been bags of gold in the boat.

He returned a high-flown phrase of thanks in a bitter, absent whisper. I knew well enough that the help he had given me was not for money, not for love—not even for loyalty to the Riegos. It was obedience to the last recommendation of Carlos. He ran risks for my safety, but gave me none of his allegiance.

He was still the same tubby, murderous little man, with a steel blade screwed to the wooden stump of his forearm, as when, swelling his breast, he had stepped on his toes before me like a bloodthirsty pigeon, in the steerage of the ship that had brought us from home. I heard him mumble, with almost incredible, sardonic contempt, that, indeed, the señor would soon have none but dead friends if he refrained from striking at his enemies. Had the señor taken the very excellent opportunity afforded by Providence, and that any sane Christian man would have taken—to let him stab the Juez O'Brien—we should not then be wandering in a little boat. What folly! What folly! One little thrust of a knife, and we should all have been now safe in our beds. . . .

*I

His tone was one of weary superiority, and I remained appalled by that truth, stripped of all chivalrous pretence. It was clear, in sparing that defenceless life, I had been guilty of cruelty for the sake of my conscience. There was Seraphina by my side; it was she who had to suffer. I had let her enemy go free, because he had happened to be near me, disarmed. Had I acted like an Englishman and a gentleman, or only like a fool satisfying his sentiment at other people's expense? Innocent people, too, like the Riego servants, Castro himself; like Seraphina, on whom my high-minded forbearance had brought all these dangers, these hardships, and this uncertain fate.

She gave no sign of having heard Castro's words. The silence of women is very impenetrable, and it was as if my hold upon the world—since she was the whole world for me—had been weakened by that shade of decency of feeling which makes a distinction between killing and murder. But suddenly I felt, without her cloaked figure having stirred, her small hand slip into mine. Its soft warmth seemed to go straight to my heart, soothing, invigorating—as if she had slipped into my palm a weapon of extraordinary and inspiring potency.

"Ah, you are generous," I whispered close to the edge of the cloak overshadowing her face.

"You must now think of yourself, Juan," she said.

"Of myself," I echoed sadly. "I have only you to think of, and you are so far away—out of my reach. There are your dead—all your loss, between you and me."

She touched my arm.

"It is I who must think of my dead," she whispered. "But you, you must think of yourself, because I have nothing of mine in this world now."

Her words affected me like the whisper of remorse. It was true. There were her wealth, her lands, her palaces; but her only refuge was that little boat. Her father's long aloofness from life had created such an isolation round his closing years that his daughter had no one but me to turn to for protection against the plots of her own Intendente. And, at the thought of our desperate plight, of the suffering awaiting us in that small boat, with the possibility of a lingering death for an end, I wavered for a moment. Was it not my duty to return to the bay and give myself up? In that case, as Castro expressed it, our throats would be cut for love of the *Juez*.

But Seraphina, the rabble would carry to the Casa on the palms of their hands—out of veneration for the family, and for fear of O'Brien.

"So, Señor," he mumbled, "if to you to-morrow's sun is as little as to me, let us pull the boat's head round."

"Let us set our hands to the side and overturn it, rather," Seraphina said, with an indignation of high command.

I said no more. If I could have taken O'Brien with me into the other world, I would have died to save her the pain of so much as a pinprick. But because I could not, she must even go with me; must suffer because I clung to her as men cling to their hope of highest good—with an exalted and selfish devotion.

Castro had moved forward, as if to show his readiness to pull round. Meantime I heard a click. A feeble gleam fell on his misty hands under the black halo of the hat rim. Again the flint and blade clicked, and a large red spark winked rapidly in the bows. He had lighted a cigarette.

CHAPTER TWO

SILENCE, stillness, breathless caution were the absolute conditions of our existence. But I hadn't the heart to remonstrate with him for the danger he caused Seraphina and myself. The fog was so thick now that I could not make out his outline, but I could smell the tobacco very plainly.

The acrid odour of *picadura* seemed to knit the events of three years into one uninterrupted adventure. I remembered the shingle beach; the deck of the old *Thames*. It brought to my mind my first vision of Seraphina, and the emblazoned magnificence of Carlos' sick bed. It all came and went in a whiff of smoke; for of all the power and charm that had made Carlos so seductive there remained no such deep trace in the world as in the heart of the little grizzled bandit who, like a philosopher, or a desperado, puffed his cigarette in the face of the very spirit of murder hovering round us, under the mask and cloak of the fog. And by the serene heaven of my life's evening, the spirit of murder became actually audible to us in hasty and rhythmical knocks, accompanied by a cheerful tinkling.

These sounds, growing swiftly louder, at last induced Castro to throw away his cigarette. Seraphina clutched my arm. The noise of oars rowing fast, to the precipitated jingling of a guitar, swooped down upon us with a gallant ferocity.

"*Caramba*," Castro muttered; "it is the fool Manuel himself!"

I said, then:

"We have eight shots between us two, Tomas."

He thrust his brace of pistols upon my knees.

"Dispose of them as your worship pleases," he muttered.

"You mustn't give up, yet," I whispered.

"What is it that I give up?" he mumbled wearily. "Besides, there grows from my forearm a blade. If I shall find myself indisposed to quit this world alone. . . . Listen to the singing of that imbecile."

A carolling falsetto seemed to hang muffled in upper space, above the fog that settled low on the water, like a dense and milky sediment of the air. The moonlight fell into it strangely. We seemed to breathe at the bottom of a shallow sea, white as snow, shining like silver, and impenetrably opaque everywhere, except overhead, where the yellow disc of the moon glittered through a thin cloud of steam. The gay truculence of the hollow knocking, the metallic jingle, the shrill trolling, went on crescendo to a burst of babbling voices, a mad speed of tinkling, a thundering shout, "*Altro, Amigos!*" followed by a great clatter of oars flung in. The sudden silence pulsated with the ponderous strokes of my heart.

To escape now seemed impossible. At least it seemed impossible while they talked. A dark spot in the shining expanse of fog swam into view. It shifted its place after I had first made it out, and then remained motionless, astern of the dinghy. It was the shadow of a big boat full of men, but when they were silent, I was not sure that I saw anything at all. I make no doubt, had they been aware of our nearness, there were amongst them eyes that could have detected us in the same elusive way. But how could they even dream of anything of the kind? They talked noisily, and there must have been a round dozen of them, at the least.

Sometimes they would fall a-shouting all together, and then keep quiet as if listening. By-and-by I began to hear answering yells, that seemed to converge upon us from all directions.

We were in the thick of it. It was Manuel's boat, as Castro had guessed, and the other boats were rallying upon it gropingly, keeping up a succession of yells:

"*Ohe! Ohe!* Where, where?"

And the people in Manuel's boat howled back at them, "*Ohe! Ohe . . e!* This way; here!"

Suddenly he struck the guitar a mighty blow, and chanted in an inspired and grandiose strain:

"Steer—for—the—song."

His fingers ran riot among the strings, and above the jingling his voice, forced to the highest pitch, declaimed, as in the midst of a tempest:

> "I adore the saints in the glory of heaven
> And, on the dust of the earth,
> The print of her footsteps."

He was improvising. Sometimes he gasped; the rill of softened tinkle ran on, and, glaring watchfully, I fancied I could detect his shape in the white vapour, like a shadow thrown from afar by a tallow dip upon a snowy sheet—the lank droop of his posturing, the greasy locks, the attentive poise of his head, the sentimental rolling of his lustrous and enormous eyes.

I had not forgotten his astonishing display in the cabin of the schooner when, after the confiding of his woes and his ambitions, he had favoured me with a sample of his art. As at that time, when he had been nursing his truculent conceit, he sang, and the unsteady twanging of his guitar lurched and staggered far behind his voice, like a drunken slave in the footsteps of a raving master. *Tinkle, tinkle, twang!* A headlong rush of muddled fingering; a sudden bang, like a heavy stumble.

"She is the proud daughter of the old Castile! *Olà! Olà!* " he chanted mysteriously at the beginning of every stanza in a rapturous and soft ecstasy, and then would shriek, as though he had been suddenly cast up on the rock. The poet of Rio Medio was rallying his crew of thieves to a rhapsody of secret and unrequited passion. *Twang, ping, tinkle tinkle.* He was the *Capataz* of the valiant *Lugareños!* The true *Capataz!* The only *Capataz. Olà! Olà! Twang, twang.* But he was the slave of her charms, the captive of her eyes, of her lips, of her hair, of her eyebrows, which, he proclaimed in a soaring shriek, were like rainbows arched over stars.

It was a love-song, a mournful parody, the odious grimacing of an ape to the true sorrow of the human face. I could have fled from it, as from an intolerable humiliation. And it would have been easy to pull away unheard while he sang, but I had a plan, the beginning of a plan, something like the beginning of a hope. And for that I should have to use the fog for the purpose of remaining within earshot.

Would the fog last long enough to serve my turn? That was the only question, and I believed it would, for it settled lower; it settled down denser, almost too heavy to be stirred by the fitful efforts of the breeze. It was a true night fog of the tropics, that, born after sunset, tries to creep back into the warm bosom of the sea before sunrise. Once in Rio Medio, taking a walk in the early morning along the sand-dunes, I had stood watching below me the heads of some people, fishing from a boat, emerge strangely in the dawn out of such a fog. It concealed their very shoulders more completely than water could have done. I trusted it would not come so

soon to our heads, emerging, though it seemed to me
that already, by merely clambering on Castro's
shoulders, I could attain to clear moonlight; see the
highlands of the coast, the masts of the English ship.
She could not be very far off if only one could tell the
direction. But an unsteady little dinghy was not the
platform for acrobatic exercises, and Castro not exactly
the man.

The slightest noise would have betrayed us, and
moreover, the thing was no good, for even supposing I
had got a hurried sight of the ship's spars, I should have
to get down into the fog to pull, and there would be
nothing visible to keep us from going astray, unless at
every dozen strokes I clambered on Castro's shoulders
again to rectify the direction—an obviously impracticable and absurd proceeding.

"She is the proud daughter of old Castile, *Olà, Olà*,"

Manuel sang confidentially with a subdued and gallant
lilt . . . Obviously impracticable. But I had another idea.

Tinkle tinkle pinnnng. . . Brrroum. Brrrroum.

"My soul yearns for the alms of a smile.
For a forgiving glance yearns my lofty soul . . ."

he sang. Ah, if one could have added another four
feet to one's stature. Four or five feet only. There
seemed to be nothing but a thin veil between me and
the moon. No more than a thin haze. But at the
level of my eyes everything was hidden. From behind
the white veil came the crying of the strings, a screeching, lugubrious and fierce in its artificial transport, as
if it were mocking my sad and ardent conviction of unworthiness, the crowning torment, and the inward

pride of pure love. In the breathless pauses I could hear the hollow bumping of gunwales knocking against each other; faint splashings of oars; the distant hail of some laggards groping their way on the shrouded sea.

The note of cruel passion that runs in the blood held these cut-throats profoundly silent in their boats, as at home I could imagine a party of smugglers (they would not stick at a murder or two, either) listening, with pensive faces, to a sentimental ditty of some "sweet Nancy," howled dismally within the walls of a wayside taproom in the smoke of pipes. I seemed to understand profoundly the difference of races that brings with it the feeling of romance or awakens hate. My gorge rose at Manuel's song. I hated his lamentations. "Alas, alas; in vain, in vain." He strummed with vertiginous speed, with fury, and the distracted clamour of his voice, wrestling madly with the ringing madness of the strings, ended in a piercing and supreme shriek.

"Finished. It is finished." A low and applauding murmur flowed to my ears, the austere acclamations of connoisseurs. "*Viva, viva, Manuele!* "—a squeak of fervid admiration. "Ah, our *Manuelito*." . . . But a gruff voice discoursed jovially, "Care not, Manuel. What of Paquita with the broken tooth? Is she not left to thee? And, *por Dios, hombres*, in the dark all women are alike."

"I will cram thy unclean mouth with live coals," Manuel drawled spitefully.

They roared with laughter at this sally. I depicted to myself their shapes, their fierce gesticulations, their earrings, bound heads, rags, and weapons, the vile scowls on their swarthy, grimacing faces. My anxiety beheld them as plainly as anything seen with the eyes of the body. And, with my sharpened hearing catching every word with preternatural distinctness, I felt as if, the ring of Gyges on my finger, I had sat invisible at the council of my enemies.

It was noisy, animated, with an issue of supreme interest for us. The ship, seen at midday standing inshore with a light wind, had not approached the bay near enough to be conveniently attacked till just after dusk. They had waited for her all the afternoon, sleeping and gambling on the spit of sand. But something heavy in her appearance had excited their craven suspicions, and checked their ardour. She appeared to them dangerous. What if she were an English man-of-war disguised? Some even pretended to recognize in her positively one of the lighter frigates of Rowley's squadron. Night had fallen whilst they squabbled, and their flotilla hung under the land, the men in a conflict of rapacity and fear, arguing among themselves as to the ship's character, but all unanimously goading Manuel—since he *would* call himself their only *Capataz* —to go boldly and find out.

It seems he had just been doing this with the help of a few choicer spirits, and under cover of the fog. They had managed to steal near enough to hear Englishmen conversing on board, orders given, and the yo-hoing of invisible sailors, trimming the yards of the ship to the fitful airs. This last, of course, was decisive. Such sounds are not heard on a man-of-war. She was a merchant ship: she would be an easy prey. And Manuel, in a state of exaltation at his venturesome bravery, had pulled back inshore, to rally all the boats round his own, and lead them to certain plunder. They would soon find out, he declaimed, what it was to have at their head their own valiant Manuel, instead of that vagabond, that stranger, that Andalusian starveling; that traitor, that infidel, that Castro. Hidden away, he seemed to spout all this for our ears alone, as though he could see us in our boat. . . . Patience; patience! Some day he would cut off that interloper's eyelids, and lay him on his back under a nice clear sun.

Castro made a brusque movement; a little shudder of disgust escaped Seraphina. . . . Meantime, Manuel declared, by his audacity, that ship was as good as theirs already. "*Viva el Capataz!*" they cheered.

The cloud-like vapours resting on the sea muffled the short roar; we heard grim laughter, excited cries. He began to make a set speech, and his voice, haranguing with vehement inflections in the shining whiteness of a cloud, had an amazing and uncorporeal character; the quality of abstract surprise; of phenomenal emotion shouted into empty space. And for me it had, also, the fascination of a revealed depth.

It was like the oration of an ambitious leader in a farce; he held his hearers with his eloquence, as much as he had done with the song of his grotesque and desecrating love. He vaunted his sagacity and his valour, and overwhelmed with invective all sorts of names—my own and Castro's among them. He revealed the unholy ideals of all that band of scoundrels—ideals that he said should find fruition under his captaincy. He boasted of secret conferences with O'Brien. There were murmurs of satisfaction.

I don't wonder at Seraphina's shudder of horror, of disgust, of dismay, and indignation. Robbed of the inexpugnable shelter of the Casa Riego, she, too, was made to look into the depths; upon the animalism, the lusts, and the reveries of that sordid, vermin-haunted crowd. I felt for her a profound and shamed sorrow. It was like a profaning touch on the sacredness of her mourning for the dead, and on her clear and passionate vision of life.

"*Hombres de Rio Medio! Amigos! Valientes!* . . ."
Manuel was beginning his peroration. He would lead
them, now, against the English ship. The terrified
heretics would surrender. There was always gold in
English ships. He stopped his speech, and then called
loudly, "Let the boats keep touch with each other, and
not stray in that fog."

"The dog," grunted Castro. We heard a resolute
bustle of preparation; oars were being shipped.

"Make ready, Tomas," I whispered.

"Ready for what?" he grumbled. "Where shall
your worship run from these swine?"

"We must follow them," I answered.

"The madness of the señor's countrymen descends
upon him," he whispered with sardonic politeness.
"Wherefore follow?"

"To find the English ship," I answered swiftly.

This, from the moment we had heard Manuel's
guitar, had been my idea. Since the fog that concealed
us from their sight made us, too, hopelessly blind, those
wretches must guide us themselves out of their own
clutches, as it were. I don't put this forward as an inspired conception. It was a most risky and almost
hopeless expedient; but the position was so critical that
there was no other alternative to sitting still and waiting
with folded hands for discovery. Castro seemed more
inclined for the latter.

Fortunately, the bandits wasted some time in
blasphemous bickerings as to the order of the boats in
the procession of attack. I urged my views upon
Castro in hurried whispers. His assent was of importance, since he could use an oar very well, and, if left to
myself, I could not hope to scull fast enough to keep
within hearing of the flotilla.

"Of what use to us would be a ship in Manuel's

power?" he argued morosely. On the other hand, if we waited near her till she had been plundered and released, neither the fog nor the night would last forever.

"My countrymen will beat them off," I affirmed confidently. "At any rate, let us be on the spot. We may take a hand. And remember, Tomas, they are not led by you, this time."

"True," he said, mollified. "But one thing more deserves the consideration of your worship. . . If we follow this plan, we take the señorita among flying bullets. And lead, alas! unlike steel, is blind, or that illustrious man would not now be dead. If we wait here, the señorita, at least, shall take no harm from these ruffians, as I have said."

"Are you afraid of the bullets?" I asked Seraphina. Before she had answered, Castro hissed at me:

"Oh, you unspeakable English. Would you sacrifice the daughter, too, only because she is brave?"

His sinister allusion made my blood boil with rage, and suddenly run cold in my veins. Swathed in the brilliant cloud, we heard the sounds of quarrelling and scrambling die away; cries of "Ready! ready!" an unexpected and brutal laugh. Seraphina leaned forward.

"Tomas, I wish this thing. I command it," she whispered imperiously. "We shall help these English on the ship. We must; I command it. For these are now my people."

I heard him mutter to himself, "Ah, dear shade of my Carlos. Her people. Where are now mine?" But he shipped his oar, and sat waiting.

In the moment before the picaroons actually started, I became the prey of the most intense anxiety. I knew we were to seaward of the cluster. But of our position relatively to the boats, and to the English ship they would make for, I was profoundly ignorant. The

dinghy might be lying right in the way. Before I could
master the sort of disorder I was thrown into by that
thought—which, strange to say, had not occurred to me
till then—with a shrill whistle Manuel led off.

We are always inclined to trust our eyes rather than
our ears; and such is the conventional temper in which
we receive the impression of our senses that I had no
idea they were so near us. The destruction of my
illusory feeling of distance was the most startling thing
in the world. Instantly, it seemed, with the second
swing and plash of the oars, the boats were right upon
us. They went clear. It was like being grazed by a
fall of rocks. I seemed to feel the wind of the rush.

The rapid clatter of rowing, the excited hum of voices,
the violent commotion of the water, passed by us with
an impetuosity that took my breath away. They had
started in a bunch. There must have been amongst
them at least one crew of negroes, because somebody was
beating a tambourine smartly, and the rowers chorused
in a quick, panting undertone, "*Ho, ho, talibambo. . . .
Ho, ho, talibambo.*" One of the boats silhouetted herself for an instant, a row of heads swaying back and
forth, towered over astern by a full-length figure as
straight as an arrow. A retreating voice thundered,
"Silence!" The sounds and the forms faded together
in the fog with amazing swiftness.

Seraphina, her cloak off, her head bare, stared forward after the fleeting murmurs and shadows we were
pursuing. Sometimes she warned us, "More to the
left"; or, "Faster!" We had to put forth our best, for
Manuel, as if in the very wantonness of confidence, had
set a tremendous pace.

I suppose he took his first direction by the light on the
point. I cannot tell what guided him after that feeble
sheen had become buried in the fog; but there was no

check in the speed, no sign of hesitation. We followed in the track of the sound, and, for the most part, kept in sight of the elusive shadow of the sternmost boat. Often, in a denser belt of fog, the sounds of rowing became muffled almost to extinction; or we seemed to hear them all round and, startled, checked our speed. Dark apparitions of boats would surge up on all sides in a most inexplicable way; to the right; to the left; even coming from behind. They appeared real, unmistakable, and, before we had time to dodge them, vanished utterly. Then we had to spurt desperately after the grind of the oars, caught, just in time, in an unexpected direction.

And then we lost them. We pulled frantically. Seraphina had been urging us, "Faster! faster!" From time to time I would ask her, "Can you see them?" "Not yet," she answered curtly. The perspiration poured down my face. Castro's panting was like the wheezing of bellows at my back. Suddenly, in a despairing tone, she said:

"Stop! I can neither see nor hear anything now."

We feathered our oars at once, and fell to listening with lowered heads. The ripple of the boat's way expired slowly. A great white stillness hung slumbrously over the sea.

It was inconceivable. We pulled once or twice with extreme energy for a few minutes after imaginary whistles or shouts. Once I heard them passing our bows. But it was useless; we stopped, and the moon, from within the mistiness of an immense halo, looked dreamily upon our heads.

Castro grunted, "Here is an end of your plan, Señor Don Juan."

The peculiar and ghastly hopelessness of our position could not be better illustrated than by this fresh difficulty. We had lost touch—with a murderous gang that had every inducement not to spare our lives. And positively it was a misfortune; an abandonment. I refused to admit to myself its finality, as if it had reflected upon the devotion of tried friends. I repeated to Castro that we should become aware of them directly —probably even nearer than we wished. And, at any rate, we were certain of a mighty loud noise when the attack on the ship began. She, at least, could not be very far now. "Unless, indeed," I admitted with exasperation, "we are to suppose that your imbecile *Lugareños* have missed their prey and got themselves as utterly lost as we ourselves."

I was irritated—by his nodding plume; by his cold, perfunctory, as if sleepy mutters, "Possibly, possibly, *puede ser*." He retorted: "Your English generosity could wish your countrymen no better luck than that my *Lugareños*, as your worship pleases to call them, should miss their way. They are hungry for loot— with much fasting. And it is hunger that makes your wolf fly straight at the throat."

All the time Seraphina breathed no word. But when I raised my voice, she put out a hushing hand to my arm. And, from her intent pose, from the turn of her shadowy head, I knew that she was peering and listening loyally.

Minutes passed—very few, I dare say—and brought no sound. The restlessness of waiting made us dip our oars in a haphazard stroke, without aim, without the means of judging whether we pulled to seaward, inshore, north, or south, or only in a circle. Once we went excitedly in chase of some splashing that must have been a leaping fish. I was hanging my head over my idle oar when Seraphina touched me.

"I see!" she said, pointing over the bows.

Both Castro and I, peering horizontally over the water, did not see anything. Not a shadow. Moreover, if they were so near, we ought to have heard something.

"I believe it is land!" she murmured. "You are looking too low, Juan."

As soon as I looked up I saw it, too, dark and beetling, like the overhang of a low cliff. Where on earth had we blundered to? For a moment I was confounded. Fiery reflections from a light played faintly above that shape. Then I recognized what I was looking at. We had found the ship.

The fog was so shallow that up there the upper bulk of a heavy, square stern, the very rails and stanchions crowning it like a balustrade, jutted out in the misty sheen like the balcony of an invisible edifice, for the lines of her run, the sides of her hull, were plunged in the dense white layer below. And, throwing back my head, I traced even her becalmed sails, pearly gray pinnacles of shadow uprising, tall and motionless, towards the moon.

A redness wavered over her, as from a blaze on her deck. Could she be on fire? And she was silent as a tomb. Could she be abandoned? I had promised myself to dash alongside, but there was a weirdness in that fragment of a dumb ship hanging out of a fog. We pulled only a stroke or two nearer to the stern, and stopped. I remembered Castro's warning—the blindness of flying lead; but it was the profound stillness that checked me. It seemed to portend something inconceivable. I hailed, tentatively, as if I had not expected to be answered, "Ship, ahoy!"

Neither was I answered by the instantaneous, "Hallo," of usual watchfulness, though she was not abandoned. Indeed, my hail made a good many men

jump, to judge by the sounds and the words that came
to me from above. "What? What? A hail?" "Boat
near?" "In English, sir."

"Dive for the captain, one of you," an authoritative
voice directed. "He's just run below for a minute.
Don't frighten the missus. Call him out quietly."

Talking, in confidential understones, followed.

"See him?" "Can't, sir." "What's the dodge, I
wonder." "Astern, I think, sir." "D——n this fog,
it lies as thick as pea-soup on the water."

I waited, and after a perplexed sort of pause, heard
a stern "Keep off."

CHAPTER THREE

They did not suspect how close I was to them. And their temper struck me at once as unsafe. They seemed very much on the alert, and, as I imagined, disposed to precipitate action. I called out, deadening my voice warily:

"I am an Englishman, escaping from the pirates here. We want your help."

To this no answer was made, but by that time the captain had come on deck. The dinghy must have drifted in a little closer, for I made out behind the shadowy rail one, two, three figures in a row, looming bulkily above my head, as men appear enlarged in mist.

"'Englishman,'" he says. "That's very likely," pronounced a new voice. They held a hurried consultation up there, of which I caught only detached sentences, and the general tone of concern. "It's perfectly well known that there *is* an Englishman here. . . . Aye, a runaway second mate. . . . Killed a man in a Bristol ship. . . . What was his name, now?"

"Won't you answer me?" I called out.

"Aye, we will answer you as soon as we see you. . . . Keep your eyes skinned fore and aft on deck there. . . . Ready, boys?"

"All ready, sir"; voices came from further off.

"Listen to me," I entreated.

Someone called out briskly, "This is a bad place for pretty tales of Englishmen in distress. We know very well where we are."

"You are off Rio Medio," I began anxiously; "and I——"

"Speaks the truth like a Briton, anyhow," commented a lazy drawl.

"I would send another man to the pump," a reflective voice suggested. "To make sure of the force, Mr. Sebright, you know."

"Certainly, sir. . . . Another hand to the brakes, bo'sun."

"I have been held captive on shore," I said. "I escaped this evening, three hours ago."

"And found this ship in the fog? You made a good shot at it, didn't you?"

"It's no time for trifling, I swear to you," I continued. "They are out looking for you, in force. I've heard them. I was with them when they started."

"I believe you."

"They seem to have missed the ship."

"So you came to have a friendly chat meantime. That's kind. Beastly weather, aint it?"

"I want to come aboard," I shouted. "You must be crazy not to believe me."

"But we do believe every single word you say," bantered the Sebright voice with serenity.

Suddenly another struck in, "Nichols, I call to mind, sir."

"Of course, of course. This is the man."

"My name's not Nichols," I protested.

"Now, now. You mustn't begin to lie," remonstrated Sebright. Somebody laughed discreetly.

"You are mistaken, on my honour," I said. "Nichols left Rio Medio some time ago."

"About three hours, eh?" came the drawl of insufferable folly in these precious minutes.

It was clear that Manuel had gone astray, but I

feared not for long. They would spread out in search. And now I had found this hopeless ship, it seemed impossible that anybody else could miss her.

"You may be boarded any moment by more than a dozen boats. I warn you solemnly. Will you let me come?"

A low whistle was heard on board. They were impressed, "Why should he tell us this?" an undertone inquired.

"Why the devil shouldn't he? It's no great news, is it? Some scoundrelly trick. This man's up to any dodge. Why, the *Jane* was taken in broad day by two boats that pretended they were going to sell vegetables."

"Look out, or by heavens you'll be taken by surprise. There's a lot of them," I said as impressively as I could.

"Look out, look out. There's a lot of them," someone yelled in a sort of panic.

"Oh, that's your game," Sebright's voice said to me. "Frighten us, eh? Never you mind what this skunk says, men. Stand fast. We shall take a lot of killing." He was answered by a sort of pugnacious uproar, a clash of cutlasses and laughter, as if at some joke.

"That's right, boys; mind and send them away with clean faces, you gunners. Jack, you keep a good lookout for that poor distressed Englishman. What's that? a noise in the fog? Stand by. Now then, cook! . . ."

"All ready to dish up, sir," a voice answered him.

It was like a sort of madness. Were they thinking of eating? Even at that the English talk made my heart expand—the homeliness of it. I seemed to know all their voices, as if I had talked to each man before. It brought back memories, like the voices of friends.

But there was the strange irrelevancy, levity, the enmity—the irrational, baffling nature of the anguishing conversation, as if with the unapproachable men we meet in nightmares.

We in the dinghy, as well as those on board, were listening anxiously. A profound silence reigned for a time.

"I don't care for myself," I tried once more, speaking distinctly. "But a lady in the boat here is in great danger, too. Won't you do something for a woman?"

I perceived, from the sort of stir on board, that this caused some sensation.

"Or is the whole ship's company afraid to let one little boat come alongside?" I added, after waiting for an answer.

A throat was cleared on board mildly, "Hem . . . you see, we don't know who you are."

"I've told you who I am. The lady is Spanish."

"Just so. But there are Englishmen *and* Englishmen in these days. Some of them keep very bad company ashore, and others afloat. I couldn't think of taking you on board, unless I know something more of you."

I seemed to detect an intention of malice in the mild voice. The more so that I overheard a rapid interchange of mutterings up there. "See him yet?" "Not a thing, sir." "Wait, I say."

Nothing could overcome the fixed idea of these men, who seemed to enjoy so much the cleverness of their suspicions. It was the most dangerous of tempers to deal with. It made them as untrustworthy as so many lunatics. They were capable of anything, of decoying us alongside, and stoving the bottom out of the boat, and drowning us before they discovered their mistake, if they ever did. Even as it was, there was danger; and yet I was extremely loath to give her up. It was impossible to give her up. But what were we to do? What to say? How to act?

"Castro, this is horrible," I said blankly. That he was beginning to chafe, to fret, and shuffle his feet only added to my dismay. He might begin at any moment to swear in Spanish, and that was sure to bring a shower of lead, blind, fired blindly. "We have nothing to expect from the people of that ship. We cannot even get on board."

"Not without Manuel's help, it seems," he said bitterly. "Strange, is it not, Señor? Your countrymen—your excellent and virtuous countrymen. Generous and courageous and perspicacious."

Seraphina said suddenly, "They have reason. It is well for them to be suspicious of us in this place." She had a tone of calm reproof, and of faith.

"They shall be of more use when they are dead," Castro muttered. "The señor's other dead countrymen served us well."

"I shall give you great, very great sums of money," Seraphina suddenly cried towards the ship. "I am the Señorita Seraphina Riego."

"There is a woman—that's a woman's voice, I'll swear," I heard them exclaim on board, and I cried again:

"Yes, yes. There is a woman."

"I dare say. But where do you come in? You are a distressed Englishman, aren't you?" a voice came back.

"You shall let us come up on your ship," Seraphina said. "I shall come myself, alone—Seraphina Riego."

"Eh, what?" the voice asked.

I felt a little wind on the back of my head. There was desperate hurry.

"We are escaping to get married," I called out.

They were beginning to shout orders on the ship.

"Oh, you've come to the wrong shop. A church is what you want for *that* trouble," the voice called back brutally, through the other cries of orders to square the yards.

I shouted again, but my voice must have been drowned in the creaking of blocks and yards. They were alert enough for every chance of getting away— for every flaw of wind. Already the ship was less distinct, as if my eyes had grown dim. By the time a voice on board her cried, "Belay," faintly, she had gone from my sight. Then the puff of wind passed away, too, and left us more alone than ever, with only the small disk of the moon poised vertically above the mists.

"Listen," said Tomas Castro, after what seemed an eternity of crestfallen silence.

He need not have spoken; there could be no doubt that Manuel had lost himself, and my belief is that the ship had sailed right into the midst of the flotilla. There was an unmistakable character of surprise in the distant tumult that arose suddenly, and as suddenly ceased for a space of a breath or two.

"Now, Castro," I shouted.

"Ha! *bueno!*"

We gave way with a vigour that seemed to lift the dinghy out of the water. The uproar gathered volume and fierceness.

From the first it was a hand-to-hand contest, engaged in suddenly, as if the assailants had at once managed to board in a body, and, as it were, in one unanimous spring. No shots had been fired. Too far to hear the blows, and seeing nothing as yet of the ship, we seemed to be hastening towards a deadly struggle of voices, of shadows with leathern throats; every cry heard in battle was there—rage, encouragement, fury, hate, and pain. And those of pain were amazingly distinct. They were yells; they were howls. And suddenly, as we approached the ship, but before we could make out any sign of her, we came upon a boat. We had to swerve to clear her. She seemed to have dropped out of the fight in utter disarray; she lay with no oars out, and full of men who writhed and tumbled over each other, shrieking as if they had been flayed. Above the writhing figures in the middle of the boat, a tall man, upright in the stern-sheets, raved awful imprecations and shook his fists above his head.

The blunt dinghy foamed past that vision within an oar's length, no more, making straight for the clamour of the fight. The last puff of wind must have thinned the fog in the ship's track; for, standing up, face forward to pull stroke, I saw her come out, stern-on to us, from truck to water-line, mistily tall and motionless, but resounding with the most fierce and desperate noises. A cluster of empty boats clung low to her port side, raft-like and vague on the water.

We heard now, mingled with the fury and hate of shouts reverberating from the placid sails, mighty thuds and crashes, as though it had been a combat with clubs and battle-axes.

Evidently, in the surprise and haste of the unexpected coming together, they had been obliged to board all on the same side. As I headed for the other a big boat, full of men, with many oars, shot across our bows, and vanished round the ship's counter in the twinkling of an eye. The defenders, engaged on the port side, were going to be taken in the rear. We were then so close to the counter that the cries of "Death, death," rang over our heads. A voice on the

K

poop said furiously in English, "Stand fast, men."
Next moment, we, too, rounded the quarter only
twenty feet behind the big boat, but with a slightly
wider sweep.

I said, "Have the pistols ready, Seraphina." And
she answered quite steadily:

"They are ready, Juan."

I could not have believed that any handiwork of man
afloat could have got so much way through the water.
To this very day I am not rid of the absurd impression
that, at that particular moment, the dinghy was travelling with us as fast as a cannon-ball. No sooner round
than we were upon them. We were upon them so fast
that I had barely the time to fling away my oar, and
close my grip on the butt of the pistols Seraphina
pressed into my hand from behind. Castro, too, had
dropped his oar, and, turning as swift as a cat, crouched
in the bows. I saw his good arm darting out towards
their boat.

They had cast a grapnel cleverly, and, swung abreast
of the main chains, were grimly busied in boarding
the undefended side in silence. One had already his
leg over the ship's rail, and below him three more were
clambering resolutely, one above the other. The rest
of them, standing up in a body with their faces to the
ship, were so oblivious of everything in their purpose,
that they staggered all together to the shock of the
dinghy, heavily, as if the earth had reeled under them.

Castro knew what he was doing. I saw his only
hand hop along the gunwale, dragging our cockle-shell
forward very swiftly. The tottering Spaniards turned
their heads, and for a moment we looked at each other
in silence.

I was too excited to shout; the surprise seemed to
have deprived them of their senses, and they all had

the same grin of teeth closed upon the naked blades of their knives, the same stupid stare fastened upon my eyes. I pulled the trigger in the nearest face, and the terrific din of the fight going on above us was overpowered by the report of the pistol, as if by a clap of thunder. The man's gaping mouth dropped the knife, and he stood stiffly long enough for the thought, "I've missed him," to flash through my mind before he tumbled clean out of the boat without touching anything, like a wooden dummy tipped by the heels. His headlong fall sent the water flying high over the stern of the dinghy. With the second barrel I took a long shot at the man sitting amazed, astride of the rail above. I saw him double up suddenly, and fall inboard sideways, but the fellow following him made a convulsive effort, and leapt out of sight on to the deck of the ship. I dropped the discharged weapon, and fired the first barrel of the other at the upper of the two men clinging halfway up the ship's side. To that one shot they both vanished as if by enchantment, the fellow I had hit knocking off his friend below. The crash of their fall was followed by a great yell.

These had been all nearly point-blank shots, and, anyhow, I had had a good deal of pistol practice. Macdonald had a little gallery at Horton Pen. The *Lugareños*, huddled together in the boat, were only able to moan with terror. They made soft, pitiful, complaining noises. Two or three took headers overboard, like so many frogs, and then one began to squeak exactly like a rat.

By that time, Castro, with his fixed blade, had cut their grapnel rope close to the ring. As the ship kept forging ahead all the time, the boat of the pirate bumped away lightly from between the vessel and our dinghy, and we remained alongside, holding to the end of the

severed line. I sent my fourth shot after them and
got in exchange a scream and a howl of "Mercy!
mercy! we surrender!" She swung clear of the quarter,
all hushed, and faded into the mist and moonlight,
with the head and arms of a motionless man hanging
grotesquely over the bows.

Leaving Seraphina with Castro, and sticking the
remaining pair of pistols in my belt, I swarmed up the
rope. The moon, the lights of several lanthorns, the
glare from the open doors, mingled violently in the
steamy fog between the high bulwarks of the ship. But
the character of the contest was changing, even as I
paused on the rail to get my bearings. The fellow
who had leapt on board to escape my shot had bolted
across the deck to his friends on the other side, yelling:

"Fly, fly! The heretics are coming, shooting from
the sea. All is lost. Fly, oh fly!"

He had jumped straight overboard, but the infection
of his panic was already visible. The cries of "*Muerte,
muerte!* Death, death!" had ceased, and the Englishmen were cheering ferociously. In a moment, under
my eyes, the seamen, who had been holding their own
with difficulty in a shower of defensive blows, began
to dart forward, striking out with their fists, catching
with their hands. I jumped upon the main hatch, and
found myself in the skirt of the final rush.

A tall *Lugareño* had possessed himself of one of the
ship's capstan bars, and, less craven than the others,
was flourishing it on high, aiming at the head of a sailor
engaged in throttling a negro whom he held at the full
length of his immense arms. I fired, and the *Lugareño*
tumbled down with all the appearance of having
knocked himself over with the bar he had that moment
uplifted. It rested across his neck as he lay stretched
at my feet.

I was not able to effect anything more after this, because the sailor, after rushing his limp antagonist overboard with terrific force, turned raging for more, caught sight of me—an evident stranger—and flew at my throat. He was English, but as he squeezed my windpipe so hard that I couldn't utter a word I brought the butt of my pistol upon his thick skull without the slightest compunction, for, indeed, I had to deal with a powerful man, well able to strangle me with his bare hands, and very determined to achieve the feat. He grunted under the blow, reeled away a few steps, then, charging back at once, gripped me round the body, and tried to lift me off my feet. We fell together into a warm puddle.

I had no idea spilt blood kept its warmth so much. And the quantity of it was appalling; the deck seemed to swim with gore, and we simply weltered in it. We rolled rapidly along the reeking scuppers, amongst the feet of a lot of men who were hopping about us in the greatest excitement, the hearty thuds of blows, aimed with all sorts of weapons, just missing my head. The pistol was kicked out of my hand.

The horror of my position was very great. Must I kill the man? must I die myself in this miserable and senseless manner? I tried to shout, "Drag this maniac off me."

He was pinning my arms to my body. I saw the furious faces bending over me, the many hands murderously uplifted. They, of course, couldn't tell that I wasn't one of the men who had boarded them, and my life had never been in such jeopardy. I felt all the fury of rage and mortification. Was I to die like this, villainously trodden underfoot, on the threshold of safety, of liberty, of love? And, in those moments of violent struggle I saw, as one sees in moments of wisdom and

meditation, my soul—all life, lying under the shadow
of a perfidious destiny. And Seraphina was there in
the boat, waiting for me. The sea! The boat! They
were in another land, and I, I should no more. . . .
never any more. . . . A sharp voice called, "Back
there, men. Steady. Take him alive." They dragged me up.

I needn't relate by what steps, from being terribly
handled as a captive, I was promoted to having my
arms shaken off in the character of a saviour. But I got
any amount of praise at last, though I was terribly
out of breath—at the very last gasp, as you might say.
A man, smooth-faced, well-knit, very elated and
buoyant, began talking to me endlessly. He was
mighty happy, and anyhow he could talk to me, because I was past doing anything but taking a moment's
rest. He said I had come in the nick of time, and was
quite the best of fellows.

"If you had a fancy to be called the Archbishop of
Canterbury, we'd 'your Grace' you. I am the mate,
Sebright. The captain's gone in to show himself to the
missus; she wouldn't like to have him too much chipped. . . . Wonderful is the love of woman. She
sat up a bit later to-night with her fancy-sewing to see
what might turn up. I told her at tea-time she had
better go in early and shut her stateroom door, because
if any of the Dagos chanced to come aboard, I couldn't
be responsible for the language of my crowd. We are
supposed to keep clear of profanity this trip, she being
a niece of Mr. Perkins of Bristol, our owner, and a
Methodist. But, hang it all, there's reason in all
things. You can't have a ship like a chapel—though
she would. Oh, bless you, she would, even when we're
beating off these picaroons."

I was sitting on the afterhatch, and leaning my head on my arms.

"Feel bad? Do you? Handled you like a bag of shavings. Well, the boys got their monkey up, hammering the Dagos. Here you, Mike, go look along the deck, for a double-barrelled pistol. Move yourself a bit. Feel along under the spars."

There was something authoritative and knowing in his personality; boyishly elated and full of business.

"We must put the ship to rights. You don't think they'd come back for another taste? The blessed old deck's afloat. That's my little dodge, boiling water for these Dagos, if they come. So I got the cook to fire up, and we put the suction-hose of the fire pump into the boiler, and we filled the coppers and the kettles. Not a bad notion, eh? But ten times as much wouldn't have been enough, and the hose burst at the third stroke, so that only one boat got anything to speak of. But Lord, *she* dropped out of the ruck as if she'd been swept with langridge. Squealed like a litter of pigs, didn't they?"

What I had taken for blood had been the water from the burst hose. I must say I was relieved. My new friend babbled any amount of joyous information into me before I quite got my wind back. He rubbed his hands and clapped me on the shoulder. But his heart was kind, and he became concerned at my collapsed state.

"I say, you don't think my chaps broke some of your ribs, do you? Let me feel."

And then I managed to tell him something of Seraphina that he would listen to.

"What, what?" he said. "Oh, heavens and earth! there's your girl. Of course. . . . Hey, bo'sun, rig a whip and chair on the yardarm to take a lady on board. Bear a hand. A lady! yes, a lady. Confound it, don't lose your wits, man. Look over the starboard rail, and you will see a lady alongside with a Dago in a small boat. Let the Dago come on board, too; the gentleman here says he's a good sort. Now, do you understand?"

He talked to me a good deal more; told me that they had made a prisoner—"a tall, comical chap; wears his hair like an old aunt of mine, a bunch of curls flapping on each side of his face"—and then said that he must go and report to Captain Williams, who had gone into his wife's stateroom. The name struck me. I said:

"Is this ship the *Lion?*"

"Aye, aye. That's her. She is," several seamen answered together, casting curious glances from their work.

"Tell your captain my name is Kemp," I shouted after Sebright with what strength of lung I had.

What luck! Williams was the jolly little ship's captain I was to have dined with on the day of execution on Kingston Point—the day I had been kidnapped. It seemed ages ago. I wanted to get to the side to look after Seraphina, but I simply couldn't remember how to stand. I sat on the hatch, looking at the seamen.

They were clearing the ropes, collecting the lamps, picking up knives, handspikes, crowbars, swabbing the decks with squashy flaps. A bare-footed, bare-armed fellow, holding a bundle of brass-hilted cutlasses under his arm, had lost himself in the contemplation of my person.

"Where are you bound to?" I inquired at large, and everybody showed a friendly alacrity in answer.

"Havana." "Havana, sir." "Havana's our next port. Aye, Havana."

The deck rang with modulations of the name.

I heard a loud, "Alas," sighed out behind me. A distracted, stricken voice repeated twice in Spanish, "Oh, my greatness; oh, my greatness." Then, shiveringly, in a tone of profound self-communion, "I have a greatly parched throat," it said. Harshly jovial voices answered:

"Stow your lingo and come before the captain. Step along."

A prisoner, conducted aft, stalked reluctantly into the light between two short, bustling sailors. Dishevelled black hair like a damaged peruke, mournful, yellow face, enormous stag's eyes straining down on me. I recognized Manuel-del-Popolo. At the same moment he sprang back, shrieking, "This is a miracle of the devil—of the devil."

The sailors fell to tugging at his arms savagely, asking, " What's come to you? " and, after a short struggle that shook his tatters and his raven locks tempestuously like a gust of wind, he submitted to be walked up repeating:

"Is it you, Señor? Is it you? Is it *you?*"

One of his shoulders was bare from neck to elbow; at every step one of his knees and part of a lean thigh protruded their nakedness through a large rent; a strip of grimy, blood-stained linen, torn right down to the waist, dangled solemnly in front of his legs. There was a horrible raw patch amongst the roots of his hair just above his temple; there was blood in his nostrils, the stamp of excessive anguish on his features, a sort of guarded despair in his eye. His voice sank while he said again, twice:

"Is it you? Is it you?" And then, for the last time, "Is it you?" he repeated in a whisper.

The seamen formed a wide ring, and, looking at me, he talked to himself confidentially.

*K

"Escaped—the *Inglez!* Then thou art doomed, Domingo. Domingo, thou art doomed. Dom . . . Señor!"

The change of tone, his effort to extend his hands towards me, surprised us all. I looked away.

"Hold hard! Hold him, mate!"

"Señor, condescend to behold my downfall. I am led here to the slaughter, Señor! To the slaughter, Señor! Pity! Grace! Mercy! And only a short while ago—behold. Slaughter . . . I . . . Manuel. Señor, I am universally admired—with a parched throat, Señor. I could compose a song that would make a priest weep. . . . A greatly parched throat, Señor," he added piteously.

I could not help turning my head. I had not been used half as hard as he. It was enough to look at him to believe in the dryness of his throat. Under the matted mass of his hair, he was grinning in amiable agony, and his globular eyes yearned upon me with a motionless and glassy lustre.

"You have not forgotten me, Señor? Forget Manuel! Impossible! Manuel, Señor. For the love of God. Manuel. Manuel-del-Popolo. I did sing, deign to remember. I offered you my fidelity, Señor. As you are a *caballero*, I charge you to remember. Save me, Señor. Speak to those men. . . . For the sake of your honour, Señor."

His voice was extraordinarily harsh—not his own. Apparently, he believed that he was going to be cut to pieces there and then by the sailors. He seemed to read it in their faces, shuddering and shrinking whenever he raised his eyes. But all these faces gaped with good-natured wonder, except the faces of his two guardians, and these expressed a state of conscientious worry. They were ridiculously anxious to suppress his sudden

contortions, as one would some gross indecency.   In the
scuffle they hissed and swore under their breath.   They
were scandalized and made unhappy by his behaviour.

"Are you ready down there?" roared the bo'sun in
the waist.

"Olla raight! Olla raight! Waita a leetle," I heard
Castro's voice coming, as if from under the ship.   I
said coldly a few words about the certain punishment
awaiting a pirate in Havana, and got on to my feet
stiffly. But Manuel was too terrified to understand
what I meant. He attempted to snatch at me with his
imprisoned hands, and got for his pains a severe jerking,
which made his head roll about his shoulders weirdly.

"Pity, Señor!" he screamed. And then, with low
fervour, "Don't go away. Listen! I am profound.
Perhaps the señor did not know that? Mercy! I am
a man of intrigue. A *politico*. You have escaped, and
I rejoice at it."   . . .   He bared his fangs, and
frothed like a mad dog. . . .   "Señor, I am made
happy because of the love I bore you from the first—
and Domingo, who let you slip out of the Casa, is
doomed. He is doomed. Thou art doomed, Domingo!
But the excessive affection for your noble person
inspires my intellect with a salutary combination.
Wait, Señor! A moment! An instant! . . . A combination! . . ."

He gasped as though his heart had burst. The seamen, open-mouthed, were slowly narrowing their circle.

"Can't he gabble!" remarked someone patiently.

His eyes were starting out of his head. He spoke
with fearful rapidity.

". . . There's no refuge from the anger of the
Juez but the grave—the grave—the grave! . . . Ha!
ha! Go into thy grave, Domingo. But you, Señor—
listen to my supplications—where will you go? To

Havana. The *Juez* is there, and I call the malediction
of the priests on my head if you, too, are not doomed.
Life! Liberty! Señor, let me go, and I shall run—I
shall ride, Señor—I shall throw myself at the feet of the
Juez, and say . . . I shall say I killed you. I am
greatly trusted by the reason of my superior intelligence.
I shall say, 'Domingo let him go—but he is dead.
Think of him no more—of that *Inglez* who escaped—
from Domingo. Do not look for him. I, your own
Manuel, have killed him.' Give me my life for yours,
Señor. I shall swear I had killed you with this right
hand! Ah!"

He hung on my lips breathless, with a face so dis-
torted that, though it might have been death alone he
hated, he looked, indeed, as if impatient to set to and
tear me to pieces with his long teeth. Men clutching at
straws must have faces thus convulsed by an eager and
despairing hope. His silence removed the spell—the
spell of his incredible loquacity. I heard the boatswain's hoarse tones:

"Hold on well, ma'am. Right! Walk away steady
with that whip!"

I ran limping forward.

"High enough," he rumbled; and I received Seraphina into my arms.

CHAPTER FOUR

I said, "This is home, at last. It is all over"; and she stood by me on the deck. She pushed the heavy black cloak from over her head, and her white face appeared above the dim black shadow of her mourning. She looked silently round her on the mist, the groups of rough men, the spatterings of light that were like violence, too. She said nothing, but rested her hand on my arm.

She had her immense griefs, and this was the home I offered her. She looked back at the side. I thought she would have liked to be in the boat again. I said:

"The people in this ship are my old friends. You can trust them—and me."

Tomas Castro, clambering leisurely over the side, followed. As soon as his feet touched the deck, he threw the corner of his cloak across his left shoulder, bent down half the rim of his hat, and assumed the appearance of a short, dark conspirator, overtopped by the stalwart sailors, who had abandoned Manuel to crowd, bare-armed, bare-chested, pushing, and craning their necks, round us.

She said, "I can trust you; it is my duty to trust you, and this is now my home."

It was like a definite pronouncement of faith—and of a line of policy. She seemed, for that moment, quite apart from my love, a thing very much above me and mine; closed up in an immense grief, but quite whole-souledly determined to go unflinchingly into a new life, breaking quietly with all her past for the sake of the traditions of that past.

The sailors fell back to make way for us. It was only by the touch of her hand on my arm that I had any hope that she trusted me, me personally, and apart from the commands of the dead Carlos; the dead father, and the great weight of her dead traditions that could be never anything any more for her—except a memory. Ah, she stood it very well; her head was erect and proud. The cabin door opened, and a rigid female figure with dry outlines, and a smooth head, stood out with severe simplicity against the light of the cabin door. The light falling on Seraphina seemed to show her for the first time. A lamentable voice bellowed:

"Señorita! . . . Señorita!" and then, in an insinuating, heart-breaking tone, "Señorita! . . ."

She walked quietly past the figure of the woman, and disappeared in the brilliant light of the cabin. The door closed. I remained standing there. Manuel, at her disappearance, raised his voice to a tremendous, incessant yell of despair, as if he expected to make her hear.

"*Señorita . . . proteccion del opprimido; oh, hija de piedad . . . Señorita.*"

His lamentable noise brought half the ship round us; the sailors fell back before the mate, Sebright, walking at the elbow of a stout man in loose trousers and jacket. They stopped.

"An unexpected meeting, Captain Williams," was all I found to say to him. He had a constrained air, and shook hands in awkward silence.

"How do you do?" he said hurriedly. After a moment he added, with a sort of confused, as if official air, "I hope, Kemp, you'll be able to explain satisfactorily . . ."

I said, rather off-handedly, "Why, the two men I killed ought to be credentials enough for all immediate purposes!"

"That isn't what I meant," he said. He spoke rather with a mumble, and apologetically. It was difficult to see in him any trace of the roystering Williams who had roared toasts to my health in Jamaica, after the episode at the Ferry Inn with the admiral. It was as if, now, he had a weight on his mind. I was tired. I said:

"Two dead men is more than you or any of your crew can show. And, as far as I can judge, you did no more than hold your own till I came."

He positively stuttered, "Yes, yes. But . . ."

I got angry with what seemed stupid obstinacy.

"You'd be having a rope twisted tight round your head, or red-hot irons at the soles of your feet, at this very moment, if it had not been for us," I said indignantly.

He wiped his forehead perplexedly. "Phew, how you do talk!" he remonstrated. "What I mean is that my wife . . ." He stopped again, then went on. "She took it into her head to come with me this voyage. For the first time. . . . And you two coming alone in an open boat like this! It's what she isn't used to."

I simply couldn't get at what he meant; I couldn't even hear him very well, because Manuel-del-Popolo was still calling out to Seraphina in the cabin. Williams and I looked at each other—he embarrassed, and I utterly confounded.

"Mrs. Williams thinks it's irregular," Sebright broke in, "you and your young lady being alone—in an open boat at night, and that sort of thing. It isn't what they approve of at Bristol."

Manuel suddenly bellowed out, "Señorita—save me

from their barbarity. I am a victim. Behold their bloody knives ready—and their eyes which gloat."

He shrank convulsively from the fellow with the bundle of cutlasses under his arm, who innocently pushed his way close to him; he threw himself forward, the two sailors hung back on his arms, nearly sitting on the deck, and he strained dog-like in his intense fear of immediate death. Williams, however, really seemed to want an answer to his absurdity that I could not take very seriously. I said:

"What do you expect us to do? Go back to our boat, or what?"

It seemed to affect him a good deal. "Wait till you are caught by a good woman yourself," he mumbled wretchedly.

Was this the roystering Williams? The jolly good fellow? I wanted to laugh, a little hysterically, because of the worry after great fatigue. Was his wife such a terrifying virago? "A good woman," Williams insisted. I turned my eyes to Sebright, who looked on amusedly.

"It's all right," he answered my questioning look. "She's a good soul, but she doesn't see fellows like us in the congregation she worships with at home." Then he whispered in my ear, "Owner's niece. Older than the skipper. Married him for love. Suspects every woman —every man, too, by George, except me, perhaps. She's learned life in some back chapel in Bristol. What can you expect? You go straight into the cabin," he added.

At that moment the cabin door opened again, and the figure of the woman I had seen before reappeared against the light.

"I was allowed to stand under the gate of the Casa, Excellency, I was in very truth. Oh, turn not the light of your face from me." Manuel, who had been silent for a minute, immediately recommenced his clamour in the hope, I suppose, that it would reach Seraphina's ears, now the door was opened.

"What is to be done, Owen?" the woman asked, with a serenity I thought very merciless.

She had precisely the air of having someone "in the house," someone rather questionable that you want, at home, to get rid of, as soon as a very small charity permitted.

"Madam," I said rather coldly, "I appeal to your woman's compassion. . . ."

"Even thus the arch-enemy sets his snares," she retorted on me a little tremulously.

"Señorita, I have seen you grow," Manuel called again. "Your father, who is with the saints, gave me alms when I was a boy. Will you let them kill a man to whom your father . . ."

"Snares. All snares. Can she be blessed in going away from her natural guardians at night, alone, with a young man? How can we, consistently with our duty . . ."

Her voice was cold and gentle. Even in the imperfect light her appearance suggested something cold and monachal. The thought of what she might have been saying, or, in the subtle way of women, making Seraphina feel, in there, made me violently angry, but lucid, too.

"She comes straight from the fresh grave of her father," I said. "I am her only guardian."

Manuel rose to the height of his appeal. "Señorita, I worshipped your childhood, I threw my hat in the air many times before your coach, when you drove out all in white, smiling, an angel from paradise. Excellency, help me. Excel . . ."

A hand was clapped on his mouth then, and we heard only a great scuffle going on behind us. The way to the cozy cabin remained barred. My heart was kindled by resentment, but by the power of love my soul was made tranquil, for come what absurdity might, I had Seraphina safe for the time. The woman in the doorway guarded the respectable ship's cuddy from the unwedded vagabondage of romance.

"What's to be done, Owen?" she asked again, but this time a little irresolutely, I thought. "You know something of this—but I. . . ."

"My dear, what an idea," began Williams; and I heard his helpless mutters, "Like a hero—one evening—admiral—old Topnambo—nothing of her—on my soul —Lord's son . . ."

Sebright spoke up from the side. "We could drive them overboard together, certainly, Mrs. Williams, but that wouldn't be quite proper, perhaps. Put them each in a bag, separately, and drown them one on each side of the ship, decently. . . ."

"You will not put me off with your ungodly levity, Mr. Sebright."

"But I am perfectly serious, Mrs. Williams. It may raise a mutiny amongst these horrid, profane sailors, but I really don't see how we are to get rid of them else. The bo'sun has cut adrift their ramshackle, old sieve of a boat, and she's now a quarter of a mile astern, half-full of water. And we can't give them one of the ship's boats to go and get their throats cut ashore. J. Perkins, Esquire, wouldn't like it. He would swear something awful, if the boat got lost. Now, don't say no, Mrs. Williams. I've heard him myself swear a pound's worth of oaths for a matter of tenpence. You know very well what your uncle is. A perfect Turk in that way."

"Don't be scandalous, Mr. Sebright."

"But I didn't begin, Mrs. Williams. It's you who are raising all this trouble for nothing; because, as a matter of fact, they did not come alone. They had a man with them. An elderly, most respectable man. There he stands yonder, with a feather in his hat. Hey! You! *Señor caballero, hidalgo, Pedro—Miguel—José*—what's your particular saint? Step this way a bit . . ."

Manuel managed to jerk a half-choked "Excellency," and Castro, muffled up to the eyes, began to walk slowly aft, pausing after each solemn stride. The dark woman in the doorway was as effectual as an angel with a flaming sword. She paralyzed me completely.

Sebright dropped his voice a little. "I don't see that's much worse than going off at six o'clock in the morning to get married on the quiet; all alone with a man in a hackney coach—you know you did—and being given away by a perfect stranger."

"Mr. Sebright! Be quiet! How dare you? . . . Owen!"

Williams made a vague, growling noise, but Sebright, after muttering hurriedly, "It's all right, sir," proceeded with the utmost coolness:

"Why, all Bristol knows it! There are those who said that you got out of the scullery window into the back street. I am only telling you . . ."

"You ought to be ashamed of yourself to believe such tales," she cried in great agitation. "I walked out at the gate!"

"Yes. And the gardener's wife said you must have sneaked the key off the nail by the side of the cradle— coming to the lodge the evening before, to see her poor, ailing baby. You ought to know what love brings the best of us to. And your uncle isn't a bloody-handed pirate either. He's only a good-hearted, hard-swearing old heathen. And you, too, are good-hearted. Come, Mrs. Williams. I know you're just longing to tuck this young lady up in bed—poor thing. Think what she has gone through! You ought to be fussing with sherry and biscuits and what not—making that good-for-nothing steward fly round. The beggar is hiding in the lazarette, I bet. Now then—allow me."

I got hold of the matter there again. I said—because I felt that the matter only needed making clear:

"This young lady is the daughter of a great Spanish noble. Her father was killed by these pirates. I am myself of noble family, and I am her appointed guardian, and am trying to save her from a very horrible fate."

She looked at me apprehensively.

"You would be committing a wicked act to try to interfere with this," I said.

I suppose I carried conviction.

"I must believe what you say," she said. She added suddenly, with a sort of tremulous, warm feeling, "There, there. I don't mean to be unkind. I knew nothing, and a married woman can't be too careful. For all I could have told, you might have been a—a libertine; one of the poor lost souls that Satan . . ."

Manuel, as if struggling with the waves, managed to free his lips.

"Excellency, help!" he spluttered, like a drowning man.

"I will give the young lady every care," Mrs. Williams said, "until light shall be vouchsafed."

She shut the door.

"You will go too far, Sebright," Williams remonstrated; "and I'll have to give you the sack."

"It's all right, captain. I can turn her round my little finger," said the young man cheerily. "Somebody has to do it if you won't—or can't. What shall we do with that yelping Dago? He's a distressful beast to have about the decks."

"Put him in the coal-hole, I suppose, as far as Havana. I won't rest till I see him on his way to the gallows. The Captain-General shall be made sick of this business, or my name isn't Williams. I'll make a breeze over it at home. You shall help in that, Kemp. You ain't afraid of big-wigs. Not you. You ain't afraid of anything. . . ."

"He's a devil of a fellow, and a dead shot," threw in Sebright. "And jolly lucky for us, too, sir. It's simply marvellous that you should turn up like this, Mr. Kemp. We hadn't a grain of powder that wasn't caked solid in the canisters. Nothing'll take it out of my head that somebody had got at the magazine while we lay in Kingston. . . ."

It did not occur to Williams to ask whether I was wounded, or tired, or hungry. And yet all through the West Indies the dinners you got on board the *Lion* were famous in shipping circles. But festive men of his stamp are often like that. They do it more for the glory and romance of the hospitality, and he could not, perhaps, under the circumstances, expect me to intone "for he is a jolly good fellow" over the wine. He was by no means a bad or unfeeling man; only he was not hungry himself, and another's mere necessity of that sort failed to excite his imagination. I know he was no worse than other men, and I have reason to remember him with gratitude; but, at the time, I was surprised and indignant at the extraordinary way he took my presence for granted, as if I had come off casually in a shore boat to idle away an hour or two on board. Since his wife appeared satisfied, he did not seem to desire any explanation. I felt as if I had for him no independent existence. When I had ceased to be a source of domestic difficulty, I became a precious sort of convenience, a most welcome person ("an English gentleman to back me up," he repeated several times), who would help him to make "these old women at the Admiralty sit up!" A burning shame, this! It had gone on long enough, God knows, but if they were to tackle an old trader, like the *Lion*, now, it was time the whole country should hear of it. His owner, J. Perkins, his wife's uncle, wasn't the man to go to sleep over the job. Parliament should hear of it. Most fortunate I was there to be produced—eye-witness—nobleman's son. He knew I could speak up in a good cause.

"And by the way, Kemp," he said, with sudden annoyance, recollecting himself, as it were, "you never turned up for that dinner—sent no word, nor anything. . . ."

Williams had been talking to me, but it was with Sebright that I felt myself growing intimate. The young mate of the *Lion* stood by, very quiet, listening with a capable smile. Now he said, in a tone of dry comment:

"Jolly sight more useful turning up here."

"I was kidnapped away from Ramon's back shop, if that's a sufficient apology. It's rather a long story."

"Well, you can't tell it on deck, that's very clear," Sebright had to shout to me. "Not while this infernal noise—what the deuce's up? It sounds more like a dog-fight than anything else."

As we ran towards the main hatch I recognized the aptness of the comparison. It was that sort of vicious, snarling, yelping clamour which arises all at once and suddenly dies.

"Castro! Thou Castro!"

"Malediction . . . My eyelids . . ."

"Thou! Englishman's dog!"

"Ha! *Porco.*"

The voices ceased. Castro ran tiptoeing lightly, mantled in ample folds. He assumed his hat with a brave tap, crouched swiftly inside his cloak. It touched the deck all round in a black cone surmounted by a peering, quivering head. Quick as thought he hopped and sank low again. Everybody watched with wonder this play, as of some large and diabolic toy. For my part, knowing the deadly purpose of these preliminaries, I was struck with horror. Had he chosen to run on him at once, nothing could have saved Manuel. The poor wretch, vigorously held in front of Castro, was far too terrified to make a sound. With an immovable sailor on each side, he scuffled violently, and cowered by starts as if tied up between two stone posts. His dumb, rapid panting was in our ears. I shouted:

"Stop, Castro! Stop! . . . Stop him, some of you! He means to kill the fellow!"

Nobody heeded my shouting. Castro flung his cloak on the deck, jumped on it, kicked it aside, all in the same moment as it seemed, dodged to the right, to the left, drew himself up, and stepped high, paunchy in his tight smalls and short jacket, making all the time a low, sibilant sound, which was perfectly blood-curdling.

"He has a blade on his forearm!" I yelled. "He's armed, I tell you!"

No one could comprehend my distress. A sailor, raising a lamp, had a broad smile. Somebody laughed outright. Castro planted himself before Manuel, nodded menacingly, and stooped ready for a spring. I was too late in my grab at his collar, but Manuel's guardians, acting with precision, put out one arm each to meet his rush, and he came flying backwards upon me, as though he had rebounded from a wall.

He had almost knocked me down, and while I staggered to keep my feet the air resounded with urgent calls to shoot, to fire, to bring him down! . . . "Kill him, Señor!" came in an entreating yell from Castro. And I became aware that Manuel had taken this opportunity to wrench himself free. I heard the hard thud of his leap. Straight from the hatch (as I was told later by the marvelling sailors) he had alighted with both feet on the rail. I only saw him already there, sitting on his heels, jabbering and nodding at us like an enormous baboon. "Shoot, sir! Shoot!" "Kill! Kill, Señor! As you love your life—kill!"

Unwittingly, without volition, as if compelled by the suggestion of the bloodthirsty cries, my hand drew the remaining pistol out of my belt. I raised it, and found myself covering the strange antics of an infuriated ape. He tore at his flanks with both hands in the idea, I suppose, of stripping for a swim. Rags flew from him in all directions; an astounding eruption of rags round a huddled-up figure crouching, wildly active, in front of the muzzle. I had him. I was sure of my shot. He was only an ape. A dead ape. But why? Wherefore? To what end? What could it matter whether he lived or died. He sickened me, and I pitied him, as I should have pitied an ape.

I lowered my arm an almost imperceptible fraction of a second before he sprang up and vanished. The sound of the heavy plunge was followed by a regretful clamour all over the decks, and a general rush to the side. There was nothing to be seen; he had gone through the layer of fog covering the water. No one heard him blow or splutter. It was as if a lump of lead had fallen overboard.

Williams wouldn't have had this happen for a five-pound note. Sebright expressed the hope that he wouldn't cheat the gallows by drowning. The two men who had held him slunk away abashed. To lower a boat for the purpose of catching him in the water would have been useless and imprudent.

"His friends can't be far off yet in the boats," growled the bo'sun; "and if they don't pick him up, they would be more than likely to pick up our chaps."

Somebody expectorated in so marked a manner that I looked behind me. Castro had resumed his cloak, and was draping himself with deliberate dignity. When this undertaking had been accomplished, he came up very close to me, and without a word looked up balefully from the heavy folds thrown across his mouth and chin under the very tip of his hooked nose.

"I could not do it," I said. "I could not. It would have been useless. Too much like murder, Tomas."

"Oh! the inconstancy, the fancifulness of these English," he generalized, with suppressed passion, right into my face. "I don't know what's worse, their fury or their pity. The childishness of it! The childishness. . . . Do you imagine, Señor, that Manuel or the Juez O'Brien shall some day spare you in their turn? If I didn't know the courage of your nation . . ."

"I despise the *Juez* and Manuel alike," I interrupted angrily. I despised Castro, too, at that moment, and he paid me back with interest. There was no mistaking his scathing tone.

"I know you well. You scorn your friends, as well as your foes. I have seen so many of you. The blessed saints guard us from the calamity of your friendship. . . ."

"No friendship could make an assassin of me, Mr. Castro. . . ."

". . . Which is only a very little less calamitous than your enmity," he continued, in a cold rage. "A very little less. You let Manuel go. . . . Manuel!

. . . Because of your mercy. . . . Mercy! Bah! It is all your pride—your mad pride. You shall rue it, Señor. Heaven is just. You shall rue it, Señor."

He denounced me prophetically, wrapped up with an air of midnight secrecy; but, after all, he had been a friend in the act, if not in the spirit, and I contented myself by asking, with some pity for his imbecile craving after murder:

"Why? What can Manuel do to me? He at least is completely helpless."

"Did the Señor Don Juan ever ask himself what Manuel could do to me—Tomas Castro? To me, who am poor and a vagabond, and a friend of Don Carlos, may his soul rest with God. Are all you English like princes that you should never think of anybody but yourselves?"

He revolted and provoked me, as if his opinion of the English could matter, or his point of view signify anything against the authority of my conscience. And it is our conscience that illumines the romantic side of our life. His point of view was as benighted and primitive as the point of view of hunger; but, in his fidelity to the dead architect of my fortunes, he reflected dimly the light of Carlos' romance, and I had taken advantage of it, not so much for the saving of my life as for the guarding of my love. I had reached that point when love displaces one's personality, when it becomes the only ground under our feet, the only sky over our head, the only light of vision, the first condition of thought—when we are ready to strive for it, as we fight for the breath of our body. Brusquely I turned my back on him, and heard the repeated clicking of flint against his blade. He lighted a cigarette, and crossed the deck to lean cloaked against the bulwark, smoking moodily under his slouched hat.

CHAPTER FIVE

MANUEL'S escape was the last event of that memorable night. Nothing more happened, and nothing more could be done; but there remained much talk and wonderment to get through. I did all the talking, of course, under the cuddy lamps. Williams, red and stout, sat staring at me across the table. His round eyes were perfectly motionless with astonishment—the story of what had happened in the Casa Riego was not what he had expected of the small, badly reputed Cuban town.

Sebright, who had all the duties of the soiled ship and chipped men to attend to, came in from the deck several times, and would stand listening for minutes with his fingers playing thoughtfully about his slight moustache. The dawn was not very far when he led me into his own cabin. I was half dead with fatigue, and troubled by an inward restlessness.

"Turn in into my berth," said Sebright.

I protested with a stiff tongue, but he gave me a friendly push, and I tumbled like a log on to the bedclothes. As soon as my head felt the pillow the fresh colouring of his face appeared blurred, and an arm, mistily large, was extended to put out the light of the lamp screwed to the bulkhead.

"I suppose you know there are warrants out in Jamaica against you—for that row with the admiral," he said.

An irresistible and unexpected drowsiness had relaxed all my limbs.

"Hang Jamaica!" I said, with difficult animation. "We are going home."

"Hang Jamaica!" he agreed. Then, in the dark, as if coming after me across the obscure threshold of sleep, his voice meditated, "I am sorry, though, we are bound for Havana. Pity. Great pity! Has it occurred to you, Mr. Kemp, that . . ."

It is very possible that he did not finish his sentence; no more penetrated, at least, into my drowsy ear. I awoke slowly from a trance-like sleep, with a confused notion of having to pick up the thread of a dropped hint. I went up on deck.

The sun shone, a faint breeze blew, the sea sparkled freshly, and the wet decks glistened. I stood still, touched by the new glory of light falling on me; it was a new world—new and familiar, yet disturbingly beautiful. I seemed to discover all sorts of secret charms that I had never seen in things I had seen a hundred times. The watch on deck were busy with brooms and buckets; a sailor, coiling a rope over a pin, paused in his work to point over the port-quarter, with a massive fore-arm like a billet of red mahogany.

I looked about, rubbing my eyes. The *Lion*, close hauled, was heading straight away from the coast, which stood out, not very far yet, outlined heavily and flooded with light. Astern, and to leeward of us, against a headland of black and indigo, a dazzling white speck resembled a snowflake fallen upon the blue of the sea.

"That's a schooner," said the seaman.

They were the first words I heard that morning, and their friendly hoarseness brushed away whatever of doubt might seem to mar the inexplicability of my new glow of my happiness. It was because we were safe— she and I—and because my undisturbed love let my heart open to the beauty of the young day and the joyousness of a splendid sea. I took deep breaths, and my eyes went all over the ship, embracing, like an affectionate contact, her elongated shape, the flashing brasses, the tall masts, the gentle curves of her sails soothed into perfect stillness by the wind. I felt that she was a shrine, for was not Seraphina sleeping in her, as safe as a child in its cradle? And presently the beauty, the serenity, the purity, and the splendour of the world would be reflected in her clear eyes, and made over to me by her glance.

There are times when an austere and just Providence, in its march along the inscrutable way, brings our hearts to the test of their own unreason. Which of us has not been tried by irrational awe, fear, pride, abasement, exultation? And such moments remain marked by indelible physical impressions, standing out of the ghostly level of memory like rocks out of the sea, like towers on a plain. I had many of these unforgettable emotions—the profound horror of Don Balthasar's death; the first floating of the boat, like the opening of wings in space; the first fluttering of the flames in the fog—many others afterwards, more cruel, more terrible, with a terror worse than death, in which the very suffering was lost; and also this—this moment of elation in the clear morning, as if the universe had shed its glory upon my feelings as the sunshine glorifies the sea. I laughed in very lightness of heart, in a profound sense of success; I laughed, irresponsible and oblivious, as one laughs in the thrilling delight of a dream.

"Do I look so confoundedly silly?" asked Sebright, speaking as though he had a heavy cold. "I am stupid —tired. I've been on my feet this twenty-four hours— about the liveliest in my life, too. You haven't slept very long either—none of us have. I'm sure I hope your young lady has rested."

He put his hands in his pockets. He might have been very tired, but I had never seen a boy fresh out of bed with a rosier face. The black pin-points of his pupils seemed to bore through distance, exploring the horizon beyond my shoulder. The man called Mike, the one I had had the tussle with overnight, came up behind the indefatigable mate, and shyly offered me my pistol. His head was bound over the top, and under the chin, as if for toothache, and his bronzed, rough-hewn face looked out astonishingly through the snowy whiteness of the linen. Only a few hours before, we had been doing our best to kill each other. In my cordial glow, I bantered him light-heartedly about his ferocity and his strength.

He stood before me, patiently rubbing the brown instep of one thick foot with the horny sole of the other.

"You paid me off for that bit, sir," he said bashfully. "It was in the way of duty."

"I'm uncommon glad you didn't squeeze the ghost out of me," I said; "a morning like this is enough to make you glad you can breathe."

To this day I remember the beauty of that rugged, grizzled, hairy seaman's eyelashes. They were long and thick, shadowing the eyes softly like the lashes of a young girl.

"I'm sure, sir, we wish you luck—to you and the young lady—all of us," he said shamefacedly; and his bass, half-concealed mutter was quite as sweet to my ears as a celestial melody; it was, after all, the sanction of simple earnestness to my desires and hopes—a witness that he and his like were on my side in the world of romance.

"Well, go forward now, Mike," Sebright said, as I took the pistol.

"It's a blessing to talk to one's own people," I said,

expansively, to him. "He's a fine fellow." I stuck
the pistol in my belt. "I trust I shall never need to use
barrel or butt again, as long as I live."

"A very sensible wish," Sebright answered, with a
sort of reserve of meaning in his tone; "especially as on
board here we couldn't find you a single pinch of powder
for a priming. Do you notice the consort we have this
morning?"

"What do I want with powder?" I asked. "Do you
mean that?" I pointed to the white sail of the
schooner. Sebright, looking hard at me, nodded several
times.

"We sighted her as soon as day broke. D'you know
what she means?"

I said I supposed she was a coaster.

"It means, most likely, that the fellow with the curls
that made me think of my maiden aunt, has managed
to keep his horse-face above water." He meant
Manuel-del-Popolo. "What mischief he may do yet
before he runs his head into a noose, it's hard to say.
The old Spaniard you brought with you thinks he has
already been busy—for no good, you may be sure."

"You mean that's one of the Rio schooners?" I asked
quickly.

That, with all its consequent troubles for me, was what
he did mean. He said I might take his word for it that,
with the winds we had had, no craft working along the
coast could be just there now unless she came out of
Rio Medio. There was a calm almost up to sunrise,
and it looked as if they had towed her out with boats
before daylight. . . . "Seems a rather unlikely
bit of exertion for the lazy brutes; but if they are as
much afraid of that confounded Irishman as you say
they are, that would account for their energy."

They would steal and do murder simply for the love of

God, but it would take the fear of a devil to make them do a bit of honest work—and pulling an oar *was* honest work, no matter why it was done. This was the combined wisdom of Sebright and of Tomas Castro, with whom he had been in consultation. As to the fear of the devil, O'Brien was very much like a devil, an efficient substitute. And there was certainly somebody or something to make them bestir themselves like this. . . .

Before my mind arose a scene: Manuel, the night before, pulled out of the water into a boat—raging, half-drowned, eloquent, inspired. The contemptible beast *was* inspired, as a politician is, a demagogue. He could sway his fellows, as I had heard enough to know. And I felt a slight chill on the warmth of my hope, because that bright sail, brilliantly and furtively dodging along in our wake, must be the product of Manuel's inspiration, urged to perseverance by the fear of O'Brien. The mate continued, staring knowingly at it:

"You know I am putting two and two together, like the old maids that come to see my aunt when they want to take away a woman's character. The Dagos are out and no mistake. The question is, Why? You must know whether those schooners can sail anything; but don't forget the old *Lion* is pretty smart. Is it likely they'll attempt the ship again?"

I negatived that at once. I explained to Sebright that the store of ammunition in Rio Medio would not run to it; that the *Lugareños* were cowardly, divided by faction, incapable, by themselves, of combining for any length of time, and still less of following a plan requiring perseverance and hardihood.

"They can't mean anything in the nature of open attack," I affirmed. "They may have attempted something of the sort in Nichols' time, but it isn't in their nature."

Sebright said that was practically Castro's opinion, too—except that Castro had emphasized his remarks by spitting all the time, "like an old tomcat. He seems a very spiteful man, with no great love for you, Mr. Kemp. Do you think it safe to have him about you? What are all these grievances of his?"

Castro seemed to have spouted his bile like a volcano, and had rather confused Sebright. He had said much about being a friend of the Spanish lord—Carlos; and that now he had no place on earth to hide his head.

"As far as I could make out, he's wanted in England," said Sebright, "for some matter of a stolen watch, years ago in Liverpool, I think. And your cousin, the grandee, was mixed up in that, too. That sounds funny; you didn't tell us about that. Damme if he didn't seem to imply that you, too. . . . But you have never been in Liverpool. Of course not. . . ."

But that had not been precisely Castro's point. He had affirmed he had enemies in Spain; he shuddered at the idea of going to France, and now my English fancifulness had made it impossible for him to live in Rio Medio, where he had had the care of a good *padrona*.

"I suppose he means a landlady," Sebright chuckled. "Old but good, he says. He expected to die there in peace, a good Christian. And what's that about the priests getting hold of his very last bit of silver? I must say that sounded truest of all his rigmarole. For the salvation of his soul, I suppose?"

"No, my cousin's soul," I said gloomily.

"Humbugs. I only understood one word in three."

Just then Tomas himself stalked into sight among the men forward. Coming round the corner of the deck-

L

house, he stopped at the galley door like a crow outside a hut, waiting. We watched him getting a light for his cigarette at the galley door with much dignified pantomime. The negro cook of the *Lion*, holding out to him in the doorway a live coal in a pair of tongs, turned his Ethiopian face and white ivories towards a group of sailors lost in the contemplation of the proceedings. And, when Castro had passed them, spurting jets of smoke, they swung about to look after his short figure, upon whose draped blackness the sunlight brought out reddish streaks as if bucketfuls of rusty water had been thrown over him from hat to toe. The end of his broken plume hung forward aggressively.

"Look how the fellow struts! Night and thunder! Hey, Don Tenebroso! Would your worship hasten hither. . . ." Sebright hailed jocularly.

Castro, without altering his pace, came up to us.

"What do you think of her now?" asked Sebright, pointing to the strange sail. "She's grown a bit plainer, now she is out of the glare."

Castro, wrapping his chin, stood still, face to the sea. After a long while:

"Malediction," he pronounced slowly, and without moving his head shot a sidelong glance at me.

"It's clear enough how *he* feels about our friends over there. Malediction. Just so. Very proper. But it seems as though he had a bone to pick with all the world," drawled Sebright, a little sleepily. Then, resuming his briskness, he bantered, "So you don't want to go to England, Mr. Castro? No friends there? *Sus. per col.*, and that sort of thing?"

Castro, contemptuous, staring straight away, nodded impatiently.

"But this gentleman you are so devoted to is going to England—to his friends."

Castro's arms shook under the mantle falling all round him straight from the neck. His whole body seemed convulsed. From his puckered dark lips issued a fiendish and derisive squeal.

"Let his friends beware, then. *Por Dios!* Let them beware. Let them pray and fast, and beg the intercession of the saints. Ha! ha! ha! . . ."

Nothing could have been more unlike his saturnine self-centred truculence of restraint. He impressed me; and even Sebright's steady, cool eyes grew perceptibly larger before this sarcastic fury. Castro choked; the rusty, black folds encircling him shook and heaved. Unexpectedly he thrust out in front of the cloak one yellow, dirty little hand, side by side with the bright end of his fixed blade.

"What do I hear? To England! Going to England! Ha! Then let him hasten there straight! Let him go straight there, I say—I, Tomas Castro!"

He lowered his tone to impress us more, and the point of the knife, as it were an emphatic forefinger, tapped the open palm forcibly. Did we think that a man was not already riding along the coast to Havana on a fast mule?—the very best mule from the stables of Don Balthasar himself—that murdered saint. The Captain-General had no such mules. His late excellency owned a sugar estate halfway between Rio Medio and Havana, and a relay of riding mules was kept there for quickness when his excellency of holy memory found occasion to write his commands to the capital. The news of our escape would reach the *Juez* next day at the latest. Manuel would take care of that—unless he were drowned. But he could swim like a fish. Malediction!

"I cried out to you to kill!" he addressed me directly; "with all my soul I cried. And why? Because he

had seen you and the señorita, too, alas! He should
have been made dumb—made dumb with your pistol,
Señor, since those two stupid English mariners were too
much for an old man like me. Manuel should have
been made dumb—dumb forever, I say. What mattered he—that gutter-born offspring of an evil *Gitana*,
whom I have seen, Señor! I, myself, have seen her
in the days of my adversity in Madrid, Señor—a red
flower behind the ear, clad in rags that did not cover
all her naked skin, looking on while they fought for her
with knives in a wine-shop full of beggars and thieves.
Si, Señor. That's his mother. *Impro isador—politico
—capataz*. Ha. . . . Dirt!"

He made a gesture of immense contempt.

"What mattered he? The coach would have returned from the cathedral, and the Casa Riego could
have been held for days—and who could have known
you were not inside. I had conversed earnestly with
Cesar the major-domo—an African, it is true, but a
man of much character and excellent sagacity. Ah,
Manuel! Manuel! If I—— But the devil himself
fathers the children of such mothers. I am no longer
in possession of my first vigour, and you, Señor, have all
the folly of your nation . . ."

He bared his grizzled head to me loftily.

". . . And the courage! Doubtless, that is
certain. It is well. You may want it all before long,
Señor . . . And the courage!"

The broken plume swept the deck. For a time he
blinked his creased, brown eyelids in the sun, then
pulled his hat low down over his brows, and, wrapping
himself up closely, turned away from me to look at the
sail to leeward.

"What an old, old, wrinkled, little, puffy beggar he
is!" observed Sebright, in an undertone. . . .

"Well, and what is your worship's opinion as to the purpose of that schooner?"

Castro shrugged his shoulders. "Who knows?" . . . He released the gathered folds of his cloak, and moved off without a look at either of us.

"There he struts, with his wings drooping like a turkey-cock gone into deep mourning," said Sebright. "Who knows? Ah, well, there's no hurry to know for a day or two. I don't think that craft could overhaul the *Lion*, if they tried ever so. They may manage to keep us in sight perhaps."

He yawned, and left me standing motionless, thinking of Seraphina. I longed to see her—to make sure, as if my belief in the possession of her had been inexplicably weakened. I was going to look at the door of her cabin. But when I got as far as the companion I had to stand aside for Mrs. Williams, who was coming up the winding stairs.

From above I saw the gray woollen shawl thrown over her narrow shoulders. Her parting made a broad line on her brown head. She mounted busily, holding up a little the front of her black, plain skirt. Her glance met mine with a pale, searching candour from below.

Overnight she had heard all my story. She had come out to the saloon whilst I had been giving it to Williams, and after saying reassuringly, "The young lady, I am thankful, is asleep," she had sat with her eyes fixed upon my lips. I had been aware of her anxious face, and of the slight, nervous movements of her hands at certain portions of my narrative under the blazing lamps. We met now, for the first time, in the daylight.

Hastily, as if barring my road to Seraphina's cabin, "Miss Riego, I would have you know," she said, "is in good bodily health. I have this moment looked upon her again. The poor, superstitious young lady is on her knees, crossing herself."

Mrs. Williams shuddered slightly. It was plain that the sight of that popish practice had given her a shock—almost a scare, as if she had seen a secret and nefarious rite. I explained that Seraphina, being a Catholic, worshipped as her lights enjoined, as we did after ours. Mrs. Williams only sighed at this, and, making an effort, proposed that I should walk with her a little. We began to pace the poop, she gliding with short steps at my side, and drawing close the skimpy shawl about her. The smooth bands of her hair put a shadow into the slight hollows of her temples. No nun, in the chilly meekness of the habit, had ever given me such a strong impression of poverty and renunciation.

But there was in that faded woman a warmth of sentiment. She flushed delicately whenever caught (and one could not help catching her continually) following her husband with eyes that had an expression of maternal uneasiness and the captivated attention of a bride. And after she had got over the idea that I, as a member of the male British aristocracy, was dissolute —it was an article of faith with her—that warmth of sentiment would bring a faint, sympathetic rosiness to her sunken cheeks.

She said suddenly and trembling, "Oh, young sir, reflect upon these things before it is too late. You young men, in your luxurious, worldly, ungoverned lives . . ."

I shall never forget that first talk with her on the poop —her hurried, nervous voice (for she was a timid woman, speaking from a sense of duty), and the extravagant forms her ignorance took. With the emotions of the past night still throbbing in my brain and heart, with the sight of the sea and the coast, with the

Rio Medio schooner hanging on our quarter, I listened to her, and had a hard task to believe my ears. She was so convinced that I was "dissolute," because of my class—as an earl's grandson.

It is difficult to imagine how she arrived at the conviction; it must have been from pulpit denunciations of the small Bethel on the outskirt of Bristol. Her uncle, J. Perkins, was a great ruffian, certainly, and Williams was dissolute enough, if one wished to call his festive imbecilities by a hard name. But these two could, by no means, be said to belong to the upper classes. And these two, apart from her favourite preacher, were the only two men of whom she could be said to have more than a visual knowledge.

She had spent her best years in domestic slavery to her bachelor uncle, an old shipowner of savage selfishness; she had been the deplorable mistress of his big, half-furnished house, standing in a damp garden full of trees. The outrageous Perkins had been a sailor in his time—mate of a privateer in the great French war, afterwards master of a slaver, developing at last into the owner of a small fleet of West Indiamen. Williams was his favourite captain, whom he would bring home in the evening to drink rum and water, and smoke churchwarden pipes with him. The niece had to sit up, too, at these dismal revels. Old Perkins would keep her out of bed to mix the grogs, till he was ready to climb the bare stone staircase, echoing from top to bottom with his stumbles. However, it seems he dozed a good deal in snatches during the evening, and this, I suppose, gave their opportunity to the pale, spiritual-looking spinster with the patient eyes, and to the thick, staring Williams, florid with good living, and utterly unused to the company of women of that sort. But in what way these two unsimilar beings had looked upon each other, what she saw in him, what he imagined her to be like, why, how, wherefore, an understanding arose between them, remains inexplicable. It was her romance—and it is even possible that he was moved by an unselfish sentiment. Sebright accounted for the matter by saying that, as to the woman, it was no wonder. Anything to get away from a bullying old ruffian, that would use bad language in cold blood just to horrify her—and then burst into a laugh and jeer; but as to Captain Williams (Sebright had been with him from a boy), he ought to have known he was quite incapable of keeping straight after all these free-and-easy years.

He used to talk a lot, about that time, of good women, of settling down to a respectable home, of leading a better life; but, of course, he couldn't. Simply couldn't, what with old friends in Kingston and Havana—and his habits formed—and his weakness for women who, as Sebright put it, could not be called good. Certainly there did not seem to have been any sordid calculation in the marriage. Williams fully expected to lose his command; but, as it turned out, the old beast, Perkins, was quite daunted by the loss of his niece. He found them out in their lodgings, came to them crying—absolutely whimpering about his white hairs, talking touchingly of his will, and promising amendment. In the end it was arranged that Williams should keep his command; and Mrs. Williams went back to her uncle. That was the best of it. Actually went back to look after that lonely old rip, out of pure pity and goodness of heart. Of course old Perkins was afraid to treat her as badly as before, and everything was going on fairly well, till some kind friend sent her an anonymous letter about Williams' goings on in Jamaica. Sebright strongly suspected the master of another regular trading ship, with whom Williams had a difference in Kingston the voyage before last—Sebright said— about a small matter, with long hair—not worth talking about. She said nothing at first, and nearly worried herself into a brain-fever. Then she confessed she had a letter—didn't believe it—but wanted a change, and would like to come for one voyage. Nothing could be said to that.

The worst was, the captain was so knocked over at the idea of his little sins coming to light, that he—Sebright —had the greatest difficulty in preventing him from giving himself away.

"If I hadn't been really fond of her," Sebright concluded, "I would have let everything go by the board. It's too difficult. And mind, the whole of Kingston was on the broad grin all the time we were there—but it's no joke. She's a good woman, and she's jealous. She wants to keep her own. Never had much of her own in this world, poor thing. She can't help herself any more than the skipper can. Luckily, she knows no more of life than a baby. But it's a most cruel set out."

Sebright had exposed the domestic situation on board the *Lion* with a force of insight and sympathy hardly to be expected from his years. No doubt his attachment to the disparate couple counted for not a little. He seemed to feel for them both a sort of exasperated affection; but I have no doubt that in his way he was a remarkable young man with his contrasted bringing up first at the hands of an old maiden lady; afterwards on board ship with Williams, to whom he was indentured at the age of fifteen, when as he casually mentioned—"a scoundrelly attorney in Exeter had run off with most of the old girl's money." Indeed, looking back, they all appear to me uncommon; even to the round-eyed Williams, cowed simply out of respect and

*L

regard for his wife, and as if dazed with fright at the conventional catastrophe of being found out before he could get her safely back to Bristol. As to Mrs. Williams, I must confess that the poor woman's ridiculous and genuine misery, inducing her to undertake the voyage, presented itself to me simply as a blessing, there on the poop. She had been practically good to Seraphina, and her talking to me mattered very little, set against that. . . . And such talk!

It was like listening to an earnest, impassioned, tremulous impertinence. She seemed to start from the assumption that I was capable of every villainy, and devoid of honour and conscience; only one perceived that she used the words from the force of unworldly conviction, and without any real knowledge of their meaning, as a precocious child uses terms borrowed from its pastors and masters.

I was greatly disconcerted at first, but I was never angry. What of it, if, with a sort of sweet absurdity, she talked in great agitation of the depravity of hearts, of the sin of light-mindedness, of the self-deception which leads men astray—a confused but purposeful jumble, in which occasional allusions to the errors of Rome, and to the want of seriousness in the upper classes, put in a last touch of extravagance?

What of it? The time was coming when I should remember the frail, homely, as if starved, woman, and thank heaven for her generous heart, which was gained for us from that moment. Far from being offended, I was drawn to her. There is a beauty in the absolute conscience of the simple; and besides, her distrust was for me, alone. I saw that she erected herself not into a judge, but into a guardian, against the dangers of our youth and our romance. She was disturbed by its origin.

There was so much of the unusual, of the unheard of in its beginning, that she was afraid of the end. I was so inexperienced, she said, and so was the young lady—poor motherless thing—wilful, no doubt—so very taking—like a little child, rather. Had I comprehended all my responsibility? (And here one of the hurried side-allusions to the errors of Rome came in with a reminder, touching the charge of another immortal soul beside my own.) Had I reflected? . . .

It seems to me that this moment was the last of my boyishness. It was as if the contact with her earnestness had matured me with a power greater than the power of dangers, of fear, of tragic events. She wanted to know insistently whether I were sure of myself, whether I had examined my feelings, and had measured my strength, and had asked for guidance. I had done nothing of this. Not till brought face to face with her unanswerable simplicity did I descend within myself. It seemed I had descended so deeply that, for a time, I lost the sound of her voice. And again I heard her.

"There's time yet," she was saying. "Think, young sir (she had addressed me throughout as "young sir.") My husband and I have been talking it over most anxiously. Think well before you commit the young lady for life. You are both so young. It looks as if we had been sent providentially. . . ."

What was she driving at? Did she doubt my love? It was rather horrible; but it was too startling and too extravagant to be met with anger. We looked at each other, and I discovered that she had been, in reality, tremendously excited by this adventure. This was the secret of her audacity. And I was also possessed by excitement. We stood there like two persons meeting in a great wind. Without moving her hands, she clasped and unclasped her fingers, looking up at me with soliciting eyes; and her lips, firmly closed, twitched.

"I am looking for the means of explaining to you how much I love her," I burst out. "And if I found a way, you could not understand. What do you know?— what can you know? . . ."

I said this not in scorn, but in sheer helplessness. I was at a loss before the august magnitude of my feeling, which I saw confronting me like an enormous presence arising from that blue sea. It was no longer a boy-and-girl affair; no longer an adventure; it was an immense and serious happiness, to be paid for by an infinity of sacrifice.

"I am a woman," she said, with a fluttering dignity. "And it is because I know how women suffer from what men say. . . ."

Her face flushed. It flushed to the very bands of her hair. She was rosy all over the eyes and forehead. Rosy and ascetic, with something outraged and inexpressibly sweet in her expression. My great emotion was between us like a mist, through which I beheld strange appearances. It was as if an immaterial spirit had blushed before me. And suddenly I saw tears—tears that glittered exceedingly, falling hard and round, like pellets of glass, out of her faded eyes.

"Mrs. Williams," I cried, "you can't know how I love her. No one in the world can know. When I think of her—and I think of her always—it seems to me that one life is not enough to show my devotion. I love her like something unchangeable and unique—altogether out of the world; because I see the world through her. I would still love her if she had made me miserable and unhappy."

She exclaimed a low "Ah!" and turned her head away for a moment.

"But one cannot express these things," I continued. "There are no words. Words are not meant for that. I love her so that, were I to die this moment, I verily believe my soul, refusing to leave this earth, would remain hovering near her. . . ."

She interrupted me with a sort of indulgent horror. "Sh! sh!" I mustn't talk like that. I really must not—and inconsequently she declared she was quite willing to believe me. Her husband and herself had not slept a wink for thinking of us. The notion of the fat, sleepy Williams, sitting up all night to consider, owlishly, the durability of my love, cooled my excitement. She thought they had been providentially thrown into our way to give us an opportunity of reconsidering our decision. There were still so many difficulties in the way.

I did not see any; her utter incomprehension began to weary me, while she still twined her fingers, wiped her eyes by stealth, as it were, and talked unflinchingly. She could not have made herself clearly understood by Seraphina. Moreover, women were so helpless—so very helpless in such matters. That is why she was speaking to me. She did not doubt my sincerity at the present time—but there was, humanly speaking, a long life before us—and what of afterwards? Was I sure of myself—later on—when all was well?

I cut her short. Seizing both her hands:

"I accept the omen, Mrs. Williams!" I cried. "That's it! When all is well! And all must be well in a very short time, with you and your husband's help, which shall not fail me, I know. I feel as if the worst of our troubles were over already. . . ."

But at that moment I saw Seraphina coming out on deck. She emerged from the companion, bare-headed, and looked about at her new surroundings with that air of imperious and childlike beauty which made her charm. The wind stirred slightly her delicate hair, and I looked at her; I looked at her stilled, as one watches the dawn or listens to a sweet strain of music caught from afar. Suddenly dropping Mrs. Williams' hand, I ran to her. . . .

When I turned round, Williams had joined his wife, and she had slipped her arm under his. Her hand, thin and white, looked like the hand of an invalid on the brawny forearm of that man bursting with health and good condition. By the side of his lustiness, she was almost ethereal—and yet I seemed to see in them something they had in common—something subtle, like the expression of eyes. It *was* the expression of their eyes. They looked at us with commiseration; one of them sweetly, the other with his owlish fixity. As we two, Seraphina and I, approached them together, I heard Williams' thick, sleepy voice asking, "And so he says he won't?" To which his wife, raising her tone with a shade of indignation, answered, "Of course not." No, I was not mistaken. In their dissimilar persons, eyes, faces, there was expressed a common trouble, doubt, and commiseration. This expression seemed to go out to meet us sadly, like a bearer of ill-news. And, as if at the sight of a downcast messenger, I experienced the clear presentiment of some fatal intelligence.

It was conveyed to me late in the afternoon of that same day out of Williams' own thick lips, that seemed as heavy and inert as his voice.

"As far as we can see," he said, "you can't stay in the ship, Kemp. It would do no one any good—not the slightest good. Ask Sebright here."

It was a sort of council of war, to which we had been summoned in the saloon. Mrs. Williams had some sewing in her lap. She listened, her hands motionless, her eyes full of desolation. Seraphina's attitude, leaning her cheek on her hand, reminded me of the time when I had seen her absorbed in watching the green-and-gold lizard in the back room of Ramon's store, with her hair falling about her face like a veil. Castro was not called in till later on. But Sebright was there, leaning his back negligently against the bulkhead behind Williams, and looking down on us seated on both sides of the long table. And there was present, too, in all our minds, the image of the Rio Medio schooner, hull down on our quarter. In all the trials of sailing, we had not been able to shake her off that day.

"I don't want to hide from you, Mr. Kemp," Sebright began, "that it was I who pointed out to the captain that you would be only getting the ship in trouble for nothing. She's an old trader and favourite with shippers; and if we once get to loggerheads with the powers, there's an end of her trading. As to missing Havana this trip, even if you, Mr. Kemp, could give a pot of money, the captain could never show his nose in there again after breaking his charter-party to help steal a young lady. And it isn't as if she were nobody. She's the richest heiress in the island. The biggest people in Spain would have their say in this matter. I suppose they could put the captain in prison or something. Anyway, good-by to the Havana business for good. Why, old Perkins would have a fit. He got over one runaway match. . . . All right, Mrs. Williams, not another word. . . . What I meant to say is that this is nothing else but a love story, and to knock on the head a valuable old-established connection for it. . . . Don't bite your lip, Mr. Kemp. I mean no disrespect to your feelings. Perkins would start up to break things—let alone his heart. I am sure the captain and Mrs. Williams think so, too."

The festive and subdued captain of the *Lion* was

staring straight before him, as if stuffed. Mrs. Williams moved her fingers, compressed her lips, and looked helplessly at all of us in turn. "Besides altering his will," Sebright breathed confidentially at the back of my head. I perceived that this old Perkins, whom I had never seen, and was never to see in the body, whose body no one was ever to see any more (he died suddenly on the echoing staircase, with a flat candlestick in his hand; was already dead at the time, so that Mrs. Williams was actually sitting in the cabin of her very own ship)—I perceived that old Perkins was present at this discussion with all the power of a malignant, bad-tempered spirit. Those two were afraid of him. They had defied him once, it is true—but even that had been done out of fear, as it were.

Dismayed, I spoke quickly to Seraphina. With her head resting on her hand, and her eyes following the aimless tracings of her finger on the table, she said:

"It shall be as God wills it, Juan."

"For Heaven's sake, don't!" said Sebright, coughing behind me. He understood Spanish fairly well. "What I've said is perfectly true. Nevertheless the captain was ready to risk it."

"Yes," ejaculated Williams profoundly, out of almost still lips, and otherwise so motionless all over that the deep sound seemed to have been produced by some person under the table. Mrs. Williams' fingers were clasped on her lap, and her eyes seemed to beg for belief all round our faces.

"But the point is that it would have been no earthly good for you two," continued Sebright. "That's the point I made. If O'Brien knows anything, he knows you are on board this ship. He reckons on it as a dead certainty. Now, it is very evident that we could refuse to give *you* up, Mr. Kemp, and that the admiral (if the flagship's off Havana, as I think she must be by now) would have to back us up. How you would get on afterwards with old Groggy Rowley, I don't know. It isn't likely he has forgotten you tried to wipe the floor with him, if I am to take the captain's yarn as correct."

"A regular hero," Williams testified suddenly, in his concealed, from-under-the-table tone. "He's not afraid of any of them; not he. Ha! ha! Old Topnambo must have. . . ." He glanced at his wife, and bit his tongue—perhaps at the recollection of his unsafe conjugal position—ending in disjointed words, "In his chaise—warrant—separationist—rebel," and all this without moving a limb or a muscle of his face, till, with a low, throaty chuckle, he fluttered a stony sort of wink to my address.

Sebright had paused only long enough for this ebullition to be over. The cool logic of his surmise appalled me. He didn't see why O'Brien or anybody in Havana should want to interfere with me personally. But if I wanted to keep my young lady, it was obvious she must not arrive in Havana on board a ship where they would be sure to look for her the very first thing. It was even worse than it looked, he declared. His firm conviction was that if the *Lion* did not turn up in Havana pretty soon, there would be a Spanish man-of-war sent out to look for her—or else Mr. O'Brien was not the man we took him for. There was lying in harbour a corvette called the *Tornado*, a very likely looking craft. I didn't expect them to fight a corvette. No doubt there would be a fuss made about stopping a British ship on the high seas; but that would be a cold comfort after the lady had been taken away from me. She was a person of so much importance that even our own admiral could be induced—say, by the Captain-General's remonstrances—to sanction such an action. There was no saying what Rowley would do if they only promised to present him with half a dozen pirates to take home for a hanging. Why! that was the very identical thing the flagship was kept dodging off Havana for! And O'Brien knew where to lay his hands on a gross of such birds, for that matter.

"No," concluded Sebright, overwhelming me from behind, as I sat looking, not at the uncertainties of the future, but at the paralyzing hopelessness of the bare to-morrow. "The *Lion* is no place for you, whether she goes into Havana or not. Moreover, into Havana she must go now. There's no help for it. It's the deuce of a situation."

"Very well," I gasped. I tried to be resolute. I felt, suddenly, as if all the air in the cabin had gone up the open skylight. I couldn't remain below another moment; and, muttering something about coming back directly, I jumped up and ran out without looking at any one lest I should give myself away. I ran out on deck for air, but the great blue emptiness of the open staggered me like a blow over the heart. I walked slowly to the side, and, planting both my elbows on the rail, stared abroad defiantly and without a single clear thought in my head. I had a vague feeling that the descent of the sun towards the waters, going on before my eyes with changes of light and cloud, was like some gorgeous and empty ceremonial of immersion belonging to a vast barren faith remote from consolation and hope. And I noticed, also, small things without importance—the hirsute aspect of a sailor; the end of a rope trailing overboard; and Castro, so different from everybody else on board that his appearance seemed to create a profound solitude round him, lounging before the cabin door as if engaged in a deep conspiracy all by himself. I heard voices talking loudly behind me, too.

I noted them distinctly, but with perfect indifference. A long time after, with the same indifference, I looked over my shoulder. Castro had vanished from the quarter-deck. And I turned my face to the sea again as a man, feeling himself beaten in a fight with death, might turn his face to the wall.

I had fought a harder battle with a more cruel foe than death, with the doubt of myself; an endless contest, in which there is no peace of victory or of defeat. The open sea was like a blank and unscalable wall imprisoning the eternal question of conduct. Right or wrong? Generosity or folly? Conscience or only weak fear before remorse? The magnificent ritual of sunset went on palpitating with an inaudible rhythm, with slow and unerring observance, went on to the end, leaving its funeral fires on the sky and a great shadow upon the sea. Twice I had honourably stayed my hand. Twice . . . to this end.

In a moment, I went through all the agonies of suicide, which left me alive, alas, to burn with the shame of the treasonable thought, and terrified by the revolt of my soul refusing to leave the world in which a young girl lived! The vast twilight seemed to take the impress of her image like wax. What did Seraphina think of me? I knew nothing of her but her features, and it was enough. Strange, this power of a woman's face upon a man's heart—this mastery, potent as witchcraft and mysterious like a miracle. I should have to go and tell her. I did not suppose she could have understood all of Sebright's argumentation. Therefore, it was for me to explain to what a pretty pass I had brought our love.

I was so greatly disinclined to stir that I let Sebright's voice go on calling my name half a dozen times from the cabin door. At last I faced about.

"Mr. Kemp! I say, Kemp! Aren't you coming in yet?"

"To say good-by," I said, approaching him.

It had fallen dark already.

"Good-by? No. The carpenter must have a day at least."

Carpenter! What had a carpenter to do in this? However, nothing mattered—as though I had managed to spoil the whole scheme of creation.

"You didn't think of making a start to-night, did you?" Sebright wondered. "Where would be the sense of it?"

"Sense," I answered contemptuously. "There is no sense in anything. There is necessity. Necessity."

He remained silent for a time, peering at me.

"Necessity, to be sure," he said slowly. "And I don't see why you should be angry at it."

I was thinking that it was easy enough for him to keep cool—the necessity being mine. He continued to philosophize with what seemed to me a shocking freedom of mind.

"Must try to put some sense into it. That's what we are here for, I guess. Anyhow, there's some room for sense in arranging the way a thing is to be done, be it as hard as it may. And I don't see any sense, either, in exposing a woman to more hardship than is absolutely necessary. We have talked it out now, and I can do no more. Do go inside for a bit. Mrs. Williams is worrying the señorita, rather, I'm afraid."

I paused a moment to try and regain the command of my faculties. But it was as if a bombshell had exploded inside my skull, scattering all my wits to the four winds of heaven. Only the conviction of failure remained, attended by a profound distress.

I fancy, though, I presented a fairly bold front. The

lamp was lit, and small changes had occurred during my absence. Williams had turned his bulk sideways to the table. Mrs. Williams had risen from her place, and was now sitting upright close to Seraphina, holding one little hand inclosed caressingly between her frail palms, as if she had there something alive that needed cherishing. And in that position she looked up at me with a strange air of worn-out youth, cast by a rosy flush over her forehead and face. Seraphina still leaned her head on her other hand, and I noted, through the soft shadow of falling hair, the heightened colour on her cheek and the augmented brilliance of her eye.

"How I wish she had been an English girl," Mrs. Williams sighed regretfully, and leaned forward to look into Seraphina's half-averted face.

"My dear, did you quite, quite understand what I have been saying to you?"

She waited.

"*Si Señora*," said Seraphina. None of us moved. Then, after a time, turning to me with sudden animation, "This woman asked me if I believed in your love," she cried. "She is old. Oh, Juan, can the years change the heart? your heart?" Her voice dropped. "How am I to know that?" she went on piteously. "I am young—and we may not live so long. I believe in mine. . . ."

The corners of her delicate lips drooped; but she mastered her desire to cry, and steadied her voice which, always rich and full of womanly charm, took on, when she was deeply moved, an imposing gravity of timbre.

"But I am a Spaniard, and I believe in my lover's honour; in your—your English honour, Juan."

With the dignity of a supreme confidence she extended her hand. It was one of the culminating moments of our love. For love is like a journey in mountainous country, up through the clouds, and down into the shadows to an unknown destination. It was a moment rapt and full of feeling, in which we seemed to dwell together high up and alone—till she withdrew her hand from my lips, and I found myself back in the cabin, as if precipitated from a lofty place.

Nobody was looking at us. Mrs. Williams sat with downcast eyelids, with her hands reposing on her lap: her husband gazed discreetly at a gold moulding on the deck-beam; and the upward cast of his eyes invested his red face with an air of singularly imbecile ecstasy. And there was Castro, too, whom I had not seen till then, though I must have brushed against him on entering. He had stood by the door a mute, and, as it were, a voluntarily unmasked conspirator with the black round of the hat lying in front of his feet. He, alone, looked at us. He looked from Seraphina to me—from me to Seraphina. He looked unutterable things, rolling his crow-footed eyes in pious horror and glowering in turns. When Seraphina addressed him, he hastened to incline his head with his usual deference for the daughter of the Riegos.

She said, "There are things that concern this *caballero*, and that you can never understand. Your fidelity is proved. It has sunk deep here. . . . It shall give you a contented old age—on the word of Seraphina Riego."

He looked down at his feet with gloomy submission.

"There is a proverb about an enamoured woman," he muttered to himself, loud enough for me to overhear. Then, stooping deliberately to pick up his hat, he flourished it with a great sweep lower than his knees. His dumpy black back flitted out of the cabin; and almost directly we heard the sharp click of his flint and blade outside the door.

CHAPTER SIX

How often the activity of our life is the least real part of it! Life, looked upon as a whole, presents itself to my fancy as a pursuit with open arms of a winged and magnificent dream, hovering just over our heads and casting its glory upon our hopes. It is in this simple vision, which is one and enduring, and not in the changing facts, that we must look for meaning and for truth. The three quiet days we spent together on board the *Lion* remain to me memorable and full of import, eventless and containing the very quintessence of existence. We shared the sunshine, always together, very close, turning hand in hand to the sea, whose unstained blueness continued under our feet the blue above our heads, as though we had been snatched up into the sky. The insignificant words we exchanged seemed informed by a sustaining certitude and an admirable gravity, as though there had been some quality of unerring wisdom in the blind love of man and woman. From the inexhaustible treasure of her feelings she drew words, glances, gestures that appeased every uneasiness of my heart. In some brief moment of illumination whose advent my man's eyes had utterly missed, she had learned all at once everything there was to know. She knew. She no longer needed to survey my actions, my words, my thoughts; but she accorded me the sincere flattery of spell-bound attention, and it was made intoxicating by her smile. In those short days of a pause, when, like a swimmer turning on his back, we lived in the trustful confidence of the sustaining depths, instead of struggling with the agitation of the surface—in these days we had the time to look at each other profoundly; and I saw her smile come back again a little changed, more meaning and a little less mirthful, as if her lips had been made stiff by sorrow. But she was young; and youth, the time of softness, of tenderness, of enthusiasm, and of pity, presents a surface as hard as marble to the finality of death.

Breathing side by side, drinking in the sunshine, and talking of ourselves not at all, but casting the sense of our love like a magnificent garment over the wide significance of a world already conquered, we could not help being made aware of the currents of excitement and sympathy that converged upon our essential isolation from the life of the ship. It was the excitement of the adventure brewing for our drinking according to Sebright's recipe. People approached us—spoke to us. We attended to them as if called down from an elevation; we were aware of the kind tone; and, remaining indistinct, they retreated, leaving us free to regain the heights of the lovers' paradise—a region of tender whispers and intense silences. Suddenly there would be a short, throaty laugh behind our backs, and Williams would begin, "I say, Kemp; do you call to mind so-and-so?" Invariably some planter or merchant in Jamaica. I never could.

Williams would grunt, "No? I wonder how you passed your time away these two years or more. The place isn't that big." His purpose was to cheer me up by some gossip, if only he could find a common acquaintance to talk over. I believe he thought me a queer fish. He told me once that everybody he knew in Jamaica had that precise opinion of me. Then with a chuckle and muttering, "Warrants—assault—Topnambo—ha, ha!" he would leave us to ourselves, and continue his waddle up and down the poop. He wore loose silk trousers, and the round legs inside moved like a contrivance made out of two gate-posts.

He was absurd. They all were that before our sweet reasonableness. But this atmosphere, full of interest and good will, was good to breathe. The very steward —the same who had been hiding in the lazarette during the fight—a hunted creature, displaying the most insignificant anatomy ever inhabited by a quailing spirit, devoted himself to the manufacture of strange cakes, which at tea-time he would deposit smoking hot in front of Seraphina's place. After each such exploit, he appeared amazed at his audacity in taking so much upon himself. The carpenter took more than a day, tinkering at an old ship's boat. He was a Shetlander— a sort of shaggy hyperborean giant with a forbidding face, an appraising, contemplative manner, and many nails in his mouth. At last the time came when he, too, approached our oblivion from behind, with a large hammer in his hand; but instead of braining us with one sweep of his mighty arm, he remarked simply in uncouth accents, "There now; I am thinking she will do well for what ye want her. I can do no more for ye."

We turned round, arm-in-arm, to look at the boat. There she was, lying careened on the deck, with patched sides, in a belt of chips, shavings, and sawdust; a few pensive sailors stood about, gazing down at her with serious eyes. Sebright, bent double, circled slowly on a prowl of minute inspection. Suddenly straightening himself up, he pronounced a curt "She'll do"; and, without looking at us at all, went off busily with his rapid stride.

A light sigh floated down upon our heads. Williams and his wife appeared on the poop above us like an

allegorical couple of repletion and starvation, conceived in a fantastic vein on a balcony. A cigar
smouldered in his stumpy red fingers. She had slipped
a hand under his arm, as she would always do the moment they came near each other. She never looked
more wasted and old-maidish than when thus affirming
her wifely rights. But her eyes were motherly.

"Ah, my dears!" (She usually addressed Seraphina
as "miss," and myself as "young sir.") "Ah, my dears!
It seems so heartless to be sending you off in such a
small boat, even for your own good."

"Never fear, Mary. Repaired. Carry six comfortably," reassured Williams in a tremendous mutter,
like a bull.

"But why can't you give them one of the others,
Owen? That big one there?"

"Nonsense, Mary. Never see boat again. Wouldn't
grudge it. Only Sebright is quite right. Didn't you
hear what Sebright said? Very sensible. Ask Sebright. He will explain to you again."

It was Sebright, with his asperity and his tact, with
fits of brusqueness subdued by an almost affectionate
contempt, who conducted all their affairs, as I have
seen a trustworthy and experienced old nurse rule the
infinite perplexities of a room full of children. His
clear-sightedness and mental grip seemed independent of age and experience, like the ability of genius.
He had an imaginative eye for detail, and, starting
from a mere hint, would go scheming onwards with
astonishing precision. His plan, to which we were
committed—committed helplessly and without resistance—was based upon the necessity of our leaving
the ship.

He had developed it to me that evening, in the cabin,
directly Castro had gone out. He had already got

Williams and his wife to share his view of our situation. He began by laying it down that in every desperate position there was a loophole for escape. Like other great men, he was conscious of his ability, and was inclined to theorize at large for a while. You had to accept the situation, go with it in a measure; and as you had walked into trouble with your eyes shut, you had only to continue with your eyes open. Time was the only thing that could defeat one. If you had no time, he admitted, you were at a dead wall. In this case he judged there would be time, because O'Brien, warned already, would sit tight for a few days, being sure to get hold of us directly the *Lion* came into port. It was only if the *Lion* failed to turn up within a reasonable term in Havana, that he would take fright, and take measures to hunt her up at sea. But I might rest assured that the *Lion* was going to Havana as fast as the winds would allow her.

What was, then, the situation? he continued, looking at me piercingly above Williams' cropped head. I had run away for dear life from Cuba (taking with me what was best in it, to be sure, he interjected, with a faint smile towards Seraphina). I had no money, no friends (except my friends in this cabin, he was good enough to say); warrants out against me in Jamaica; no means to get to England; no safety in the ship. It was no use shirking that little fact. We must leave the *Lion*. This was a hopeless enough position. But it was hopeless only because it was not looked upon in the right way. We assumed that we had to leave her forever, while the whole secret of the trick was in this, that we need only leave her for a time. After O'Brien's myrmidons had gone through her, and had been hooted away empty-handed, she became again, if not absolutely safe, then at least possible—the only possible refuge for us—the only decent means of reaching England together, where, he understood, our trouble would cease. Williams nodded approval heavily.

"The friends of Miss Riego would be glad to know she had made the passage under the care of a respectable married lady," Sebright explained, in that imperturbable manner of his, which reflected faintly all his inner moods—whether of recklessness, of jocularity or anxiety—and often his underlying scorn. His gravity grew perfectly portentous. "Mrs. Williams," he continued, "was, of course, very anxious to do her part creditably. As it happened, the *Lion* was chartered for London this voyage; and notwithstanding her natural desire to rejoin, as soon as possible, her home and her aged uncle in Bristol, she intended to go with the young lady in a hackney coach to the very door."

I had previously told them that the lately appointed Spanish ambassador in London was a relation of the Riegos, and personally acquainted with Seraphina, who, nearly two years before, had been on a short visit to Spain, and had lived for some months with his family in Madrid, I believe. No trouble or difficulty was to be apprehended as to proper recognition, or in the matter of rights and inheritance, and so on. The ambassador would make that his own affair. And for the rest I trusted the decision of her character and the strength of her affection. I was not afraid she would let any one talk her out of an engagement, the dying wish of her nearest kinsman, sealed, as it were, with the blood of her father. This matter of temporary absence from the *Lion*, however, seemed to present an insuperable difficulty. We could not, obviously, be left for days floating in an open boat outside Havana harbour, waiting till the ship came out to pick us up. Sebright himself admitted that at first he did not see how it could be contrived. He didn't see at all. He thought and thought. It was enough to sicken one of every sort of thinking. Then, suddenly, the few words Castro had let drop about the sugar estate and the relay of mules came into his head—providentially, as Mrs. Williams would say. He fancied that the primitive and grandiose manner for a gentleman to keep a relay of mules—any amount of mules—in case he should want to send a letter or two, caused the circumstance to stick in his mind. At once he had "our little *hidalgo*" in, and put him through an examination.

"He turned fairly sulky, and tried constantly to break out against you, till Doña Seraphina here gave him a good talking to," Sebright said.

Otherwise it was most satisfactory. The place was accessible from the sea through a narrow inlet, opening into a small, perfectly sheltered basin at the back of the sand-dunes. The little river watering the estate emptied itself into that basin. One could land from a boat there, he understood, as if in a dock—and it was the very devil if I and Miss Riego could not lie hidden for a few days on her own property, the more so that, as it came out in the course of the discussion, while I had "rushed out to look at the sunset," that the manager, or whatever they called him—the fellow in charge—was the husband of Doña Seraphina's old nurse-woman. Of course, it behoved us to make as little fuss as possible—try to reach the house along by-paths early in the morning, when all the slaves would be out at work in the fields. Castro, who professed to know the locality very well indeed, would be of use. Meantime, the *Lion* would make her way to Havana, as if nothing was the matter. No doubt all sorts of confounded *alguazils* and custom-house hounds would be ready to swarm on board in full cry. They would be made very welcome. Any strangers on board? Certainly not. Why should there be? . . . Rio Medio? What about Rio Medio? Hadn't been within miles and miles of Rio Medio; tried this trip to beat up well clear of the coast. Search the ship? With pleasure—every nook and cranny. He didn't suppose they would have the cheek to talk of the pirates; but if they did venture—what then? Pirates? That's very serious and dishonourable to the power of Spain. Personally, had seen nothing of pirates. Thought they had all been captured and hanged quite lately. Rumours of the *Lion* having been attacked obviously untrue. Some other ship, perhaps. . . . That was the line to take. If it didn't convince them, it would puzzle them altogether. Of course, Captain Williams, in his great regard for me, had abandoned the intention of making an affair of state of the outrage committed on his ship. He would not lodge any complaint in Havana—nothing at all. The old women of the Admiralty wouldn't be made to sit up this time. No report would be sent to the admiral either. Only, if the ship were interfered with, and bothered under any pretence whatever, once they had been given every facility to have one good look everywhere, the admiral would be asked to stop it. And the Spanish authorities would have not a leg to stand on either, for this simple reason, that they could not very well own to the sources of their information. Meantime, all hands on board the *Lion* had to be taken into confidence; that could not be avoided. He, Sebright, answered for their discretion while sober, anyhow; and he promised me that no leave or money would be given in Havana, for fear they should get on a spree, and let out something in the grog-shops on shore. We all knew what a sailor-man was after a glass or two. So that was settled. Now, as to our rejoining the *Lion*. This, of necessity, must be left to me. Counting from the time we parted from her to land on the coast, the *Lion* would remain in Havana sixteen days; and if we did not turn up in that time, and the cargo was all on board by then, Captain Williams would 'try to remain in harbour on one pretence or another a few days longer. But sixteen days should be ample, and it was even better not to hurry up too much. To arrive on the fifteenth day would be the safest proceeding in a way, but for the cutting of the thing too fine, perhaps. With all these mules at our disposal, Sebright didn't see why we should not make our way by land, pass through the town at night, or in the earliest morning, and go straight on board the *Lion*—perhaps use some sort of disguise. He couldn't say. He was out of it there. Blackened faces or something. Anyway, we would be looked out for on board night and day.

Later on, however, we had learned from Castro that the estate possessed a sailing craft of about twenty tons, which made frequent trips to Havana. These sugar *droghers* belonging to the plantations (every estate on the coast had one or more) went in and out of the harbour without being taken much notice of. Sometimes the battery at the water's edge on the north side or a custom-house guard would hail them, but not often—and even then only to ask the name, where from, and for the number of sugar-hogsheads on board. "By heavens! That's the very thing!" rejoiced Sebright. And it was agreed that this would be our best way. We should time our arrival for early morning, or else at dusk. The craft that brought us in should be made, by a piece of unskillful management, to fall aboard the *Lion*, and remain alongside long enough to give us time to sneak in through an open deck-port.

The whole occurrence must be so contrived as to wear the appearance of a pure accident to the onlookers, should there be any. Shouting and an exchange of abuse on both parts should sound very true. Then the *drogher*, getting herself clear, would proceed innocently to the custom-house steps, where all such coasters had to report themselves on arrival. "Never fear. We shall put in some loud and scandalous cursing," Sebright assured me. "The boys will greatly enjoy that part, I dare say."

Remained to consider the purpose of the schooner that had come out of Rio Medio to hang on our skirts. It was doubtful whether it was in our power to shake her off. Sebright was full of admiration for her sailing qualities, coupled with infinite contempt for the "lubberly gang on board."

"If I had the handling of her, now," he said, "I would take my position as near as I liked, and stick there. It seems almost as if she would do it of herself, if those imbeciles would only let her have her own way. I never yet saw a Spaniard, good or bad, that was anything of a sailor. As it is, we may maintain a distance that would make it difficult for them to see what we are about. And if not, then—why, you must take your leave of us at night."

He didn't know that, but for the dismalness of such a departure, it were not just as well. Who could tell what eyes might be watching on shore.

"You know I never pretended my plan was quite safe. But have you got another?"

I made no answer, because I had no other, and could not think of one. Incredible as it may appear, not only my heart, but my mind, also, in the awakened comprehension of my love, refused to grapple with difficulties. My thoughts raced ahead of ships and pursuing men, into a dream of cloudless felicity without end. And I don't think Sebright expected any suggestion from me. This took place during one of our busy talks—only he and I—alone in his cabin. He had been washing his hands, making ready for tea.

"Do you know," he said, turning full on me, and wiping his fingers carefully with a coarse towel—"do you know, I shouldn't wonder if that schooner were not keeping watch on us, in suspicion of just some such move on our part. 'Tis extraordinary how clever the greatest fool may show himself sometimes. Only, with their lubberly Spanish seamanship, they would expect us, probably, to make a whole ceremony of your landing: ship hove to for hours close in shore, a boat going off to land and returning, and all such pother. 'We are sure to see their little show,' they think to themselves. Eh? What? Whereas we shall keep well clear of the land when the time comes, and drop you in the dark without as much check on our way as there is in the wink of an eye. Hey? . . . Mind, Mr. Kemp, you take the boat out of sight up that little river, in case they should have a fancy, as they go along after us, to peep into that inlet. As I have said, it wouldn't do to trust too much in any fool's folly."

And now the time was approaching; the time to awake and step forth out of the temple of sunshine and love—of whispers and silences. It had come. The night before both Williams and Sebright had been on deck, working the ship with an anxious care to take the utmost advantage of every favouring flaw in the contrary breeze. In the morning I was told there was a norther brewing. A norther is a tempestuous gale. I saw no signs of it. The realm of the sun, like the vanished one of the stars, appeared to my senses to be profoundly asleep, and breathing as gently as a child

M

upon the ship. The *Lion*, too, seemed to lie wrapped in an enchanted slumber from the water-line to the tops of her upright masts. And yet she moved with the breath of the world, but so imperceptibly that it was the coast that seemed to be nearing her like a line of low vapour blown along the water. Between Williams and Sebright Castro pointed with his one arm, and a splutter of guttural syllables fell like hail out of his lips. The other two seemed incredulous. He stamped with both his feet angrily. Finally they went below together, to look at the chart, I suppose. They came up again very fast, one after another, and stood in a row, looking on as before. Three more dissimilar human beings it would have been difficult to imagine.

Dazzling white patches, about the size of a man's hand, came out between sky and water. They grew in width, and ran together with a hummocky outline into a continuous undulation of sand-dunes. Here and there this rampart had a gap like a breach made by guns. Mrs. Williams, behind me, blew her nose faintly; her eyes were red, but she did not look at us. No eye was turned our way, and the spell of the coast was on her, too. A low, dark headland broke out to view through the dunes, and stood there conspicuous amongst the heaps of dazzling sand, like a small man frowning. A voice on deck pronounced:

"That's right. Here's his landmark. The fellow knew very well what he was talking about."

It was Sebright's voice, and Castro, strolling away triumphantly, affected to turn his back on the land. He had recognized the formation of the coast about the inlet long before anybody else could distinguish the details. His word had been doubted. He was offended, and passed us by, wrapping himself up closely. One of Seraphina's locks blew against my cheek, and this last effort of the breeze remained snared in the silken meshes of her hair.

"There's not enough wind to fill the sail of a toy boat," grumbled Sebright; "and you can't pull this heavy gig ashore with only that one-armed man at the other oar." He was sorry he could not send us off with four good rowers. The norther might be coming on before they could return to the ship, and—apart from the presence of four English sailors on the coast being sure to get talked about—there was the difficulty in getting them back on board in Havana. We could, no doubt, smuggle ourselves in; but six people would make too much of a show. On the other hand, the absence of four men out of the ship's company could not be accounted for very well to the authorities. "We can't say they all died, and we threw them overboard. It would be too startling. No; you must go alone, and leave us at the first breath of wind; and that, I fear, 'll be the first of the norther, too."

He threw his head back, and hailed, "Do you see anything of that schooner from aloft there?"

"Nothing of her, sir," answered a man perched, with dangling feet, astride the very end of the topsail yard-arm. He paused, scanned the space from under the flat of his hand, and added, shouting with deliberation, "There's—a—haze—to seaward, sir." The ship, with her decks sprinkled over with men in twos and threes, sent up to his ears a murmur of satisfaction.

If we could not see her, she could not see us. This was a favourable circumstance. To the infinite gratification of everyone on board, it had been discovered at daylight that the schooner had lost touch with us during the hours of darkness—either through unskillful handling, or from some accidental disadvantage of the variable wind. I had been informed of it, directly I showed myself on deck in the morning, by several men who had radiant grins, as if some great piece of luck had befallen them, one and all. They shared their unflagging attention between the land and the sea-horizon, pointing out to each other, with their tattooed arms, the features of the coast, nodding knowingly towards the open. At midday most of them brought out their dinners on deck, and could be seen forward, each with a tin plate in the left hand, gesticulating amicably with clasp knives. A small white handkerchief hung from Mrs. Williams' fingers, and now and then she touched her eyes lightly, one after the other. Her husband and Sebright, with a grave mien, stamped busily around the binnacle aft, changing places, making way for each other, stooping in turns to glance carefully along the compass card at the low bluff, like two gunners laying a piece of heavy ordnance for an important shot. The steward, emerging out of the companion, rang a handbell violently, and remained scared at the failure of that appeal. After waiting for a moment, he produced a further feeble tinkle, and sank down out of sight, with resignation.

A white sun, as if blazing with the pallor of fury, swung past the zenith in a profound and universal stillness. There was not a wrinkle on the sea; it presented a lustrous and glittering level, like the polished facet of a gem. In the cabin we sat down to the meal, not even pretending a desire to eat, exchanging vague phrases, hanging our heads over the empty plates. But the regular footsteps of the boatswain left in charge hesitated, stopped near the skylight. He said in an imperfectly assured voice, "Seems as if there was a steadier draught coming now." At this we rose from the table impetuously, as though he had shouted an alarm of fire, and Mrs. Williams, with a little cry,

ran round to Seraphina. Leaving the two women
locked in a silent embrace, the captain, Sebright and
myself hurried out on deck.

Every man in the ship had done the same. Even
the shiny black cook had come out of his galley, and was
already comfortably seated on the rail, baring his white
teeth to the sunshine.

"Just about enough to blow out a farthing dip," said
Sebright, in a disappointed mutter.

He thought, however, we had better not wait for
more. There would be too much presently. Some
sailors hauled the boat alongside, the rest lined the rail
as for a naval spectacle, and Williams stared blankly.
We were waiting for Seraphina, who appeared, attended
by Mrs. Williams, looking more kind, bloodless, and
ascetic than ever. But my girl's cheeks glowed; her
eyes sparkled audaciously. She had done up her hair
in some way that made it fit her head like a cap. It
became her exceedingly, and the decision of her movements, the white serenity of her brow, dazzled me as if I
had never seen her before. She seemed less childlike,
older, ripe for this adventure in a new development of
strength and courage. She inclined her head slowly
at the gaping sailors, who had taken their caps off.

As soon as she appeared, Castro, who had been leaning against the bulwark, started up, and with a muttered "*Adios, Señores,*" went down the overside ladder
and ensconced himself in the bow of the boat. The
leave-taking was hurried over. Williams gave no sign
of feeling, except, perhaps, for the greater intensity of
his stare, which passed beyond our shoulders in the
very act of handshaking. Sebright helped Seraphina
down into the boat, and ran up again nimbly. Mrs.
Williams, with her slim hand held in both mine, uttered
a few incoherent words—about men's promises and

the happiness of women, as I thought; but, truth to say, my own suppressed excitement was too considerable for close attention. I only knew that I had given her my confidence, that complete and utter confidence which neither wisdom nor power alone, can command. And, suddenly, it occurred to me that the heiress of a splendid name and fortune, down in the boat there, had no better friend in the world than this woman, who had come to us out of the waste of the sea, opening her simple heart to our need, like a pious and naïve hermit in a wilderness throwing open the door of his cell to strange wayfarers.

"Mrs. Williams," I stammered. "If we—if I—there's no saying what may happen to any of us. If she ever comes to you—if she ever is in want of help. . . ."

"Yes, yes. Always, always—like my own daughter."

And the good woman broke down, as if, indeed, I were taking her own daughter away.

"Nonsense, Mary!" Williams advanced, muttering tremendously. "They are not going round the world. Dare say get ashore in time for supper."

He stared through her without expression, as if she had been thin air, but she seized his arm, of course, and he gave me, then, an amazingly rapid wink which, I suppose, meant that I should go. . . .

"All right there?" asked Sebright from above, as soon as I had taken my seat in the stern sheets by the side of Seraphina. He was standing on the poop deck ready with a sign for letting go the end of our painter on deck; but before I could answer in the affirmative, Castro, ensconced forward under his hat, drew his ready blade across the rope, as it were a throat.

At once a narrow strip of water opened between the boat and the ship, and our long-prepared departure, hastened thus by half a second, seemed to strike every-body dumb with surprise, as if we had taken wings to ourselves to fly away. Hastily I grasped the tiller to give the boat a sheer, and heard a sort of loud gasp in the air above. A row of heads, posed on chins all along the rail, stared after us with unanimous fixity. Mrs. Williams averted her face on her husband's shoulder. Behind the couple, Sebright raised his cap gravely.

Our little sail filled to a breeze which was much too feeble to produce a perceptible effect on the ship, and we left behind us her towering form, as one recedes from a tall white spire on a plain. I laid the boat's head straight for the dwarf headland, marking the mouth of the inlet on the interminable range of sand-dunes. We drove on with a smart ripple, but before we felt sufficiently settled to exchange a few words the animated sound languished suddenly, paused altogether, and, with a renewed murmur under our feet, seemed to lose itself below the glassy waters.

CHAPTER SEVEN

THE calm had returned. The sea, changing from the warm glitter of a gem, and attuned to the grays and blacks of space, resembled a monstrous cinder under a sky of ashes.

The sun had disappeared, smothered in these clouds that had formed themselves all at once and everywhere, like some swift corruption of the upper air. For the best part of the afternoon the ship and the boat remained lying at right angles, within half a mile of each other. What light was left in the world, cut off from the source of life, seemed to sicken with a strange decay. The long stretch of sands and the sails of the motionless vessel stood out lividly pale in universal gloom. And yet the state of the atmosphere was such that we could see clear-cut the very folds in the steep face of the dunes, and the figures of the people moving on the poop of the *Lion*. There was always somebody there that had the aspect of watching us. Then, with some excitement, we saw them on board haul up the mainsail and lower the gig.

The four oars beat the sombre water, rising and falling apparently in the same place. She was an interminable time coming on, but as she neared us I was surprised at her dashing speed. Sebright, who steered, laid her alongside smartly, and two of his men, clambering over without a word, lowered our lug at once.

"We came to reef your sail for you. You couldn't manage that very well with a one-armed crew," said the young mate quietly in the enormous stillness. In his opinion, we couldn't expect now any wind till the first squall came down. This flurry, as he called it, would send us in smoking, and he was sure it would help the ship, as well, into Havana, in about twenty-four hours. He didn't think that it would come *very* heavy at first; and, once landed, we need not care how hard it blew.

He tendered me over the gunwale a pocket-flask covered with leather, and with a screwed silver stopper in the shape of a cup. It was from the captain; full of prime rum. We were pretty sure to get wet. He thrust, also, into my hands a gray woollen shawl. Mrs. Williams thought my young lady might be glad of it at night. "The dear old woman has shut herself up inside their stateroom, and is praying for you now," he concluded. "Look alive, boys."

His men did not answer him, but at some words he addressed to Castro, the latter, in the bows and looking at the coast, growled with a surly impatience. He was perfectly sure of the entrance. Had been in and out several times. Yes. At night, too. Sebright then turned to me. After all, it was not so difficult. The inlet bore due south from us, and the wind would come true from the north. Always did in these bursts. I had only to keep dead before it. "The clouds will light you in at the last," he added meaningly, glancing upwards.

The two sailors, having finished reefing, hoisted, lowered, and hoisted again the yard to see that the gear ran clear, and without one look at us, stepped back into the gig, and sat down in their places. For a moment longer we lay together, touching sides. Sebright extended his hand from boat to boat.

"You are in God's care now, Kemp," he said, looking up at me, and with an unexpected depth of feeling in his

*M

tone. "Take no turn with the sheet on any account, and if you feel it coming too heavy, let fly and chance it. Did I tell you we have sighted the schooner from aloft? No? We can just make her out from the main-yard away astern under the land. That don't matter now. . . . Señorita, I kiss your hands." He liked to air his Spanish. . . . "Keep cool whatever happens. Dead before it—mind. And count on sixteen days from to-morrow. Well. No more. Give way, boys."

He never looked back. We watched the boat being hoisted and secured. Shortly afterwards, as we were observing the *Lion* shortening sail, the first of the rain descended between her and us like a lowered veil. For a time she remained mistily visible, dark and gaunt with her bared spars. The downpour redoubled; she disappeared; and our hearts were stirred to a faster beat.

The shower fell on us, around us, descending perpendicularly, with a steady force; and the thunder rolled far off, as if coming from under the sea. Sometimes the muffled rumbling stopped, and let us hear plainly the gentle hiss and the patter of the drops falling upon a vast expanse. Suddenly, mingled with a loud detonation right over our heads, a burst of light outlined under the bellying strip of our sail the pointed crown of Castro's hat, reposing on a heap of black clothing huddled in the bows. The darkness swallowed it all. I swung Seraphina in front of me, and made her sit low on the stern sheets beneath my feet. A lot of foam boiled up around the boat, and we had the sensation of having been sent flying from a catapult.

Everything was black—perfectly black. At intervals, headlong gusts of rain swept over our heads. I suppose I did keep sufficiently cool, but in every flash of lightning the wind, the sea, the clouds, the rain, and the boat appeared to rush together thundering upon the coast. The line of sands, bordered with a belt of foam, zigzagged dazzlingly upon an earth as black as the clouds; only the headland, with every vision, remained sombre and unmoved. At last it rose up right before the boat. Blue lightning streamed on a lane of tumbling waters at its foot. Was this the entrance? With the vague notion of shortening sail, I let the sheet go from my hand. There was a jerk, the crack of snapped wood, and the next flash showed me Castro emerging from the ruins of mast and sail. He uprose, hurling the wreck from him overboard, then flickered out of sight with his arm waving to the left, and I bore accordingly on the tiller. In a moment I saw him again, erect forward, with the arm pointing to the right, and I obeyed his signal. The clouds, straining with water and fire, were, indeed, lighting us on our way. A wave swelled astern, chasing us in; rocking frightfully, we glanced past a stationary mass of foam—a sandbar—breakers. . . . It was terrible. . . . Suddenly, the motion of the boat changed, and the flickers of lightning fell into a small, land-locked basin. The wind tore deep furrows in it, howling and scuffling behind the dunes. Spray flew from the whole surface, the entire pool of a bay seemed to heave bodily upwards, and I saw Castro again, with his face to me this time. His black cloak was blowing straight out from his throat, his mouth yawned wide; he shouted directions, but in an instant darkness sealed my eyes with its impenetrable impress. It was impossible to steer now; the boat swung and reeled where she listed; a violent shock threw me sideways off my seat. I felt her turning over, and, gathering Seraphina in my arms, I leaped out before she capsized. I leaped clear out into shallow water.

I should never in my life have thought myself capable of such a feat, and yet I did it with assurance, with no effort that I can remember. More than that—I managed, after the leap, to keep my feet in the clinging, staggering clutch of water charged with sand, which swirled heavily about my knees. It kept on hurling itself at my legs from behind, while I waded across the narrow strip of sand with an inspired firmness of step defying all the power of the elements. I felt the harder ground at last, but not before I had caught a momentary glimpse of a black and bulky object tumbling over and over in the advancing and withdrawing liquid flurry of the beach.

"Sit still here on the ground," I shouted to Seraphina, though flights of spray enveloped us completely. "I am going back for Castro."

I faced about, putting my head down. He had been undoubtedly knocked over; and an old man, with only one hand to help himself with, ran a very serious risk of being buffeted into insensibility, and thus coming to his death in some four feet of water. The violent glare disclosed a body, entangled in a cloak, rolling about helplessly between land and water, as it were. I dashed on in the dark; a wave went over my head as I stooped, nearly waist-deep, groping. His rotary motion, in that smother, made it extremely difficult to obtain any sort of hold. A little more, and he would have knocked my legs from under me, but it was as if my grim determination were by itself of a saving nature. He submitted to being hauled up the beach, passively, like a sack. It was a heavy drag on the sand; I felt him bump behind me on the edge of the harder ground, and a deluge fell uninterruptedly from above. He lay prone on his face, like a corpse, between Seraphina and myself. We could not remain there, however.

But where to go? What to do? In what direction to look for a refuge? Was there any shelter near by? How were we to reach it? How were we to move at all? No doubt he had expired; and the earth, swept, deluged, glimmering fiercely and devastated with an awful uproar, appeared no longer habitable. A thunder-clap seemed to crash new life into him; the world flared all round, as if turning to a spark, and he was seen sitting up dazedly, like one called up from the dead. Through it all he had preserved his hat.

It was fixed firmly down under his chin with a handkerchief, the side rims over his ears like flaps, and, for the rest, presenting the appearance of a coal-scuttle bonnet behind, as well as in front. We followed its peculiar aspect. Driving on under this indestructible headgear, he flickered in and out of the world, while, with entwined arms and leaning back against the wind with all our might, Seraphina and myself were borne along in his train. He knew of a shelter; and this knowledge, perhaps, and also his evident familiarity with the topography of the country, made him appear indomitably confident in the storm.

A small plain of coarse grass was bounded by the steep spur of a rise. To the left a little river would burst, all at once, in all its windings into a bluish sulphurous glow; and between the crashes of thunder there was heard the long-drawn, whistling swish of the rushes and cane-brakes springing on the boggy ground. We skirted the rise. The rain beat against it; the lightning showed its streaming and furrowed surface. We stumbled in the gusts. We felt under our feet, mud, sand, rocky inequalities of the ground, and the moving stones in the bed of a torrent, which broke headlong against our ankles. The entrance of a deep ravine opened.

Its lower sides palpitated with the ceaseless tossing

of dwarf trees and bushes; and, motionless above the sombre tumult of the slopes, the monumental stretch of bare rock rose on high, level at the top, and emitting a ghastly yellow sheen in the flashes. The thunderclaps rolled ponderously between the narrowing walls of that chasm, that was all aflame one moment, and all black the next. A torrent springing at its head, and dashing with inaudible fury along the bottom, seemed to gleam placidly amongst the rounded forms of inky bushes and pale boulders below our path. Enormous eddies of wind from above made us stop short and totter breathless, clinging to each other.

Castro sustained Seraphina on the other side; but frequently he had to leave us and move ahead, looking for the way. There was, in fact, a half-obliterated path winding along the less steep of the two sides; and we struggled after our guide with the unthinking fortitude of despair. He was being disclosed to us so suddenly, extinguished so swiftly, that he appeared, always, as if motionless and posturing in a variety of climbing attitudes. The rise of the bottom was very steep, and the last hundred yards really stiff. We did them practically on our hands and knees. The dislodged stones bounded away from under our feet, unheard, like puff-balls.

At the top I tried to make of my body a shelter for Seraphina. The wind howled and roared over us.

"Up! *Vamos!* The worst is yet before us," shrieked Castro in my ear.

What could he mean by this? The play of lightning opened to view only a vast and rolling upland. Fire flowed in sheets undulating with the expanses of long grass amongst the trees, here and there, in coal-black clumps, and flashed violently against a low edge of forests very dark and far away.

"Let us go!" he cried. "Courage, Señorita!"

Courage! The populace said of her that she had never needed to put her foot to the ground. If courage consists, for a being so tender, in toiling and enduring without faltering and plaint,—even to the very limit of physical power,—then she was the most courageous woman in the world, as she was the most charming, most faithful, most generous, and the most worthy of love. I tried not to think of her racked limbs, for the very pain and pity of it. We retraced our steps, but now following the edge of that precipice out of which we had emerged. I had peremptorily insisted on carrying her. She put her arms round my neck and, to my uplifted heart, she weighed no heavier than a feather. Castro, grasping my arm, guided my steps and gave me support against the wind.

There was a distinct lull. Even the thunder had rolled away, dwindling to a deep mutter. Castro fell on his knees in front of me.

"It is here," I heard him scream.

I set Seraphina down. A hooked dart of fire tore in two the thick canopy of clouds. I started back from the edge.

"What! Here?" I yelled.

"Señor—*Si!* There is a cavern below. . . ."

I had seen a ledge clinging to the face of the rock.

It was a cornice inclining downwards upon the wall of the precipice, as you see, sometimes, a flight of stairs built against the outside wall of a house. And it resembled a stair roughly, with long, sloping steps, wet with rain.

"*Por Dios*, Señor, do not let us stay to think here, or we shall perish in this tempest."

He howled, gesticulated, shrieked with all the strength of his lungs. He knew these tornadoes. Brute beasts would be found lying dead in the fields in the morning. This was the beginning only. The lightning showed his kneeling form, the eager upturned face, and a finger pointing urgently into the abyss. The wind was nothing! Nothing to what would come after. As he shrieked these words I was feeling the crust of the earth vibrate, absolutely vibrate, under the soles of my feet, with the sound of thunder.

He unfastened his cloak, and was seen to struggle above his head with the hovering and flapping cloth, as though he had captured a black and pugnacious bird. We mastered at last a corner each, and then we started to twist the whole, as if to wring the water out. We produced, thus, a sort of short rope, the thickness of a cable, and the descent began.

"Do not look behind you. Do not look," Castro screeched.

The first downward steps were terrible, but as soon as our heads had sunk below the level of the plain it was better, for we had turned about to the rock, moving sideways, cautiously, one step at a time, as if inspecting its fractured roughness for traces of a mysterious inscription. Castro, with one end of the twisted cloak in his hand, went first; I held the other; and between us, Seraphina, the rope at her back, imitated our movements, with her loosened hair flying high in the wind, and her pale, rigid head as if deaf to the crashes. I saw the drawn stillness of her face, her dilated eyes staring within three inches of the strata. The strain of our prudence was tremendous. The knowledge of the precipice behind must have affected me. Explain it as you will, several times during that descent I felt my brain slip away from my control, and suggest a desire to fling myself over backwards. The twigs of the bushes, growing a little below the outer edge of the path, swished at my calves.

Castro stopped. The cornice ended as a broken stairway hangs upon nothing. A tall, narrow arch stood back in the rock, with a sill three feet high at least. Castro clambered over; his head and torso, when he turned about, were lighted up blindingly between the inner walls at every flash. Seeing me lay hold of Seraphina, he yelled:

"Señor, mind! It's death if you stagger back."

I lifted her up, and put her over like a child; and, no sooner in myself, felt my strength leave all my limbs as water runs out of an overturned vessel. I could not have lifted up a child's doll then. Directly, with a wild little laugh, she said to me:

"Juan—I shall never dare come out."

I hugged her silently to my breast.

Castro went ahead. It was a narrow passage; our elbows touched the sides all the way. He struck at his flint regularly, sparks streamed down from his hand; we felt a freshness, a sense of space, as though we had come into another world. His voice directed us to turn to the left, then cried in the dark, "Stand still." A blue gleam darted after us, and retired without having done anything against the tenebrous body of gloom, and the thunder rolled far in, unobstructed, in leisurely, organ-like peals, as if through an amazingly vast emptiness of a temple. But where was Castro? We heard snappings, rustlings, mutters; sparks streamed, now here, now there. We dared not move. There might have been steep ridges—deep holes in that cavern. And suddenly we discovered him on all-fours, puffing out his cheeks above a small flame kindled in a heap of dry sticks and leaves.

It was an abode of darkness, enormous, without sonority. Feeble currents of air, passing on our faces, gave us a feeling of being in the open air on a

night more black than any known night had been before. One's voice lost itself in there without resonance,
as if on a plain; the smoke of our blaze drove aslant,
scintillating with red sparks, and went trailing afar,
as if under the clouds of a starless sky. Ultimately,
it must have escaped through some imperceptible
crevices in the roof of rock. In one place, only, the
light of the fire illuminated a small part of the rugged
wall, where the shadows of our bodies would surge up,
repeating our movements, and suddenly be gone from
our side. Everywhere else, pressing upon the reflection
of the flames, the blind darkness of the vault might
have extended away for miles and miles.

Castro thought it probable. He made me observe
the incline of the floor. It sloped down deep and far.
For miles, no doubt. Nobody could tell; no one had
seen the end of it. This cavern had been known of
old. This brushwood, these dead leaves, that would
make a couch for her Excellency, had been stored for
years—perhaps by men who had died long ago. Look
at the dry rot. These large piles of branches were
found stacked up when he first beheld this place. *Caramba!* What toil! What fatigue! Let us thank the
saints, however.

Nevertheless, he shook his head at the strangeness
of it. His cloak, spread out wide, was drying in the
light, while he busied himself with his hat, turning
it before the blaze in both hands, tenderly; and his
tight little figure, lit up in front from head to foot,
steamed from every limb. His round, plump shoulders
and gray shock head smoked quietly at the top. Suddenly, the fine mesh of wrinkles on his face ran together,
shrinking like a torn cobweb; a spasmodic sound, quite
new to me, was heard. He had laughed.

The warmth of the fire had penetrated our chilled

bodies with a feeling of comfort and repose. Williams' flask was empty; and this was a new Castro, mellowed, discoursive, almost genial. It was obvious to me that, had it not been for him, we two, lost and wandering in the storm, should have died from exposure and exhaustion—from some accident, perhaps. On the other hand I had indubitably saved his life, and he had already thanked me in high-flown language; very grave, but exaggerating the horrors of his danger, as a woman might have done for the better expression of gratitude. He had been greatly shocked. Spaniards, as a race, have never, for all their conquests, been on intimate terms with the sea. As individuals I have often observed in them, especially in the lower classes, a sort of dread, a dislike of salt water, mingled with contempt and fear.

Castro, lifting up his right arm, protested that I had given a proof of very noble devotion in rushing back for an old man into that black water. Ough! He shuddered. He had given himself up—*por Dios!* He hinted that, at his age, he could not have cared much for life; but then, drowning in the sea was a death abhorrent to an old Christian. You died brutally—without absolution, and unable, even, to think of your sins. He had had his mouth filled with horrid, bitter sand, too. Tfui! He gave me a thousand thanks. But these English were wonderful in their way. . . . Ah! *Caramba!* They were. . . .

A large protuberance of the rocky floor had been roughly chipped into the semblance of a seat, God only knows by what hands and in what forgotten age. Seraphina's inclined pose, her torn dress, the wet tresses lying over her shoulders, her homeless aspect, made me think of a beautiful and miserable gypsy girl drying her hair before a fire. A little foot advanced, gleamed white on the instep in front of the ruddy glare; her clasped fingers nursed one raised knee; and, shivering no longer, her head drooping in still profile, she listened to us, frowning thoughtfully upon the flames.

In the guise of a beggar-maid, and fair, like a fugitive princess of romance, she sat concealed in the very heart of her dominions. This cavern belonged to her, as Castro remarked, and the bay of the sea, and the earth above our heads, the rolling upland, herds of cattle, fields of sugar-cane—even as far as the forest away there; the forest itself, too. And there were on that estate, alone, over two hundred Africans, he was able to tell us. He boasted of the wealth of the Riegos. Her Excellency, probably, did not know such details. Two hundred—certainly. The estate of Don Vincente Salazar was on the other side of the river. Don Vincente was at present suffering the indignity of a prison for a small matter of a quarrel with another *caballero*—who had died lately—and all, he understood, through the intrigues of the prior of a certain convent; the uncle, they said, of the dead *caballero*. Bah! There was something to get. These fat friars were like the lean wolves of Russia—hungry for everything they could see. Never enough, *Cuerpo de Dios!* Never enough! Like their good friend who helped them in their iniquities, the Juez O'Brien, who had been getting rich for years on the sublime generosity of her Excellency's blessed father. In the greatness of his nobility, Don Balthasar of holy memory had every right to be obstinate. . . . *Basta!* He would speak no more; only there is a saying in Castile that fools and obstinate people make lawyers rich. . . .

"*Vuestra Señoria,*" he cried, checking himself, slapping his breast penitently, "deign to forgive me. I have been greatly exalted by the familiarity of the two last men of your house—allowed to speak freely because of my fidelity. . . . Alas! Alas!"

Seraphina, on the other side of the fire, made a vague gesture, and took her chin in her hand without looking at him.

"Patience," he mumbled to himself very audibly. "He is rich, this picaro, O'Brien. But there is, also, a proverb—that no riches shall avail in the day of vengeance."

Noticing that we had begun to whisper together, he threw himself before the fire, and was silent.

"Promise me one thing, Juan," murmured Seraphina. I was kneeling by the side of her seat.

"By all that's holy," I cried, "I shall force him to come out and fight fair—and kill him as an English gentleman may."

"Not that! Not that!" she interrupted me. She did not mean me to do that. It was what she feared. It would be delivering myself into that man's hands. Did I think what that meant? It would be delivering her, too, into that man's power. She would not survive it. And if I desired her to live on, I must keep out of O'Brien's clutches.

"In my thoughts I have bound my life to yours, Juan, so fast that the stroke which cuts yours, cuts mine, too. No death can separate us."

"No," I said.

And she took my head in her hands, and looked into my eyes.

"No more mourning," she whispered rapidly. "No more. I am too young to have a lover's grave in my life—and too proud to submit. . . ."

"Never," I protested ardently. "That couldn't be."

"Therefore look to it, Juan, that you do not sacrifice your life which is mine, either to your love—or—or—to revenge." She bowed her head; the falling hair concealed her face. "For it would be in vain."

"The cloak is perfectly dry now, Señorita," said Castro, reclining on his elbow on the edge of the darkness.

We two stepped out towards the entrance, leaving her on her knees, in silent prayer, with her hands clasped on her forehead, and leaning against the rugged wall of rock. Outside, the earth, enveloped in fire and uproar, seemed to have been given over to the fury of a devil.

Yes. She was right. O'Brien was a formidable and deadly enemy. I wished ourselves on board the *Lion* chaperoned by Mrs. Williams, and in the middle of the Atlantic. Nothing could make us really safe from his hatred but the vastness of the ocean. Meantime we had a shelter, for that night, at least, in this cavern that seemed big enough to contain, in its black gloom of a burial vault, all the dust and passions and hates of a nation. . . .

Afterwards Castro and I sat murmuring by the diminished fire. He had much to say about the history of this cave. There was a tradition that the ancient buccaneers had held their revels in it. The stone on which the señorita had been sitting was supposed to have been the throne of their chief. A ferocious band they were, without the fear of God or devil—mostly English. The Rio Medio picaroons had used this cavern, occasionally, up to a year or so ago. But there were always ugly affairs with the people on the estate—the *vaqueros*. In his younger days Don Balthasar, having whole leagues of grass land here, had introduced a herd of cattle; then, as the Africans are useless for that work, he had ordered some peons from Mexico to be brought over with their families—igno-

rant men, who hardly knew how to make the sign of the
cross. The quarrels had been about the cattle, which
the *Lugareños* killed for meat. The peons rode over
them, and there were many wounds on both sides.
Then, the last time a Rio Medio schooner was lying
here (after looting a ship outside), there was some gambling going on (they played round this very stone),
and Manuel—(*Si, Señor,* this same Manuel the singer—
Bestia !)—in a dispute over the stakes, killed a peon,
striking him unexpectedly with a knife in the throat.
No vengeance was taken for this, because the *Lugareños* sailed away at once; but the widow made a great
noise, and some rumours came to the ears of Don
Balthasar himself—for he, Castro, had been honoured
with a mission to visit the estate. That was even the
first occasion of Manuel's hate for him—Castro.
And, as usual, the Intendente after all settled the matter
as he liked, and nothing was done to Manuel. Don
Balthasar was old, and, besides, too great a noble to be
troubled with the doings of such vermin. . . . And
Castro began to yawn.

At daybreak—he explained—he would start for the
hacienda early, and return with mules for Seraphina
and myself. The buildings of the estate were nearly
three leagues away. All this tract of the country on
the side of the sea was very deserted, the sugar-cane
fields worked by the slaves lying inland, beyond the
habitations. Here, near the coast, there were only the
herds of cattle ranging the *savannas* and the peons
looking after them, but even they sometimes did not
come in sight of the sea for weeks together. He had no
fear of being seen by anybody on his journey; we, also,
could start without fear in daylight, as soon as he
brought the mules. For the rest, he would make proper
arrangements for secrecy with the husband of Sera-

phina's nurse—Enrico, he called him: a silent Galician; a graybeard worthy of confidence.

One of his first cares had been to grub out of his soaked clothes a handful of tobacco, and now he turned over the little drying heap critically. He hunted up a fragment of maize leaf somewhere upon his bosom. His face brightened. "*Bueno*," he muttered, very pleased.

"Señor—good-night," he said, more humanized than I had supposed possible; or was it only that I was getting to know him better? "And thanks. There's that in life which even an old tired man. . . . Here I, Castro . . . old and sad, Señor. Yes, Señor—nothing of mine in all the world—and yet. . . . But what a death! Ouch! the brute water . . . *Caramba!* Altogether improper for a man who has escaped from a great many battles and the winter of Russia. . . . The snow, Señor. . . ."

He drowsed, garrulous, with the blackened end of his cigarette hanging from his lower lip, swayed sideways—and let himself go over gently, pillowing his head on the stump of his arm. The thin, viperish blade, stuck upwards from under his temple, gleamed red before the sinking fire.

I raised a handful of flaring twigs to look at Seraphina. A terrible night raged over the land; the inner arch of the opening growled, winking bluishly time after time, and, like an enchanted princess enveloped in a beggar's cloak, she was lying profoundly asleep in the heart of her dominions.

CHAPTER EIGHT

THE first thing I noted, on opening my eyes, was that Castro had gone already; I was annoyed. He might have called me. However, we had arranged everything the evening before. The broad day, penetrating through the passage, diffused a semicircle of twilight over the flooring. It extended as far as the emplacement of the fire, black and cold now with a gray heap of ashes in the middle. Farther away in the darkness, beyond the reach of light, Seraphina on her bed of leaves did not stir. But what was that hat doing there? Castro's hat. It asserted its existence more than it ever did on the head of its master; black and rusty, like a battered cone of iron, reposing on a wide flange near the ashes. Then he was not gone. He would not start to walk three leagues, bare-headed. He would appear presently; and I waited, vexed at the loss of time. But he did not appear. "Castro," I cried in an undertone. The leaves rustled; Seraphina sat up.

We were pleased to be with each other in an inexpugnable retreat, to hear our voices untinged by anxiety; and, going to the outer end of the short passage, we breathed with joy the pure air. The tops of the bushes below glittered with drops of rain, the sky was clear, and the sun, to us invisible, struck full upon the face of the rock on the other side of the ravine. A great bird soared, all was light and silence, and we forgot Castro for a time. I threw my legs over the sill, and sitting on the stone surveyed the cornice. The bright day robbed the ravine of half its horrors. The

path was rather broad, if there was a frightful sheer
drop of ninety feet at least. Two men could have
walked abreast on that ledge, and with a hand-rail one
would have thought nothing of it. The most dangerous part yet was at the entrance, where it ended in a
rounded projection not quite so wide as the rest. I
bantered Seraphina as to going out. She said she was
ready. She would shut her eyes, and take hold of my
hand. Englishmen, she had heard, were good at climbing. Their heads were steady. Then we became
silent. There were no signs of Castro. Where could
he have gone? What could he be doing? It was un-
imaginable.

I grew nervous with anxiety at last, and begged
Seraphina to go in. She obeyed without a word, and I
remained just within the entrance, watching. I had
no means to tell the time, but it seemed to me that an
hour or two passed. Hadn't we better, I thought,
start at once on foot for the *hacienda?* I did not know
the way, but by descending the ravine again to the sea,
and walking along the bank of the little river, I was sure
to reach it. The objection to this was that we should
miss Castro. Hang Castro! And yet there was
something mysterious and threatening in his absence.
Could he—could he have stepped out for some reason
in the dark, perhaps, and tumbled off the cornice?
I had seen no traces of a slip—there would be none
on the rock; the twigs of the growth below the edge
would spring back, of course. But why should he
fall? The footing was good—however, a sudden attack
of vertigo. . . . I tried to look at it from every
side. He was not a somnambulist, as far as I knew.
And there was nothing to eat—I felt hungry already—
or drink. The want of water would drive us out very
soon to the spring bubbling out at the head of the

ravine, a mile in the open. Then why not go at once, drink, and return to our lair as quickly as possible.

But I did not like to think of her going up and down the cornice. I remembered that we had a flask, and went in hastily to look for it. First, I looked near the hat; then, Seraphina and I, bent double with our eyes on the ground, examined every square inch of twilight; we even wandered a long way into the darkness, feeling about with our hands. It was useless! I called out to her, and then we desisted, and coming together, wondered what might have become of the thing. He had taken it—that was clear.

But if, as one might suppose, he had taken it away to get some water for us, he ought to have been back long before. I was beginning to feel rather alarmed, and I tried to consider what we had better do. It was necessary to learn, first, what had become of him. Staring out of the opening, in my perplexity, I saw, on the other side of the ravine, the lower part of a man from his waist to his feet.

By crouching down at once, I brought his head into view. This was not Castro. He wore a black sombrero, and on his shoulder carried a gun. He turned his back on the ravine, and began to walk straight away, sinking from my sight till only his hat and shoulders remained visible. He lifted his arm then—straight up—evidently as a signal, and waited. Presently another head and shoulders joined him, and they glided across my line of sight together. But I had recognized their bandit-like aspect with infinite consternation. *Lugareños!*

I caught Seraphina's hand. My first thought was that we should have to steal out of the cavern with the first coming of darkness. Castro must be lying low in hiding somewhere above. The thing was plain. We must try to make our way to the *hacienda* under the cover of the night, unseen by those two men. Evidently they were emissaries sent from Rio Medio to watch this part of the coast against our possible landing. I was to be hunted down, it seems: and I reproached myself bitterly with the hardships I was bringing upon her continually. Thinking of the fatigues she had undergone—(I did not think of dangers—that was another thing—the romance of dying together like all the lovers in the tradition of the world)—I shook with rage and exasperation. The firm pressure of her hands calmed me. She was content. But what if they took it into their heads to come into the cavern?

The emptiness of the blue sky above the sheer yellow rock opposite was frightful. It was a mere strip, stretched like a luminous bandage over our eyes. They were, perhaps, even now on their way round the head of the ravine. I had no weapon except the butt of my pistol. The charges had been spoilt by the salt water, of course, and I had been tempted to fling it out of my belt, but for the thought of obtaining some powder somewhere. And those men I had seen were armed. At once we abandoned the neighbourhood of the entrance, plunging straight away into the profound obscurity of the cave. The rocky ground under our feet had a gentle slope, then dipped so sharply as to surprise us; and the entrance, diminishing at our backs, shone at last no larger than the entrance of a mousehole. We made a few steps more, gropingly. The bead of light disappeared altogether when we sat down, and we remained there hand-in-hand and silent, like two frightened children placed at the centre of the earth. There was not a sound, not a gleam. Seraphina bore the crushing strain of this perfect and black stillness in an almost heroic immobility; but, as to me, it seemed to lie upon my limbs, to embarrass my breathing like a numbness full of dread; and to shake that feeling off I jumped up repeatedly to look at that luminous bead, that point of light no bigger than a pearl in the infinity of darkness. And once, just as I was looking, it shut and opened at me slowly, like the deliberate drooping and rising of the lid upon a white eyeball.

Somebody had come in.

We watched side by side. Only one. Would he go out? The point of light, like a white star setting in a coal-black firmament, remained uneclipsed. Whoever had entered was in no haste to leave. Moreover, we had no means of telling what another obscuring of the light might mean; a departure or another arrival. There were two men about, as we knew; and it was even possible that they had entered together in one wink of the light, treading close upon each other's heels. We both felt the sudden great desire to know for certain. But, especially, we needed to find out if perchance this was not Castro who had returned. We could not afford to lose his assistance. And should he conclude we were out—should he risk himself outside again, in order to find us and be discovered himself, and thus lost to us when we felt him so necessary? And the doubt came. If this man was Castro, why didn't he penetrate further, and shout our names? He ought to have been intelligent enough to guess. . . . And it was this doubt that, making suspense intolerable, put us in motion.

We circled widely in that subterranean darkness, which, unlike the darkest night on the surface of the earth, had no suggestion of shape, no horizon, and seemed to have no more limit than the darkness of infinite space. On this floor of solid rock we moved with noiseless steps, like a pair of timid phantoms. The spot of light grew in size, developed a shape—stretching from a pearly bead to a silvery thread; and, approaching from the side, we scanned from afar the circumscribed region of twilight about the opening. There was a man in it. We contemplated for a time his rounded back, his drooping head. It was gray. The man was Castro. He sat rocking himself sorrowfully over the ashes. He was mourning for us. We were touched by this silent faithfulness of grief.

He started when I put my hand on his shoulder, looked up, then, instead of giving any signs of joy, dropped his head again.

"You managed to avoid them, Castro?" I said.

"Señor, behold. Here I am. I, Castro."

His tone was gloomy, and after sitting still for a while under our gaze, he slapped his forehead violently. He was in his tantrums, I judged, and, as usual, angry with me—the cause of every misfortune. He was upset and annoyed beyond reason, as I thought, by this new difficulty. It meant delay—a certain measure of that sort of danger of which we had thought ourselves free for a time—night travelling for Seraphina. But I had an idea to save her this. We did not all want to go. Castro could start, alone, for the *hacienda* after dark, and bring, besides the mules, half a dozen peons with him for an escort. There was nothing really to get so upset about. The danger would have been if he had let himself be caught. But he had not. As to his temper, I knew my man; he had been amiable too long. But by this time we were so sure of his truculent devotion that Seraphina spoke gently to him, saying how anxious we had been—how glad we were to see him safe with us. . . .

He would not be conciliated easily, it seemed, and let

out only a blood-curdling dismal groan. Without looking at her, he tried hastily to make a cigarette. He was very clever at it generally, rolling it with one hand on his knee somehow; but this time all his limbs seemed to shake, he lost several pinches of tobacco, dropped the piece of maize leaf. Seraphina, stooping over his shoulder, took it up, twisted the thing swiftly.

"Take, *amigo*," she said.

He was looking up at her, as if struck dumb, rolling his eye wildly. He jumped up.

"You—Señorita! For a miserable old man! You break my heart."

And with long strides he disappeared in the darkness, leaving us wondering.

We sat side by side on the couch of leaves. With Castro there I felt we were quite equal to dealing with the two *Lugareños* if they had the unlucky idea of intruding upon us. Indeed, a vigilant man, posted on one side of the end of the passage, could have disputed the entrance against ten, twenty, almost any number, as long as he kept his strength and had something heavy enough to knock them over. Faint sounds reached me, as if at a great distance Castro had been shouting to himself. I called to him. He did not answer, but unexpectedly his short person showed itself in the brightest part of the light.

"Señor!" he called out with a strange intonation.

I got up and went to him. He seemed to be listening intently with his ear turned to the opening. Then suddenly:

"Look at me, Señor. Am I Castro—the same Castro? old and friendless?"

He stood biting his forefinger and looking up at me from under his knitted eyebrows. I didn't know what to say. What was this nonsense?

He ejaculated a sort of incomprehensible babble, and, passing by me, rushed towards Seraphina; she sat up, startled, on her couch of leaves. Falling before her on his plump knees, he seized her hand, pressed it against his ragged moustache.

"Excellency, forgive me! No—no forgiveness! Ha! old man! Ha—thou old man. . . ."

He bowed before her shadowy figure, that sustained the pale oval of the face, till his forehead struck the rock. Plunging his hand into the ashes, he poured a fistful with inarticulate low cries over his gray hairs; and the agitation of that obese little body on its knees had a lamentable and grotesque inconsequence, as inexplicable in itself as the sorrow of a madman. Full of wonder before his abject collapse, she murmured:

"What have you done?"

He tried to fling himself upon her feet, but my hand was in his collar, and after an unmerciful shaking, I sat him down by main force. He gulped, blinked the whites of his eyes, then, in a whisper full of rage:

"Horror, shame, misery, and malediction; I have betrayed you."

At once she said soothingly, "Tomas. I do not believe this"; while I thought to myself: How? Why? For what reason? In what manner betrayed? How was it possible? And, if so, why did he come back to us? But, as things stood, he would never dare approach a *Lugareño*. If he had, they would never have let him go again.

"You told them we were here?" I asked, so perfectly incredulous that I was not at all surprised to hear him protest, by all the saints, that he never did—never would do. Never. Never. . . . But why should he? Was he the prey of some strange hallucination? Rocking himself, he struck his breast with his clenched hand, then suddenly caught at his hair and remained perfectly motionless. Minutes passed; this despairing stillness inspired in me a feeling of awe at last—the awe of something inconceivable. My head buzzed so with the effort to think that I had the illusions of faint murmurs in the cave, the very shadows of murmurs. And all at once a real voice—his voice—burst out fearfully rapid and voluble.

He had really gone out to get a provision of water. Waking up early, he saw us sleeping, and felt a great pity for the señorita. As to the *caballero*—his saviour from drowning, alas!—the señorita would need every ounce of his strength. He would let us sleep till his return from the spring; and, there being a blessed freshness in the air, he caught up the flask and started bare-headed. The sun had just risen. Would to God he had never seen it! After plunging his face in the running water, he remained on his knees and busied himself in rinsing and filling the flask. The torrent, gushing with force, made a loud noise, and after he had done screwing the top on, he was about to rise, when, glancing about carelessly, he saw two men leaning on their *escopetas* and looking at him in perfect silence. They were standing right over him; he knew them well; one they called El Rubio; the other, the little one, was José—squinting José. They said nothing; nothing at all. With a sudden and mighty effort he preserved his self-command, affected unconcern and, instead of getting up, only shifted his pose to a sitting position, took off his shoes and stockings, and proceeded to bathe his feet. But it was as if a blazing fire had been kindled in his breast, and a tornado had been blowing in his head.

He could not tell whence these two had come, with what object, or how much they knew. They might

N

have been only messengers from Rio Medio to Havana. They generally went in couples. If Manuel had escaped alive out of the sea, everything was known in Rio Medio. From where he sat he beheld the empty, open sea over the dunes, but the edge of the upland, cleft by many ravines (of which the one we had ascended was the deepest), concealed from him the little basin and the inlet. He was certain these men had not come up that way. They had approached him over the plain. But there was more than one way by which the upland could be reached from below. The thoughts rushed round and round his head. He remembered that our boat must be floating or lying stranded in the little bay, and resolved, in case of necessity, to say that we two were dead, that we had been drowned.

It was El Rubio who put the very question to him, in an insolent tone, and sitting on the ground out of his reach, with his gun across his knees. His long knife ready in his hand, squinting José remained standing over Castro. Those two men nodded to each other significantly at the intelligence. He perceived that they were more than half disposed to credit his story. They had nearly been drowned themselves pursuing that accursed heretic of an Englishman. When, from their remarks, he learned that the schooner was in the bay, he began putting on his shoes, though the hope of making a sudden dash for his life down the ravine abandoned him.

The schooner had been run in at night during the gale, and in such distress that they let her take the ground. She was not injured, however, and some of them were preparing to haul her off. Our boat, as I conceived, after bumping along the beach, had drifted within the influence of the current created by the little river, or else by the water forced into the basin by the tempest, seeking to escape, and had been carried out towards the inlet. She was seen at daylight, knocking about amongst the breakers, bottom up, and in such shallow water that three or four men wading out knee-deep managed to turn her over. They had found Mrs. Williams' woollen shawl and my cap floating underneath. At the same time the broken mast and sail were made out, tossing upon the waves, not very far off to seaward. That the boat had been in the bay at all did not seem to have occurred to them. It had been concluded that she had capsized outside the entrance. It was very possible that we had been drowned under her. Castro hastened to confirm the idea by relating how he had been clinging to the bottom of the boat for a long time. Thus he had saved himself, he declared.

"Manuel will be glad," observed El Rubio then, with an evil laugh. And for a long time nobody said a word.

El Rubio, cross-legged, was observing him with the eyes of a basilisk, but Castro swore a great oath that, as to himself, he showed no signs of fear. He looked at the water gushing from the rock, bubbling up, sparkling, running away in a succession of tiny leaps and falls. Why should he fear? Was he not old, and tired, and without any hope of peace on earth? What was death? Nothing. It was absolutely nothing. It comes to all. It was rest after much vain trouble—and he trusted that, through his devotion to the Mother of God, his sins would be forgiven after a short time in purgatory. But, as he had made up his mind not to fall into Manuel's hands, he resolved that presently he would stab himself to the heart, where he sat—over this running water. For it would not be like a suicide. He was doomed, and surely God did not want his body to be tormented by such a devil as Manuel before death.

He would lean far over before he struck his faithful blade into his breast, so as to fall with his face in the water. It looked deliciously cool, and the sun was heavy on his bare head. Suddenly, El Rubio sprang to his feet, saying:

"Now, José."

It is clear that these ruffians stood in awe of his blade. In their cowardly hearts they did not think it quite safe (being only two to one) to try and disarm that old man. They backed away a step or two, and, levelling their pieces, suddenly ordered him to get up and walk before. He threw at them an obscene word. He thought to himself, "*Bueno!* They will blow my head off my shoulders." No emotion stirred in him, as if his blood had already ceased to run in his veins. They remained, all three, in a state of suspended animation, but at last El Rubio hissed through his teeth with vexation, and grunted:

"Attention, José. Take aim. We will break his legs and take away the sting of this old scorpion."

Castro's blood felt chilly in his limbs, but instead of planting his knife in his breast, he spoke up to ask them where, supposing he consented, they wished to conduct him.

"To Manuel—our captain. He would like to embrace you before you die," said El Rubio, advancing a stride nearer, his gun to his shoulder. "Get up! March!"

And Castro found himself on his feet, looking straight into the black holes of the barrels.

"Walk!" they exclaimed together, stepping upon him. The time had come to die.

"Ha! *Canalla!*" he said.

They made a menacing clamour, "Walk *viejo*, traitor; walk."

"Señorita—I walked." The heartrending effort of the voice, the trembling of this gray head, the sobs under the words, oppressed our breast with dismay and dread. Ardently he would have us believe that at this juncture he was thinking of us only—of us wondering, alone, ignorant of danger, and hidden blindly under the earth. His purpose was to provoke the two *Lugareños* to shoot, so that we should be warned by the reports. Besides, an opportunity for escape might yet present itself in some most unlikely way, perhaps at the very last moment. Had he not his own life in his own hands? He cared not for it. It was in his power to end it at any time. And there would be dense thickets on the way; long grass where one could plunge suddenly—who knows! And overgrown ravines where one could hide—creep under the bushes—escape—and return with help. . . . But when he faced the plains its greatness crushed his poor strength. The uncovered vastness imprisoned him as effectually as a wall. He knew himself for what he was: an old man, short of breath, heavy of foot; nevertheless he walked on hastily, his eyes on the ground. The footsteps of his captors sounded behind him, and he tried to edge towards the ravine. When nearly above the opening of the cavern he would, he thought, swerve inland, and dash off as fast as he was able. Then they would have to fire at him; we would be sure to hear the shots, the warning would be clear . . . and suddenly, looking up, he saw that a small band of *Lugareños*, having just ascended the brow of the upland, were coming to meet him. Now was the time to get shot; he turned sharply, and began to run over that great plain towards a distant clump of trees.

Nobody fired at him. He heard only the mingled jeers and shouts of the two men behind, "Quicker,

Castro; quicker!" They followed him, holding their sides. Those ahead had already spread themselves out over the plain, yelling to each other, and were converging upon him. That was the time to stop, and with one blow fall dead at their feet. He doubled round in front of Manuel, who stood waving his arms and screeching orders, and ran back towards the ravine. The plain rang with furious shouts. They rushed at him from every side. He would throw himself over. It was a race for the precipice. He won it.

I suppose he found it not so easy to die, to part with the warmth of sunshine, the taste of food; to break that material servitude to life, contemptible as a vice, that binds us about like a chain on the limbs of hopeless slaves. He showered blows upon his chest, sitting before us, he battered with his fist at the side of his head till I caught his arm. We could always sell our lives dearly, I said. He would have to defend the entrance with me. We two could hold it till it was blocked with their corpses.

He jumped up with a derisive shriek; a cloud of ashes flew from under his stumble, and he vanished in the darkness with mad gesticulations.

"Their corpses—their corpses—their . . . Ha! ha! ha!"

The snarling sound died away; and I understood, then, what meant this illusion of ghostly murmurs that once or twice had seemed to tremble in the narrow region of gray light around the arch. The sunshine of the earth, and the voices of men, expired on the threshold of the eternal obscurity and stillness in which we were imprisoned, as if in a grave with inexorable death standing between us and the free spaces of the world.

CHAPTER NINE

FOR it meant that. Imprisoned! Castro's derisive shriek meant that. And I had known it before. He emerged back out of the black depths, with livid, swollen features, and foam about his mouth, to splutter:

"Their corpses, you say. . . . Ha! Our corpses," and retreated again, where I could only hear incoherent mutters.

Seraphina clutched my arm. "Juan—together—no separation."

I had known it, even as I spoke of selling our lives dearly. They could only be surrendered. Surrendered miserably to these wretches, or to the everlasting darkness in which Castro muttered his despair. I needed not to hear this ominous and sinister sound— nor yet Seraphina's cry. She understood, too. They would never come down unless to look upon us when we were dead. I need not have gone to the entrance of the cave to understand all the horror of our fate. The *Lugareños* had already lighted a fire. Very near the brink, too.

It was burning some thirty feet above my head; and the sheer wall on the other side caught up and sent across into my face the crackling of dry branches, the loud excited talking, the arguments, the oaths, the laughter; now and then a very shriek of joy. Manuel was giving orders. Some advanced the opinion that the cursed *Inglez*, the spy who came from Jamaica to see whom he could get for a hanging without a priest, was down there, too. So that was it! O'Brien knew

how to stir their hate. I should get a short shrift.
"He was a fiend, the *Inglez:* look how many of us he has
killed!" they cried; and Manuel would have loved to
cut my flesh, in small pieces, off my bones—only, alas!
I was now beyond his vengeance, he feared. However,
somebody was left.

He must have thrown himself flat, with his head over
the brink, for his yell of "Castro!" exploded, and
rolled heavily between the rocks.

"Castro! Castro! Castro!" he shouted twenty
times, till he set the whole ravine in an uproar. He
waited, and when the clamour had quieted down amongst
the bushes below, called out softly, "Do you hear me,
Castro, my victim? Thou art my victim, Castro."

Castro had crept into the passage after me. He
pushed his head beyond my shoulder.

"I defy thee, Manuel," he screamed.

A hubbub arose. "He's there! He is there!"

"Bravo, Castro," Manuel shouted from above. "I
love thee because thou art my victim. I shall sing
a song for thee. Come up. Hey! Castro! Castro!
Come up. . . . No? Then the dead to their grave,
and the living to their feast."

Sometimes a little earth, detached from the layer of
soil covering the rock, would fall streaming from
above. The men told off to guard the cornice walked
to and fro near the edge, and the confused murmur of
voices hung subdued in the air of the cleft, like a
modulated tremor. Castro, moaning gently, stumbled
back into the cave.

Seraphina had remained sitting on the stone seat.
The twilight rested on her knees, on her face, on the
heap of cold ashes at her feet. But Castro, who had
stood stock-still, with a hand to his forehead, turned
to me excitedly:

"The peons, *por Dios!*" Had I ever thought of the peons belonging to the *estancia?*

Well, that was a hope. I did not know exactly how matters stood between them and the *Lugareños*. There was no love lost. A fight was likely; but, even if no actual collision took place, they would be sure to visit the camp above in no very friendly spirit; a chance might offer to make our position known to these men, who had no reason to hate either me or Castro—and would not be afraid of thwarting the miserable band of ghouls sitting above our grave. How our presence could be made known I was not sure. Perhaps simply by shouting with all our might from the mouth of the cave. We could offer rewards—say who we were, summon them for the service of their own señorita. But, probably, they had never heard of her. No matter. The news would soon reach the *hacienda*, and Enrico had two hundred slaves at his back. One of us must always remain at the mouth of the cave listening to what went on above. There would be the trampling of horses' hoofs—quarrelling, no doubt—anyway, much talk—new voices—something to inform us. Only, how soon would they come? They were not likely to be riding where there were no cattle. Had Castro seen any signs of a herd on the uplands near by?

His face fell. He had not. There were many *savannas* within the belt of forests, and the herds might be miles away, stampeded inland by the storm. Sitting down suddenly, as if overcome, he averted his eyes and began to scratch the rock between his legs with the point of his blade.

We were all silent. How long could we wait? How long could people live? . . . I looked at Seraphina. How long could she live? . . . The thought

*N

seared my heart like a hot iron. I wrung my hands
stealthily.

"Ha! my blade!" muttered Castro. "My sting. . . .
Old scorpion! They did not take my sting away. . . .
Only—bah!"

He, a man, had not risen to the fortitude of a venomous creature. He was defeated. He groaned profoundly. Life was too much. It clung to one. A
scorpion—an insect—within a ring of flames, would
lift its sting and stab venom into its own head. And
he—Castro—a man—a man, *por Dios*—had less
firmness than a creeping thing. Why—why, did he
not stab this dishonoured old heart?

"Señorita," he cried agonizingly, "I swear I did shout
to them to fire—so—into my breast—and then . . ."

Seraphina leaned over him pityingly.

"Enough, Castro. One lives because of hope. And
grieve not. Thy death would have done no good."

Her face had a splendid pallor, the radiant whiteness
and majesty of marble; it had never before appeared to
me more beautiful: and her hair unrolling its dark un-
dulations, as if tinged deep with the funereal gloom
of the background, covered her magnificently right
down to her elbows. Her eyes were incredibly profound. Her person had taken on an indefinable beauty,
a new beauty, that, like the comeliness that comes
from joy, love, or success, seemed to rise from the
depths of her being, as if an unsuspected and sombre
quality of her soul had responded to the horror of our
situation. The fierce trials had gradually developed
her, as burning sunshine opens the bud of a flower; and I
beheld her now in the plenitude of her nature. From
time to time Castro would raise up to her his blinking
old eyes, full of timidity and distress.

He had not been young enough to throw himself

over—he had worn the chain for too many years, had lived well and softly too long, was too old a slave. And yet—if he had had the courage of the act! Who knows? I rejected the thought far from me. It returned, and I caught myself looking at him with irritated eyes. But this first day passed not intolerably. We ignored our sufferings. Indeed, I felt none for my part. We had kept our thoughts bound to the slow blank minutes. And if we exchanged a few words now and then, it was to speak of patience, of resolution to endure and to hope.

At night, from the hot ravine full of shadows, came the cool fretting of the stream. The big blaze they kept up above crackled distinctly, throwing a fiery, restless stain on the face of the rock in front of the cave, high up under the darkness and the stars of the sky— and a pair of feet would appear stamping, the shadow of a pair of ankles and feet, fantastic, sustaining no gigantic body, but enormous, tramping slowly, resembling two coffins leaping to a slow measure. I see them in my dreams now, sometimes. They disappeared.

Manuel would sing; far in the night the monotonous staccato of the guitar went on, accompanying plaintive murmurs, outbursts of anger and cries of pain, the tremulous moans of sorrow. My nerves vibrated, I broke my nails on the rock, and seemed to hear once more the parody of all the transports and of every anguish, even to death—a tragic and ignoble rendering of life. He was a true artist, powerful and scorned, admired with derision, obeyed with jeers. It was a song of mourning; he sat on the brink with his feet dangling over the precipice that sent him back his inspired tones with a confused noise of sobs and desolation. . . . His idol had been snatched from the humility of his adoring silence, like a falling star from the sight of the worm that crawls. . . . He stormed on the strings; and his voice emerged like the crying of a castaway in the tumult of the gale. He apostrophized his instrument. . . . Woe! Woe! No more songs. He would break it. Its work was done. He would dash it against the rock. . . . His palm slapped the hollow wood furiously. . . . So that it should lie shattered and mute like his own heart!

A frenzied explosion of yells, jests, and applause covered the finale.

A complete silence would follow, as if in the acclamations they had exhausted at once every bestial sound. Somebody would cough pitifully for a long time—and when he had done spluttering and cursing, the world outside appeared lost in an even more profound stillness. The red stain of the fire wavered across to play under the dark brow of the rock. The irritated murmur of the torrent, tearing along below, returned timidly at first, expanded, filled the ravine, ran through my ears in an angry babble. The deadened footfalls on the brink sometimes dislodged a pebble: it would start with a feeble rattle and be heard no more.

In the daytime, too, there were silences up there, perfect, profound. No prowl of feet disturbed them; the sun blazed between the rocks, and even the hum of insects could be heard. It seemed impossible not to believe that they had all died by a miracle, or else had been driven away by a silent panic. But two or more were always on the watch, directly above, with their heads over the edge; and suddenly they would begin to talk together in drowsy tones. It was as if some barbarous somnambulists had mumbled in the daytime the bizarre atrocity of their thoughts.

They discussed Williams' flask, which had been

picked up. Was the cup made of silver, they wondered. Manuel had appropriated it for his own use, it seems. Well—he was the *capataz*. The *Inglez*, should he appear by an impossible chance, was to be shot down at once; but Castro must be allowed to give himself up. And they would snigger ferociously. Sometimes quarrels arose, very noisy, a great hubbub of bickerings touching their jealousies, their fears, their unspeakable hopes of murder and rapine. They did not feel very safe where they were. Some would maintain that Castro could not have saved himself, alone. The *Inglez* was there, and even the señorita herself . . . Manuel scouted the idea with contempt. He advanced the violence of the storm, the fury of the waves, the broken mast, the position of the boat. How could they expect a woman! . . . . No. It was as his song had it. And he defended his point of view angrily, as though he could not bear being robbed of that source of poetical inspiration. He emitted profound sighs and superb declamations.

Castro and I listened to them at the mouth of the cave. Our tongues were dry and swollen in our mouths, there was the pressure of an iron clutch on our windpipes, fire in our throats, and the pangs of hunger that tore at us like iron pincers. But we could hear that the bandits above were anxious to be gone; they had but very few charges for their guns, and it was apparent that they were afraid of a collision with the peons of the *hacienda*. Glaring at each other with bloodshot, uncertain eyes, Castro and I imagined longingly a vision of men in *ponchos* spurring madly out of the woods, bent low, and swinging *riatas* over the necks of their horses—with the thunder of the galloping hoofs in the cave. Seraphina had withdrawn further into the darkness. And, with a shrinking fear, I would join her, to eat my heart out by the side of her tense and mute contemplation.

Sometimes Manuel would begin again, "Castro! Castro! Castro!" till he seemed to stagger the rocks and disturb the placid sunshine with an immense wave of sound. He called upon his victim to drink once more before he died. Long shrieks of derision rent the air, as if torn out of his breast by far greater torments than any his fancy delighted to invent. There was something terrible and weird in the abundance of words screeched continuously, without end, as if in desperation. No wonder Castro fled from the passage. And Seraphina and I, within, would be startled out of our half-delirious state by the sudden appearance of that old man, disordered, sordid, with a white beard sprouting, who wandered, weeping aloud in the twilight.

More than once I would stagger off far away into the depths of the cavern in an access of rage, fling myself on the floor, bite my arms, beat my head on the rock. I would give myself up. She must be saved from this tortured death. She had said she would throw herself over if I left her. But would she have the strength? It was impossible to know. For days it seemed she had been lying perfectly still, on her side, one hand under her wan cheek, and only answering "Juan" when I pronounced her name. There was something awful in our dry whispers. They were lifeless, like the tones of the dead, if the dead ever speak to each other across the earth separating the graves. The moral suffering, joined to the physical torture of hunger and thirst, annihilated my will in a measure, but also kindled a vague, gnawing feeling of hostility against her. She asked too much of me. It was too much. And I would drag myself back to sit for hours, and with an aching heart look towards her couch from a distance.

My eyes, accustomed to obscurity, traced an indistinct and recumbent form. Her forehead was white; her hair merged into the darkness which was gathering slowly upon her eyes, her cheeks, her throat. She was perfectly still. It was cruel, it was odious, it was intolerable to be so still. This must end. I would carry her out by main force. She said no word, but there was in the embrace of those arms instantly thrown around my neck, in the feel of those dry lips pressed upon mine, in the emaciated face, in the big shining eyes of that being as light as a feather, a passionate mournfulness of seduction, a tenacious clinging to the appointed fate, that suddenly overawed my movement of rage. I laid her down again, and covered my face with my hands. She called out to Castro. He reeled, as if drunk, and waited at the head of her couch, with his chin dropped on his breast.

"*Vuestra, Señoria*," he muttered.

"Listen well, Castro." Her voice was very faint, and each word came alone, as if shrunk and parched. "Can my gold—the promise of much gold—you know these men—save the lives . . . ?"

He uttered a choked cry, and began to tremble, groping for her hand.

"*Si, Señorita*. Excellency, *si*. It would. Mercy. Save me. I am too old to bear this. Gold, yes; much gold. Manuel. . . ."

"Listen, Castro. . . . And Don Juan?"

His head fell again.

"Speak the truth, Castro."

He struggled with himself; then, rattling in his throat, shrieked "No!" with a terrible effort. "No. Nothing can save thy English lover."

"Why?" she breathed feebly.

He raged at her in his weakness. Why? Because

the order had gone forth; because they dared not disobey. Because she had only gold in the palm of her hand, while Señor O'Brien held all their lives in his. The accursed *Juez* was for them like death itself that walks amongst men, taking this one, leaving another.

He was their life, and their law, and their safety, and their death—and the *caballero* had not killed him. . . .

His voice seemed to wither and dry up gradually in his throat. He crawled away, and we heard him chuckling horribly somewhere, like a madman. Seraphina stretched out her hand.

"Then, Juan—why not together—like this?"

If she had the courage of this death, I must have even more. It was a point of honour. I had no wish, and no right, to seek for some easier way out of life. But she had a woman's capacity for passive endurance, a serenity of mind in this martyrdom confessing to something sinister in the power of love that, like faith, can move mountains and order cruel sacrifices. She could have walked out in perfect safety—and it was that thought that maddened me. And there was no sleep; there were only intervals in which I could fall into a delirious reverie of still lakes, of vast sheets of water. I waded into them up to my lips. Never further. They were smooth and cold as ice; I stood in them shivering and straining for a draught, burning within with the fire of thirst, while a phantom all pale, and with its hair streaming, called to me "Courage" from the brink in Seraphina's voice. As to Castro, he was going mad. He was simply going mad, as people go mad for want of food and drink. And yet he seemed to keep his strength. He was never still. It was a factitious strength, the restlessness of incipient insanity. Once, while I was trying to talk with him about our only hope—the peons—he gave me a look of such sombre distraction that I left off, intimidated, to wonder vaguely at this glimpse of something hidden and excessive springing from torments which surely could be no greater than mine.

He had the strength, and sometimes he could find the voice, to hurl abuse, curses, and imprecations from the mouth of the cave. Great shouts of laughter exploded above, and they seemed to hold their breath to hear more; or Manuel, hanging over, would praise in mocking, mellifluous accents the energy of his denunciations. I tried to pull him away from there, but he turned upon me fiercely; and from prudence—for all hope was not dead in me yet—I left him alone.

That night I heard him make an extraordinary sound chewing; at the same time he was sobbing and cursing stealthily. He had found something to eat, then! I could not believe my ears, but I began to creep towards the sound, and suddenly there was a short, mad scuffle in the darkness, during which I nearly spitted myself on his blade. At last, trembling in every limb, with my blood beating furiously in my ears, I scrambled to my feet, holding a small piece of meat in my hands. Instantly, without hesitating, without thinking, I plunged my teeth into it only to fling it far away from me with a frantic execration. This was the first sound uttered since we had grappled. Lying prone near me, Castro, with a rattle in his throat, tried to laugh.

This was a supreme touch of Manuel's art; they were pressed for time, and he had hit upon that deep and politic invention to hasten the surrender of his beloved victim. I nearly cried with the fiery pain on my cracked lips. That piece of half-putrid flesh was salt—horribly salt—salt like salt itself. Whenever they heard him rave and mutter at the mouth of the cave, they would throw down these prepared scraps. It was as if I had put a live coal into my mouth.

"Ha!" he croaked feebly. "Have you thrown it away? I, too; the first piece. No matter. I can no more swallow anything, now."

His voice was like the rustling of parchment at my feet.

"Do not look for it, Don Juan. The sinners in hell. . . . Ha! Fiend. I could not resist."

I sank down by his side. He seemed to be writhing on the floor muttering, "Thirst—thirst—thirst." His blade clicked on the rock; then all was still. Was he dead? Suddenly he began with an amazingly animated utterance.

"Señor! For this they had to kill cattle."

This thought had kept him up. Probably, they had been firing shots. But there was a way of hamstringing a stalked cow silently; and the plains were vast, the grass on them was long; the carcasses would lie hidden out of sight; the herds were rounded up only twice every year. His despairing voice died out in a mournful fall, and again he was as still as death.

"No! I can bear this no longer," he uttered with force. He refused to bear it. He suffered too much. There was no hope. He would overwhelm them with maledictions, and then leap down from the ledge. "*Adios, Señor.*"

I stretched out my arm and caught him by the leg. It seemed to me I could not part with him. It would have been disloyal, an admission that all was over, the beginning of the end. We were exhausting ourselves by this sort of imbecile wrestling. Meantime, I kept on entreating him to be a man; and at last I managed to clamber upon his chest. "A man!" he sighed. I released him. For a space, unheard in the dark-

ness, he seemed to be collecting all his remaining
strength.

"Oh, those strange *Inglez!* Why should I not leap?
and whom do you love best or hate more, me or the
señorita? Be thou a man, also, and pray God to give
thee reason to understand men for once in thy life.
Ha! Enamoured woman—he is a fool! But I, Castro. . . ."

His whispering became appallingly unintelligible,
then ceased, passing into a moan. My will to restrain
him abandoned me. He had brought this on us. And
if he really wished to give up the struggle. . . .

"Señor," he mumbled brokenly, "a thousand thanks.
Br-r-r! Oh, the ugly water—water—water—water—
salt water—salt! You saved me. Why? Let God
be the Judge. I would have preferred a malignant
demon for a friend. I forgive you. *Adios!* And—
her excellency—poor Castro. . . . Ha! Thou old
scorpion, encircled by fire—by fire and thirst. No.
No scorpion, alas! Only a man—not like you—therefore—a Mass—or two—perhaps. . . ."

The freshness of the night penetrated through the
arch, as far as the faint twilight of the day. I heard his
tearful muttering creep away from my side. "Thirst—
thirst—thirst." I did not stir; and an incredulity, a
weariness, the sense of our common fate, mingled with
an unconfessed desire—the desire of seeing what would
come of it—a desire that stirred my blood like a glimmer
of hope, and prevented me from making a movement or
uttering a whisper. If his sufferings were so great, who
was I to . . . Mine, too. I almost envied him.
He was free.

As if an inward obscurity had parted in two I looked
to the very bottom of my thoughts. And his action
appeared like a sacrifice. It could liberate us two from

this cave before it was too late. He, he alone, was the
prey they had trapped. They would be satisfied,
probably. Nay! There could be no doubt. Directly
he was dead they would depart. Ah! he wanted to
leap. He must not be allowed. Now that I understood perfectly what this meant, I had to prevent him.
There was no choice. I must stop him at any cost.

The awakening of my conscience sent me to my feet;
but before I had stumbled halfway through the passage
I heard his shout in the open air, "Behold me!"

A man outside cried excitedly, "He is out!"

An exulting tumult fell into the arch, the clash of
twenty voices yelling in different keys, "He is out—the
traitor! He is out!" I was too late, but I made three
more hesitating steps and stood blinded. The flaming
branches they were holding over the precipice showered
a multitude of sparks, that fell disappearing continuously in the lurid light, shutting out the night from
the mouth of the cave. And in this light Castro could
be seen kneeling on the other side of the sill.

With his fingers clutching the edge of the slab, he
hung outwards, his head falling back, his spine arched
tensely, like a bow; and the red sparks coming from
above with the dancing whirl of snowflakes, vanished in
the air before they could settle on his face.

"Manuel! Manuel!"

They answered with a deep, confused growl, jostling
and crowding on the edge to look down into his eyes.
Meantime I stared at the convulsive heaving of his
breast, at his upturned chin, his swelling throat. He
defied Manuel. He would leap. Behold! he was
going to leap—to his own death—in his own time. He
challenged them to come down on the ledge; and the
blade of the maimed arm waved to and fro stiffly,
point up, like a red-hot weapon in the light. He de-

voted them to pestilence, to English gallows, to the infernal powers: while all the time commenting murmurs passed over his head, as though he had extorted their sinister appreciation.

"*Canalla!* dogs, thieves, prey of death, vermin of hell—I spit on you—like this!"

He had not the force, nor the saliva, and remained straining mutely upwards while they laughed at him all together, with something sombre, and as if doomed in their derision. . . . "He will jump! No, he will not!" "Yes! Leap, Castro! Spit, Castro!" "He will run back into the cave! *Maladetta!*" . . . Manuel's voiced cooed lovingly on the brink:

"Come to us and drink, Castro."

I waited for his leap with doubt, with disbelief, in the helpless agitation of the weak. Gradually he seemed to relax all over.

"Drink deep; drink, and drink, and drink, Castro. Water. Clear water, cool water. Taste, Castro!"

He called on him in tones that were almost tender in their urgency, to come and drink before he died. His voice seemed to cast a spell, like an incantation, upon the tubby little figure, with something yearning in the upward turn of the listening face.

"Drink!" Manuel repeated the word several times; then, suddenly he called, "Taste, Castro, taste," and a descending brightness, as of a crystal rod hurled from above, shivered to nothing on the upturned face. The light disappearing from before the cave seemed scared away by the inhuman discord of his shriek; and I flung myself forward to lick the splash of moisture on the sill. I did not think of Castro, I had forgotten him. I raged at the deception of my thirst, exploring with my tongue the rough surface of the stone till I tasted my own blood. Only then, raising my head to gasp, and clench my fists with a baffled and exasperated desire, I noticed how profound was the silence, in which the words, "Take away his sting," seemed to pronounce themselves over the ravine in the impersonal austerity of the rock, and with the tone of a tremendous decree.

CHAPTER TEN

HE HAD surrendered to his thirst. What weakness! He had not thrown himself over, then. What folly! One splash of water on his face had been enough. He was contemptible; and lying collapsed, in a sort of tormented apathy, at the mouth of the cave, I despised and envied his good fortune. It could not save him from death, but at least he drank. I understood this when I heard his voice, a voice altogether altered—a firm, greedy voice saying, "More," breathlessly. And then he drank again. He was drinking. He was drinking up there in the light of the fire, in a circle of mortal enemies, under Manuel's gloating eyes. Drinking! O happiness! O delight! What a miserable wretch! I clawed the stone convulsively; I think I would have rushed out for my share if I had not heard Manuel's cruel and caressing voice:

"How now? You do not want to throw yourself over, my Castro?"

"I have drunk," he said gloomily.

I think they must have given him something to eat then. In my mind there are many blanks in the vision of that scene, a vision built upon a few words reaching me, suddenly, with great intervals of silence between, as though I had been coming to myself out of a dead faint now and then. A ferocious hum of many voices would rise sometimes impatiently, the scrambling of feet near the edge; or, in a sinister and expectant stillness, Manuel the artist would be speaking to his "beloved victim Castro" in a gentle and insinuating voice that seemed to tremble slightly with eagerness. Had he eaten and drunk enough? They had kept their promises, he said. They would keep them all. The water had been cool—and presently he, Manuel-del-Popolo, would accompany with his guitar and his voice the last moments of his victim. Bursts of laughter punctuated his banter. Ah! that Manuel, that Manuel! Some actually swore in admiration. But was Castro really at his ease? Was it not good to eat and drink? Had he quite returned to life? But, *Caramba, amigos*, what neglect! The *caballero* who has honoured us must smoke. They shouted in high glee:

"Yes. Smoke, Castro. Let him smoke."

I suppose he did; and Manuel expounded to him how pleasant life was in which one could eat, and drink, and smoke. His words tortured me. Castro remained mute—from disdain, from despair, perhaps. Afterwards they carried him along clear of the cornice, and I understood they formed a half-circle round him, drawing their knives. Manuel, screeching in a high falsetto, ordered the bonds of his feet to be cut. I advanced my head out as far as I dared; their voices reached me deadened; I could only see the profound shadow of the ravine, a patch of dark clear sky opulent with stars, and the play of the firelight on the opposite side. The shadow of a pair of monumental feet, and the lower edge of a cloak, spread amply like a skirt, stood out in it, intensely black and motionless, right in front of the cave. Now and then, elbowed in the surge round Castro, the guitar emitted a deep and hollow resonance. He was tumultuously ordered to stand up and, I imagine, he was being pricked with the points of their knives till he did get on his feet. "Jump" they roared all together—and Manuel began to finger the strings, lifting up his voice between the gusts of savage hilarity, mingled with cries of death. He exhorted his followers to close on the traitor inch by inch, presenting their knives.

"He runs here and there, the blood trickling from his limbs—but in vain, this is the appointed time for the leap. . . ."

It was an improvisation; they stamped their feet to the slow measure; they shouted in chorus the one word "Leap!" raising a ferocious roar; and between whiles the song of voice and strings came to me from a distance, softened and lingering in a voluptuous and pitiless cadence that wrung my heart, and seemed to eat up the remnants of my strength. But what could I have done, even if I had had the strength of a giant, and a most fearless resolution? I should have been shot dead before I had crawled halfway up the ledge. A piercing shriek covered the guitar, the song, and the wild merriment.

Then everything seemed to stop—even my own painful breathing. Again Castro shrieked like a madman:

"Señorita—your gold. Señorita! Hear me! Help!"

Then all was still.

"Hear the dead calling to the dead," sneered Manuel.

An awestruck sort of hum proceeded from the Spaniards. Was the señorita alive? In the cave? Or where?

"Her nod would have saved thee, Castro," said Manuel slowly. I got up. I heard Castro stammer wildly:

"She shall fill both your hands with gold. Do you hear, *hombres*? I, Castro, tell you—each man—both hands——"

He had done it. The last hope was gone now. And all that there remained for me to do was to leap over or give myself up, and end this horrible business.

"She was a creature born to command the moon and

the stars," Manuel mused aloud in a vibrating tone, and suddenly smote the strings with emphatic violence. She could even stay his vengeance. But was it possible! No, no. It could not be—and yet. . . .

"Thou art alive yet, Castro," he cried. "Thou hast eaten and drunk; life is good—is it not, old man?—and the leap is high."

He thundered "Silence!" to still the excited murmurs of his band. If she lived Castro should live, too—he, Manuel, said so; but he threatened him with horrible tortures, with two days of slow dying, if he dared to deceive. Let him, then, speak the truth quickly.

"Speak, *viejo*. Where is she?"

And at the opening, fifty yards away, I was tempted to call out, as though I had loved Castro well enough to save him from the shame and remorse of a plain betrayal. That the moment of it had come I could have no doubt. And it was I myself, perhaps, who could not face the certitude of his downfall. If my throat had not been so compressed, so dry with thirst and choked with emotion, I believe I should have cried out and brought them away from that miserable man with a rush. Since we were lost, he at least should be saved from this. I suffered from his spasmodic, agonized laugh away there, with twenty knives aimed at his breast and the eighty-foot drop of the precipice at his back. Why did he hesitate?

I was to learn, then, that the ultimate value of life to all of us is based on the means of self-deception. Morally he had his back against the wall, he could not hope to deceive himself; and after Manuel had cried again at him, "Where are they?" in a really terrible tone, I heard his answer:

"At the bottom of the sea."

He had his own courage after all—if only the courage

not to believe in Manuel's promises. And he must have
been weary of his life—weary enough not to pay that
price. And yet he had gone to the very verge, calling
upon Seraphina as if she could hear him. Madness of
fear, no doubt—succeeded by an awakening, a heroic
reaction. And yet sometimes it seems to me as if the
whole scene, with his wild cries for help, had been the
outcome of a supreme exercise of cunning. For, indeed, he could not have invented anything better to
bring the conviction of our death to the most sceptical
of those ruffians. All I heard after his words had been a
great shout, followed by a sudden and unbroken silence.
It seemed to last a very long time. He had thrown
himself over! It is like the blank space of a swoon to
me, and yet it must have been real enough, because,
huddled up just inside the sill, with my head reposing
wearily on the stone, I watched three moving flames of
lighted branches carried by men follow each other
closely in a swaying descent along the path on the
other side of the ravine. They passed on downwards,
flickering out of view. Then, after a time, a voice
below, to the left of the cave, ascended with a hooting
and mournful effect from the depths.

"Manuel! Manuel! We have found him! . . .
Es muerte ! "

And from above Manuel's shout rolled, augmented,
between the rocks.

"*Bueno !* Turn his face up—for the birds!"

They continued calling to each other for a good while.
The men below declared their intention of going on to
the sea shore; and Manuel shouted to them not to forget
to send him up a good rope early in the morning.
Apparently, the schooner had been refloated some time
before; many of the *Lugareños* were to sleep on board.
They purposed to set sail early next day.

This revived me, and I spent the night between Seraphina's couch and the mouth of the cave, keeping tight hold of my reason that seemed to lose itself in this hope, in this darkness, in this torment. I touched her cheek, it was hot—while her forehead felt to my fingers as cold as ice. I had no more voice, but I tried to force out some harsh whispers through my throat. They sounded horrible to my own ears, and she endeavoured to soothe me by murmuring my name feebly. I believe she thought me delirious. I tried to pray for my strength to last till I could carry her out of that cave to the side of the brook—then let death come. "Live, live," I whispered into her ear, and would hear a sigh so faint, so feeble, that it swayed all my soul with pity and fear, "Yes, Juan." . . . And I would go away to watch for the dawn from the mouth of the cave, and curse the stars that would not fade.

Manuel's voice always steadied me. A languor had come over them above, as if their passion had been exhausted; as if their hearts had been saddened by an unbridled debauch. There was, however, their everlasting quarrelling. Several of them, I understood, left the camp for the schooner, but avoiding the road by the ravine as if Castro's dead body down there had made it impassable. And the talk went on late into the night. There was some superstitious fear attached to the cave—a legend of men who had gone in and had never come back any more. All they knew of it was the region of twilight; formerly, when they used the shelter of the cavern, no one, it seems, ever ventured outside the circle of the fire. Manuel disdained their fears. Had he not been such a profound *politico*, a man of stratagems, there would have been a necessity to go down and see. . . . They all protested.

Who was going down? Not they. . . . Their craven cowardice was amazing.

He begged them to keep themselves quiet. They had him for *Capataz* now. A man of intelligence. Had he not enticed Castro out? He had never believed there was any one else in there. He sighed. Otherwise Castro would have tried to save his life by confessing. There had been nothing to confess. But he had the means of making sure. A voice suggested that the *Inglez* might have withdrawn himself into the depths. These English were not afraid of demons, being devils themselves; and this one was fiendishly reckless. But Manuel observed, contemptuously, that a man trapped like this would remain near the opening. Hope would keep him there till he died—unless he rushed out like Castro. Manuel laughed, but in a mournful tone: and, listening to the craven talk of their doubts and fears, it seemed to me that if I could appear at one bound amongst them, they would scatter like chaff before my glance. It seemed intolerable to wait; more than human strength could bear. Would the day never come? A drowsiness stole upon their voices.

Manuel kept watch. He fed the fire, and his incomplete shadow, projected across the chasm, would pass and return, obscuring the glow that fell on the rock. His footsteps seemed to measure the interminable duration of the night. Sometimes he would stop short and talk to himself in low, exalted mutters. A big bright star rested on the brow of the rock opposite, shining straight into my eyes. It sank, as if it had plunged into the stone. At last. Another came to look into the cavern. I watched the gradual coming of a gray sheen from the side of Seraphina's couch. This was the day, the last day of pain, or else of life. Its ghostly edge invaded slowly the darkness of the cave towards its appointed limit, creeping slowly, as colour-less as spilt water on the floor. I pressed my lips silently upon her cheek. Her eyes were open. It seemed to me she had a smile fainter than her sighs. She was very brave, but her smile did not go beyond her lips. Not a feature of her face moved. I could have opened my veins for her without hesitation, if it had not been a forbidden sacrifice.

Would they go? I asked myself. Through Castro's heroism or through his weakness, perhaps through both the heroism and the weakness of that man, they must be satisfied. They must be. I could not doubt it; I could not believe it. Everything seemed improbable; everything seemed possible. If they descended I would, I thought, have the strength to carry her off, away into the darkness. If there was any truth in what I had overheard them saying, that the depths of the cavern concealed an abyss, we would cast ourselves into it.

The feeble, consenting pressure of her hand horrified me. They would not come down. They were afraid of that place, I whispered to her—and I thought to myself that such cowardice was incredible. Our fate was sealed. And yet from what I had heard. . . .

We watched the daylight growing in the opening; at any moment it might have been obscured by their figures. The tormenting incertitudes of that hour were cruel enough to overcome, almost, the sensations of thirst, of hunger, to engender a restlessness that had the effect of renewed vigour. They were like a nightmare; but that nightmare seemed to clear my mind of its feverish hallucinations. I was more collected, then, than I had been for the last forty-eight hours of our imprisonment. But I could not remain there, waiting. It was ab-solutely necessary that I should watch at the entrance for the moment of their departure.

The morning was serenely cool and, in its stillness, their talk filled with clear-cut words the calm air of the ravine. A party—I could not tell how many—had already come up from the schooner in a great state of excitement. They feared that their presence had, in some way, become known to the peons of the *hacienda*. There was much abuse of a man called Carneiro, who, the day before, had fired an incautious shot at a fat cow on one of the inland *savannas*. They cursed him. Last night, before the moon rose, those on board the schooner had heard the whinnying of a horse. Somebody had ridden down to the water's edge in the darkness and, after waiting a while, had galloped back the way he came. The prints of hoofs on the beach showed that.

They feared these horsemen greatly. A vengeance was owing for the man Manuel had killed; and I could guess they talked with their faces over their shoulders. "And what about finding out whether the *Inglez* was there, dead or alive?" asked some.

I was sure, now, that they would not come down in a body. It would expose them to the danger of being caught in the cavern by the peons. There was no time for a thorough search, they argued.

For the first time that morning I heard Manuel's voice, "Stand aside."

He came down to the very brink.

"If the *Inglez* is down there, and if he is alive, he is listening to us now."

He was as certain as though he had been able to see me. He added:

"But there's no one."

"Go and look, Manuel," they cried.

He said something in a tone of contempt. The voices above my head sank into busy murmurs.

"Give me the rope here," he said aloud.

I had a feeling of some inconceivable danger nearing me; and in my state of weakness I began to tremble, backing away from the orifice. I had no strength in my limbs. I had no weapons. How could I fight? I would use my teeth. With a light knocking against the rock above the arch, Williams' flask, tied by its green cord to the end of a thick rope, descended slowly, and hung motionless before the entrance.

It had been freshly filled with water; it was dripping wet outside, and the silver top, struck by the sunbeams, dazzled my eyes.

This was the danger—this bait. And it seems to me that if I had had the slightest inkling of what was coming, I should have rushed at it instantly. But it took me some time to understand—to take in the idea that this was water, there, within reach of my hand. With a great effort I resisted the madness that incited me to hurl myself upon the flask. I hung back with all my power. A convulsive spasm contracted my throat. I turned about and fled out of the passage.

I ran to Seraphina. "Put out your hand to me," I panted in the darkness. "I need your help."

I felt it resting lightly on my bowed head. She did not even ask me what I meant; as if the greatness of her soul was omniscient. There was, in that silence, a supreme unselfishness, the unquestioning devotion of a woman.

"Patience, patience," I kept on muttering. I was losing confidence in myself. If only I had been free to dash my head against the rock. I had the courage for that, yet. But this was a situation from which there was no issue in death.

"We are saved," I murmured distractedly.

"Patience," she breathed out. Her hand slipped languidly off my head.

And I began to creep away from her side. I am here to tell the truth. I began to creep away towards the flask. I did not confess this to myself; but I know now. There was a devilish power in it. I have learned the nature of feelings in a man whom Satan beguiles into selling his soul—the horror of an irresistible and fatal longing for a supreme felicity. And in a drink of water for me, then, there was a greater promise than in universal knowledge, in unbounded power, in unlimited wealth, in imperishable youth. What could have been these seductions to a drink? No soul had thirsted after things unlawful as my parched throat thirsted for water. No devil had ever tempted a man with such a bribe of perdition.

I suffered from the lucidity of my feelings. I saw, with indignation, my own wretched self being angled for like a fish. And with all that, in my forlorn state, I remained prudent. I did not rush out blindly. No. I approached the inner end of the passage, as though I had been stalking a wild creature, slowly, from the side. I crept along the wall of the cavern, and protruded my head far enough to look at the fiendish temptation.

There it was, a small dark object suspended in the light, with the yellow rock across the ravine for a background. The silver top shivered the sunbeams brilliantly. I had half hopes they had taken it away by this time. When I drew my head back I lost sight of it, but all my being went out to it with an almost pitiful longing. I remembered Castro for the first time in many hours. Was I nothing better than Castro? He had been angled for with salted meat. I shuddered.

A darkness fell into the passage. I put down my
o

uplifted foot without advancing. The unexpectedness
of that shadow saved me, I believe. Manuel had descended the cornice.

He was alone. Standing before the outer opening, he
darkened the passage, through which his talk to the
people above came loudly into my ears. They could
see now if he were not a worthy *Capataz*. If the
Iglez was in there he was a corpse. And yet, of these
living hearts above, of these *valientes* of Rio Medio,
there was not one who would go alone to look upon a
dead body. He had contrived an infallible test, and
yet they would not believe him. Well, his valiance
should prove it; his valiance, afraid neither of light nor
of darkness.

I could not hear the answers he got from up there; but
the vague sounds that reached me carried the usual
commingling of derision and applause, the resentment
of their jeers at the admiration he knew how to extort
by the display of his talents.

They must kill the cattle, these *caballeros*. He
scolded ironically. Of course. They must feed on
meat like lions; but their souls were like the souls of
hens born on dunghills. And behold! there was he,
Manuel, not afraid of shadows.

He was coming in, there could be no doubt. Out
there in the full light, he could not possibly have detected that rapid appearance of my head darted forward and withdrawn at once; but I had a view of his
arm putting aside the swinging flask, of his leg raised
to step over the high sill. I saw him, and I ran noiselessly away from the opening.

I had the time to charge Seraphina not to move, on
our lives—on the wretched remnant of our lives—when
his black shape stood in the frame of the opening, edged
with a thread of light following the contour of his hat,

of his shoulders, of his whole body down to his feet—
whence a long shadow fell upon the pool of twilight on
the floor.

What had made him come down? Vanity? The
exacting demands of his leadership? Fear of O'Brien?
The *Juez* would expect to hear something definite,
and his band pretended not to believe in the stratagem
of the bottle. I think that, for his part, from his
knowledge of human nature, he never doubted its efficacy. He could not guess how very little, only, he was
wrong. How very little! And yet he seemed rooted
in incertitude on the threshold. His head turned from
side to side. I could not make out his face as he stood,
but the slightest of his movements did not escape me.
He stepped aside, letting in all the fullness of the light.

Would he have the courage to explore at least the immediate neighbourhood of the opening? Who could tell
his complex motives? Who could tell his purpose or his
fears? He had killed a man in there once. But, then,
he had not been alone. If he were only showing off
before his unruly band, he need not stir a step further.
He did not advance. He leaned his shoulders against
the rock just clear of the opening. One half of him was
lighted plainly; his long profile, part of his raven locks,
one listless hand, his crossed legs, the buckle of one shoe.

"Nobody," he pronounced slowly, in a dead whisper.

While I looked at him, the profound *politico*, the
artist, the everlastingly questioned *Capataz*, the man of
talent and ability, he thought himself alone, and allowed
his head to drop on his breast, as if saddened by the
vanity of human ambition. Then, lifting it with a
jerk, he listened with one ear turned to the passage;
afterwards he peered into the cavern. Two long
strides, over the cold heap of ashes, brought him to the
stone seat.

It was very plain to me from his starting movements and attitudes, that he shared his uneasy attention between the inside and the outside of the cave. He sat down, but seemed ready to jump up; and I saw him turn his eyes upwards to the dark vault, as if on the alert for a noise from above. I am inclined to think he was expecting to hear the galloping hoofs of the peons' horses every moment. I think he did. The words "I am safer here than they above," were perfectly audible to me in the mumbling he kept up nervously. He wished to hear the sound of his own voice, as a timid person whistles and talks on a lonely road at night. Only the year before he had killed a man in that cavern, under circumstances that were, I believe, revolting even to the honour of these bandits. He sat there between the shadow of his murder and the reality of the vengeance. I asked myself what could be the outcome of a struggle with him. He was armed; he was not weakened by hunger; but he stood between us and the water. My thirst would give me strength; the desire to end Seraphina's sufferings would make me invincible. On the other hand, it was dangerous to interfere. I could not tell whether they would not try to find out what became of him. It was safest to let him go. It was extremely improbable that they would sail without him.

I am not conscious of having stirred a limb; neither had Seraphina moved, I am ready to swear; but plainly something, some sort of sound, startled him. He bounded out of his seated immobility, and in one leap had his shoulders against the rock standing at bay before the darkness, with his knife in his hand. I wonder he did not surprise me into an exclamation. I was as startled as himself. His teeth and the whites of his eyes gleamed straight at me from afar; he hissed with fear; for an instant I was firmly convinced he had seen me. All this took place so quickly that I had no time to make one movement towards receiving his attack, when I saw him make a great sign of the cross in the air with the point of his dagger.

He sheathed it slowly, and sidled along the few feet to the entrance, his shoulders rubbing the wall. He blocked out the light, and in a moment had backed out of sight.

Before he got to the further end I was already, at the inner, creeping after him. I had started at once, as if his disappearance had removed a spell, as though he had drawn me after him by an invisible bond. Raising myself on my forearms I saw him, from his knees up, standing outside the sill, with his back to the precipice and his face turned up.

"There is nobody in there," he shouted.

I sank down and wriggled forward on my stomach, raising myself on my elbows, now and then, to look. Manuel was looking upwards conversing with the people above, and holding Williams' flask in both his hands. He never once glanced into the passage; he seemed to be trying to undo the cord knotted to the end of the thick rope, which hung in a long bight before him. The flask captured my eyes, my thought, my energy. I would tear it away from him directly. There was in me, then, neither fear nor intelligence; only the desire of possessing myself of the thing; but an instinctive caution prevented my rushing out violently. I proceeded with an animal-like stealthiness, with which cool reason had nothing to do.

He had some difficulty with the knot, and evidently did not wish to cut the green silk cord. How well I remember his fumbling fingers. He sat down sideways on the sill, with his legs outside, of course, his face and hands turned to the light, very absorbed in his endeavour. They shouted to him from above.

"I come at once," he cried to them, without lifting his head.

I had crept up almost near enough to grab the flask. It never occurred to me that by flinging myself on him, I could have pushed him off the sill. My only idea was to get hold. He did not exist for me. The leather-covered bottle was the only real thing in the world. I was completely insane. I heard a faint detonation, and Manuel got up quickly from the sill. The flask was out of my reach.

There were more popping sounds of shots fired, away on the plain. The peons were attacking an outpost of the *Lugareños.* A deep voice cried, "They are driving them in." Then several together yelled:

"Come away, Manuel. Come away. *Por Dios. . . .*"

Stretched at full length in the passage, and sustaining myself on my trembling arms, I gazed up at him. He stood very rigid, holding the flask in both hands. Several muskets were discharged together just above, and in the noise of the reports I remember a voice crying urgently over the edge, "Manuel! Manuel!" The shadow of irresolution passed over his features. He hesitated whether to run up the ledge or bolt into the cave. He shouted something. He was not answered, but the yelling and the firing ceased suddenly, as if the *Lugareños* had given up and taken to their heels. I became aware of a sort of increasing throbbing sound that seemed to come from behind me, out of the cave; then, as Manuel lifted his foot hastily to step over the sill, I jumped up deliriously, and with outstretched hands lurched forward at the flask in his fingers.

I believe I laughed at him in an imbecile manner.

Somebody laughed; and I remember the superior smile
on his face passing into a ghastly grin, that disappeared
slowly, while his astonished eyes, glaring at that gaunt
and dishevelled apparition rising before him in the dusk
of the passage, seemed to grow to an enormous size.
He drew back his foot, as though it had been burnt; and
in a panic-stricken impulse, he flung the flask straight
into my face, and staggered away from the sill.

I made a catch at it with a scream of triumph, whose
unearthly sound brought me back to my senses.

"In the name of God, retire," he cried, as though I
had been an apparition from another world.

What took place afterwards happened with an inconceivable rapidity, in less time than it takes to draw
breath. He never recognized me. I saw his glare of
incredulous awe change, suddenly, to horror and despair. He had felt himself losing his balance.

He had stepped too far back. He tried to recover
himself, but it was too late. He hung for a moment
in his backward fall; his arms beat the air, his body
curled upon itself with an awful striving. All at once
he went limp all over, and, with the sunlight full
upon his upturned face, vanished downwards from my
sight.

But at the last moment he managed to clutch the bight
of the hanging rope. The end of it must have been
lying quite loose on the ground above, for I saw its
whole length go whizzing after him, in the twinkling
of an eye. I pressed the flask fiercely to my breast,
raging with the thought that he could yet tear it out of
my hands; but by the time the strain came, his falling
body had acquired such a velocity that I didn't feel
the slightest jerk when the green cord snapped—no
more than if it had been the thread of a cobweb.

I confess that tears, tears of gratitude, were running

down my face. My limbs trembled. But I was sane enough not to think of myself any more.

"Drink! Drink," I stammered, raising Seraphina's head on my shoulder, while the galloping horses of the peons in hot pursuit passed with a thundering rumble above us. Then all was still.

Our getting out of the cave was a matter of unremitting toil, through what might have been a year of time; the recollection is of an arduous undertaking, accomplished without the usual incentives of men's activity. Necessity, alone, remained; the iron necessity without the glamour of freedom of choice, of pride.

Our unsteady feet crushed, at last, the black embers of the fires scattered by the hoofs of horses; and the plain appeared immense to our weakness, swept of shadows by the high sun, lonely and desolate as the sea. We looked at the litter of the *Lugareños'* camp, rags on the trodden grass, a couple of abandoned blankets, a musket thrown away in the panic, a dirty red sash lying on a heap of sticks, a wooden bucket from the schooner, smashed water-gourds. One of them remained miraculously poised on its round bottom and full to the brim, while everything else seemed to have been overturned, torn, scattered haphazard by a furious gust of wind. A scaffolding of poles, for drying strips of meat, had been knocked over; I found nothing there except bits of hairy hide; but lumps of scorched flesh adhered to the white bones scattered amongst the ashes of the camp—and I thanked God for them.

We averted our eyes from our faces in very love, and we did not speak from pity for each other. There was no joy in our escape, no relief, no sense of freedom. The *Lugareños* and the peons, the pursued and the pursuers, had disappeared from the upland without leaving as much as a corpse in view. There were no moving things on the earth, no bird soared in the pellucid air, not even a moving cloud on the sky. The sun declined, and the rolling expanse of the plain frightened us, as if space had been something alive and hostile.

We walked away from that spot, as if our feet had been shod in lead; and we hugged the edge of the cruel ravine, as one keeps by the side of a friend. We must have been grotesque, pathetic, and lonely; like two people newly arisen from a tomb, shrinking before the strangeness of the half-forgotten face of the world. And at the head of the ravine we stopped.

The sensation of light, vastness, and solitude, rolled upon our souls emerging from the darkness, overwhelmingly, like a wave of the sea. We might have been an only couple sent back from the underworld to begin another cycle of pain on a depopulated earth. It had not for us even the fitful caress of a breeze; and the only sound of greeting was the angry babble of the brook dashing down the stony slope at our feet.

We knelt over it to drink deeply and bathe our faces. Then looking about helplessly, I discovered afar the belt of the sea inclosed between the undulating lines of the dunes and the straight edge of the horizon. I pointed my arm at the white sails of the schooner creeping from under the land, and Seraphina, resting her head on my shoulder, shuddered.

"Let us go away from here."

Our necessity pointed down the slope. We could not think of another way, and the extent of the plain with its boundary of forests filled us with the dread of things unknown. But, by getting down to the inlet of the sea, and following the bank of the little river, we were sure to reach the *hacienda*, if only a hope could buoy our sinking hearts long enough.

*O

From our first step downwards the hard, rattling noise of the stones accompanied our descent, growing in volume, bewildering our minds. We had missed the indistinct beginning of the trail on the side of the ravine, and had to follow the course of the stream. A growth of wiry bushes sprang thickly between the large fragments of fallen rocks. On our right the shadows were beginning to steal into the chasm. Towering on our left the great stratified wall caught at the top of the glow of the low sun in a rich, tawny tint, right under the dark blue strip of sky, that seemed to reflect the gloom of the ravine, the sepulchral arid gloom of deep shadows and gray rocks, through which the shallow torrent dashed violently with glassy gleams between the sombre masses of vegetation.

We pushed on through the bunches of tough twigs; the massive boulders closed the view on every side; and Seraphina followed me with her hands on my shoulders. This was the best way in which I could help her descent till the declivity became less steep; and then I went ahead, forcing a path for her. Often we had to walk into the bed of the stream. It was icy cold. Some strange beast, perhaps a bird, invisible somewhere, emitted from time to time a faint and lamentable shriek. It was a wild scene, and the orifice of the cave appeared as an inaccessible black hole some ninety feet above our heads.

Then, as I stepped round a large fragment of rock, my eyes fell on Manuel's body.

Seraphina was behind me. With a wave of my hand I arrested her. It had not occurred to me before that, following the bottom of the ravine, we must come upon the two bodies. Castro's was lower down, of course. I would have spared her the sight, but there was no retracing our steps. We had no strength and no time. Manuel was lying on his back with his hands under him, and his feet nearly in the brook.

The lower portion of the rope made a heap of cordage on the ground near him, but a great length of it hung perpendicularly above his head. The loose end he had snatched over the edge of his fall had whipped itself tight round the stem of a dwarf tree growing in a crevice high up the rock; and as he fell below, the jerk must have checked his descent, and had prevented him from alighting on his head. There was not a sign of blood anywhere upon him or on the stones. His eyes were shut. He might have lain down to sleep there, in our way; only from the slightly unnatural twist in the position of his arms and legs, I saw, at a glance, that all his limbs were broken.

On the other side of the boulder Seraphina called to me, and I could not answer her, so great was the shock I received in seeing the flutter of his slowly opening eyelids.

He still lived, then! He looked at me! It was an awful discovery to make, and the contrast of his anxious and feverish stare with the collapsed posture of his body was full of intolerable suggestions of fate blundering unlawfully, of death itself being conquered by pain. I looked away only to perceive something pitiless, belittling, and cruel in the precipitous immobility of the sheer walls, in the dark funereal green of the foliage, in the falling shadows, in the remoteness of the sky.

The unconsciousness of matter hinted at a weird and mysterious antagonism. All the inanimate things seemed to have conspired to throw in our way this man just enough alive to feel pain. The faint and lamentable sounds we had heard must have come from him. He was looking at me. It was impossible to say

whether he saw anything at all. He barred our road
with his remnant of life; but, when suddenly he spoke,
my heart stood still for a moment in my motionless
body.

"You, too!" he droned awfully. "Behold! I have
been precipitated, alive, into this hell by another ghost.
Nothing else could have overcome the greatness of my
spirit."

His red shirt was torn open at the throat. His bared
breast began to heave. He cried out with pain.
Ready to fly from him myself, I shouted to Seraphina
to keep away.

But it was too late. Imagining I had seen some new
danger in our path, she had advanced to stand by my
side.

"He is dying," I muttered in distraction. "We can
do nothing."

But could we pass him by before he died?

"This is terrible," said Seraphina.

My real hope had been that, after driving the
Lugareños away, the peons would off-saddle near the
little river to rest themselves and their horses. This is
why I had almost pitilessly hurried Seraphina, after
we had left the cave, down the steep but short descent
of the ravine. I had kept to myself my despairing conviction that we could never reach the *hacienda* unaided,
even if we had known the way. I had pretended confidence in ourselves, but all my trust was in the assistance I expected to get from these men. I understood
so well the slenderness of that hope that I had not
dared to mention it to her and to propose she should
wait for me on the upland, while I went down by myself
on that quest. I could not bear the fear of returning
unsuccessful only to find her dead. That is, if I had
the strength to return after such a disappointment.

And the idea of her, waiting for me in vain, then wandering off, perhaps to fall under a bush and die alone, was too appalling to contemplate. That we must keep together, at all costs, was like a point of honour, like an article of faith with us—confirmed by what we had gone through already. It was like a law of existence, like a creed, like a defence which, once broken, would let despair upon our heads. I am sure she would not have consented to even a temporary separation. She had a sort of superstitious feeling that, should we be forced apart, even to the manifest saving of our lives, we would lay ourselves open to some calamity worse than mere death could be.

I loved her enough to share that feeling, but with the addition of a man's half-unconscious selfishness. I needed her indomitable frailness to prop my grosser strength. I needed that something not wholly of this world, which women's more exalted nature infuses into their passions, into their sorrows, into their joys; as if their adventurous souls had the power to range beyond the orbit of the earth for the gathering of their love, their hate—and their charity.

"He calls for death," she said, shrinking with horror and pity before the mutters of the miserable man at our feet. Every moment of daylight was of the utmost importance, if we were to save our freedom, our happiness, our very lives; and we remained rooted to the spot. For it seemed as though, at last, he had attained the end of his enterprise. He had captured us, as if by a very cruel stratagem.

A drowsiness would come at times over those big open eyes, like a film through which a blazing glance would break out now and then. He had recognized us perfectly; but, for the most part, we seemed to him to be the haunting ghosts of his inferno.

"You came from heaven," he raved feebly, rolling his straining eyes towards Seraphina. His internal injuries must have been frightful. Perhaps he dared not shift his head—the only movement that was in his power. "I reached up to the very angels in the inspiration of my song," he droned, "and would be called a demon on earth. *Manuel el Demonio*. And now precipitated alive. . . . Nothing less. There is a greatness in me. Let some dew fall upon my lips."

He moaned from the very bottom of his heart. His teeth chattered.

"The blessed may not know anything of the cold and thirst of this place. A drop of dew—as on earth you used to throw alms to the poor from your coach— for the love of God."

She sank on the stones nearer to him than I would willingly have done, brave as a woman, only, can be before the atrocious depths of human misery. I leaned my shoulders against the boulder and crossed my arms on my breast, as if giving up an unequal struggle. Her hair was loose, her dress stained with ashes, torn by brambles; the darkness of the cavern seemed to linger in her hollow cheeks, in her sunken temples.

"He is thirsty," she murmured to me.

"Yes," I said.

She tore off a strip of her dress, dipped it in the running water at her side, and approached it, all dripping, to his lips which closed upon it with avidity. The walls of the rock looked on implacably, but the rushing stream seemed to hurry away, as if from an accursed spot.

"Dew from heaven," he sighed out.

"You are on earth, Manuel," she said. "You are given time to repent. This is earth."

"Impossible," he muttered with difficulty.

He had forced his human fellowship upon us, this man whose ambition it had been to be called demon on the earth. He held us by the humanity of his broken frame, by his human glance, by his human voice. I wonder if, had I been alone, I would have passed on as reason dictated, or have had the courage of pity and finished him off, as he demanded. Whenever he became aware of our presence, he addressed me as "Thou, English ghost," and directed me, in a commanding voice, to take a stone and crush his head, before I went back to my own torments. I withdrew, at last, where he could not see me; but Seraphina never flinched in her task of moistening his lips with the strip of cloth she dipped in the brook, time after time, with a sublime perseverance of compassion.

It made me silent. Could I have stood there and recited the sinister detail of that man's crimes, in the hope that she would recoil from him to pursue the road of safety? It was not his evil, but his suffering that confronted us now. The sense of our kinship emerged out of it like a fresh horror after we had escaped the sea, the tempest; after we had resisted untold fatigues, hunger, thirst, despair. We were vanquished by what was in us, not in him. I could say nothing. The light ebbed out of the ravine. The sky, like a thin blue veil stretched between the earth and the spaces of the universe, filtered the gloom of the darkness beyond.

I thought of the invisible sun ready to set into the sea, of the peons riding away, and of our helpless, hopeless state.

"For the love of God," he mumbled.

"Yes, for the love of God," I heard her expressionless voice repeat. And then there was only the greedy sound of his lips sucking at the cloth, and the impatient ripple of the stream.

"Come, death," he sighed.

Yes, come, I thought, to release him and to set us free. All my prayer, now, was that we should be granted the strength to struggle from under the malignant frown of these crags, to close our eyes forever in the open.

And the truth is that, had we gone on, we should have found no one by the sea. The routed *Lugareños* had been able to embark under cover of a fusillade from those on board the schooner. All that would have met our despair, at the end of our toilsome march, would have been three dead pirates lying on the sand. The main body of the peons had gone, already, up the valley of the river with their few wounded. There would have been nothing for us to do but to stumble on and on upon their track, till we lay down never to rise again. They did not draw rein once, between the sea and the *hacienda*, sixteen miles away.

About the time when we began our descent into the ravine, two of the peons, detached from the main body for the purpose of observing the schooner from the upland, had topped the edge of the plain. We had then penetrated into Manuel's inferno, too deep to be seen by them. These men spent some time lying on the grass, and watching over the dunes the course of the schooner on the open sea. Their horses were grazing near them. The wind was light; they waited to see the vessel far enough down the coast to make any intention of return improbable.

It was Manuel who saved our lives, defeating his own aim to the bitter end. Had not his vanity, policy, or the necessity of his artistic soul, induced him to enter the cave; had not his cowardice prevented him joining the *Lugareños* above, at the moment of the attack; had he not recoiled violently in a superstitious fear before my apparition at the mouth of the cave—we should have been released from our entombment, only to look once more at the sun. He paid the price of our ransom, to the uttermost farthing, in his lingering death. Had he killed himself on the spot, he would have taken our only slender chance with him into that nether world where he imagined himself to have been "precipitated alive." Finding him dead, we should have gone on. Less than ten minutes, no more than another ten paces beyond the spot, we should have been hidden from sight in the thickets of denser growth in the lower part of the ravine. I doubt whether we should have been able to get through; but, even so, we should have been going away from the only help within our reach. We should have been lost.

The two *vaqueros*, after seeing the schooner hull down under the low, fiery sun of the west, mounted and rode home over the plain, making for the head of the ravine, as their way lay. And, as they cantered along the side opposite to the cave, one of them caught sight of the length of rope dangling down the precipice. They pulled up at once.

The first I knew of their nearness was the snorting of a horse forced towards the edge of the chasm. I saw the animal's forelegs planted tensely on the very brink, and the body of the rider leaning over his neck to look down. And, when I wished to shout, I found I could not produce the slightest sound.

The man, rising in his stirrups, the reins in one hand and turning up the brim of his sombrero with the other, peered down at us over the pricked ears of his horse. I pointed over my head at the mouth of the cave, then down at Seraphina, lifting my hands to show that I was unarmed. I opened my lips wide. Surprise, agitation, weakness, had robbed me of every vestige of my

voice. I beckoned downwards with a desperate energy,
Horse and rider remained perfectly still, like an eques-
trian statue set up on the edge of a precipice. Seraphina had never raised her head.

The man's intent scrutiny could not have mistaken
me for a *Lugareño*. I think he gazed so long because
he was amazed to discover down there a woman on her
knees, stooping over a prostrate body, and a bare-
headed man in a ragged white shirt and black breeches,
reeling between the bushes and gesticulating violently,
like an excited mute. But how a rope came to hang
down from a tree, growing in a position so inaccessible
that only a bird could have attached it there struck
him as the most mysterious thing of all. He pointed his
finger at it interrogatively, and I answered this inquir-
ing sign by indicating the stony slope of the ravine.
It seemed as if he could not speak for wonder. After
a while he sat back in his saddle, gave me an encouraging wave of the hand, and wheeled his horse away from
the brink.

It was as if we had been casting a spell of extinction
on each other's voices. No sooner had he disappeared
than I found mine. I do not suppose it was very loud
but, at my aimless screech, Seraphina looked upwards
on every side, saw no one anywhere, and remained on
her knees with her eyes, full of apprehension, fixed
upon me.

"No! I am not mad, dearest," I said. "There was
a man. He has seen us."

"Oh, Juan!" she faltered out, "pray with me that God
may have mercy on this poor wretch and let him die."

I said nothing. My thin, quavering scream after the
peon had awakened Manuel from his delirious dream of
an inferno. The voice that issued from his shattered
body was awfully measured, hollow, and profound.

"You live!" he uttered slowly, turning his eyes full upon my face, and, as if perceiving for the first time in me the appearance of a living man. "Ha! You English walk the earth unscathed."

A feeling of pity came to me—a pity distinct from the harrowing sensations of his miserable end. He had been evil in the obscurity of his life, as there are plants growing harmful and deadly in the shade, drawing poison from the dank soil on which they flourish. He was as unconscious of his evil as they—but he had a man's right to my pity.

"I am b—roken," he stammered out.

Seraphina kept on moistening his lips.

"Repent, Manuel," she entreated fervently. "We have forgiven thee the evil done to us. Repent of thy crimes—poor man."

"Your voice, Señorita. What? You! You yourself bringing this blessing to my lips! In your childhood I had cried '*viva*' many times before your coach. And now you deign—in your voice—with your hand. Ha! I could improvise—The star stoops to the crushed worm. . . ."

A rising clatter of rolling stones mingled from afar with the broken moanings of his voice. Looking over my shoulder, I saw one peon beginning the descent of the slope, and, higher up, motionless between the heads of two horses, the head of another man—with the purple tint of an enlarged sky beyond, reflecting the glow of an invisible sun setting into the sea.

Manuel cried out piercingly, and we shuddered. Seraphina shrank close to my side, hiding her head on my breast. The peon staggered awkwardly down the slope, descending sideways in small steps, embarrassed by the enormous rowels of his spurs. He had a striped *serape* over his shoulder, and grasped a broad-bladed *machete* in his right hand. His stumbling, cautious feet sent into the ravine a crashing sound, as though we were to be buried under a stream of stones.

"*Vuestra Señoria*," gasped Manuel. "I shall be silent. Pity me! Do not—do not withdraw your hand from my extreme pain."

I felt she had to summon all her courage to look at him again. She disengaged herself, resolutely, from my enfolding arms.

"No, no; unfortunate man," she said, in a benumbed voice. "Think of thy end."

"A crushed worm, señorita," he mumbled.

The peon, having reached the bottom of the slope, became lost to view amongst the bushes and the great fragments of rocks below. Every sound in the ravine was hushed; and the darkening sky seemed to cast the shadow of an everlasting night into the eyes of the dying man.

Then the peon came out, pushing through, in a great swish of parted bushes. His spurs jingled at every step, his footfalls crunched heavily on the pebbles. He stopped, as if transfixed, muttering his astonishment to himself, but asking no questions. He was a young man with a thin black moustache twisted gallantly to two little points. He looked up at the sheer wall of the precipice; he looked down at the group we formed at his feet. Suddenly, as if returning from an abyss of pain, Manuel declared distinctly:

"I feel in me a greatness, an inspiration. . . ."

These were his last words. The heavy dark lashes descended slowly upon the faint gleam of the eyeballs, like a lowered curtain. The deep folds of the ravine gathered the falling dusk into great pools of absolute blackness, at the foot of the crags.

Rising high above our littleness, that watched,

fascinated, the struggle of lights and shadows over the soul entangled in the wreck of a man's body, the rocks had a monumental indifference. And between their great, stony faces, turning pale in the gloom, with the amazed peon as if standing guard, *machete* in hand, Manuel's greatness and his inspiration passed away without as much as an exhaled sigh. I did not even know that he had ceased to breathe, till Seraphina rose from her knees with a low cry, and flung far away from her, nervously, the strip of cloth upon which his parted lips had refused to close.

My arms were ready to receive her. "Ah! At last!" she cried. There was something resentful and fierce in that cry, as though the pity of her woman's heart had been put to too cruel a test.

I, too, had been humane to that man. I had had his life on the end of my pistol, and had spared him from an impulse that had done nothing but withhold from him the mercy of a speedy death. This had been my pity.

But it was Seraphina's cry—this "At last," showing the stress and pain of the ordeal—that shook my faith in my conduct. It had brought upon our heads a retribution of mental and bodily anguish, like a criminal weakness. I was young, and my belief in the justice of life had received a shock. If it were impossible to foretell the consequences of our acts, if there was no safety in the motives within ourselves, what remained for our guidance?

And the inscrutable immobility of towering forms, steeped in the shadows of the chasm, appeared pregnant with a dreadful wisdom. It seemed to me that I would never have the courage to lift my hand, open my lips, make a step, obey a thought. A long sun-ray shot to the zenith from the beclouded west, crossing obliquely in a faint red bar the purple band of sky above the ravine.

The young *vaquero* had taken off his hat before the might of death, and made a perfunctory sign of the cross. He looked up and down the lofty wall, as if it could give him the word of that riddle. Twice his spurs clashed softly, and, with one hand grasping the rope, he stooped low in the twilight over the body.

"We looked for this *Lugareño*," he said, replacing his hat on his head carelessly. "He was a mad singer, and I saw him once kill one of us very swiftly. They used to call him in jest, *El Demonio*. Ah! But you . . . But you. . . ."

His wonder overcame him. His bewildered eyes glimmered, staring at us in the deepening dusk.

"Speak, *hombre*," he cried. "Who are you and who is she? Whence came you? Where are you going with this woman? . . ."

CHAPTER ELEVEN

Not a soul stirred in the one long street of the negro village. The yellow crescent of the diminished moon swam low in the pearly light of the dawn; and the bamboo walls of huts, thatched with palm leaves, glistened here and there through the great leaves of bananas. All that night we had been moving on and on, slowly crossing clear *savannas*, in which nothing stirred beside ourselves but the escort of our own shadows, or plunging through dense patches of forest of an obscurity so impenetrable that the very forms of our rescuers became lost to us, though we heard their low voices and felt their hands steadying us in our saddles. Then our horses paced softly on the dust of a road, while athwart an avenue of orange trees whose foliage seemed as black as coal, the blind walls of the *hacienda* shone dead white like a vision of mists. A Brazilian aloe flowered by the side of the gate; we drooped in our saddles; and the heavy knocks against the wooden portal seemed to go on without cause, and stop without reason, like a sound heard in a dream. We entered Seraphina's *hacienda*. The high walls inclosed a square court deep as the yard of a prison, with flat-roofed buildings all around. It rang with many voices suddenly. Every moment the daylight increased; young negresses in loose gowns ran here and there, cackling like chased hens, and a fat woman waddled out from under the shadow of a veranda.

She was Seraphina's old nurse. She was scolding volubly, and suddenly she shrieked, as though she had been stabbed. Then all was still for a long time. Sitting high on the back of my patient mount, with my fingers twisted in the mane, I saw in a throng of woolly heads and bright garments Seraphina's pale face. An increasing murmur of sobs and endearing names mounted up to me. Her hair hung down, her eyes seemed immense; these people were carrying her off—and a man with a careworn, bilious face and a straight, gray beard, neatly clipped on the edges, stood at the head of my horse, blinking with astonishment.

The fat woman reappeared, rolling painfully along the veranda.

"Enrico! It is her lover! Oh! my treasure, my lamb, my precious child. Do you hear, Enrico? Her lover! Oh! the poor darling of my heart."

She appeared to be giggling and weeping at the same time. The sky above the yard brightened all at once, as if the sun had emerged with a leap from the distant waters of the Atlantic. She waved her short arms at me over the railing, then plunged her dark fingers in the shock of iron-gray hair gathered on the top of her head. She turned away abruptly, a yellow head-kerchief dodged in her way, a slap resounded, a cry of pain, and a negro girl bolted into the court, nursing her cheek in the palms of her hands. Doors slammed; other negro girls ran out of the veranda dismayed, and took cover in various directions.

I swayed to and fro in the saddle, but faithful to the plan of our escape, I tried to make clear my desire that these peons should be sworn to secrecy immediately. Meantime, somebody was trying to disengage my feet from the stirrups.

"Certainly. It is as your worship wishes."

The careworn man at the head of my horse was utterly in the dark.

"Attention!" he shouted. "Catch hold, *hombres*. Carry the *caballero*."

What *caballero*? A rosy flush tinged a boundless expanse above my face, and then came a sudden contraction of space and dusk. There were big earthenware jars ranged in a row on the floor, and the two *vaqueros* stood bareheaded, stretching their arms over me towards a black crucifix on a wall, taking their oaths, while I rested on my back. A white beard hovered about my face, a voice said, "It is done," then called anxiously twice, "Señor! Señor!" and when I had escaped from the dream of a cavern, I found myself with my head pillowed on a fat woman's breast, and drinking chicken broth out of a basin held to my lips. Her large cheeks quivered, she had black twinkling eyes and slight moustaches at the corners of her lips. But where was her white beard? And why did she talk of an angel, as if she were Manuel?

"Seraphina!" I cried, but Castro's cloak swooped on my head like a sable wing. It was death. I struggled. Then I died. It was delicious to die. I followed the floating shape of my love beyond the worlds of the universe. We soared together above pain, strife, cruelty, and pity. We had left death behind us and everything of life but our love, which threw a radiant halo around two flames which were ourselves—and immortality inclosed us in a great and soothing darkness.

Nothing stirred in it. We drifted no longer. We hung in it quite still—and the empty husk of my body watched our two flames side by side, mingling their light in an infinite loneliness. There were two candles burning low on a little black table near my head. Enrico, with his white beard and zealous eyes, was bending over my couch, while a chair, on high runners, rocked empty behind him. I stared.

"Señor, the night is far advanced," he said sooth-ingly, "and Dolores, my wife, watches over Doña Seraphina's slumbers, on the other side of this wall."

I had been dead to the world for nearly twenty hours, and the awakening resembled a new birth, for I felt as weak and helpless as an infant.

It is extraordinary how quickly we regained so much of our strength; but I suppose people recover sooner from the effects of privation than from the weakness of disease. Keeping pace with the return of our bodily vigour, the anxieties of mind returned, augmented tenfold by all the weight of our sinister experience. And yet, what worse could happen to us in the future? What other terror could it hold? We had come back from the very confines of destruction. But Seraphina, reclining back in an armchair, very still, with her eyes fixed on the high white wall facing the veranda across the court, would murmur the word "Separa-tion!"

The possibility of our lives being forced apart was terrible to her affection, and intolerable to her pride. She had made her choice, and the feeling she had sur-rendered herself to so openly must have had a supreme potency. She had disregarded for it all the traditions of silence and reserve. She had looked at me fondly through the very tears of her grief; she had followed me —leaving her dead unburied and her prayers unsaid. What more could she have done to proclaim her love to the world? Could she, after that, allow anything short of death to thwart her fidelity? Never! And if she were to discover that I could, after all, find it in my heart to support an existence in which she had no share, then, indeed, it would be more than enough to make her die of shame.

"Ah, dearest!" I said, "you shall never die of shame."

We were different, but we had read each other's natures by a fierce light. I understood the point of honour in her constancy, and she never doubted the scruples of my true devotion, which had brought so many dangers on her head. We were flying not to save our lives, but to preserve inviolate our truth to each other and to ourselves. And if our sentiments appear exaggerated, violent, and overstrained, I must point back to their origin. Our love had not grown like a delicate flower, cherished in tempered sunshine. It had never known the atmosphere of tenderness; our souls had not been awakened to each other by a gentle whisper, but as if by the blast of a trumpet. It had called us to a life whose enemy was not death, but separation.

The enemy sat at the gate of our shelter, as death sits at the gate of life. These high walls could not protect us, nor the tearful mumble of the old woman's prayers, nor yet the careworn fidelity of Enrico. The couple hung about us, quivering with emotion. They peeped round the corners of the veranda, and only rarely ventured to come out openly. The silent Galician stroked his clipped beard; the obese woman kept on crossing herself with loud, resigned sighs. She would waddle up, wiping her eyes, to stroke Seraphina's head and murmur endearing names. They waited on us hand and foot, and would stand close together, ready for the slightest sign, in a rapt contemplation. Now and then she would nudge her husband's ribs with her thick elbow and murmur, "Her lover."

She was happy when Seraphina let her sit at her feet, and hold her hand. She would pat it with gentle taps, squatting shapelessly on a low stool.

"Why go so far from thy old nurse, darling of my heart? Ah! love is love, and we have only one life to live, but this England is very far—very far away."

She nodded her big iron-gray head slowly; and to our longing England appeared very distant, too, a fortunate isle across the seas, an abode of peace, a sanctuary of love.

There was no plan open to us but the one laid down by Sebright. The secrecy of our sojourn at the *hacienda* had, in a measure, failed, though there was no reason to suppose the two peons had broken their oath. Our arrival at dawn had been unobserved, as far as we knew, and the domestic slaves, mostly girls, had been kept from all communication with the field hands outside. All these square leagues of the estate were very much out of the world, and this isolation had not been broken upon by any of O'Brien's agents coming out to spy. It seemed to be the only part of Seraphina's great possessions that remained absolutely her own.

Not a whisper of any sort of news reached us in our hiding-place till the fourth evening, when one of the *vaqueros* reported to Enrico that, riding on the inland boundary, he had fallen in with a company of infantry encamped on the edge of a little wood. Troops were being moved upon Rio Medio. He brought a note from the officer in command of that party. It contained nothing but a requisition for twenty head of cattle. The same night we left the *hacienda*.

It was a starry darkness. Behind us the soft wailing of the old woman at the gate died out:

"So far! So very far!"

We left the long street of the slave village on the left, and walked down the gentle slope of the open glade towards the little river. Seraphina's hair was concealed

in the crown of a wide sombrero and, wrapped up in a
serape, she looked so much like a cloaked *vaquero* that
one missed the jingle of spurs out of her walk. Enrico
had fitted me out in his own clothes from top to toe.
He carried a lanthorn, and we followed the circle of light
that swayed and trembled upon the short grass. There
was no one else with us, the crew of the *drogher* being
already on board to await our coming.

Her mast appeared above the roof of some low sheds
grouped about a short wooden jetty. Enrico raised the
lamp high to light us, as we stepped on board.

Not a word was spoken; the five negroes of the crew
(Enrico answered for their fidelity) moved about noiselessly, almost invisible. Blocks rattled feebly aloft.

"Enrico," said Seraphina, "do not forget to put a
stone cross over poor Castro's grave."

"No, Señorita. May you know years of felicity.
We would all have laid down our lives for you. Remember that, and do not forget the living. Your
childhood has been the consolation of the poor woman
there for the loss of our little one, your foster brother,
who died. We have given to you much of our affection
for him who was denied to our old age."

He stepped back from the rail. "Go with God," he
said.

The faint air filled the sail, and the outlines of wharf
and roof fell back into the sombre background of the
land, but the lanthorn in Enrico's hand glimmered
motionless at the end of the jetty, till a bend of the
stream hid it from our sight.

We glided smoothly between the banks. Now and
then a stretch of osiers and cane brakes rustled alongside in the darkness. All was strange; the contours
of the land melted before our advance. The earth
was made of shifting shadows, and only the stars re-

mained in unchanged groups of glitter on the black sky.
We floated across the land-locked basin, and under the
low headland we had steered for from the sea in the
storm. All this, seen only once under streams of
lightning, was unrecognizable to us, and seemed
plunged in deep slumber. But the fresh feel of the sea
air, and the freedom of earth and sky wedded on the sea
horizon, returned to us like old friends, the companions
of that time when we communed in words and silences
on board the *Lion*, that fragment of England found in a
mist, boarded in battle, with its absurd and warm-
hearted protection. On our other hand, the rampart
of white dunes intruded the line of a ghostly shore
between the depth of the sea and the profundity of the
sky; and when the faint breeze failed for a moment, the
negro crew troubled the silence with the heavy splashes
of their sweeps falling in slow and solemn cadence.
The rudder creaked gently; the black in command was
old and of spare build, resembling Cesar, the major-
domo, without the splendour of maroon velvet and gold
lace. He was a very good sailor, I believe, taciturn
and intelligent. He had seen the *Lion* frequently on
his trips to Havana, and would recognize her, he
assured me, amongst a whole host of shipping. When
I had explained what was expected of him, according
to Sebright's programme, a bizarre grimace of a smile
disturbed the bony, mournful cast of his African face.

"Fall on board by accident, Señor. *Si!* Now, by
St. Jago of Compostella, the patron of our *hacienda*, you
shall see this old Pedro—who has been set to sail the
craft ever since she was built—as overcome by an accident as a little rascal of a boy that has stolen a boat."

After this wordy declaration he never spoke to us
again. He gave his short orders in low undertones,
and the others, four stalwart blacks, in the prime of

life, executed them in silence. Another night brought the unchanging stars to look at us in their multitudes, till the dawn put them out just as we opened the entrance of the harbour. The daylight discovered the arid colouring of the coast, a castle on a sandy hill, and a few small boats with ragged sails making for the land. A brigantine, that seemed to have carried the breeze with her right in, threw up the Stars and Stripes radiantly to the rising sun, before rounding the point. The sound of bells came out to sea, and met us while we crept slowly on, abreast of the battery at the water's edge.

"A feast-day in the city," said the old negro at the helm. "And here is an English ship of war."

The sun-rays struck from afar full at her belted side; the water was like glass along the shore. She swam into the very shade of the hill, before she wore round, with great deliberation, in an ample sweep of her headgear through a complete half-circle. She came to the wind on the other tack under her short canvas; her lower deck ports were closed, the hammock cloths made like a ridge of unmelted snow lying along her rail.

It was evident she was kept standing off and on outside the harbour, as an armed man may pace to and fro before a gate. With the hum of six hundred wakeful lives in her flanks, the tap-tapping of a drum, and the shrill modulations of the boatswain's calls piping some order along her decks, she floated majestically across our path. But the only living being we saw was the red-coated marine on sentry by the lifebuoys, looking down at us over the taffrail. We passed so close to her that I could distinguish the whites of his eyes, and the tompions in the muzzles of her stern-chasers protruding out of the ports belonging to the admiral's quarters.

I knew her. She was Rowley's flagship. She had

thrown the shadow of her sails upon the end of my first sea journey. She was the man-of-war going out for a cruise on that day when Carlos, Tomas, and myself arrived in Jamaica in the old *Thames*. And there she was meeting me again, after two years, before Havana —the might of the fortunate isle to which we turned our eyes, part and parcel of my inheritance, formidable with the courage of my countrymen, humming with my native speech—and as foreign to my purposes as if I had forfeited forever my birthright in her protection. I had drifted into a sort of outlaw. You may not break the king's peace and be made welcome on board a king's ship. You may not hope to make use of a king's ship for the purposes of an elopement. There was no room on board that seventy-four for our romance.

As it was, I very nearly hailed her. What would become of us if the *Lion* had already left Havana? I thought. But no. To hail her meant separation—the only forbidden thing to those who, in the strength of youth and love, are permitted to defy the world together.

I did not hail; and the marine dwindled to a red speck upon the noble hull forging away from us on the off-shore tack. The brazen clangour of bells seemed to struggle with the sharp puff of the breeze that sent us in.

The shipping in harbour was covered with bunting in honour of the feast-day; for the same reason, there was not a sign of the usual crowd of small boats that give animation to the waters of a port; the middle of the harbour was strangely empty. A solitary bumboat canoe, with a yellow bunch of bananas in the bow, and an old negro woman dipping a languid paddle at the stern, were all that met my eye. Presently, however, a six-oared custom-house galley darted out from the tier of ships, pulling for the American brigantine. I noticed in her, beside the ordinary port officials, several soldiers, and a person astonishingly like the *alguazil* of the illustrations to Spanish romances. One of the uniformed sitters waved his hand at us, recognizing an estate *drogher*, and shouted some directions, of which we only caught the words:

"Steps—examination—to-morrow."

Our steersman took off his old hat humbly, to hail back, "*Muy bien, Señor.*"

I breathed freely, for they gave us no more of their attention. Soldiers, *alguazil*, and custom-house officers were swarming aboard the American, as if bent on ransacking her from stem to stern in the shortest possible time, so as not to be late for the procession.

The absence of movement in the harbour, the festive and idle appearance of the ships, with the flutter of innumerable flags on the forest of masts, and the great uproar of church bells in the air, made an impressive greeting for our eyes and ears. And the deserted aspect of the harbour front of the city was very striking, too. The feast had swept the quays of people so completely that the tiny pair of sentries at the foot of a tall yellow building caught the eye from afar. Seraphina crouched on a coil of rope under the bulwark; old Pedro, at the tiller, peered about from under his hand, and I, trying to expose myself to view as little as possible, helped him to look for the *Lion*. There she is. Yes! No! There she was. A crushing load fell off my chest. We had made her out together, old Pedro and I.

And then the last part of Sebright's plan had to be carried out at once. The foresheet of the *drogher* appeared to part, our mainsail shook, and before I could gasp twice, we had drifted stern foremost into the *Lion's* mizzen chains with a crash that brought a

P

genuine expression of concern to the old negro's face. He had managed the whole thing with a most convincing skill, and without even once glancing at the ship. We had done our part, but the people of the *Lion* seemed to fail in theirs unaccountably. Of all the faces that crowded her rail at the shock, not one appeared with a glimmer of intelligence. All the cargo ports were down. Their surprise and their swearing appeared to me alarmingly unaffected; with a most imbecile alacrity they exerted themselves, with small spars and boathooks, to push the *drogher* off. Nobody seemed to recognize me; Seraphina might have been a peon sitting on deck, cloaked from neck to heels and under a sombrero. I dared not shout to them in English, for fear of being heard on board the other ships around. At last Sebright himself appeared on the poop.

He gave one look over the side.

"What the devil . . ." he began. Was he blind, too?

Suddenly I saw him throw up his arms above his head. He vanished. A port came open with a jerk at the last moment. I lifted Seraphina up: two hands caught hold of her, and, in my great hurry to scramble up after her, I barked my shins cruelly. The port fell; the *drogher* went on bumping alongside, completely disregarded. Seraphina dropped the cloak at her feet and flung off her hat.

"Good-morning, *amigos*," she said gravely.

A hissed "Damn you fools—keep quiet!" from Sebright, stifled the cheer in all those bronzed throats. Only a thin little poor "hooray" quavered along the deck. The timid steward had not been able to overcome his enthusiasm. He slapped his head in despair, and rushed away to bury himself in his pantry.

"Turned up, by heavens! . . . Go in. . . ."

Good God! . . . Bucketfuls of tears. . . ." stammered Sebright, pushing us into the cuddy. "Go in! Go in at once!"

Mrs. Williams rose from behind the table wide-eyed, clasping her hands, and stumbled twice as she ran to us.

"What have you done to that child, Mr. Kemp!" she cried insanely at me. "Oh, my dear, my dear! You look like your own ghost."

Sebright, burning with impatience, pulled me away. The cabin door fell upon the two women, locked in a hug, and, stepping into his stateroom, we could do nothing at first but slap each other on the back and ejaculate the most unmeaning exclamations, like a couple of jocular idiots. But when, in the expansion of my heart, I tried to banter him about not keeping his word to look out for us, he bent double in trying to restrain his hilarity, slapped his thighs, and grew red in the face.

The excellent joke was that, for the past six days, we had been supposed to be dead—drowned; at least Doña Seraphina had been provided with that sort of death in her own name; I was drowned, too, but in the disguise of a piratical young English nobleman.

"There's nothing too bad for them to believe of us," he commented, and guffawed in his joy at seeing me unscathed. "Dead! Drowned! Ha! Ha! Good, wasn't it?"

Mrs. Williams—he said—had been weeping her eyes out over our desolate end; and even the skipper had sulked with his food for a day or two.

"Ha! Ha! Drowned! Excellent!" He shook me by the shoulders, looking me straight in the eyes—and the bizarre, nervous hilarity of my reception, so unlike his scornful attitude, proved that he, too, had believed the rumour. Indeed, nothing could have been more natural, considering my inexperience in handling boats and the fury of the norther. It had sent the *Lion* staggering into Havana in less than twenty hours after we had parted from her on the coast.

Suddenly a change came over him. He pushed me on to the settee.

"Speak! Talk! What has happened? Where have you been all this time? Man, you look ten years older."

"Ten years. Is that all?" I said.

And after he had heard the whole story of our passages he appeared greatly sobered.

"Wonderful! Wonderful!" he muttered, lost in deep thought, till I reminded him it was his turn, now, to speak.

"You are the talk of the town," he said, recovering his elasticity of spirit as he went on. The death of Don Balthasar had been the first great sensation of Havana, but it seemed that O'Brien had kept that news to himself, till he heard by an overland messenger that Seraphina and I had escaped from Casa Riego.

Then he gave it to the world; he let it be inferred that he had the news of both events together. The story, as sworn to by various suborned rascals, and put out by his creatures, ran that an English desperado, arriving in Rio Medio with some Mexicans in a schooner, had incited the rabble of the place to attack the Casa Riego. Don Balthasar had been shot while defending his house at the head of his negroes; and Don Balthasar's daughter had been carried off by the English pirate.

The amazement and sensation were extreme. Several of the first families went into mourning. A service for the repose of Don Balthasar's soul was sung in the Cathedral. Captain Williams went there out of

curiosity, and returned full of the magnificence of the
sight; nave draped in black, an enormous catafalque,
with silver angels, more than life-size, kneeling at the
four corners with joined hands, an amazing multitude
of lights. A demonstration of unbounded grief from
the Judge of the Marine Court had startled the distinguished congregation. In his place amongst the body
of higher magistrature, Don Patricio O'Brien burst into
an uncontrollable paroxysm of sobs, and had to be
assisted out of the church.

It was almost incredible, but I could well believe it.
With the thunderous strains of *Dies Irae* rolling over
his bowed head, amongst all these symbols and trap-
pings of woe, he must have seen, in the black anguish of
his baffled passion, the true image of death itself, and
tasted all the profound deception of life. Who could
tell how much secret rage, jealousy, regret, and despair
had gone to that outburst of grief, whose truth had
fluttered a distinguished company of mourners, and had
nearly interrupted their official supplications for the
repose of that old man, who had been dead to the world
for so many years? I believe that, on that very day,
just as he was going to the service, O'Brien had received the news of our supposed death by drowning.
The music, the voices, the lights of the grave, the
pomp of mourning, awe, and supplication crying for
mercy upon the dead, had been too much for him. He
had presumed too much upon his fortitude. He
wept aloud for his love lost, for his vengeance defeated,
for the dreams gone out of his life, for the inaccessible
consummation of his desire.

"And, you know, with all these affairs, he feels himself wobbling in his socket," Sebright began again, after
musing for a while. Indeed, the last events in Rio
Medio were endangering his position. He could no

more present his reports upon the state of the province with incidental reflections upon the bad faith of the English Government (who encouraged the rebels against the Catholic king), the arrogance of the English admiral, and concluding with the loyalty and honesty of the Rio Medio population, "who themselves suffered many acts of molestation from the Mexican pirates." The most famous of these papers, printed at that time in the official *Gazette*, had recommended that the loyal town should be given a battery of thirty-six pounders for purposes of self-defence. They had been given them just in time to be turned on Rowley's boats; it is known with what deadly effect. O'Brien's report after that event had made it clear that that virtuous population of the bay, exasperated by the intrusions of the *Mexicanos* upon their peaceful state, and abhorring in their souls the rebellion trying to lift its envenomed head, etc., etc., . . . heroically manned the battery to defend their town from the boats which they took to be these very pirates the British admiral was in search of. He pleaded for them the uncertain light of the early morning, the ardour of citizens, valorous, but naturally inexperienced in matters of war, and the impossibility to suppose that the admiral of a friendly power would dispatch an armed force to land on these shores. I have read these things with my own eyes; there were old files of the *Gazette* on board, and Sebright, who had been reading up his O'Brien, pointed them out to me with his finger, muttering:

"Here—look there. Pretty, ain't it?"

But that was all over. The bubble had burst. It was reported in town that the private audience the *Juez* had lately from the Captain-General was of a most stormy description. They say old Marshal What-d'ye-call-'um ended by flinging his last report in his face, and asking him how dared he work his lawyer's tricks upon an old soldier. Good old fighting cock. But stupid. All these old soldiers were stupid, Sebright declared. Old admirals, too. However, the land troops had arrived in Rio Medio by this time; the *Tornado* frigate, too, no doubt, having sailed four days ago, with orders to burn the villages to the ground; and the good *Lugareños* must be catching colds trying to hide from the carabineers in the deep, damp woods.

Our admiral was awaiting the issue of that expedition. Returning home under a cloud, Rowley wanted to take with him the assurance of the pirate nest being destroyed at last, as a sort of diplomatic feather in his cap.

"He may think," Sebright commented, "that it's his sailorly bluff that has done it, but, as far as I can see, nobody but you yourself, Kemp, had anything to do with bringing it about. Funny, is it not? Old Rowley keeps his ship dodging outside because it's cooler at sea than stewing in this harbour, but he sends in a boat for news every morning. What he is most anxious for is to get the notorious Nichols into his hands; take him home for a hanging. It seems clear to me that they are humbugging him ashore. Nichols! Where's Nichols? There are people here who say that Nichols has had free board and lodging in Havana jail for the last six months. Others swear that it is Nichols who has killed the old gentleman, run off with Doña Seraphina, and got drowned. Nichols! Who's Nichols? On that showing you are Nichols. Anybody may be Nichols. Who has ever seen him outside Rio Medio? I used to believe in him at one time, but, upon my word I begin to doubt whether there ever was such a man."

"But the man existed, at any rate," I said. "I knew him—I've talked with him. He came out second mate in the same ship with me—in the old *Thames*. Ramon took charge of him in Kingston, and that's the last positive thing I can swear to, of him. But that he was in Rio Medio for two years, and vanished from there almost directly after that unlucky boat affair, I am absolutely certain."

"Well, I suppose O'Brien knows where to lay his hand on him. But no matter where the fellow is, in jail or out of it, the admiral will never get hold of him. If they had him they could not think of giving him up. He knows too much of the game; and remember that O'Brien, if he wobbles in the socket, is by no means down yet. A man like that doesn't get knocked over like a ninepin. You may be sure he has twenty skeletons put away in good places, that he will haul out one by one, rather than let himself be squashed. He's not going to give in. A few days since, a priest—your priest, you know—turned up here on foot from Rio Medio, and went about wringing his hands, declaring that he knew all the truth, and meant to make a noise about it, too. O'Brien made short work of him, though; got the archbishop to send him into retreat, as they call it, to a Franciscan convent a hundred miles from here. These things are whispered about all along the gutters of this place."

I imagined the poor Father Antonio, with his simple resignation, mourning for us in his forced retreat, brokenhearted, and murmuring, "Inscrutable, inscrutable." I should have liked to see the old man.

"I tell you the town is fairly buzzing with the atrocities of this business," Sebright went on. "It's the thing for fashionable people to go and see what I may call the relics of the crime. They are on show in the waiting-hall of the Palace of Justice. Why, I went there myself. You go through a swing door into

a big place that, for cheerfulness, is no better than a
monster coal cellar, and there you behold, laid out on a
little black table, Mrs. Williams' woollen shawl, your
señorita's tortoise-shell comb, that had got entangled in
it somehow, and my old cap that I lent you—you remember. I assure you, it gave me the horrors to see
the confounded things spread out there in that dim
religious light. Dash me, if I didn't go queer all over.
And all the time swell carriages stopping before the
portico, dressed-up women walking up in pairs and
threes, sighing before the missus' shawl, turning up
their eyes, 'Ah! *Pobrecita! Pobrecita!* But what a
strange wrap for her to have. It is very coarse.
Perished in the flower of her youth. Incredible! Oh,
the savage, cruel Englishman.' The funniest thing in
the world."

But if this was so, Manuel's *Lugareños* were now in
Havana. Sebright pointed out that, as things stood, it
was the safest place for them, under the wing of their
patron. Sebright had recognized the schooner at once.
She came in very early one morning, and hauled herself
unostentatiously out of sight amongst a ruck of small
craft moored in the lower part of the harbour. He
took the first opportunity to ask one of the guards on
the quay what was that pretty vessel over there, just
to hear what the man would say. He was assured that
she was a Porto Rico trader of no consequence, well
known in the port.

"Never mind the scoundrels; they can do nothing
more to you."

Sebright dismissed the *Lugareños* out of my life. The
unfavourable circumstance for us was that the captain
had gone ashore. The ship was ready for sea; absolutely cleared; papers on board; could go in an hour if it
came to that; but, at any rate, next morning at day-

*P

light, before O'Brien could get wind of the Riego *drogher* arriving. Every movement in port was reported to the *Juez;* but this was a feast, and he would not hear of it probably till next day. Even *fiestas* had their uses sometimes. In his anxiety to discover Seraphina, O'Brien had played such pranks amongst the foreign shipping (after the *Lion* had been drawn blank) that the whole consular body had addressed a joint protest to the Governor, and the *Juez* had been told to moderate his efforts. No ship was to be visited more than once. Still I had seen, myself, soldiers going in a boat to board the American brigantine: a garlic-eating crew, poisoning the cabins with their breath, and poking their noses everywhere. Of course, since our supposed drowning, there had been a lull; but the least thing might start him off again. He was reputed to be almost out of his mind with sorrow, arising from his great attachment for the family. He walked about as if distracted, suffered from insomnia, and had not been fit to preside in his court for over a week, now.

"But don't you expect Williams back on board directly?"

He shook his head.

"No. Not even to-night. He told the missus he was going to spend the day out of town with his consignee, but he tipped me the wink. This evening he will send a note that the consignee detains him for the night, because the letters are not ready, and I'll have to go to her and lie, the best I am able, that it's quite the usual thing. Damn!"

I was appalled. This was too bad. And, as I raged against the dissolute habits of the man, Sebright entreated me to moderate my voice so as not to be heard in the cabin. Did I expect the man to change his

skin? He had been doing the gay bachelor about here
all his life; had never suspected he was doing anything
particularly scandalous either.

"He married the old girl out of chivalry,—the romantic fat beggar,—and never realized what it meant
till she came out with him," Sebright went on whispering to me. "He loves and honours her more than you
may think. That is so, for all your shrugs, Mr. Kemp.
It is not so easy to break the old connection as you
imagine. Why, the other evening, two of his dissolute
habits (as you call them) came off, with *mantillas* over
their heads, in a boat, in company with a male scallawag
of sorts, pinching a mandolin, and serenaded the ship
for him. We were all in the cabin after supper, and
poor Mrs. Williams, with her eyes still red from weeping
over you people, says to us, 'How sweet and melancholy
that sounds,' says she. You should have seen the
skipper rolling his eyes at me. The perspiration of
fright was simply pouring down his face. I rushed on
deck, and it took me all my Spanish to stop them from
coming aboard. I had to swear by all the saints, and
the honour of a *caballero*, that there was a wife. They
went away laughing at last. They did not want to
make trouble. They simply had not believed the tale
before. Thought it was some dodge of his. I could
hear their peals of laughter all the way up the harbour.
These are the difficulties we have. The old girl must
be protected from that sort of eye-opener, if I've to
forswear my soul. I've been keeping guard over her
ever since we arrived here—besides looking out for you
people, as long as there was any hope."

I was greatly cast down. Perhaps Williams was
justified in making concessions to the associates of his
former jolly existence to save some outrage to the feelings of his consort. I did not want to criticise his

motives—but what about getting him back on board at once?

Sebright was biting his lip. The necessity was pressing, he admitted.

He had an idea where to find him. But for himself he could not go—that was evident. Neither would I wish him to leave the ship, even for a moment, now Seraphina was on board. An unexpected visit from some zealous police understrapper, a momentary want of presence of mind on the part of the timid steward; there was enough to bring about our undoing. Moreover, as he had said, he must remain on guard over the missus. But whom to send? There was not a single boatman about. The harbour was a desert of water and dressed ships; but even the crews of most of them were ashore—"on a regular spree of praying," as he expressed it vexedly. As to our own crew, not one of them knew anything more of Spanish than a few terms of abuse, perhaps. Their hearts were in the right place, but as to their wits, he wouldn't trust a single one of them by himself—no, not an inch away from the ship. How could he send one of them ashore with the wine-shops yawning wide on all sides, and not enough lingo to ask for the way. Sure to get drunk, to get lost, to get into trouble in some way, and in the end get picked up by the police. The slightest hitch of that sort would call attention upon the ship—and with O'Brien to draw inferences. . . . He rubbed his head.

"I suppose I'll have to go," he grunted. "But I am known; I may be followed. They may wonder why I rush to fetch my skipper. And yet I feel this is the time. The very time. Between now and four o'clock to-morrow morning we have an almost absolute certitude of getting away with you two. This is our chance and your chance."

He was lost in perplexity. Then, as if inspired, I cried:

"I will go!"

"The devil!" he said, amazed. "Would you?"

I rushed at him with arguments. No one would know me. My clothes were all right and clean enough for a feast-day. I could slip through the crowds unperceived. The principal thing was to get Seraphina out of O'Brien's reach. At the worst, I could always find means to get away from Cuba by myself. There was Mrs. Williams to look after her, and if I missed Williams by some mischance, and failed to make my way back to the ship in time, I charged them solemnly not to wait, but sail away at the earliest possible moment.

I said much more than this. I was eloquent. I became as if suddenly intoxicated by the nearness of freedom and safety. The thought of being at sea with her in a few hours away from all trouble of mind or heart, made my head swim. It seemed to me I should go mad if I was not allowed to go. My limbs tingled with eagerness. I stuttered with excitement.

"Well—after all!" Sebright mumbled.

"I must go in and tell her," I said.

"No. Don't do that," said that wise young man. "Have you made up your mind?"

"Yes, I have," I answered. "But she's reasonable."

"Still," he argued, "the old girl is sure to say that nothing of the kind is necessary. The captain told her that he was coming back for tea. What could we say to that? We can't explain the true state of the case, and if you persist in going, it will look like pig-headed folly on your part."

He threw his writing-desk open for me.

"Write to her. Write down your arguments—what

you have been telling me. It's a fact that the door stands open for a few hours. As to the rest," he pursued, with a weary sigh, "I'll do the lying to pass it off with Mrs. Williams."

Thus it came about that, with only two flimsy bulkheads between us, I wrote my first letter to Seraphina, while Sebright went on deck to make arrangements to send me ashore. He was some time away; long enough for me to pour out on paper the exultation of my thought, the confidence of my hope, my desire to have her safe at last with me upon the blue sea. One must seize a propitious moment lest it should slip away and never return, I wrote. I begged her to believe I was acting for the best, and only from my great love, that could not support the thought of her being so near O'Brien, the arch-enemy of our union. There was no separation on the sea.

Sebright came in brusquely.

"Come along."

The American brigantine was berthed by then, close astern of the *Lion*, and Sebright had the idea of asking her mate to let his boat (it was in the water) put ashore a visitor he had on board. His own were hoisted, he explained, and there were no boatmen plying for hire.

His request was granted. I was pulled ashore by two American sailors, who never said a word to each other, and evidently took me for a Spaniard.

It was an excellent idea. By borrowing the Yankee's boat, the track of my connection with the *Lion* was covered. The silent seamen landed me, as asked by Sebright, near the battery on the sand, quite clear of the city.

I thanked them in Spanish, and, traversing a piece of open ground, made a wide circle to enter the town from the land side, to still further cover my tracks. I passed through a sort of squalid suburb of huts, hovels, and negro shanties. I met very few people, and these mostly old women, looking after the swarms of children of all colours and sizes, playing in the dust. Many curs sunned themselves among heaps of rubbish, and took not the trouble to growl at me. Then I came out upon a highroad, and turned my face towards the city lying under a crude sunshine, and in a ring of metallic vibrations.

Better houses with plastered fronts washed yellow or blue, and even pinky red, alternated with tumble-down wooden structures. A crenellated squat gateway faced me with a carved shield of stone above the open gloom. A young smooth-faced mulatto, in some sort of dirty uniform, but wearing new straw slippers with blue silk rosettes over his naked feet, lounged cross-legged at the door of a kind of guardroom. He held a big cigar tilted up between his teeth, and ogled me, like a woman, out of the corners of his languishing eyes. He said not a word.

Fortunately my face had tanned to a dark hue. Enrico's clothes would not attract attention to me, of course. The light colour of my hair was concealed by the handkerchief bound under my hat; my footsteps echoed loudly under the vault, and I penetrated into the heart of the city.

And directly, it seemed to me, I had stepped back three hundred years. I had never seen anything so old; this was the abandoned inheritance of an adventurous race, that seemed to have thrown all its might, all its vigour, and all its enthusiasm into one supreme effort of valour and greed. I had read the history of the Spanish Conquest; and, looking at these great walls of stone, I felt my heart moved by the same wonder, and by the same sadness. With what a fury of heroism and faith had this whole people flung itself upon the opulent mystery of the New World. Never had a nation clasped closer to its heart its dream of greatness, of glory, and of romance. There had been a moment in its destiny, when it could believe that Heaven itself smiled upon its massacres. I walked slowly, awed by the solitude. They had conquered and were no more, and these wrought stones remained to testify gloomily to the death of their success. Heavy houses, immense walls, pointed arches of the doorways, cages of iron bars projecting balconywise around each square window. And not a soul in sight, not a head looking out from these dwellings, these houses of men, these ancient abodes of hate, of base rivalries, of avarice, of ambitions —these old nests of love, these witnesses of a great romance now past and gone below the horizon. They seemed to return mournfully my wondering glances; they seemed to look at me and say, "What do you here? We have seen other men, heard other footsteps!" The peace of the cloister brooded over these aged blocks of masonry, stained with the green trails of mosses, infiltrated with shadows.

At times the belfry of a church would volley a tremendous crash of bronze into the narrow streets; and between whiles I could hear the faint echoes of far-off chanting, the brassy distant gasps of trombones. A woman in black whisked round a corner, hurrying towards the route of the procession. I took the same direction. From a wine-shop, yawning like a dirty cavern in the basement of a palatial old building, issued suddenly a brawny ruffian in rags, wiping his thick beard with the back of a hairy paw. He lurched a little, and began to walk before me hastily. I noticed the glitter of a gold earring in the lobe of his huge ear.

His cloak was frayed at the bottom into a perfect

fringe and, as he flung it about, he showed a good deal of
naked skin under it. His calves were bandaged cross-
wise; his peaked hat seemed to have been trodden upon
in filth before he had put it on his head. Suddenly
I stopped short. A *Lugareño!*

We were then in the empty part of a narrow street,
whose lower end was packed close with a crowd viewing
the procession which was filing slowly past, along the
wide thoroughfare. It was too late for me to go back.
Moreover, the ruffian paid no attention to me. It was
best to go on. The people, packed between the houses
with their backs to us, blocked our way. I had to wait.

He took his position near me in the rear of the last
rank of the crowd. He must have been inclined to
repentance in his cups, because he began to mumble and
beat his breast. Other people in the crowd were also
beating their breasts. In front of me I had the façade
of a building which, according to the little plan of my
route Sebright drew for me, was the Palace of Justice.
It had a peristyle of ugly columns at the top of a flight
of steps. A cordon of infantry kept the roadway clear.
The singing went on without interruption; and I saw
tall saints of wood, gilt and painted red and blue, pass,
borne shoulder-high, swaying and pitching above the
heads of the crowd like the masts of boats in a seaway.
Crucifixes were carried, flashing in the sun; an enormous Madonna, which must have weighed half a ton,
tottered across my line of sight, dressed up in gold
brocade and with a wreath of paper roses on her head.
A military band sent a hurricane blast of brasses as it
went by. Then all was still at once, except the silvery
tinkling of hand-bells. The people before me fell on
their knees together and left me standing up alone.

As a matter of fact I had been caught gaping at the
ceremony quite new to me, and had not expected a

move of that sort. The ruffian kneeling within a foot of me thumped and bellowed in an ecstasy of piety. As to me, I own I stood there looking with impatience at a passing canopy that seemed all gold, with three priests in gorgeous capes walking slowly under it, and I absolutely forgot to take off my hat. The bearded ruffian looked up from the midst of his penitential exercises, and before I realized I was outraging his or anybody else's feelings, leaped up with a yell, "Thou sacrilegious infidel," and sent my hat flying off my head.

Just then the band crashed again, the bells pealed out, and no one heard his shout. With one blow of my fist I sent him staggering backwards. The procession had passed; people were rising from their knees and pouring out of the narrow street. Swearing, he fumbled under his cloak; I watched him narrowly; but in a moment he sprang away and lost himself amongst the moving crowd. I picked up my hat.

For a time I stood very uneasy, and then retreated under a doorway. Nothing happened, and I was anxious to get on. It was possible to cross the wide street now. That *Lugareño* did not know me. He was a *Lugareño*, though. No doubt about it. I would make a dash now; but first I stole a hasty glance at the plan of my route which I kept in the hollow of my palm.

"Señor," said a voice. I lifted my head.

An elderly man in black, with a white moustache and imperial, stood before me. The ruffian was stalking up to his side, and four soldiers with an officer were coming behind. I took in the whole disaster at a glance.

"The señor is no doubt a foreigner—perhaps an Englishman," said the official in black. He had a lace collar, a chain on his neck, velvet breeches, a well-turned leg in black stockings. His voice was soft.

I was so disconcerted that I nodded at him.

"The señor is young and inconsiderate. Religious feelings ought to be respected." The official in black was addressing me in sad and measured tones. "This good Catholic," he continued, eying the bearded ruffian dubiously, "has made a formal statement to me of your impious demonstration."

What a fatal accident, I thought, appalled; but I tried to explain the matter. I expressed regret. The other gazed at me benevolently.

"Nevertheless, Señor, pray follow me. Even for your own safety. You must give some account of yourself."

This I was firmly resolved not to give. But the *Lugareño* had been going through a pantomime of scrutinizing my person. He crouched up, stepped back, then to one side.

"This worthy man," began the official in black, "complains of your violence, too. . . ."

"This worthy man," I shouted stupidly, "is a pirate. He is a Rio Medio *Lugareño*. He is a criminal."

The official seemed astounded, and I saw my idiotic mistake at once—too late!

"Strange," he murmured, and, at the same time, the ruffianly wretch began to shout:

"It is he! The traitor! The heretic! I recognize him!"

"Peace, peace!" said the man in black.

"I demand to be taken before the Juez Don Patricio for a deposition," shrieked the *Lugareño*. A crowd was beginning to collect.

The official and the officer exchanged consulting glances. At a word from the latter, the soldiers closed upon me.

I felt utterly overcome, as if the earth had crumbled under my feet, and the heavens had been rent in twain.

I walked between my captors across the street amongst hooting knots of people, and up the steps of the portico, as if in a frightful dream.

In the gloomy, chilly hall they made me wait. A soldier stood on each side of me, and there, absolutely before my eyes on a little table, reposed Mrs. Williams' shawl and Sebright's cap. This was the very hall of the Palace of Justice of which Sebright had spoken. It was more than ever like an absurd dream, now. But I had the leisure to collect my wits. I could not claim the Consul's protection simply because I should have to give him a truthful account of myself, and that would mean giving up Seraphina. The Consul could not protect her. But the *Lion* would sail on the morrow. Sebright would understand it if Williams did not. I trusted Sebright's sagacity. Yes, she would sail to-morrow evening. A day and a half. If I could only keep the knowledge of Seraphina from O'Brien till then—she was safe, and I should be safe, too, for my lips would be unsealed. I could claim the protection of my Consul and proclaim the villainy of the *Juez*.

"Go in there now, Señor, to be confronted with your accuser," said the official in black, appearing before me. He pointed at a small door to the left. My heart was beating steadily. I felt a sort of intrepid resignation.

PART FIFTH

THE LOT OF MAN

CHAPTER ONE

"WHY have I been brought here, your worships?" I asked, with a great deal of firmness.

There were two figures in black, the one beside, the other behind a large black table. I was placed in front of them, between two soldiers, in the centre of a large, gaunt room, with bare, dirty walls, and the arms of Spain above the judge's seat.

"You are before the *Juez de la Primiera Instancia*," said the man in black beside the table. He wore a large and shadowy tricorn. "Be silent, and respect the procedure."

It was, without doubt, excellent advice. He whispered some words in the ear of the Judge of the First Instance. It was plain enough to me that the judge was a quite inferior official, who merely decided whether there were any case against the accused; he had, even to his clerk, an air of timidity, of doubt.

I said, "But I insist on knowing. . . ."

The clerk said, "In good time. . . ." And then, in the same tone of disinterested official routine, he spoke to the *Lugareño*, who, from beside the door, rolled very frightened eyes from the judges and the clerk to myself and the soldiers—"Advance."

The judge, in a hurried, perfunctory voice, put questions to the *Lugareño;* the clerk scratched with a large quill on a sheet of paper.

"Where do you come from?"

"The town of Rio Medio, excellency."

"Of what occupation?"

"Excellency—a few goats. . . ."

"Why are you here?"

"My daughter, excellency, married Pepe of the *posada* in the *Calle*. . . ."

The judge said, "Yes, yes," with an unsanguine impatience. The *Lugareño's* dirty hands jumped nervously on the large rim of his limp hat.

"You lodge a complaint against the señor there."

The clerk pointed the end of his quill towards me.

"I? God forbid, excellency," the *Lugareño* bleated. "The *Alguazil* of the Criminal Court instructed me to be watchful. . . ."

"You lodge an information, then?" the *Juez* said.

"Maybe it is an information, excellency," the *Lugareño* answered, "as regards the señor there."

The *Alguazil* of the Criminal Court had told him, and many other men of Rio Medio, to be on the watch for me, "undoubtedly touching what had happened, as all the world knew, in Rio Medio."

He looked me full in the face with stupid insolence, and said:

"At first I much doubted, for all the world said this man was dead—though others said worse things. Perhaps, who knows?"

He had seen me, he said, many times in Rio Medio, outside the Casa; on the balcony of the Casa, too. And he was sure that I was a heretic and an evil person.

It suddenly struck me that this man—I was undoubtedly familiar with his face—must be the lieutenant of Manuel-del-Popolo, his boon companion. Without doubt, he had seen me on the balcony of the Casa.

He had gained a lot of assurance from the conciliatory manner of the *Juez*, and said suddenly, in a tentative way:

"An evil person; a heretic? Who knows? Perhaps it was he who incited some people there to murder his señoria, the illustrious Don."

I said almost contemptuously, "Surely the charge against me is most absurd? Everyone knows who I am."

The old judge made a gentle, tired motion with his hand.

"Señor," he said, "there is no charge against you—except that no one knows who you are. You were in a place where very lamentable and inexplicable things happened; you are now in Havana: you have no passport. I beg of you to remain calm. These things are all in order."

I hadn't any doubt that, as far as he knew, he was speaking the truth. He was a man, very evidently, of a weary and naïve simplicity. Perhaps it was really true—that I should only have to explain; perhaps it was all over.

O'Brien came into the room with the casual step of an official from an office entering another's room.

It was as if seeing me were a thing that he very much disliked—that he came because he wanted to satisfy himself of my existence, of my identity, and my being alone. The slow stare that he gave me did not mitigate the leisureliness of his entry. He walked behind the table; the judge rose with immense deference; with his eternal smile, and no word spoken, he motioned the judge to resume the examination; he stood looking at the clerk's notes meditatively, the smile still round lips that had a nervous tremble, and eyes that had dark marks beneath them. He seemed as if he were still smiling just after having been violently shaken.

The judge went on examining the *Lugareño*.

"Do you know whence the señor came?"

"Excellency, excellency. . . ." The man stuttered, his eyes on O'Brien's face.

"Nor how long he was in the town of Rio Medio?" the judge went on.

O'Brien suddenly drooped towards his ear. "All those things are known, señor, my colleague," he said, and began to whisper.

The old judge showed signs of very naïve astonishment and joy.

"Is it possible?" he exclaimed. "This man? He is very young to have committed such crimes."

The clerk hurriedly left the room. He returned with many papers. O'Brien, leaning over the judge's shoulder, emphasized words with one finger. What new villainies could O'Brien be meditating? It wasn't possibly the *Lugareño's* suggestion that I had lured men to murder Don Balthasar? Was it merely that I had infringed some law in carrying off Seraphina?

The old judge said, "How lucky, Don Patricio! We may now satisfy the English admiral. What good fortune!"

He suddenly sat straight in his chair; O'Brien behind him scrutinized my face—to see how I should bear what was coming.

"What is your name?" the judge asked peremptorily.

I said, "Juan—John Kemp. I am of noble English family; I am well enough known. Ask the Señor O'Brien."

On O'Brien's shaken face the smile hardened.

"I heard that in Rio Medio the señor was called . . . was called . . ." He paused and appealed to the *Lugareño*.

"What was he called—the *capataz*, the man who led the picaroons?"

The *Lugareño* stammered, "Nikola . . . Nikola el Escoces, Señor Don Patricio."

"You hear?" O'Brien asked the judge. "This villager identifies the man."

"Undoubtedly—undoubtedly," the *Juez* said. "We need no more evidence. . . . You, Señor, have seen this villain in Rio Medio, this villager identifies him by name."

I said, "This is absurd. A hundred witnesses can say that I am John Kemp. . . ."

"That may be true," the *Juez* said dryly, and then to his clerk:

"Write here, 'John Kemp, of noble British family, called, on the scene of his crimes, Nikola el Escoces, otherwise El Demonio.'"

I shrugged my shoulders. I did not, at the moment, realize to what this all tended.

The judge said to the clerk, "Read the Act of Accusation. Read here. . . ." He was pointing to a paragraph of the papers the clerk had brought in. They were the Act of Accusation, prepared long before, against the man Nichols.

This particular villainy suddenly became grotesquely and portentously plain. The clerk read an appalling catalogue of sordid crimes, working into each other like kneaded dough—the testimony of witnesses who had signed the record. Nikola had looted fourteen ships, and had apparently murdered twenty-two people with his own hand—two of them women—and there was the affair of Rowley's boats. "The pinnace," the clerk read, "of the British came within ten yards. The said Nikola then exclaimed, 'Curse the bloodthirsty hounds,' and fired the grapeshot into the boat. Seven were killed by that discharge. This I saw with my own eyes. . . . Signed, Isidoro Alemanno." And another swore, "The said Nikola was below, but he came running up, and with one blow of his knife severed the throat of the man who was kneeling on the deck. . . ."

There was no doubt that Nikola had committed these crimes; that the witnesses had sworn to them and signed the deposition. . . . The old judge had evidently never seen him, and now O'Brien and the *Lugareño* had sworn that I was Nikola el Escoces, alias El Demonio.

My first impulse was to shout with rage; but I checked it because I knew I should be silenced. I said:

"I am not Nikola el Escoces. That I can easily prove."

The Judge of the First Instance shrugged his shoulders and looked, with implicit trust, up into O'Brien's face.

"That man," I pointed at the *Lugareño*, "is a pirate. And, what is more, he is in the pay of the Señor Juez O'Brien. He was the lieutenant of a man called Manuel-del-Popolo, who commanded the *Lugareños* after Nikola left Rio Medio."

"You know very much about the pirates," the *Juez* said, with the sardonic air of a very stupid man. "Without doubt you were intimate with them. I sign now your order for committal to the *carcel* of the Marine Court."

I said, "But I tell you I am not Nikola. . . ."

The *Juez* said impassively, "You pass out of my hands into those of the Marine Court. I am satisfied that you are a person deserving of a trial. That is the limit of my responsibility."

I shouted then, "But I tell you this O'Brien is my personal enemy."

The old man smiled acidly.

"The señor need fear nothing of our courts. He will be handed over to his own countrymen. Without doubt of them he will obtain justice." He signed to the *Lugareño* to go, and rose, gathering up his papers; he bowed to O'Brien. "I leave the criminal at the disposal of your worship," he said, and went out with his clerk.

O'Brien sent out the two soldiers after him, and stood there alone. He had never been so near his death. But for sheer curiosity, for my sheer desire to know what he *could* say, I would have smashed in his brains with the clerk's stool. I was going to do it; I made one step towards the stool. Then I saw that he was crying.

"The curse—the curse of Cromwell on you," he sobbed suddenly. "You send me back to hell again." He writhed his whole body. "Sorrow!" he said, "I know it. But what's this? What's *this?*"

The many reasons he had for sorrow flashed on me like a procession of sombre images.

"Dead and done with a man can bear," he muttered. "But this—Not to know—perhaps alive—perhaps hidden—She may be dead. . . ." With a change like a flash he was commanding me.

"Tell me how you escaped."

I had a vague inspiration of the truth.

"You aren't fit for a decent man's speaking to," I said.

"You let her drown."

It gave me suddenly the measure of his ignorance; he did not know anything—nothing. His hell was uncertainty. Well, let him stay there.

"Where is she?" he said. "Where is she?"

"Where she's no need to fear you," I answered.

He had a sudden convulsive gesture, as if searching for a weapon.

"If you'll tell me she's alive . . ." he began.

"Oh, I'm not dead," I answered.

"Never a drowned puppy was more," he said, with a flash of vivacity. "You hang here—for murder—or in England for piracy."

"Then I've little to want to live for," I sneered at him.

"You let her drown," he said. "You took her from that house, a young girl, in a little boat. And you can hold up your head."

"I was trying to save her from you," I answered.

"By God," he said. "These English—I've seen them, spit the child on the mother's breast. I've seen them set fire to the thatch of the widow and childless. But this. . . . But this. . . . I can save you, I tell you."

"You can't make me go through worse than I've borne," I answered. Sorrow and all he might wish on my head, my life was too precious to him till I spoke. I wasn't going to speak.

"I'll search every ship in the harbour," he said passionately.

"Do," I said. "Bring your *Lugareños* to the task."

Upon the whole, I wasn't much afraid. Unless he got definite evidence he couldn't—in the face of the consul's protests, and the presence of the admiral—touch the *Lion* again. He fixed his eyes intently upon me.

"You came in the American brigantine," he said. "It's known you landed in her boat."

I didn't answer him; it was plain enough that the *drogher's* arrival had either not been reported to him, or it had been searched in vain.

"In her boat," he repeated. "I tell you I know she is not dead; even you, an Englishman, must have a different face if she were."

"I don't at least ask you for life," I said, "to enjoy with her."

"She's alive," he said. "Alive! As for where, it matters little. I'll search every inch of the island, every road, every *hacienda*. You don't realize my power."

"Then search the bottom of the sea," I shouted.

"Let's look at the matter in the right light."

He had mastered his grief, his incertitude. He was himself again, and the smile had returned—as if at the moment he forced his features to their natural lines.

"Send one of your friars to heaven—you'll never go there yourself to meet her."

"If you will tell me she's alive, I'll save you."

I made a mute, obstinate gesture.

"If she's alive, and you don't tell me, I can't but find her. And I'll make you know the agonies of suspense— a long way from here."

I was silent.

"If she's dead, and you'll tell me, I'll save you some trouble. If she's dead and you don't, you'll have your own remorse and the rest, too."

I said, "You're too Irish mysterious for me to understand. But you've a choice of four evils for me— choose yourself."

He continued with a quivering, taut good-humour: "Prove to me she's dead, and I'll let you die sharply and mercifully."

"You won't believe!" I said; but he took no notice.

"I tell you plainly," he smiled. "If we find . . . if we find her dear body—and I can't but help, I've men on the watch all along the shores—I'll give you up to your admiral for a pirate. You'll have a long slow agony of a trial; I know what English justice is. And a disgraceful felon's death."

I was thinking that, in any case, a day or so might be gained, the *Lion* would be gone; they could not touch

her while the flagship remained outside. I certainly
didn't want to be given up to the admiral; I might
explain the mistaken identity. But there was the charge
of treason in Jamaica. I said:

"I only ask to be given up; but you daren't do it
for your own credit. I can show you up."

He said, "Make no mistake! If he gets you, he'll
hang you. He's going home in disgrace. Your whole
blundering Government will work to hang you."

"They know pretty well," I answered, "that there
are queer doings in Havana. I promise you, I'll clear
things up. I know too much. . . ."

He said, with a sudden, intense note of passion,
"Only tell me where her grave is, I'll let you go free.
You couldn't, you dare not, dastard that you are,
go away from where she died—without . . . without making sure."

"Then search all the new graves in the island," I
said, "I'll tell you nothing. . . . Nothing!"

He came at me again and again, but I never spoke
after that. He made all the issues clearer and clearer—
his own side involuntarily and all the griefs I had to
expect. As for him, he dare not kill me—and he dare
not give me up to the admiral. In his suspense, since,
for him, I was the only person in the world who knew
Seraphina's fate, he dare not let me out of his grip.
And all the while he had me he must keep the admiral
there, waiting for the surrender either of myself or of
some other poor devil whom he might palm off as
Nikola el Escoces. While the admiral was there the
Lion was pretty safe from molestation, and she would
sail pretty soon.

At the same time, except for the momentary sheer
joy of tormenting a man whom I couldn't help regarding
as a devil, I had more than enough to fear. I had

suffered too much; I wanted rest, woman's love, slackening off. And here was another endless coil—endless. If it didn't end in a knife in the back, he might keep me for ages in Havana; or he might get me sent to England, where it would take months, an endless time, to prove merely that I wasn't Nikola el Escoces. I should prove it; but, in the meantime, what would become of Seraphina? Would she follow me to England? Would she even know that I had gone there? Or would she think me dead and die herself? O'Brien knew nothing; his spies might report a hundred uncertainties. He was standing rigidly still now, as if afraid to move for fear of breaking down. He said suddenly:

"You came in some ship; you can't deceive me, I shall have them all searched again."

I said desperately, "Search and be damned—whatever ships you like."

"You cold, pitiless, English scoundrel," he shrieked suddenly. The breaking down of his restraint had let him go right into madness. "You have murdered her. You cared nothing; you came from nowhere. A beggarly fool, too stupid to be even an adventurer. A miserable blunderer, coming in blind; coming out blind; and leaving ruin and worse than hell. What good have you done yourself? What could you? What did you see? What did you hope? . . . Sorrow? Ruin? Death? I am acquainted with them. It is in the blood; 'tis in the tone; in the entrails of us, in our mother's milk. Your accursed land has brought always that on our own dear and sorrowful country. . . . You waste, you ruin, you spoil. What for? . . . Tell me what for? Tell me? Tell me? What did you gain? What will you ever gain? An unending curse! . . . But, ah, ye've no souls."

Q

He called very loudly, as if with a passionate relief, his voice giving life to an unsuspected, misgiving echo:

"Guards! Soldiers! . . . You shall be shot, now!"

He was going to cut the knot that way. Two soldiers pushed the door noisily open, their muskets advanced. He took no notice of them; and they retained an attitude of military stupidity, their eyes upon him. He whispered:

"No, no! Not yet!"

Then he looked at me searchingly, as if he still hoped to get some certainty from my face, some inkling, perhaps some inspiration of what would persuade me to speak. Then he shook his wrists violently, as if in fear of himself.

"Take him away," he said. "Away! Out of reach of my hands. Out of reach of my hands."

I was trembling a good deal; when the soldiers entered I thought I had got to my last minute. But, as it was, he had not learnt a thing from me. Not a thing. And I did not see where else he could go for information.

CHAPTER TWO

THE entrance to the common prison of Havana was a sort of lofty tunnel, finished by great, iron-rusted, wooden gates. A civil guard was exhibiting the judge's warrant for my committal to a white-haired man, with a red face and blue eyes, that seemed to look through tumbled bushes of silver eyebrows—the *al-cayde* of the prison. He bowed, and rattled two farcically large keys. A practicable postern was ajar on the yellow wood of the studded gates. It was as if it afforded a glimpse of the other side of the world. The venerable turnkey, a gnome in a steeple-crowned hat, protruded a blood-red hand backwards in the direction of the postern.

"Señor Caballero," he croaked, "I pray you to consider this house your own. My servants are yours."

Within was a gravel yard, shut in by portentous lead-white house-sides with black window holes. Under each row of windows was a vast vaulted tunnel, caged with iron bars, for all the world like beasts' dens. It being day, the beasts were out and lounging about the *patio*. They had an effect of infinite tranquillity, as if they were ladies and gentlemen parading in a Sunday avenue. Perhaps twenty of them, in snowy white shirts and black velvet knee-breeches, strutted like pigeons in a knot, some with one woman on the arm, some with two. Bundles of variegated rags lay against the walls, as if they were sweepings. Well, they were the sweepings of Havana jail. The men in white and black were the great thieves . . . and there were children, too—the place was the city orphanage. For the fifth part of a second my advent made no difference. Then, at the far end, one of the men in black and white separated himself, and came swiftly to me across the sunny *patio*. The others followed slowly, with pea-fowl steps, their women hanging to them and whispering. The bundles of rags rose up towards me; others slunk furtively out of the barred dens. The man who was approaching had the head of a Julius Cæsar of fifty, for all the world as if he had stolen a bust and endowed it with yellow skin and stubby gray and silver hair. He saluted me with intense gravity and an imperial glance of yellow eyes along a hooked nose. His linen was the most spotless broidered and embossed stuff; from the crimson scarf round his waist protruded the shagreen and silver handle of a long dagger. He said:

"Señor, I have the honour to salute you. I am Crisostomo Garcia. I ask the courtesy of your trousers."

I did not answer him. I did not see what he wanted with my trousers, which weren't anyway as valuable as his own. The others were closing in on me like a solid wall. I leant back against the gate; I was not frightened, but I was mightily excited. The man like Cæsar looked fiercely at me, swayed a long way back on his haunches, and imperiously motioned the crowd to recede.

"Señor Inglesito," he said, "the gift I have the honour to ask of you is the price of my protection. Without it these, my brothers, will tear you limb from limb, there will nothing of you remain."

His brothers set up a stealthy, sinister growl, that went round among the heads like the mutter of an obscene echo among the mountain-tops. I wondered whether this, perhaps, was the man who, O'Brien said, would put a knife in my back. I hadn't any knife; I might knock the fellow's teeth down his throat, though.

The *alcayde* thrust his immense hat, blood-red face, and long, ragged, silver locks out of the little door. His features were convulsed with indignation. He had been whispering with the Civil Guard.

"Are you mad, gentlemen?" he said. "Do you wish to visit hell before your times? Do you know who the señor is? Did you ever hear of Carlos el Demonio? This is the *Inglesito* of Rio Medio!"

It was plain that my deeds, such as they were, reported by O'Brien spies, by the *Lugareños*, by all sorts of credulous gossipers, had got me the devil of a reputation in the *patio* of the jail. Men detached themselves from the crowd, and went running about to announce my arrival. The *alcayde* drew his long body into the *patio*, and turned to lock the little door with an immense key. In the crowd all sorts of little movements happened. Women crossed themselves, and furtively thrust pairs of crooked, skinny, brown, black-nailed fingers in my direction. The man like Cæsar said:

"I ask your pardon, Señor Caballero. I did not know. How could I tell? You are free of all the *patios* in this land."

The tall *alcayde* finished grinding the immense key in the lock, and touched me on the arm.

"If the señor will follow me," he said. "I will do the honours of this humble mansion, and indicate a choice of rooms where he may be free from the visits of these gentry."

We went up steps, and through long, shadowy corridors, with here and there a dark, lounging figure, like a stag seen in the dim aisles of a wood. The *alcayde* threw open a door.

The room was like a blazing oblong box, filled with light, but without window or chimney. Two men were fencing in the illumination of some twenty candles stuck all round the mildewed white walls on lumps of clay. There was a blaze of silver things, like an altar of a wealthy church, from a black, carved table in the far corner. The two men, in shirts and breeches, revolved round each other, their rapiers clinking, their left arms scarved, holding buttoned daggers. The *alcayde* proclaimed:

"Don Vincente Salazar, I have the honour to announce an English señor."

The man with his face to me tossed his rapier impatiently into a corner. He was a plump, dark Cuban, with a brooding truculence. The other faced round quickly. His cheeks shone in the candle-light like polished yellow leather, his eyes were narrow slits, his face lugubrious. He scrutinized me intently, then drawled:

"My! You? . . . Hang me if I didn't think it would be you!"

He had the air of surveying a monstrosity, and pulled the neck of his dirty print shirt open, panting. He slouched out into the corridor, and began whispering eagerly to the *alcayde*. The little Cuban glowered at me; I said I had the honour to salute him.

He muttered something contemptuous between his teeth. Well, if he didn't want to talk to me, I didn't want to talk to him. It had struck me that the tall, sallow man was undoubtedly the second mate of the *Thames*. Nicholas, the real Nikola el Escoces! The Cuban grumbled suddenly:

"You, Señor, are without doubt one of the spies of

that friend of the priests, that O'Brien. Tell him to
beware—that I bid him beware. I, Don Vincente
Salazar de Valdepeñas y Forli y . . ."

I remembered the name; he was once the suitor of
Seraphina—the man O'Brien had put out of the way.
He continued with a grotesque frown of portentous
significance:

"To-morrow I leave this place. And your com-
patriot is very much afraid, Señor. Let him fear!
Let him fear! But a thousand spies should not save
him."

The tall *alcayde* came hurriedly back and stood bowing between us. He apologized abjectly to the Cuban
for introducing me upon him. But the room was the
best in the place at the disposal of the prisoners of the
Juez O'Brien. And I was a noted *caballero*. Heaven
knows what I had not done in Rio Medio. Burnt,
slain, ravished. . . . The Señor Juez was understood to be much incensed against me. The gloomy
Cuban at once rushed upon me, as if he would have
taken me into his arms.

"The *Inglesito* of Rio Medio!" he said. "Ha, ha!
Much have I heard of you. Much of the señor's
valiance! Many tales! That foul eater of the carrion
of the priests wishes your life! Ah, but let him beware!
I shall save you, Señor—I, Don Vincente Salazar."

He presented me with the room—a remarkably bare
place but for his properties: silver branch candlesticks,
a silver chafing-dish as large as a basin. They might
have been chased by Cellini—one used to find things
like that in Cuba in those days, and Salazar was the
person to have them. Afterwards, at the time of the
first insurrection, his eight-mule harness was sold for
four thousand pounds in Paris—by reason of the gold
and pearls upon it. The atmosphere, he explained, was

fetid, but his man was coming to burn sandal-wood and beat the air with fans.

"And to-morrow!" he said, his eyes rolling. Suddenly he stopped. "Señor," he said, "is it true that my venerated friend, my more than father, has been murdered—at the instigation of that fiend? Is it true that the señorita has disappeared? These tales are told."

I said it was very true.

"They shall be avenged," he declared, "to-morrow! I shall seek out the señorita. I shall find her. I shall find her! For me she was destined by my venerable friend."

He snatched a black velvet jacket from the table and put it on.

"Afterwards, Señor, you shall relate. Have no fear. I shall save you. I shall save all men oppressed by this scourge of the land. For the moment afford me the opportunity to meditate." He crossed his arms, and dropped his round head. "Alas, yes!" he meditated.

Suddenly he waved towards the door. "Señor," he said swiftly, "I must have air; I stifle. Come with me to the corridor. . . ."

He went towards the window giving on to the *patio;* he stood in the shadow, his arms folded, his head hanging dejectedly. At the moment it grew suddenly dark, as if a veil had been thrown over a lamp. The sun had set outside the walls. A drum began to beat. Down below in the obscurity the crowd separated into three strings and moved slowly towards the barren tunnels. Under our feet the white shirts disappeared; the ragged crowd gravitated to the left; the small children strung into the square cage-door. The drum beat again and the crowd hurried. Then there was a clang of closing grilles and lights began to show behind the bars from deep recesses. In a little time there was a repulsive hash of heads and limbs to be seen under the arches vanishing a long way within, and a little light washed across the gravel of the *patio* from within.

"Señor," the Cuban said suddenly, "I will pronounce his panegyric. He was a man of a great gentleness, of an inevitable nobility, of an invariable courtesy. Where, in this degenerate age, shall we find the like!" He stopped to breathe a sound of intense exasperation.

"When I think of these Irish, . . ." he said. "Of that O'Brien. . . ." A servant was arranging the shining room that we had left. Salazar interrupted himself to give some orders about a banquet, then returned to me. "I tell you I am here for introducing my knife to the spine of some sort of Madrid *embustero*, a man who was insolent to my *amiga* Clara. Do you believe that for that this O'Brien, by the influence of the priests whose soles he licks with his tongue, has had me inclosed for many months? Because he feared me! Aha! I was about to expose him to the noble don who is now dead! I was about to wed the señorita who has disappeared. But to-morrow . . . I shall expose his intrigue to the Captain-General. You, Señor, shall be my witness! I extend my protection to you. . . ." He crossed his arms and spoke with much deliberation. "Señor, this Irishman incommodes me, Don Vincente Salazar de Valdepeñas y Forli. . . ." He nodded his head expressively. "Señor, we offered these Irish the shelter of our robe for that your Government was making martyrs of them who were good Christians, and it behoves us to act in despite of your Government, who are heretics and not to be tolerated upon God's Christian earth. But, Señor, if they incommoded your Government as they do us, I do not wonder that there was a desire to remove

*Q

them. Señor, the life of that man is not worth the
price of eight mules, which is the price I have paid
for my release. I might walk free at this moment,
but it is not fitting that I should slink away under
cover of darkness. I shall go out in the daylight with
my carriage. And I will have an offering to show my
friends who, like me, are incommoded by this. . . ."
The man was a monomaniac; but it struck me that, if
I had been O'Brien, I should have felt uncomfortable.

In the dark of the corridor a long shape appeared,
lounging. The Cuban beside me started hospitably
forward.

"*Vamos*," he said briskly; "to the banquet. . . ."
He waved his hand towards the shining door and stood
aside. We entered.

The other man was undoubtedly the Nova Scotian
mate of the *Thames*, the man who had dissuaded me
from following Carlos on the day we sailed into Kingston Harbour. He was chewing a toothpick, and at the
ruminant motion of his knife-jaws I seemed to see
him, sitting naked to the waist in his bunk, instead of
upright there in red trousers and a blue shirt—an
immense lank-length of each. I pieced his history
together in a sort of flash. He was the true Nikola el
Escoces; his name was Nichols, and he came from Nova
Scotia. He had been the chief of O'Brien's *Lugareños*.
He surveyed me now with a twinkle in his eyes, his
yellow jaws as shiny-shaven as of old; his arms as much
like a semaphore. He said mockingly:

"So you went there, after all?"

But the Cuban was pressing us towards his banquet;
there was *gaspacho* in silver plates, and a man in livery
holding something in a napkin. It worried me. We
surveyed each other in silence. I wondered what
Nichols knew; what it would be safe to tell him; how

much he could help me? One or other of these men undoubtedly might. The Cuban was an imbecile; but he might have some influence—and if he really were going out on the morrow, and really did go to the Captain-General, he certainly could further his own revenge on O'Brien by helping me. . . . But as for Nichols. . .

Salazar began to tell a long, exaggerated story about his cook, whom he had imported from Paris.

"Think," he said; "I bring the fool two thousand miles—and then—not even able to begin on a land-crab. A fool!"

The Nova Scotian cast an uninterested side glance at him, and said in English, which Salazar did not understand:

"So you went there, after all? And now *he's* got you." I did not answer him. "I know all about yeh," he added.

"It's more than I do about you," I said.

He rose and suddenly jerked the door open, peered on each side of the corridor, and then sat down again. "I'm not afraid to tell," he said defiantly. "I'm not afraid of anything. I'm safe."

The Cuban said to me in Spanish: "This señor is my friend. Everyone who hates that devil is my friend."

"I'm safe," Nichols repeated. "I know too much about our friend the raparee." He lowered his voice. "They say you're to be given up for piracy, eh?" His eyes had an extraordinary anxious leer. "You are now, eh? For how much? Can't you tell a man? We're in the same boat! I kin help yeh!"

Salazar accidentally knocked a silver goblet off the table and, at the sound, Nichols sprang half off his chair. He glared in a wild stare around him then grasped at a flagon of *aguardiente* and drank.

"I'm not afraid of any damn thing," he said. "I've got a hold on that man. He dursen't give me up. I kin see! He's going to give you up and say you're responsible for it all."

"I don't know what he's going to do," I answered.

"Will you not, Señor," Salazar said suddenly, "relate, if you can without distress, the heroic death of that venerated man?"

I glanced involuntarily at Nichols. "The distress," I said, "would be very great. I was Don Balthasar's kinsman. The Señor O'Brien had a great fear of my influence in the Casa. It was in trying to take me away that Don Balthasar, who defended me, was slain by the *Lugareños* of O'Brien."

Salazar said, "Aha! Aha! We are kindred spirits. Hated and loved by the same souls. This fiend, Señor. And then. . . ."

"I escaped by sea—in an open boat, in the confusion. When I reached Havana, the *Juez* had me arrested."

Salazar raised both hands; his gestures, made for large, grave men, were comic in him. They reduced Spanish manners to absurdity. He said:

"That man dies. That man dies. To-morrow I go to the Captain-General. He shall hear this story of yours, Señor. He shall know of these machinations which bring honest men to this place. We are a band of brothers. . . ."

"That's what I say." Nichols leered at me. "We're all in the same boat."

I expect he noticed that I wasn't moved by his declaration. He said, still in English:

"Let us be open. Let's have a council of war. This O'Brien hates me because I wouldn't fire on my own countrymen." He glanced furtively at me. "I wouldn't," he asserted; "he wanted me to fire into their boats; but I wouldn't. Don't you believe the tales they tell about me! They tell worse about you. Who says I would fire on my countrymen? Where's the man who says it?" He had been drinking more brandy and glared ferociously at me. "None of your tricks, my hearty," he said. "None of your getting out and spreading tales. O'Brien's my friend; he'll never give me up. He dursen't. I know too much. You're a pirate! No doubt it was you who fired into them boats. By God I'll be witness against you if they give me up. I'll show you up."

All the while the little Cuban talked swiftly and with a saturnine enthusiasm. He passed the wine rapidly.

"My own countrymen!" Nichols shouted. "Never! I shot a Yankee lieutenant—Allen he was—with my own hand. That's another thing. I'm not a man to trifle with. No, sir. Don't you try it. . . . Why, I've papers that would hang O'Brien. I sent them home to Halifax. I know a trick worth his. By God, let him try it! Let him only try it. He dursen't give me up. . . ."

The man in livery came in to snuff the candles. Nichols sprang from his seat in a panic and drew his knife with frantic haste. He continued, glaring at me from the wall, the knife in his hand:

"Don't you dream of tricks. I've cut more throats than you've kissed gals in your little life."

Salazar himself drew an immense pointed knife with a shagreen hilt. He kissed it rapturously.

"Aha! . . . Aha!" he said, "bear this kiss into his ribs at the back." His eyes glistened with this mania. "I swear it; when I next see this dog; this friend of the priests." He threw the knife on the table. "Look," he said, "was ever steel truer or more thirsty?"

"Don't you make no mistake," Nichols continued to me. "Don't you think to presume. O'Brien's my friend. I'm here snug and out of the way of the old fool of an admiral. That's why he's kept waiting off the Morro. When he goes, I walk out free. Don't you try to frighten me. I'm not a man to be frightened."

Salazar bubbled: "Ah, but now the wine flows and is red. We are a band of brothers, each loving the other. Brothers, let us drink."

The air of close confinement, the blaze, the feel of the jail, pressed upon me, and I felt sore, suddenly, at having eaten and drunk with those two. The idea of Seraphina, asleep perhaps, crying perhaps, something pure and distant and very blissful, came in upon me irresistibly.

The little Cuban said, "We have had a very delightful conversation. It is very plain this O'Brien must die."

I rose to my feet. "Gentlemen," I said in Spanish, "I am very weary; I will go and sleep in the corridor."

The Cuban sprang towards me with an immense anxiety of hospitableness. I was to sleep on his couch, the couch of cloth of gold. It was impossible, it was insulting, that I should think of sleeping in the corridor. He thrust me gently down upon it, making with his plump hands the motions of smoothing it to receive me. I laid down and turned my face to the wall.

It wasn't possible to sleep, even though the little Cuban, with a tender solicitude, went round the walls blowing out the candles. He might be useful to me, might really explain matters to the Captain-General, or might even, as a last resource, take a letter from me to the British Consul. But I should have to be alone with him. Nichols was an abominable scoundrel; bloodthirsty to the defenceless; a liar; craven before the ghost of a threat. No doubt O'Brien did not want to give him up. Perhaps he *had* papers. And no doubt, once he could find a trace of Seraphina's whereabouts, O'Brien would give me up under the name of Nichols. All I could do was to hope for a gain of time. And yet, if I gained time, it could only mean that I should in the end be given up to the admiral.

And Seraphina's whereabouts. It came over me lamentably that I myself did not know. The *Lion* might have sailed. It was possible. She might be at sea. Then, perhaps, my only chance of ever seeing her again lay in my being given up to the admiral, to stand in England a trial, perhaps for piracy, perhaps for treason. I might meet her only in England, after many years of imprisonment. It wasn't possible. I would not believe in the possibility. How I loved her! How wildly, how irrationally—this woman of another race, of another world, bound to me by sufferings together, by joys together. Irrationally! Looking at the matter now, the reason is plain enough. Before then I had not lived. I had only waited—for her and for what she stood for. It was in my blood, in my race, in my tradition, in my training. We, all of us for generations, had made for efficiency, for drill, for restraint. Our Romance was just this very Spanish contrast, this obliquity of vision, this slight tilt of the convex mirror that shaped the same world so differently to onlookers at different points of its circle.

I could feel a little of it even then, when there was only the merest chance of my going back to England and getting back towards our old position on the rim of the mirror. The deviousness, the wayward passion, even the sempiternal abuses of the land were already beginning to take the aspect of something like quaint impotence. It was charm that, now I was on the road away, was becoming apparent. The inconveniences of life, the physical discomforts, the smells of streets, the heat, dropped into the background. I felt that I did not want to go away, irrevocably from a land sanctioned by her presence, her young life. I turned uneasily to the other side. At the heavy black table, in the light of a single candle, the Cuban and the Nova Scotian were discussing, their heads close together.

"I tell you no," Nichols was saying in a fluent, abominable, literal translation into Spanish. "Take the knife so . . . thumb upwards. Stab down in the soft between the neck and the shoulder-blade. You get right into the lungs with the point. I've tried it: ten times. Never stick the back. The chances are he moves, and you hit a bone. There are no bones there. It's the way they kill pigs in New Jersey."

The Cuban bent his brows as if he were reflecting over a chessboard. "Ma. . . ." he pondered. His knife was lying on the table. He unsheathed it, then got up, and moved behind the seated Nova Scotian.

"You say . . . there?" he asked, pressing his little finger at the base of Nichols' skinny column of a neck. "And then . . ." He measured the length of the knife on Nichols's back twice with elaborate care, breathing through his nostrils. Then he said with a convinced, musing air, "It is true. It would go down into the lungs."

"And there are arteries and things," Nichols said.

"Yes, yes," the Cuban answered, sheathing the knife and thrusting it into his belt.

"With a knife that length it's perfect." Nichols waved his shadowy hand towards Salazar's scarf. Salazar moved off a little.

"I see the advantages," he said. "No crying out, because of the blood in the lungs. I thank you, Señor Escoces."

Nichols rose, lurching to his full height, and looked in my direction. I closed my eyes. I did not wish him to talk to me. I heard him say:

"Well, *hasta mas ver*. I shall get away from here. Good-night."

He swayed an immense shadow through the door. Salazar took the candle and followed him into the corridor.

Yes, that was it, why she was so great a part, a whole wall, a whole beam of my life's house. I saw her suddenly in the blackness, her full red lips, her quivering nostrils, the curve of her breasts, her lithe movements from the hips, the way she set her feet down, the white flower waxen in the darkness of her hair, and the robin-wing flutter of her lids over her gray eyes when she smiled. I moved convulsively in my intense desire. I would have given my soul, my share of eternity, my honour, only to see that flutter of the lids over the shining gray eyes. I never felt I was beneath the imponderable pressure of a prison's wall till then. She was infinite miles away; I could not even imagine what inanimate things surrounded her. She must be talking to someone else; fluttering her lids like that. I recognized with a physical agony that was more than jealousy how slight was my hold upon her. It was not in her race, in her blood as in mine, to love me and my type. She had lived all her life in the middle of Romance, and the very fire and passion of her South must make me dim prose to her. I remember the flicker of Salazar's returning candle, cast in lines like an advancing scythe across the two walls from the corridor. I slept.

I had the feeling of appalled horror suddenly invading my sleep; a vast voice seemed to be exclaiming:

"Tell me where she is!"

I looked at the glowing horn of a lanthorn. It was O'Brien who held it. He stood over me, very sombre.

"Tell me where she is," he said, the moment my eyes opened.

I said, "She's . . . she's—— I don't know."

It appalls me even now to think how narrow was my escape. It was only because I had gone to sleep in the thought that I did not know, that I answered that I did not know. Ah—he was a cunning devil! To suddenly wake one; to get one's thoughts before one had had time to think! I lay looking at him, shivering. I couldn't even see much of his face.

"Where is she?" he said again. "Where? Dead? Dead? God have mercy on your soul if the child is dead!"

I was still trembling. If I had told him!—I could hardly believe I had not. He continued bending over me with an attitude that hideously mocked solicitude.

"Where is she?" he asked again.

"Ransack the island," I said. He glared at me, lifting the lamp. "The whole earth, if you like."

He ground his teeth, bending very low over me; then stood up, raising his head into the shadow above the lamp.

"What do I care for all the admirals?" he was speaking to himself. "No ship shall leave Havana till. . . ." He groaned. I heard him slap his forehead, and say distractedly, "But perhaps she is not in a ship."

There was a silence in which I heard him breathe heavily, and then he amazed me by saying:

"Have pity."

I laughed, lying on my back. "On you!"

He bent down. "Fool! on yourself."

A vast and towering shadow ran along the wall.

There wasn't a sound. The face of Salazar appeared behind him, and an uplifted hand grasping a knife. O'Brien saw the horror in my eyes. I gasped to him: "Look. . . ." and before he could move the knife went softly home between neck and shoulder. Salazar glided to the door and turned to wave his hand at me. O'Brien's lips were pressed tightly together, the handle of the knife was against his ear, the lanthorn hung at the end of his rigid arm for a moment. As he lowered it, the blood spurted from his shoulder as if from a burst stand-pipe, only black and warm. It fell over my face, over my hands, everywhere. For a minute of eternity his agonized eyes searched my features, as if to discern whether I had connived, whether I condoned.

I had started up, my face coming right against his. I felt an immense horror. What did it mean? What had he done? He had been such a power for so long, so inevitably, over my whole life that I could not even begin to understand that this was not some new subtle villainy of his. He shook his head slowly, his ear disturbing the knife.

Then he turned jerkily on his heel, the lanthorn swinging round and leaving me in his shadow. There were ten paces to reach the door. It was like the finish of a race whether he would cover the remaining seven after the first three steps. The dangling lanthorn shed small patches of light through the holes in the metal top, like sunlight through leaves, upon the gloom of the remote ceiling. At the fifth step he pressed his hand spasmodically to his mouth; at the sixth he wavered to one side. I made a sudden motion as if to save him from falling. He was dying! He was dying! I hardly realized what it meant. This immense weight was being removed from me. I had

no need to fear him any more. I couldn't understand, I could only look. This was his passing.
This. . . .

He sank, knelt down, placing the lanthorn on the
floor. He covered his face with his hands and began
to cough incessantly, like a man dying of consumption.
The glowing top of the lanthorn hissed and sputtered
out in little sharp blows, like hammer strokes . . .
Carlos had coughed like that. Carlos was dead. Now
O'Brien! He was going. I should escape. It was all
over. Was it all over? He bowed stiffly forward,
placing his hands on the stones, then lay over on his
side with his face to the light, his eyes glaring at it.
I sat motionless, watching him. The lanthorn lit the
carved leg of the black table and a dusty circle of the
flags. The spurts of blood from his shoulder grew less
long in answer to the pulsing of his heart; his fists
unclenched, he drew his legs up to his body, then sank
down. His eyes looked suddenly at mine and, as the
features slowly relaxed, the smile seemed to come back,
enigmatic, round his mouth.

He was dead; he was gone; I was free! He would
never know where she was; never! He had gone, with
the question on his lips; with the agony of uncertainty
in his eyes. From the door came an immense, grotesque, and horrible chuckle.

"Aha! Aha! I have saved you, Señor, I have
protected you. We are as brothers."

Against the tenuous blue light of the dawn Salazar
was gesticulating in the doorway. I felt a sudden
repulsion; a feeling of intense disgust. O'Brien lying
there, I almost wished alive again—I wanted to have
him again, rather than that I should have been relieved
of him by that atrocious murder. I sat looking at both
of them.

Saved! By that lunatic? I suddenly appreciated the agony of mind that alone could have brought O'Brien, the cautious, the all-seeing, into this place— to ask me a question that for him was answered now. Answered for him more than for me.

Where was Seraphina? Where? How should I come to her? O'Brien was dead. And I. . . . Could I walk out of this place and go to her? O'Brien was dead. But I . . .

I suddenly realized that now I was the pirate Nikola el Escoces—that now he was no more there, nothing could save me from being handed over to the admiral. Nothing.

Salazar outside the door began to call boastfully towards the sound of approaching footsteps.

"Aha! Aha! Come all of you! See what I have done! Come, Señor Alcayde! Come, brave soldiers . . ."

In that way died this man whose passion had for so long hung over my life like a shadow. Looking at the matter now, I am, perhaps, glad that he fell neither by my hand nor in my quarrel. I assuredly had injured him the first; I had come upon his ground; I had thwarted him; I had been a heavy weight at a time when his fortunes had been failing. Failing they undoubtedly were. He had run his course too far.

And, if his death removed him out of my path, the legacy of his intrigue caused me suffering enough. Had he lived, there is no knowing what he might have done. He was bound to deliver someone to the British —either myself or Nichols. Perhaps, at the last moment, he would have kept me in Havana. There is no saying.

Undoubtedly he had not wished to deliver Nichols;

either because he really knew too much, or because he had scruples. Nichols had certainly been faithful to him. And, with his fine irony, it was certainly delightful to him to think that I should die a felon's death in England. For those reasons he had identified me with Nikola el Escoces, intending to give up whichever suited him at the last moment.

Now that was settled for him and for me. The delivery was to take place at dawn, and O'Brien not being to be found, the old Judge of the First Instance had been sent to identify the prisoner. He selected me, whom, of course, he recognized. There was no question of Nichols, who had been imprisoned on a charge of theft trumped up by O'Brien.

Salazar, whether he would have gone to the Captain-General or not, was now entirely useless. He was retained to answer the charge of murder. And to any protestations I could make, the old *Juez* was entirely deaf.

"The señor must make representations to his own authorities," he said. "I have warrant for what I have done."

It was impossible to expose O'Brien to him. The soldiers of the escort, in the dawn before the prison gates, simply laughed at me.

They marched me down through the gray mists, to the water's edge. Two soldiers held my arms; O'Brien's blood was drying on my face and on my clothes. I was, even to myself, a miserable object. Among the negresses on the slimy boat-steps a thick, short man was asking questions. He opened amazed eyes at the sight of me. It was Williams—the *Lion* was not yet gone then. If he spoke to me, or gave token of connection with Seraphina, the Spaniards would understand. They would take her from him certainly; perhaps immure her in a convent. And now that I was bound irrevocably for England, she must go, too. He was shouldering his way towards my guards.

"Silence!" I shouted, without looking at him. "Go away, make sail. . . . Tell Sebright. . . ."

My guards seemed to think I had gone mad; they laid hands upon me. I didn't struggle, and we passed down towards the landing steps, brushing Williams aside. He stood perturbedly gazing after me; then I saw him asking questions of a civil guard. A man-of-war's boat, the ensign trailing in the glassy water, the glazed hats of the seamen bobbing like clockwork, was flying towards us. Here was England! Here was home! I should have to clear myself of felony, to strain every nerve and cheat the gallows. If only Williams understood, if only he did not make a fool of himself. I couldn't see him any more; a jabbering crowd all round us was being kept at a distance by the muskets of the soldiers. My only chance was Sebright's intelligence. He might prevent Williams making a fool of himself. The commander of the guard said to the lieutenant from the flagship, who had landed, attended by the master-at-arms:

"I have the honour to deliver to your worship's custody the prisoner promised to his excellency the English admiral. Here are the papers disclosing his crimes to the justice. I beg for a receipt."

A shabby *escrivano* from the prison advanced bowing, with an inkhorn, shaking a wet goose-quill. A *guardia civil* offered his back. The lieutenant signed a paper hastily, then looking hard at me, gave the order:

"Master-at-arms, handcuff one of the prisoner's hands to your own wrist. He is a desperate character."

CHAPTER THREE

THE first decent word I had spoken to me after that for months came from my turnkey at Newgate. It was when he welcomed me back from my examination before the Thames Court magistrate. The magistrate, a bad-tempered man, snuffy, with red eyes, and the air of being a piece of worn and dirty furniture of his court, had snapped at me when I tried to speak:

"Keep your lies for the Admiralty Session. I've only time to commit you. Damn your Spaniards; why can't they translate their own papers;" had signed something with a squeaky quill, tossed it to his clerk, and grunted, "Next case."

I had gone back to Newgate.

The turnkey, a man with the air of an innkeeper, bandy-legged, with a bulbous, purple-veined nose and watering eyes, slipped out of the gatehouse door, whilst the great, hollow-sounding gate still shook behind me. He said:

"If you hurries up you'll see a bit of life. . . . Do you good. Condemned sermon. Being preached in the chapel now; sheriffs and all. They swing to-morrow—three of them. Quick with the stumps."

He hurried me over the desolate mossy-green cobbles of the great solitary yard into a square, tall, bare, white-washed place. Already from the outside one caught a droning voice. There might have been three hundred people there, boxed off in pews, with turnkeys at each end. A vast king's arms, a splash of red and blue gilt, sprawled above a two-tiered pulpit that was like the trunk of a large broken tree. The turnkey pulled my hat off, and nudged me into a box beside the door.

"Kneel down," he whispered hoarsely.

I knelt. A man with a new wig was droning out words, waving his hands now and then from the top of the tall pulpit. Beneath him a smaller man in an old wig was dozing, his head bent forward. The place was dirty, and ill-lighted by the tall, grimy windows, heavily barred. A pair of candles flickered beside the preacher's right arm. . . .

"They that go down to the Sea in ships, my poor brethren," he droned, "lying under the shadow . . ."

He directed his hands towards a tall deal box painted black, isolated in the centre of the lower floor. A man with a red head sat in it, his arms folded; another had his arms covering his head, which leant abjectly forward on the rail in front. There were large rusty gyves upon his wrists.

"But observe, my poor friends," the chaplain droned on, "the psalmist saith, 'At the last He shall bring them unto the desired haven.' Now. . . ."

The turnkey whispered suddenly into my ear: "Them's the condemned he's preaching at, them in the black pew. See Roguey Cullen wink at the woman prisoners up there in the gallery. . . . Him with the red hair. . . . All swings to-morrow."

"After they have staggered and reeled to and fro, and been amazed . . . observe. After they have been tempted; even after they have fallen. . . ."

The sheriffs had their eyes decorously closed. The clerk reached up from below the preacher, and snuffed one of the candles. The preacher paused to rearrange his shining wig. Little clouds of powder flew out where he touched it. He struck his purple velvet cushion, and continued:

"At the last, I say, He shall bring them to the haven they had desired."

A jarring shriek rose out of the black pew, and an insensate jangling of irons rattled against the hollow wood. The ironed man, whose head had been hidden, was writhing in an epileptic fit. The governor began signalling to the jailers, and the whole dismal assembly rose to its feet, and craned to get a sight. The jailers began hurrying them out of the building. The red-headed man was crouching in the far corner of the black box.

The turnkey caught the end of my sleeve, and hurried me out of the door.

"Come away," he said. "Come out of it. . . . Damn my good nature."

We went swiftly through the tall, gloomy, echoing stone passages. All the time there was the noise of the prisoners being marshalled somewhere into their distant yards and cells. We went across the bottom of a well, where the weeping December light struck ghastly down on to the stones, into a sort of rabbit-warren of black passages and descending staircases, a horror of cold, solitude, and night. Iron door after iron door clanged to behind us in the stony blackness. After an interminable traversing, the turnkey, still with his hand on my sleeve, jerked me into my familiar cell. I hadn't thought to be glad to get back to that dim, frozen, damp-chilled little hole; with its hateful stone walls, stone ceiling, stone floor, stone bed-slab, and stone table; its rope mat, foul stable-blanket, its horrible sense of eternal burial, out of sound, out of sight under a mined mountain of black stones. It was so tiny that the turnkey, entering after me, seemed to be pressed close up to my chest, and so dark that I could not see the colour of the dirty hair that fell matted from the bald patch on the top of his skull; so familiar that I knew the feel of every little worming of rust on the iron candlestick. He wiped his face with a brown rag of handkerchief, and said:

"Curse me if ever I go into that place again." After a time he added: "Unless 'tis a matter of duty."

I didn't say anything; my nerves were still jangling to that shrieking, and to the clang of the iron doors that had closed behind me. I had an irresistible impulse to get hold of the iron candlestick and smash it home through the skull of the turnkey—as I had done to the men who had killed Seraphina's father . . . to kill this man, then to creep along the black passages and murder man after man beside those iron doors until I got to the open air.

He began again. "You'd think we'd get used to it—you'd think we would—but 'tis a strain for us. You never knows what the prisoners will do at a scene like that there. It drives 'em mad. Look at this scar. Machell the forger done that for me, 'fore he was condemned, after a sermon like that—a quiet, gentlemanly man, much like you. Lord, yes, 'tis a strain. . . ." He paused, still wiping his face, then went on: "*And* I swear that when I sees them men sit there in that black pew, an' hev heard the hammers going clack, clack on the scaffolding outside, and knew that they hadn't no more chance than you have to get out of there . . ." He pointed his short thumb towards the handkerchief of an opening, where the little blurr of blue light wavered through the two iron frames crossed in the nine feet of well. "Lord, you *never* gets used to it. You *wants* them to escape; 'tis in the air through the whole prison, even the debtors. I tells myself again and again, 'You're a fool for your pains.' But it's the same with the

others—my mates. You can't get it out of your mind.
That little kid now. I've seen children swing; but
that little kid—as sure to swing as what . . . as
what *you* are. . . ."

"You think I am going to swing?" I asked.

I didn't want to kill him any more; I wanted too much
to hear him talk. I hadn't heard anything for months
and months of solitude, of darkness—on board the admiral's ship, stranded in the guardship at Plymouth,
bumping round the coast, and now here in Newgate.
And it had been darkness all the time. Jove! That
Cuban time, with its movements, its pettiness, its
intrigue, its warmth, even its villainies showed plainly
enough in the chill of that blackness. It had been
romance, that life.

Little, and far away, and irrevocably done with, it
showed all golden. There wasn't any romance where I
lay then; and there had been irons on my wrists; gruff
hatred, the darkness, and always despair.

On board the flagship coming home I had been
chained down in the cable-tier—a place where I could
feel every straining of the great ship. Once these had
risen to a pandemonium, a frightful tumult. There
was a great gale outside. A sailor came down with a
lanthorn, and tossed my biscuit to me.

"You d——d pirate," he said, "maybe it's you saving
us from drowning."

"Is the gale very bad?" I had called.

He muttered—and the fact that he spoke to me at all
showed how great the strain of the weather must have
been to wring any words out of him:

"Bad—there's a large Indiaman gone. We saw her
one minute and then . . ." He went away, muttering.

And suddenly the thought had come to me. What

if the Indiaman were the *Lion*—the *Lion* with Seraphina on board? The man would not speak to me when he came again. No one would speak to me; I was a pirate who had fired on his own countrymen. And the thought had pursued me right into Newgate— if she were dead; if I had taken her from that security, from that peace, to end there. . . . And to end myself.

"Swing!" the turnkey said; "you'll swing right enough." He slapped the great key on his flabby hand. "You can tell that by the signs. You, being an Admiralty case, ought to have been in the Marshalsea. And you're ordered solitary cell, and I'm tipped the straight wink against your speaking a blessed word to a blessed soul. Why don't they let you see an attorney? Why? Because they *mean* you to swing."

I said, "Never mind that. Have you heard of a ship called the *Lion*? Can you find out about her?"

He shook his head cunningly, and did not answer. If the *Lion* had been here, I must have heard. They couldn't have left me here.

I said, "For God's sake find out. Get a shipping gazette."

He affected not to hear.

"There's money in plenty," I said.

He winked ponderously and began again. "Oh, you'll swing all right. A man with nothing against him has a chance; with the rhino he has it, even if he's guilty. But you'll *swing*. Charlie, who brought you back just now, had a chat with the 'Torney-General's devil's clerk's clerk, while old Nog o' Bow Street was trying to read their Spanish. He says it's a Gov'nment matter. They wants to hang you bad, they do, so's to go to the Jacky Spaniards and say, 'He were a nob, a nobby nob.' (So you are, aren't you? One uncle an earl and t'other a dean, if so be what they say's true.) 'He were a nobby nob and we swung 'im. Go you'n do likewise.' They want a striking example t' keep the West India trade quiet . . ." He wiped his forehead and moved my water jug of red earth on the dirty deal table under the window, for all the world like a host in front of a guest. "They means you to swing," he said. "They've silenced the Thames Court reporters. Not a noospaper will publish a correct report t'morrer. And you haven't see nobody, nor you won't, not if I can help it."

He broke off and looked at me with an expression of candour.

"Mind you," he said, "I'm not uffish. To 'n ornery gentleman—of the road or what you will—I'm not, if so be he's the necessary. I'd take a letter like another. But for you, no—fear. Not that I've my knife into you. What I can do to make you comfor'ble I will do, *both* now an' hereafter. But when I gets the wink, I looks after my skin. So'd any man. You don't see nobody, nor you won't; nor your nobby relations won't have the word. Till the Hadmir'lty trile. Charlie says it's unconstitutional, you ought to see your 'torney, if you've one, or your father's got one. But Lor', I says, 'Charlie, if they wants it they gets it. This ain't no *habeas carpis*, give the man a chance case. It's the Hadmir'lty. And not a man tried for piracy this thirty year. See what a show it gives them, what bloody Radicle knows or keeres what the perceedin's should be? Who's a-goin' t' make a question out of it? Go away,' says I to Charlie. And that's it straight."

He went towards the door, then turned.

"You should be in the Marshalsea common yard; even I knows that. But they've the wink there. 'Too full,' says they. Too full be d——d. I've know'd the time—after the Vansdell smash it were—when they found room for three hundred more improvident debtors over and above what they're charted for. Too full! Their common yard! They don't want you to speak to a soul, an' you won't till this day week, when the Hadmir'lty Session is in full swing." He went out and locked the door, snorting, "Too full at the Marshalsea! . . . Go away!"

"Find out about the *Lion*," I called, as the door closed.

It cleared the air for me, that speech. I understood that they wanted to hang me, and I wanted not to be hung, desperately, from that moment. I had not much cared before; I had—call it, moped. I had not really believed, really sensed it out. It isn't easy to conceive that one is going to be hanged, I doubt if one does even with the rope round one's neck. I hadn't much wanted to live, but now I wanted to fight—one good fight before I went under for good and all, condemned or acquitted. There wasn't anything left for me to live for, Seraphina could not be alive. The *Lion* must have been lost.

But I was going to make a fight for it; curse it, I was going to give them trouble. My "them" was not so much the Government that meant to hang me as the unseen powers that suffered such a state of things, that allowed a number of little meannesses, accidents, fatalities, to hang me. I began to worry the turnkey. He gave me no help, only shreds of information that let me see more plainly than ever how set "they" were on sacrificing me to their exigencies.

The whole West Indian trade in London was in an uproar over the Pirate Question and over the Slave Question. Jamaica was still squealing for Separation

before the premonitory grumbles of Abolition. Horton
Pen, over there, came back with astonishing clearness
before me. I seemed to hear old, wall-eyed, sandy-
headed Macdonald, agitating his immense bulk of ill-
fitting white clothes in front of his newspaper, and
bellowing in his ox-voice:

"Abolition, they give us Abolition . . . or ram
it down our throats. *They* who haven't even the
spunk to rid us o' the d——d pirates, not the spunk to
catch and hang one. . . . Jock, me lahd, we's
abolush them before they sall touch our neegurs. . . .
Let them clear oor seas, let them hang *one* pirate, and
then talk."

I was the one they were going to hang, to consolidate
the bond with the old island. The cement wanted a
little blood in the mixing. Damn them! I was going
to make a fight; they had torn me from Seraphina, to
fulfill their own accursed ends. I felt myself grow
harsh and strong, as a tree feels itself grow gnarled by
winter storms. I said to the turnkey again and again:

"Man, I will promise you a thousand pounds or a
pension for life, if you will get a letter through to my
mother or Squire Rooksby of Horton."

He said he daren't do it; enough was known of him to
hang him if he gave offence. His flabby fingers trembled,
and his eyes grew large with successive shocks of
cupidity. He became afraid of coming near me; of the
strain of the temptation. On the next day he did not
speak a word, nor the next, nor the next. I began to
grow horribly afraid of being hung. The day before the
trial arrived. Towards noon he flung the door open.

"Here's paper, here's pens," he said. "You can
prepare your defence. You may write letters. Oh,
hell! why did not they let it come sooner, I'd have had
your thousand pounds. I'll run a letter down to your

people fast as the devil could take it. I know a man, a gentleman of the road. For twenty pun promised, split between us, he'll travel faster'n Turpin did to York." He was waving a large sheet of newspaper agitatedly.

"What does it mean?" I asked. My head was whirling.

"Radical papers got a-holt of it," he said. "Trust them for nosing out. And the Government's answering them. They say you're going to suffer for your crimes. Hark to this . . . um, um . . . 'The wretched felon now in Newgate will incur the just penalty . . .' Then they slaps the West Indies in the face. 'When the planters threaten to recur to some other power for protection, they, of course, believe that the loss of the colonies would be severely felt. But . . .'"

"The *Lion's* home," I said.

It burst upon me that she was—that she must be. Williams—or Sebright—he was the man, had been speaking up for me. Or Seraphina had been to the Spanish ambassador.

She was back; I should see her. I started up.

"The *Lion's* home," I repeated.

The turnkey snarled, "She was posted as overdue three days ago."

I couldn't believe it was true.

"I saw it in the papers," he grumbled on. "I dursn't tell you." He continued violently, "Blow my dickey. It would make a cat sick."

My sudden exaltation, my sudden despair, gave way to indifference.

"Oh, coming, coming!" he shouted, in answer to an immense bellowing cry that loomed down the passage without.

I heard him grumble, "Of course, of course. I shan't make a penny." Then he caught hold of my arm. "Here, come along, someone to see you in the press-yard."

He pulled me along the noisome, black warren of passages, slamming the inner door viciously behind him.

The press-yard—the exercising ground for the condemned—was empty; the last batch had gone out, *my* batch would be the next to come in, the turnkey said suddenly. It was a well of a place, high black walls going up into the desolate, weeping sky, and quite tiny. At one end was a sort of slit in the wall, closed with tall, immense windows. From there a faint sort of rabbit's squeak was going up through the immense roll and rumble of traffic on the other side of the wall. The turnkey pushed me towards it.

"Go on," he said. "I'll not listen; I ought to. But, curse me, I'm not a bad sort," he added gloomily; "I dare say you'll make it worth my while."

I went and peered through the bars at a faint object pressed against other bars in just another slit across a black passage.

"What, Jackie, boy; what, Jackie?"

Blinking his eyes, as if the dim light were too strong for them, a thin, bent man stood there in a brilliant new court coat. His face was meagre in the extreme, the nose and cheekbones polished and transparent like a bigaroon cherry. A thin tuft of reddish hair was brushed back from his high, shining forehead. It was my father. He exclaimed:

"What, Jackie, boy! How old you look!" then waved his arm towards me. "In trouble?" he said. "You in trouble?"

He rubbed his thin hands together, and looked round the place with a cultured man's air of disgust. I said, "Father!" and he suddenly began to talk very fast and agitatedly of what he had been doing for me. My mother, he said, was crippled with rheumatism, and Rooksby and Veronica on the preceding Thursday had set sail for Jamaica. He had read to my mother, beside her bed, the newspaper containing an account of my case; and she had given him money, and he had started with violent haste for London. The haste and the rush were still dazing him. He had lived down there in the farmhouse beneath the downs, with the stackyards under his eyes, with his books of verse and his few prints on the wall—— My God, how it all came back to me.

In his disjointed speeches, I could see how exactly the same it all remained. The same old surly man with a squint had driven him along the muddy roads in the same ancient gig, past the bare elms, to meet the coach. And my father had never been in London since he had walked the streets with the Prince Regent's friends.

Whilst he talked to me there, lines of verse kept coming to his lips; and, after the habitual pleasure of the apt quotation, he felt acutely shocked at the inappropriateness of the place, the press-yard, with the dim light weeping downwards between immensely high walls, and the desultory snowflakes that dropped between us. And he had tried so hard, in his emergency, to be practical. When he had reached London, before even attempting to see me, he had run from minister to minister trying to influence them in my favour—and he reached me in Newgate with nothing at all effected.

I seemed to know him then, so intimately, so much better than anything else in the world.

He began, "I had my idea in the up-coach last night. I thought, 'A very great personage was indebted to me in the old days (more indebted than you are aware of, Johnnie). I will intercede with him.' That was why my first step was to my old tailor's in Conduit Street.

Because . . . what is fit for a farm for a palace were low." He stopped, reflected, then said, "What is fit for *the* farm for *the* palace were low."

He felt across his coat for his breast pocket. It was what he had done years and years ago, and all these years between, inscribe ideas for lines of verse in his pocket-book. I said:

"You have seen the king?"

His face lengthened a little. "Not *seen* him. But I found one of the duke's secretaries, a pleasant young fellow . . . not such as we used to be. But the duke was kind enough to interest himself. Perhaps my name has lived in the land. I was called Curricle Kemp, as I may have told you, because I drove a vermilion one with green and gilt wheels. . . ."

His face, peering at me through the bars, had, for a moment, a flush of pride. Then he suddenly remembered, and, as if to propitiate his own reproof, he went on:

"I saw the Secretary of State, and he assured me, very civilly, that not even the highest personage in the land. . . ." He dropped his voice, "Jackie, boy," he said, his narrow-lidded eyes peering miserably across at me, "there's not even hope of a reprieve afterwards."

I leaned my face wearily against the iron bars. What, after all, was the use of fighting if the *Lion* were not back?

Then, suddenly, as the sound of his words echoed down the bare, black corridors, he seemed to realize the horror of it. His face grew absolutely white, he held his head erect, as if listening to a distant sound. And then he began to cry—horribly, and for a long time.

It was I that had to comfort him. His head had bowed at the conviction of his hopeless uselessness; all through his own life he had been made ineffectual by his indulgence in perfectly innocent, perfectly trivial enjoyments, and now, in this extremity of his only son, he was rendered almost fantastically of no avail.

"No, no, sir! You have done all that any one could; you couldn't break these walls down. Nothing else would help."

Small, hopeless sobs shook him continually. His thin, delicate white fingers gripped the black grille, with the convulsive grasp of a very weak man. It was more distressing to me than anything I had ever seen or felt. The mere desire, the intense desire to comfort him, made me get a grip upon myself again. And I remembered that, now that I could communicate with the outer air, it was absolutely easy; he would save my life. I said:

"You have only to go to Clapham, sir."

And the moment I was in a state to command him, to direct him, to give him something to do, he became a changed man. He looked up and listened. I told him to go to Major Cowper's. It would be easy enough to find him at Clapham. Cowper, I remembered, could testify to my having been seized by Tomas Castro. He had seen me fight on the decks. And what was more, he would certainly know the addresses of Kingston planters, if any were in London. They could testify that I had been in Jamaica all the while Nikola el Escoces was in Rio Medio. I knew there were some. My father was fidgeting to be gone. He had his line marked for him, and a will directing his own. He was not the same man. But I particularly told him to send me a lawyer first of all.

"Yes, yes!" he said, fidgeting to go, "to Major Cowper's. Let me write his address."

"And a solicitor," I said. "Send him to me on your way there."

"Yes, yes," he said, "I shall be able to be of use to the

solicitor. As a rule, they are men of no great per-
spicacity."

And he went hurriedly away.

.　　.　　.　　.　　.　　.　　.　　.

The real torture, the agony of suspense began then.
I steadied my nerves by trying to draw up notes for my
speech to the jury on the morrow. That was the
turnkey's idea.

He said, "Slap your chest, 'peal to the honour of a
British gent, and pitch it in strong."

It was not much good; I could not keep to any logical
sequence of thought, my mind was forever wandering
to what my father was doing. I pictured him in his
new blue coat, running agitatedly through crowded
streets, his coat-tails flying behind his thin legs. The
hours dragged on, and it was a matter of minutes. I
had to hold upon the table edge to keep myself from
raging about the cell. I tried to bury myself again in
the scheme for my defence. I wondered whom my
father would have found. There was a man called
Cary who had gone home from Kingston. He had a
bald head and blue eyes; he must remember me. If he
would corroborate! And the lawyer, when he came,
might take another line of defence. It began to fall
dusk slowly, through the small barred windows.

The entire night passed without a word from my
father. I paced up and down the whole time, compos-
ing speeches to the jury. And then the day broke. I
calmed myself with a sort of frantic energy.

Early the jailer came in, and began fussing about my cell.

"Case comes on about one," he said. "Grand jury
at half after twelve. No fear they won't return a true
bill. Grand jury, five West India merchants. They
means to have you. 'Torney-General, S'lic'tor-General,

S'r Robert Mead, and five juniors agin you. . . . You take my tip. Throw yourself on the mercy of the court, and make a rousing speech with a young 'ooman in it. Not that you'll get much mercy from them. They Admir'lty jedges is all hangers. 'S we say, 'Oncet the anchor goes up in the Old Bailey, there ain't no hope. We begins to clean out the c'ndemned cell, here. Sticks the anchor up over their heads, when it is Hadmir'lty case,'" he commented.

I listened to him with strained attention. I made up my mind to miss not a word uttered that day. It was my only chance.

"You don't know any one from Jamaica?" I asked.

He shook his bullet head, and tapped his purple nose. "Can't be done," he said. "You'd get a ornery hallybi fer a guinea a head, but they'd keep out of this case. They've necks like you and me."

Whilst he was speaking, the whole of the outer world, as far as it affected me, came suddenly in upon me— that was what I meant to the great city that lay all round, the world, in the centre of which was my cell. To the great mass, I was matter for a sensation; to them I might prove myself beneficial in this business. Perhaps there were others who were thinking I might be useful in one way or another. There were the ministers of the Crown, who did not care much whether Jamaica separated or not. But they wanted to hang me because they would be able to say disdainfully to the planters, "Separate if you like; we've done our duty, we've hanged a man."

All those people had their eyes on me, and they were about the only ones who knew of my existence. That was the end of my Romance! Romance! The broad-sheet sellers would see to it afterwards with a "Dying confession."

CHAPTER FOUR

I NEVER saw my father again until I was in the prisoner's anteroom at the Old Bailey. It was full of lounging men, whose fleshy limbs bulged out against the tight, loud checks of their coats and trousers. These were jailers waiting to bring in their prisoners. On the other side of one black door the Grand Jury was deliberating on my case, behind another the court was in waiting to try me. I was in a sort of tired lull. All night I had been pacing up and down, trying to bring my brain to think of points—points in my defence. It was very difficult. I knew that I must keep cool, be calm, be lucid, be convincing; and my brain had reeled at times, even in the darkness of the cell. I knew it had reeled, because I remembered that once I had fallen against the stone of one of the walls, and once against the door. Here, in the light, with only a door between myself and the last scene, I regained my hold. I was going to fight every inch from start to finish. I was going to let no chink of their armour go untried. I was going to make a good fight. My teeth chattered like castanets, jarring in my jaws until it was painful. But that was only with the cold.

A hubbub of expostulation was going on at the third door. My turnkey called suddenly:

"Let the genman in, Charlie. Pal o' ourn," and my father ran huntedly into the room. He began an endless tale of a hackney coachman who had stood in front of the door of his coach to prevent his number being taken; of a crowd of caddee-smashers, who had hustled him and filched his purse. "Of course, I made a fight for it," he said, "a damn good fight, considering. It's in the blood. But the watch came, and, in short—on such an occasion as this there is no time for words—I passed the night in the watch-house. Many and many a night I passed there when I and Lord—— But I am losing time."

"You ain't fit to walk the streets of London alone, sir," the turnkey said.

My father gave him a corner of his narrow-lidded eyes. "My man," he said, "I walked the streets with the highest in the land before your mother bore you in Bridewell, or whatever jail it was."

"Oh, no offence," the turnkey muttered.

I said, "Did you find Cowper, sir? Will he give evidence?"

"Jackie," he said agitatedly, as if he were afraid of offending me, "he said you had filched his wife's rings."

That, in fact, was what Major Cowper *had* said—that I had dropped into their ship near Port Royal Heads, and had afterwards gone away with the pirates who had filched his wife's rings. My father, in his indignation, had not even deigned to ask him for the address of Jamaica planters in London; and on his way back to find a solicitor he had come into contact with those street rowdies and the watch. He had only just come from before the magistrates.

A man with one eye poked his head suddenly from behind the Grand Jury door. He jerked his head in my direction.

"True bill against that 'ere," he said, then drew his head in again.

"Jackie, boy," my father said, putting a thin hand on my wrist, and gazing imploringly into my eyes, "I'm . . . I'm . . . I can't tell you how. . . ."

I said, "It doesn't matter, father." I felt a foretaste of how my past would rise up to crush me. Cowper had let that wife of his coerce him into swearing my life away. I remembered vividly his blubbering protestations of friendship when I persuaded Tomas Castro to return him his black deed-box with the brass handle, on that deck littered with rubbish. . . . "Oh, God bless you, God bless you. You have saved me from starvation. . . ." There had been tears in his old blue eyes. "If you need it I will go anywhere . . . do anything to help you. On the honour of a gentleman and a soldier." I had, of course, recommended his wife to give up her rings when the pirates were threatening her in the cabin. The other door opened, another man said:

"Now, then, in with that carrion. D'you want to keep the judges waiting?"

I stepped through the door straight down into the dock; there was a row of spikes in the front of it. I wasn't afraid; three men in enormous wigs and ermine robes faced me; four in short wigs had their heads together like parrots on a branch. A fat man, bareheaded, with a gilt chain round his neck, slipped from behind into a seat beside the highest placed judge. He was wiping his mouth and munching with his jaws. On each side of the judges, beyond the short-wigged assessors, were chairs full of ladies and gentlemen. They all had their eyes upon me. I saw it all very plainly. I was going to see everything, to keep my eyes open, not to let any chance escape. I wondered why a young girl with blue eyes and pink cheeks tittered and shrugged her shoulders. I did not know what was amusing. What astonished me was the smallness, the dirt, the want of dignity of the room itself. I thought they must be trying a case of my importance there by mistake.

Presently I noticed a great gilt anchor above the judges' head. I wondered why it was there, until I remembered it was an Admiralty Court. I thought suddenly, "Ah! if I had thought to tell my father to go and see if the *Lion* had come in in the night!"

A man was bawling out a number of names. . . . "Peter Plimley, gent., any challenge. . . . Lazarus Cohen, merchant, any challenge. . . ."

The turnkey beside me leant with his back against the spikes. He was talking to the man who had called us in.

"Lazarus Cohen, West Indian merchant. . . . Lord, well, I'd challenge. . . ."

The other man said, "S—sh."

"His old dad give me five shiners to put him up to a thing if I could," the turnkey said again.

I didn't catch his meaning until an old man with a very ragged gown was handing up a book to a row of others in a box so near that I could almost have touched them. Then I realized that the turnkey had been winking to me to challenge the jury. I called out at the highest of the judges:

"I protest against that jury. It is packed. Half of them, at least, are West Indian merchants."

There was a stir all over the court. I realized then that what had seemed only a mass of stuffs of some sort were human beings all looking at me. The judge I had called to opened a pair of dim eyes upon me, clasped and unclasped his hands, very dry, ancient, wrinkled. The judge on his right called angrily:

"Nonsense, it is too late. . . . They are being sworn. You should have spoken when the names were read." Underneath his wig was an immensely broad face with glaring yellow eyes.

I said, "It is scandalous. You want to murder me.

How should I know what you do in your courts? I say the jury is packed."

The very old judge closed his eyes, opened them again, then gasped out:

"Silence. We are here to try you. This is a court of law."

The turnkey pulled my sleeve under cover of the planking. "Treat him civil," he whispered, "Lord Justice Stowell of the Hadmir'lty. 'Tother's Baron Garrow of the Common Law; a beast; him as hanged that kid. You can sass him; it doesn't matter."

Lord Stowell waved his hand to the clerk with the ragged gown; the book passed from hand to hand along the faces of the jury, the clerk gabbling all the while. The old judge said suddenly, in an astonishingly deep, majestic voice:

"Prisoner at the bar, you must understand that we are here to give you an impartial trial according to the laws of this land. If you desire advice as to the procedure of this court you can have it."

I said, "I still protest against that jury. I am an innocent man, and——"

He answered querulously, "Yes, yes, afterwards." And then creaked, "Now the indictment. . . ."

Someone hidden from me by three barristers began to read in a loud voice not very easy to follow. I caught:

"For that the said John Kemp, *alias* Nichols, *alias* Nikola el Escoces, *alias* el Demonio, *alias* el Diabletto, on the twelfth of May last, did feloniously and upon the high seas piratically seize a certain ship called the *Victoria* . . . um . . . um, the properties of Hyman Cohen and others . . . and did steal and take therefrom six hundred and thirty barrels of coffee of the value of . . . um . . . um . . . um . . . one hundred and one barrels of coffee of the value of . . . ninety-four half kegs . . . and divers others . . ."

I gave an immense sigh. . . . That was it, then. I had heard of the *Victoria;* it was when I was at Horton that the news of her loss reached us. Old Macdonald had sworn; it was the day a negro called Apollo had taken to the bush. I ought to be able to prove that. Afterwards, one of the judges asked me if I pleaded guilty or not guilty. I began a long wrangle about being John Kemp but not Nikola el Escoces. I was going to fight every inch of the way. They said:

"You will have your say afterwards. At present, guilty or not guilty?"

I refused to plead at all; I was not the man. The third judge woke up, and said hurriedly:

"That is a plea of not guilty, enter it as such." Then he went to sleep again. The young girl on the bench beside him laughed joyously, and Mr. Baron Garrow nodded round at her, then snapped viciously at me:

"You don't make your case any better by this sort of foolery." His eyes glared at me like an awakened owl's.

I said, "I'm fighting for my neck . . . and you'll have to fight, too, to get it."

The old judge said angrily, "Silence, or you will have to be removed."

I said, "I am fighting for my life."

There was a sort of buzz all round the court.

Lord Stowell said, "Yes, yes;" and then, "Now, Mr. King's Advocate, I suppose Mr. Alfonso Jervis opens for you."

A dusty wig swam up from just below my left hand, almost to a level with the dock.

The old judge shut his eyes, with an air of a man who is going a long journey in a post-chaise. Mr. Baron

Garrow dipped his pen into an invisible ink-pot, and
scratched it on his desk. A long story began to drone
from under the wig, an interminable farrago of dull nonsense, in a hypochondriacal voice; a long tale about
piracy in general; piracy in the times of the Greeks,
piracy in the times of William the Conqueror . . .
pirata nequissima Eustachio, and thanking God that a
case of the sort had not been heard in that court for an
immense lapse of years. Below me was an array of
wigs, on each side a compressed mass of humanity,
squeezed so tight that all the eyeballs seemed to be
starting out of the heads towards me. From the wig
below, a translation of the florid phrases of the Spanish
papers was coming:

"His very Catholic Majesty, out of his great love for
his ancient friend and ally, his Britannic Majesty, did
surrender the body of the notorious El Demonio, called
also . . ."

I began to wonder who had composed that precious
document, whether it was the *Juez de la Primeria
Instancia*, bending his yellow face and sloe-black eyes
above the paper, over there in Havana—or whether it
was O'Brien, who was dead since the writing.

All the while the barrister was droning on. I did not
listen because I had heard all that before—in the room
of the Judge of the First Instance at Havana. Suddenly
appearing behind the backs of the row of gentlefolk on
the bench was the pale, thin face of my father. I
wondered which of his great friends had got him his seat.
He was nodding to me and smiling faintly. I nodded,
too, and smiled back. I was going to show them that
I was not cowed. The voice of the barrister said:

"M'luds and gentlemen of the jury, that finishes the
Spanish evidence, which was taken on commission on
the island of Cuba. We shall produce the officer of H.

M. S. *Elephant*, to whom he was surrendered by the Spanish authorities at Havana, thus proving the prisoner to be the pirate Nikola, and no other. We come, now, to the specific instance, m'luds and gentlemen, an instance as vile . . . ."

It was some little time before I had grasped how absolutely the Spanish evidence damned me. It was as if, once I fell into the hands of the English officer on Havana quays, the identity of Nikola could by no manner of means be shaken from round my neck. The barrister came to the facts.

A Kingston ship had been boarded . . . and there was the old story over again. I seemed to see the Rio Medio schooner rushing towards where I and old Cowper and old Lumsden looked back from the poop to see her come alongside; the strings of brown pirates pour in empty-handed, and out laden. Only in the case of the *Victoria* there were added the ferocities of "the prisoner at the bar, m'luds and gentlemen of the jury, a fiend in human shape, as we shall prove with the aid of the most respectable witnesses. . . ."

The man in the wig sat down, and, before I understood what was happening, a fat, rosy man—the Attorney-General—whose cheerful gills gave him a grotesque resemblance to a sucking pig, was calling "Edward Sadler," and the name blared like sudden fire leaping up all over the court. The Attorney-General wagged his gown into a kind of bunch behind his hips, and a man, young, fair, with a reddish beard and a shiny suit of clothes, sprang into a little box facing the jury. He bowed nervously in several directions, and laughed gently; then he looked at me and scowled. The Attorney-General cleared his throat pleasantly . . .

"Mr. Edward Sadler, you were, on May 25th, chief mate of the good ship *Victoria*. . . ."

The fair man with the beard told his story, the old story of the ship with its cargo of coffee and dye-wood; its good passage past the Gran Caymanos; the becalming off the Cuban shore in latitude so and so, and the boarding of a black schooner, calling itself a Mexican privateer. I could see all that.

"The prisoner at the bar came alongside in a boat, with seventeen Spaniards," he said, in a clear, expressionless voice, looking me full in the face.

I called out to the old judge, "My Lord . . . I protest. This is perjury. I was not the man. It was Nichols, a Nova Scotian."

Mr. Baron Garrow roared, "Silence," his face suffused with blood.

Old Lord Stowell quavered, "You must respect the procedure. . . ."

"Am I to hear my life sworn away without a word?" I asked.

He drew himself frostily into his robes. "God forbid," he said; "but at the proper time you can cross-examine, if you think fit."

The Attorney-General smiled at the jury-box and addressed himself to Sadler, with an air of patience very much tried:

"You swear the prisoner is the man?"

The fair man turned his sharp eyes upon me. I called, "For God's sake, don't perjure yourself. You are a decent man."

"No, I won't swear," he said slowly. "I think he was. He had his face blacked then, of course. When I had sight of him at the Thames Court I thought he was; and seeing the Spanish evidence, I don't see where's the room. . . ."

"The Spanish evidence is part of the plot," I said.

The Attorney-General snickered. "Go on, Mr.

Sadler," he said. "Let's have the rest of the plot unfolded."

A juryman laughed suddenly, and resumed an abashed sudden silence. Sadler went on to tell the old story. . . . I saw it all as he spoke; only gaunt, shiny-faced, yellow Nichols was chewing and hitching his trousers in place of my Tomas, with his sanguine oaths and jerked gestures. And there was Nichol's wanton, aimless ferocity.

"He had two pistols, which he fired twice each, while we were hoisting the studding-sails by his order, to keep up with the schooner. He fired twice into the crew. One of the men hit died afterwards. . . ."

Later, another vessel, an American, had appeared in the offing, and the pirates had gone in chase of her. He finished, and Lord Stowell moved one of his ancient hands. It was as if a gray lizard had moved on his desk, a little toward me.

"Now, prisoner," he said.

I drew a deep breath. I thought for a minute that, after all, there was a little of fair play in the game—that I had a decent, fair, blue-eyed man in front of me. He looked hard at me; I hard at him; it was as if he were going to wrestle for a belt. The young girl on the bench had her lips parted and leant forward, her head a little on one side.

I said, "You won't swear I was the man . . . Nikola el Escoces?"

He looked meditatively into my eyes; it was a duel between us.

"I won't swear," he said. "You had your face blacked, and didn't wear a beard."

A soft growth of hair had come out over my cheeks whilst I lay in prison. I rubbed my hand against it, and thought that he had drawn first blood.

"You must not say 'you,'" I said. "I swear I was not the man. Did he talk like me?"

"Can't say that he did," Sadler answered, moving from one foot to the other.

"Had he got eyes like me, or a nose, or a mouth?"

"Can't say," he answered again. "His face was blacked."

"Didn't he talk Blue Nose—in the Nova Scotian way?"

"Well, he did," Sadler assented slowly. "But any one could for a disguise. It's as easy as . . ."

Beside me, the turnkey whispered suddenly, "Pull him up; stop his mouth."

I said, "Wasn't he an older man? Didn't he look between forty and fifty?"

"What do *you* look like?" the chief mate asked.

"I'm twenty-four," I answered; "I can prove it."

"Well, you look forty and older," he answered negligently. "So did he."

His cool, disinterested manner overwhelmed me like the blow of an immense wave; it proved so absolutely that I had parted with all semblance of youth. It was something added to the immense waste of waters between myself and Seraphina; an immense waste of years. I did not ask much of the next witness; Sadler had made me afraid. Septimus Hearn, the master of the *Victoria*, was a man with eyes as blue and as cold as bits of round blue pebble; a little goat's beard, iron-gray; apple-coloured cheeks, and small gold earrings in his ears. He had an extraordinarily mournful voice, and a retrospective melancholy of manner. He was just such another master of a trader as Captain Lumsden had been, and it was the same story over again, with little different touches, the hard blue eyes gazing far over the top of my head; the gnarled hands moving restlessly on the rim of his hat.

"Afterwards the prisoner ordered the steward to give us a drink of brandy. A glass was offered me, but I refused to drink it, and he said, 'Who is it that refuses to drink a glass of brandy?' He asked me what countryman I was, and if I was an American."

There were two others from the unfortunate *Victoria* —a Thomas Davis, boatswain, who had had one of Nikola's pistol-balls in his hip; and a sort of steward—I have forgotten his name—who had a scar of a cutlass wound on his forehead.

It was horrible enough; but what distressed me more was that I could not see what sort of impression I was making. Once the judge who was generally asleep woke up and began to scratch furiously with his quill; once three of the assessors—the men in short wigs—began an animated conversation; one man with a thin, dark face laughed noiselessly, showing teeth like a white waterfall. A man in the body of the court on my left had an enormous swelling, blood-red, and looking as if a touch must burst it, under his chin; at one time he winked his eyes furiously for a long time on end. It seemed to me that something in the evidence must be affecting all these people. The turnkey beside me said to his mate, "Twig old Justice Best making notes in his stud-calendar," and suddenly the conviction forced itself upon me that the whole thing, the long weary trial, the evidence, the parade of fairness, was being gone through in a spirit of mockery, as a mere formality; that the judges and the assessors, and the man with the goitre took no interest whatever in my case. It was a foregone conclusion.

A tiny, fair man, with pale hair oiled and rather long for those days, and with green and red signet rings on fingers that he was forever running through that hair, came mincingly into the witness-box. He held for a long time what seemed to be an amiable conversation with Sir Robert Gifford, a tall, portentous-looking man, who had black beetling brows, like tufts of black horse-hair sticking in the crannies of a cliff. The conversation went like this:

"You are the Hon. Thomas Oldham?"

"Yes, yes."

"You know Kingston, Jamaica, very well?"

"I was there four years—two as the secretary to the cabinet of his Grace the Duke of Manchester, two as civil secretary to the admiral on the station."

"You saw the prisoner?"

"Yes, three times."

I drew an immense breath; I thought for a moment that they had delivered themselves into my hands. The thing must prove of itself that I had been in Jamaica, not in Rio Medio, through those two years. My heart began to thump like a great solemn drum, like Paul's bell when the king died—solemn, insistent, dominating everything. The little man was giving an account of the "'bawminable" state of confusion into which the island's trade was thrown by the misdeeds of a pirate called Nikola el Demonio.

"I assure you, my luds," he squeaked, turning suddenly to the judges, "the island was wrought up in-to a pitch of . . . ah . . . almost disloyalty. The . . . ah . . . planters were clamouring for . . . ah . . . separation. And, to be sure, I trust you'll hang the prisoner, for if you don't . . ."

Lord Stowell shivered, and said suddenly with haste, "Mr. Oldham, address yourself to Sir Robert."

I was almost happy; the cloven hoof had peeped so

damningly out. The little man bowed briskly to the
old judge, asked for a chair, sat himself down, and
arranged his coat-tails.

"As I was saying," he prattled on, "the trouble and
the worry that this man caused to His Grace, myself,
and Admiral Rowley were inconceivable. You have no
idea, you . . . ah . . . can't conceive. And
no wonder, for, as it turned out, the island was simply
honeycombed by his spies and agents. You have no
idea; people who seemed most respectable, people we
ourselves had dealings with . . ."

He rattled on at immense length, the barrister taking
huge pinches of yellow snuff, and smiling genially with
the air of a horse-trainer watching a pony go faultlessly
through difficult tricks. Every now and then he
flicked his whip.

"Mr. Oldham, you saw the prisoner three times. If
it does not overtax your memory pray tell us." And
the little creature pranced off in a new direction.

"Tax my memory! Gad, I like that. You remember a man who has had your blood as near as could
be, don't you?"

I had been looking at him eagerly, but my interest
faded away now. It was going to be the old confusing
of my identity with Nikola's. And yet I seemed to
know the little beggar's falsetto; it was a voice one does
not forget.

"Remember!" he squeaked. "Gad, gentlemen of
the jury, he came as near as possible—— You have no
idea what a ferocious devil it is."

I was wondering why on earth Nichols should have
wanted to kill such a little thing. Because it was
obvious that it must have been Nichols.

"As near as possible murdered myself and Admiral
Rowley and a Mr. Topnambo, a most enlightened and

loyal . . . ah . . . inhabitant of the island, on the steps of a public inn."

I had it then. It was the little man David Macdonald had rolled down the steps with, that night at the Ferry Inn on the Spanish Town road.

"He was lying in wait for us with a gang of assassins. I was stabbed on the upper lip. I lost so much blood . . . had to be invalided . . . cannot think of horrible episode without shuddering."

He had seen me then, and when Ramon ("a Spaniard who was afterwards proved to be a spy of El Demonio's —of the prisoner's. He was hung since") had driven me from the place of execution after the hanging of the seven pirates; and he had come into Ramon's store at the moment when Carlos ("a piratical devil if ever there was one," the little man protested) had drawn me into the back room, where Don Balthasar and O'Brien and Seraphina sat waiting. The men who were employed to watch Ramon's had never seen me leave again, and afterwards a secret tunnel was discovered leading down to the quay.

"This, apparently, was the way by which the prisoner used to arrive and quit the island secretly," he finished his evidence in chief, and the beetle-browed, portly barrister sat down. I was not so stupid but what I could see a little, even then, how the most innocent events of my past were going to rise up and crush me; but I was certain I could twist him into admitting the goodness of my tale which hadn't yet been told. He knew I had been in Jamaica, and, put what construction he liked on it, he would have to admit it. I called out:

"Thank God, my turn's come at last!"

The faces of the Attorney-General, the King's Advocate, Sir Robert Gifford, Mr. Lawes, Mr. Jervis, of all the seven counsel that were arrayed to crush me, lengthened into simultaneous grins, varying at the jury-box. But I didn't care; I grinned, too. I was going to show them.

It was as if I flew at the throat of that little man. It seemed to me that I must be able to crush a creature whose malice was as obvious and as nugatory as the green and red rings that he exhibited in his hair every few minutes. He wanted to show the jury that he had rings; that he was a mincing swell; that I hadn't and that I was a bloody pirate. I said:

"You know that during the whole two years Nicholas was at Rio I was an improver at Horton Pen with the Macdonalds, the agents of my brother-in-law, Sir Ralph Rooksby. You must know these things. You were one of the Duke of Manchester's spies."

We used to call the Duke's privy council that.

"I certainly know nothing of the sort," he said, folding his hands along the edge of the witness-box, as if he had just thought of exhibiting his rings in that manner. He was abominably cool. I said:

"You must have heard of me. The Topnambos knew me."

"The Topnambos used to talk of a blackguard with a name like Kemp who kept himself mighty out of the way in the Vale."

"You knew I was on the island," I pinned him down.

"You used to *come* to the island," he corrected. "I've just explained how. But you were not there much, or we should have been able to lay hands on you. We wanted to. There was a warrant out after you tried to murder us. But you had been smuggled away by Ramon."

I tried again:

"You have heard of my brother-in-law, Sir Ralph Rooksby?"

I wanted to show that, if I hadn't rings, I had relations.

"Nevah heard of the man in my life," he said.

"He was the largest land proprietor on the island," I said.

"Dessay," he said; "I knew forty of the largest. Mostly sharpers in the boosing-kens." He yawned.

I said viciously:

"It was your place to know the island. You knew Horton Pen—the Macdonalds?"

The face of jolly old Mrs. Mac. came to my mind—the impeccable, Scotch, sober respectability.

"Oh, I knew the Macdonalds," he said—"*of* them. The uncle was a damn rebellious, canting, planting Scotchman. Horton Pen was the centre of the Separation Movement. We could have hung *him* if we'd wanted to. The nephew was the writer of an odious blackmailing print. He calumniated all the decent, loyal inhabitants. He was an agent of you pirates, too. We arrested him—got his papers; know all about your relations with him."

I said, "That's all nonsense. Let us hear"—the Attorney-General had always said that—"what you know of myself."

"What I know of you," he sniffed, "if it's a pleasuah, was something like this. You came to the island in a mysterious way, gave out that you were an earl's son, and tried to get into the very excellent society of . . . ah . . . people like my friends, the Topnambos. But they would not have you, and after that you kept yourself mighty close; no one ever saw you but once or twice, and then it was riding about at night with that humpbacked scoundrel of a blackmailer.

You, in fact, weren't on the island at all, except when you came to spy for the pirates. You used to have long confabulations with that scoundrel Ramon, who kept you posted about the shipping. As for the blackmailer with the humpback, David Macdonald, you kept him, you . . . ah . . . subsidized his filthy print to foment mutiny and murder among the black fellows, and preach separation. You wanted to tie our hands, and prevent our . . . ah . . . prosecuting the preventive measures against you. When you found that it was no good you tried to murder the admiral and myself, and that very excellent man Topnambo, coming from a ball. After that you were seen encouraging seven of your . . . ah . . . pirate fellows whom we were hanging, and you drove off in haste with your agent, Ramon, before we could lay hands on you, and vanished from the island."

I didn't lose my grip; I went at him again, blindly, as if I were boxing with my eyes full of blood, but my teeth set tight. I said:

"You used to buy things yourself of old Ramon; bought them for the admiral to load his frigates with; things he sold at Key West."

"That was one of the lies your scoundrel David Macdonald circulated against us."

"You bought things . . . even whilst you were having his store watched."

"Upon my soul!" he said.

"You used to buy things. . . ." I pinned him. He looked suddenly at the King's Advocate, then dropped his eyes.

"Nevah bought a thing in my life," he said.

I knew the man had; Ramon had told me of his buying for the admiral more than three hundred barrels of damaged coffee for thirty pounds. I was in a mad temper. I smashed my hand upon the spikes of the rail in front of me, and although I saw hands move impulsively towards me all over the court, I did not know that my arm was impaled and the blood running down.

"Perjurer," I shouted, "Ramon himself told me."

"Ah, you were mighty thick with Ramon . . ." he said.

I let him stand down. I was done. Someone below said harshly, "That closes our case, m'luds," and the court rustled all over. Old Lord Stowell in front of me shivered a little, looked at the window, and then said:

"Prisoner at the bar, our procedure has it that if you wish to say anything, you may now address the jury. Afterwards, if you had a counsel, he could call and examine your witnesses, if you have any."

It was growing very dark in the court. I began to tell my story; it was so plain, so evident, it shimmered there before me . . . and yet I knew it was so useless.

I remembered that in my cell I had reasoned out that I must be very constrained; very lucid about the opening. "On such and such a day I landed at Kingston, to become an improver on the estate of my brother-in-law. He is Sir Ralph Rooksby of Horton Priory in Kent." I *did* keep cool; I *was* lucid; I spoke like that. I had my eyes fixed on the face of the young girl upon the bench. I remember it so well. Her eyes were fixed, fascinated, upon my hand. I tried to move it, and found that it was stuck upon the spike on which I had jammed it. I moved it carelessly away, and only felt a little pain, as if from a pin-prick; but the blood was dripping on to the floor, pat, pat. Later on, a man lit the candles on the judge's desk, and the court looked different. There were deep shadows everywhere;

and the illuminated face of Lord Stowell looked grimmer, less kind, more ancient, more impossible to bring a ray of sympathy to. Down below, the barristers of the prosecution leaned back with their arms all folded, and the air of men resting in an interval of cutting down a large tree. The barristers who were merely listeners looked at me from time to time. I heard one say, "That man ought to have his hand bound up." I was telling the story of my life, that was all I could do.

"As for Ramon, how could I know he was in the pay of the pirates, even if he were. I swear I did not know. Everyone on the island had dealings with him, the admiral himself. That is not calumny. On my honour, the admiral did have dealings. Some of you have had dealings with forgers, but that does not make you forgers."

I warmed to it; I found words. I was telling the story for that young girl. Suddenly I saw the white face of my father peep at me between the head of an old man with an enormous nose, and a stout lady in a brown cloak that had a number of little watchmen's capes. He smiled suddenly, and nodded again and again, opened his eyes, shut them; furtively waved a hand. It distracted me, threw me off my balance, my coolness was gone. It was as if something had snapped. After that I remembered very little; I think I may have quoted the "Prisoner of Chillon," because he put it into my head.

I seemed to be back again in Cuba. Down below me the barristers were talking. The King's Advocate pulled out a puce-coloured bandanna, and waved it abroad preparatorily to blowing his nose. A cloud of the perfume of a West Indian bean went up from it, sweet and warm. I had smelt it last at Rio, the sensation was so strong that I could not tell where I was.

The candles made a yellow glow on the judge's desk; but it seemed to be the blaze of light in the cell where Nichols and the Cuban had fenced. I thought I was back in Cuba again. The people in the court disappeared in the deepening shadows. At times I could not speak. Then I would begin again.

If there were to be any possibility of saving my life, I had to tell what I had been through—and to tell it vividly—I had to narrate the story of my life; and my whole life came into my mind. It was Seraphina who was the essence of my life; who spoke with the voice of all Cuba, of all Spain, of all Romance. I began to talk about old Don Balthasar Riego. I began to talk about Manuel-del-Popolo, of his red shirt, his black eyes, his mandolin; I saw again the light of his fires flicker on the other side of the ravine in front of the cave.

And I rammed all that into my story, the story I was telling to that young girl. I knew very well that I was carrying my audience with me; I knew how to do it, I had it in the blood. The old pale, faded, narrow-lidded father who was blinking and nodding at me, had been one of the best raconteurs that ever was. I knew how. In the black shadows of the wall of the court I could feel the eyes upon me; I could see the parted lips of the young girl as she leaned further towards me. I knew it because, when one of the barristers below raised his voice, someone hissed "S—sh" from the shadows. And suddenly it came into my head, that even if I did save my life by talking about these things, it would be absolutely useless. I could never go back again; never be the boy again; never hear the true voice of the Ever Faithful Island. What did it matter even if I escaped; even if I could go back? The sea would be there, the sky, the silent dim hills, the listless surge; but *I* should never be there,

I should be altered for good and all. I should never see the breathless dawn in the pondwater of Havana harbour, never be there with Seraphina close beside me in the little *drogher*. All that remained was to see this fight through, and then have done with fighting. I remember the intense bitterness of that feeling and the oddity of it all; of the one "I" that felt like that, of the other that was raving in front of a lot of open-eyed idiots, three old judges, and a young girl. And, in a queer way, the thoughts of the one "I" floated through into the words of the other, that seemed to be waving its hands in its final struggle, a little way in front of me.

"Look at me . . . look at what they have made of me, one and the other of them. I was an innocent boy. What am I now? They have taken my life from me, let them finish it how they will, what does it matter to me, what do I care?"

There was a rustle of motion all round the court. On board Rowley's flagship the heavy irons had sawed open my wrists. I hadn't been ironed in Newgate, but the things had healed up very little. I happened to look down at my claws of hands with the grime of blood that the dock spikes had caused.

"What sort of a premium is it that you set on sticking to the right? Is this how you are going to encourage the others like me? What do I care about your death? What's life to me? Let them get their scaffold ready. I have suffered enough to be put out of my misery. God, I have suffered enough with one and another. Look at my hands, I say. Look at my wrists, and say if I care any more." I held my ghastly paws high, and the candle light shone upon them.

Out of the black shadows came shrieks of women and curses. I saw my young girl put her hands over her face and slip slowly, very slowly, from her chair, down out of sight. People were staggering in different directions. I had had more to say, but I forgot in my concern for the young girl. The turnkey pulled my sleeve and said:

"I say, that ain't *true*, is it, it ain't *true?*" Because he seemed not to want it to have been true, I glowed for a moment with the immense pride of my achievement. I had made them see things.

A minute after, I understood how futile it was. I was not a fool even in my then half-mad condition. The real feeling of the place came back upon me, the "Court of Law" of it. The King's Advocate was whispering to the Attorney-General, he motioned with his hand, first in my direction, then towards the jury; then they both laughed and nodded. They knew the ropes too well for me, and there were seven West India merchants up there who would remember their pockets in a minute. But I didn't care. I had made them see things.

CHAPTER FIVE

I HAD shot my bolt and I was going to die; I could see it in the way the King's Advocate tossed his head back, fluttered his bands, looked at the jury-box, and began to play with the seals on his fob. The court had resumed its stillness. A man in some sort of livery passed a square paper to the Lord Mayor, the Lord Mayor passed it to Lord Stowell, who opened it with a jerking motion of an ancient fashion that impressed me immensely. It was as if I, there at the end of my life, were looking at a man opening a letter of the reign of Queen Anne. The shadows of his ancient, wrinkled face changed as he read, raising his eyebrows and puckering his mouth. He handed the unfolded paper to Mr. Baron Garrow, then with one wrinkled finger beckoned the Attorney-General to him. The third judge was still asleep.

"What the devil's this?" the turnkey beside me said to his companion.

I was in a good deal of pain, and felt sickly that every pulse of my heart throbbed in my mangled hand. The other spat straight in front of him.

"Damme if I know," he said. "This cursed business ought to have been over and done with an hour agone. I told Jinks to have my rarebit and noggin down by the gate-house fire at half-past five, and it's six now."

They began an interminable argument under their breaths.

"It's that wager of Lord March's . . . run a

mile, walk a mile, eat five pounds of mutton, drink five pints of claret. No, it ain't . . . . Medmenham coach ain't in yet . . . roads too heavy. . . . It is. What else would stop the Court at this time of night? It isn't, or Justice Best 'd be awake and hedging his bets."

In a dizzy way I noted the Attorney-General making his way carefully back between the benches to his knot of barristers, and their wigs went all together in a bunch like ears of corn drawn suddenly into a sheaf. The heads of the other barristers were like unreaped ears. A man with a face like a weasel's called to a man with a face like a devil's—he was leaving the court—something about an ambassador. The other stopped, turned, and deposited his bag again. I heard the deep voice of Sir Robert Gifford say: "What! . . . Never! . . . too infamous, . . ." and then the interest and the light seemed to flicker out together. I could hardly see. Voices called out to each other, harsh, dry, as if their owners had breathed nothing but dust for years and years.

One loud one barked, "You can't hear him, m'luds; in *Rex* v. *Marsupenstein.* . . ."

A lot began calling all together, "Ah, but that was different, Mr. Attorney. You couldn't subpœna him, he being in the position of *extra lege commune*. But if he offers a statement. . . ."

The candles seemed to be waving deliberately like elm-tops in a high wind.

Someone called, "Clerk, fetch me volume xiii. . . . I think we shall find there. . . . You recollect the case of *Hildeshein* v. *Roe*. . . . Wasn't it *Hildegaulen and another*, m'lud?" . . . "I tried the case myself. The Prussian Plenipotentiary. . . ."

I wanted to call out to them that it was not worth

while to try their dry throats any more; that having shot my bolt, I gave in. But I could not think of any words, I was so tired. "I didn't sleep at all last night," I found myself saying to myself.

The sleeping judge woke up suddenly and snarled, "Why in Heaven's name don't we get on? We shall be all night. Let him call the second name on the list. We can take the Spanish ambassador when you have settled. For my part I think we ought to hear him. . . ."

Lord Stowell said suddenly, "Prisoner at the bar, some gentlemen have volunteered statements on your behalf. If you wish it, they can be called?"

I didn't answer; I did not understand; I wanted to tell him I did not care, because the *Lion* was posted as overdue and Seraphina was drowned. The Court seemed to be moving slowly up and down in front of me like the deck of a ship. I thought I was bound again, and on the sofa in the gorgeous cabin of the *Madre-de-Dios*. Someone seemed to be calling, "Prisoner at the bar . . . Prisoner at the bar. . . ." It was as if the candles had been lit in front of the Madonna with the pink child, only she had a gilt anchor instead of the spiky gilt glory above her head. Somebody was saying, "Hello there. . . . Hold up! . . . Here, bring a chair, . . ." and there were arms around me. Afterwards I sat down. A very old judge's voice said something rather kindly, I thought. I knew it was the very old judge, because he was called the star of Cuban law. Someone would be bending over me soon, with a lanthorn, and I should be wiping the flour out of my eyes and blinking at the red velvet and gilding of the cabin ceiling. In a minute Carlos and Castro would come . . . or was it O'Brien who would come? No, O'Brien was dead;

stabbed, with a knife in his neck; the blood was still sticky between my first and second fingers. I could feel it. I ought to have been allowed to wash my hands before I was tried; or was it before I spoke to the admiral? One would not speak to a man with hands like that.

A loud, high-pitched voice called from up in the air, "I will give any of you gentlemen of the robe down there fifty pounds to conduct the remainder of the case for him. I am the prisoner's father."

My father's voice broke the spell. I was in the court; the candles were still burning; all the faces, lit up or in the shadow, were bunched together in little groups; hands waved. The barrister whose face was like the devil's under his wig held in his hands the paper that had been handed to Lord Stowell; my father was talking to him from the bench. The barrister, tall, his robes old and ragged, silhouetted against the light, glanced down the paper, fluttered it in his hand, nodded to my father, and began a grotesque, nasal drawl:

"M'luds, I will conduct the case for the prisoner, if your lordships will bear with me a little. He obviously can't call his own witnesses. If he has been treated as he says, it has been one of the most abominable . . ."

Old Lord Stowell said, "Ch't, ch't, Mr. Walker; you know you must not make a speech for the prisoner. Call your witness. It is all that is needed."

I wondered what he meant by that. The barrister was calling a man of the name of Williams. I seemed to know the name. I seemed to know the man, too.

"Owen Williams, Master of the ship *Lion*. . . . Coffee and dye-wood. . . . Just come in under a jury-rig. Had been dismasted and afterwards be-

calmed. Heard of this trial from the pilot in Graves-
end. Had taken post-chaises . . ."

I only heard snatches of his answers.

"On the twenty-fifth of August last I was close in
with the Cuban coast. . . . The mate, Sebright,
got boiling water for them. . . . Afterwards a
heavy fog. They boarded us in many boats. . . ."
He was giving all the old evidence over again, fastening
another stone around my neck. But suddenly he said:
"This gentleman came alongside in a leaky dinghy. A
dead shot. He saved all our lives."

His bullet-head, the stare of his round blue eyes
seemed to draw me out of a delirium. I called out:

"Williams, for God's sake, Williams, where is Seraphina? Did she come with you?" There was an immense roaring in my head, and the ushers were shouting, "Silence! Silence!" I called out again.

Williams was smiling idiotically; then he shook his
head and put his finger to his mouth to warn me to keep
silence. I only noted the shake of the head. Seraphina had not come. The Havana people must have
taken her. It was all over with me. The roaring noise
made me think that I was on a beach by the sea, with
the smugglers, perhaps, at night down in Kent. The
silence that fell upon the court was like the silence of a
grave. Then someone began to speak in measured,
portentous Spanish, that seemed a memory of the past.

"I, the ambassador of his Catholic Majesty, being
here upon my honour and on my oath, demand the re-
surrender of this gentleman, whose courage equals his
innocence. Documents which have just reached my
hands establish clearly the mistake of which he is the
victim. The functionary who is called *Alcayde* of the
carcel at Havana confused the men. Nikola el Escoces
escaped, having murdered the judge whose place it was

to identify. I demand that the prisoner be set at liberty . . ."

A long time after a harsh voice said:

"Your excellency, we retire, of course, from the prosecution."

A different one directed:

"Gentlemen of the jury, you will return a verdict of 'Not Guilty' . . ."

Down below they were cheering uproariously because my life was saved. But it was I that had to face my saved life. I sat there, my head bowed into my hands. The old judge was speaking to me in a tone of lofty compassion:

"You have suffered much, as it seems, but suffering is the lot of us men. Rejoice now that your character is cleared; that here in this public place you have received the verdict of your countrymen that restores you to the liberties of our country and the affection of your kindred. I rejoice with you who am a very old man, at the end of my life. . . ."

It was rather tremendous, his deep voice, his weighted words. Suffering is the lot of us men! . . . The formidable legal array, the great powers of a nation, had stood up to teach me that, and they had taught me that—suffering is the lot of us men!

It takes long enough to realize that someone is dead at a distance. I had done that. But how long, how long it needs to know that the life of your heart has come back from the dead. For years afterwards I could not bear to have her out of my sight.

Of our first meeting in London all I remember is a speechlessness that was like the awed hesitation of our overtried souls before the greatness of a change from the verge of despair to the opening of a supreme joy.

The whole world, the whole of life, with her return, had changed all around me; it enveloped me, it enfolded me so lightly as not to be felt, so suddenly as not to be believed in, so completely that that whole meeting was an embrace, so softly that at last it lapsed into a sense of rest that was like the fall of a beneficent and welcome death.

For suffering is the lot of man, but not inevitable failure or worthless despair which is without end—suffering, the mark of manhood, which bears within its pain a hope of felicity like a jewel set in iron. . . .

Her first words were:

"You broke our compact. You went away from me whilst I was sleeping." Only the deepness of her reproach revealed the depth of her love, and the suffering she too had endured to reach a union that was to be without end—and to forgive.

And, looking back, we see Romance—that subtle thing that is mirage—that is life. It is the goodness of the years we have lived through, of the old time when we did this or that, when we dwelt here or there. Looking back, it seems a wonderful enough thing that I who am this, and she who is that, commencing so far away a life that, after such sufferings borne together and apart, ended so tranquilly there in a world so stable—that she and I should have passed through so much, good chance and evil chance, sad hours and joyful, all lived down and swept away into the little heap of dust that is life. That, too, is Romance!

THE END

JOSEPH CONRAD

Born at Berdiczew, Poland, 3rd December 1857;
christened Józef Teodor Konrad Nalęcz Korzeniowski.
Travelled to Marseilles, 1874, and became a seaman,
first reaching England in 1878. Became a naturalized
British subject, and obtained Master Mariner's
Certificate, 1886. Married Miss Jessie George,
1896; two sons: Borys (*b.* 1899), John (*b.* 1906).
Died at Bishopsbourne, Kent, 3rd August 1924.

CHRONOLOGICAL LIST OF CONRAD'S WORKS

(*Names of the original publishers, or their
present successors, are given in brackets*)

1. *Almayer's Folly—A Story of an Eastern River.* 1895. (Benn.)
2. *An Outcast of the Islands.* 1896. (Benn.)
3. *The Nigger of the 'Narcissus'—A Tale of the Sea.* 1897. (Heinemann.)
4. *Tales of Unrest.* (Contents: 'Karain, a Memory,' 'The Idiots,' 'An
   Outpost of Progress,' 'The Return,' 'The Lagoon.') 1898. (Benn.)
5. *Lord Jim—A Tale.* 1900. (Blackwood.)
6. *The Inheritors—An Extravagant Story.* (In collaboration with Ford
   Madox Hueffer.) 1901. (Heinemann.)
7. *Youth—A Narrative; and Two Other Stories.* (Contents: 'Youth,'
   'Heart of Darkness,' 'The End of the Tether.') 1902. (Blackwood.)
8. *Typhoon, and Other Stories.* (Contents: 'Typhoon,' 'Amy Foster,'
   'Falk,' 'To-morrow.') 1903. (Heinemann.)
9. *Romance—A Novel.* (In collaboration with Ford Madox Hueffer.)
   1903. (Smith Elder.)
10. *Nostromo—A Tale of the Seaboard.* 1904. (Dent.)
11. *The Mirror of the Sea—Memories and Impressions.* 1906. (Methuen.)
12. *The Secret Agent—A Simple Tale.* 1907. (Methuen.)
13. *A Set of Six.* (Contents: 'Gaspar Ruiz,' 'The Informer,' 'The Brute,'
    'An Anarchist,' 'The Duel,' 'Il Conde.') 1908. (Methuen.)
14. *Under Western Eyes.* 1911. (Methuen.)
15. *A Personal Record.* 1912. (Dent.)
16. *'Twixt Land and Sea—Tales.* (Contents: 'A Smile of Fortune,'
    'The Secret Sharer,' 'Freya of the Seven Isles.') 1912. (Dent.)
17. *Chance—A Tale in Two Parts.* 1913. (Methuen.)
18. *Victory—An Island Tale.* 1915. (Methuen.)
19. *Within the Tides—Tales.* (Contents: 'The Planter of Malata,' 'The
    Partner,' 'The Inn of the Two Witches,' 'Because of the Dollars.')
    1915. (Dent.)
20. *The Shadow Line—A Confession.* 1917. (Dent.)
21. *The Arrow of Gold—A Story between Two Notes.* 1919. (Benn.)
22. *The Rescue—A Romance of the Shallows.* 1920. (Dent.)

23. *Notes on Life and Letters.* 1921. (Dent.)
24. *The Rover.* 1923. (Benn.)
25. *The Secret Agent—A Drama in Four Acts.* 1923. (Werner Laurie.)
26. *Laughing Anne* and *One Day More.* (One-act plays, the first from the story 'Because of the Dollars,' and the second from 'To-morrow.') 1924. (John Castle.)
27. *Suspense—A Napoleonic Novel.* 1925. (Dent.)
28. *Tales of Hearsay.* (Contents: 'The Warrior's Soul,' 'Prince Roman,' 'The Tale,' 'The Black Mate.') 1925. (Benn.)
29. *Last Essays.* 1926. (Dent.)

Uniform Edition of the Works of Joseph Conrad, 1923–8 (22 volumes including all the above except the plays, Nos. 25 and 26). (Dent.)

THE PRESENT COLLECTED EDITION is reprinted from the Uniform Edition and includes the Prefatory Notes written by the Author for the latter. Two books are contained in one volume, as follows: Nos. 1 and 4, Nos. 3 and 8, Nos. 11 and 15, Nos. 19 and 20, and Nos. 28 and 29.

LIFE AND LETTERS OF CONRAD
The Life and Letters of Joseph Conrad (2 vols.), edited by G. Jean Aubry. 1927.

Letters from Conrad, 1895–1924, edited, with an Introduction, by Edward Garnett, 1928.

Letters from Joseph Conrad to Richard Curle, 1928.

SOME CRITICAL & BIOGRAPHICAL WRITINGS ABOUT CONRAD
Joseph Conrad, A Study, by Richard Curle, 1914.

Essay in *Notes on Novelists*, by Henry James, 1914.

Joseph Conrad, by Hugh Walpole, 1916.

Essay on Conrad in *A Book of Prefaces*, by H. L. Mencken, 1917.

Joseph Conrad, his Romantic Realism, by Ruth M. Stauffer, 1922.

Joseph Conrad, a Personal Remembrance, by Ford Madox Ford, 1924.

Essay on Conrad in *The Common Reader*, by Virginia Woolf, 1925.

Joseph Conrad as I knew Him, by Jessie Conrad, 1926.

'Reminiscences of Conrad' and 'Preface to Conrad's Plays' in *Castles in Spain*, by John Galsworthy, 1927.

The Last Twelve Years of Joseph Conrad, by Richard Curle, 1928.

The Polish Heritage of Joseph Conrad, by Gustav Morf, 1930.

Joseph Conrad's Mind and Method, by R. L. Mégroz, 1931.

Joseph Conrad, Some Aspects of the Art of the Novel, by Edward Crankshaw, 1936.

Introductory Essay by Edward Garnett to *Conrad's Prefaces to his Works*, 1937.

Joseph Conrad, England's Polish Genius, by M. C. Bradbrook, 1941.

Biographical Introduction by A. J. Hoppé to *The Conrad Reader*, 1946.

The Great Tradition (George Eliot, Henry James, and Joseph Conrad), by F. R. Leavis, 1948.

BIBLIOGRAPHIES
A Bibliography of the Writings of Joseph Conrad, 1895–1921, by T. J. Wise, London, 1921. *A Conrad Library*, collected by T. J. Wise, London, 1928.

A Conrad Memorial Library, collected by G. T. Keating, New York, 1929, with 'Check List of Additions,' 1938.